Once Upon a Country Lane

Once Upon a Country Lane

A Tribute
to
The Gaelic Spirit
of
Old West Huntley

Carleton County, Ontario
Canada

by

Garfield Thomas Ogilvie

[signature: Garfield Ogilvie]

PENUMBRA PRESS
www.penumbrapress.ca

Copyright 2005 © Garfield Thomas Ogilvie and
Penumbra Press
Cover art is after a painting by Marjorie O'Grady Orange,
"Farm and St. Michael's Church"

Published by PENUMBRA PRESS
Printed and bound in Canada
Originally published by House of Airlie, 1992

LIBRARY AND ARCHIVES CANADA CATALOGUING IN PUBLICATION

Ogilvie, Garfield Thomas, 1931-
    Once upon a country lane : a tribute to the Gaelic spirit of old West
Huntley, Carleton County, Ontario, Canada / by Garfield Thomas Ogilvie. --
2nd ed.
Includes bibliographical references.
ISBN 1-894131-88-6
    1. Irish Canadians--Ontario--Ottawa--History. 2. Huntley (Ont. :
Township)--History. 3. Huntley (Ont. : Township)--Biography. 4. Ottawa
(Ont.)--History. 5. Ottawa (Ont.)--Biography. I. Title.
FC3095.H83O5 2005   971.3'83   971.3'84 C2005-905970-2

Canada

Penumbra Press gratefully acknowledges the financial support of the
Government of Canada through the Book Publishing Industry
Development Program (BPIDP) for our publishing activities.
We also acknowledge the Government of Ontario through the Ontario
Media Development Corporation's Ontario Book Initiative.

Contents

For

Marilyn

Preface

Huntley Township no longer exists. Up until 1974, it was part of Carleton County; in 1974, it became absorbed by the Municipality of the Township of West Carleton. I have taken the liberty in this book of referring to this old township as if it still exists in name, identity and geographical borders.

As Huntley filled up its Twelve Concessions with immigrants from 1818 onwards, the population tended to divide itself geographically into two sections: the first six concessions from above Carp to the Seventh Line (called East Huntley) were largely of the Protestant persuasion while the other six (called West Huntley) were made up mostly of the Roman faith. This book is about West Huntley which is often affectionately referred to as Corkery.

West Huntley is divided by two valleys. The first runs parallel with and between the Ninth and Seventh Lines; the second parallel with and between the Ninth and the Twelfth. As a young lad on the farm, my haunts were mostly on this second one whose south and north extremities ran from the Old Almonte Road, south of Highway 44, to the Township of Fitzroy (also defunct). In this valley, which I shall call West Huntley Valley, most of the Irish settlements took root. The Tenth and Eleventh Lines are now the main arteries. They have new names: the Peter Robinson Road and the Upper Dwyer Hill Road.

Introduction

This writing then is mainly about the Irish people who lived in and around the valley between the Ninth and Tenth lines. It is about the generations I have known and those that have gone before me. It is about wonderful men and women who welcomed me first as a boy, then as a teenager and finally as an adult. Over the last fifty-four years, I have been in more than eighty of their homes. I have never forgotten the fine hospitality I received in each. The thoughts of youth are long, long thoughts. You don't forget! Especially kindnesses!

My mother was born in the valley at a place called O'Keefe's Corners. I started going there for my summer holidays at the age of six. During the nine glorious summers that followed, I was given far more than I gave. Within this haven of Irish ways, I stored up lessons and experiences which were to form the backbone of my character. I received sets of values that would remain with me the rest of my life. I made friendships which stood the test of time and for which I am deeply grateful.

The ebb and flow of their daily lives taught me, for example, that success is not necessarily to the swiftest, strongest or richest, that a man's goodness is his best measure and that ambitious desires often find fulfilment in our own backyards and by our own firesides. This little oasis called West Huntley Valley has helped keep me sane. It has been my tree house, my friendly tavern, my Shangri-la.

Over the years, whenever the tensions of life became too much, I would go into this pocket of serenity to soothe my ruffled nature and recharge my batteries. The genuine simplicity of their daily living freshened my spirit. Their wry wits and sweet charities rejuvenated my heart and I always returned home with renewed vigour and peace.

Even today, as I drive through this garden of my youth, my heart saddens at the thought of how many of my Irish friends are gone ... I have stood too many times by their coffins ... with each death the valley loses a bit of its heart and the church bell tolls all too frequently ... each crank in the road brings to mind a face, a tear, a laugh ... each old farmhouse reminds me that nothing stays the same ... each lane and field reinforces the passing vanity of all things ... and I am left only with the presence of the day and the reminder that tomorrow will be different from any yesterday ... the past in fact becomes part of my present as the memories of the good times with these good people give me strength to withstand each day's trials. Their spirits hover near as I go about my appointed rounds.

Naturally the old O'Keefe homestead at the corner of the Eleventh Line and the Carroll Side Road shall always be particularly dear. My grandmother O'Keefe, as all my relatives, was very kind to a "green" kid with one foot in the country and the other on the streets of Westboro Village in Nepean.

As I look back, I realize how little of this world's possessions they really had. According to today's monetary standards, many people of West Huntley would be classified well below the poverty line. Cash flow for them was a dollar floating in the creek.

Yet money could not buy what they gave me, nor could it buy the attributes they had: nobility of bearing, refinement of character, the wisdom of saints and scholars, and a humility fired in the furnace of pain. In spite of depressions, wars, famines and epidemics, they always had time to dance at the crossroads and give the bag of life a squeeze.

I can still see my grandmother's face at her kitchen window ... I can still hear her son Ignatius calling me to fetch the cows ... I can smell those freshly cooked crusty brown loaves lying face down like dead soldiers on the kitchen table ... I can taste the cream, the butter, the Johnnycakes, the tea biscuits and preserves. The lonesome cry of a train, the buzz of a fly, the bawling of a cow, the dry taste of a summer breeze still stir my heart ... the images are real; they are cut deep in my mind.

Let these pages be feeble scratchings of thanks to all the Irish of West Huntley. Let this work be a testimony of my appreciation. It is not enough, I know, but let it be at least a token and I will be happy.

This book also includes anecdotes, stories, history, and folklore about Ireland itself. I have been there five times and I felt the reader might be interested in my impressions. They might help a person better understand the West Huntley Irish and serve to show that West Huntley is really a bit of Ireland.

Every fact in the sections on West Huntley is based on firsthand experiences, research into newspapers, books, records and scrapbooks, and on interviews with countless persons from West Huntley. Most interviews were in person; a good many were over the phone.

It is my hope that while reading this book, you will be entertained, informed, and become more appreciative of the Irish people, especially those from my beloved West Huntley.

Garfield Thomas Ogilvie
Nepean, Ontario, Canada
August 15, 1992

Qu'est-ce que c'est Corkery?

No one's sure when Corkery got its name. It might have been during the pastorship of Reverend Patrick Corkery (1885-1904), or perhaps when it became a postal station. Equally undetermined have been the territorial boundaries of Corkery! Was it just the land around the church, presbytery, hall, graveyard and one or two houses? Was it the length and breadth of its postal limits? Or was it, in actuality, the entire area of West Huntley from which St. Michael's church drew its parishioners? The latter explanation is the most plausible: that the Catholic faithful living within the borders of St. Michael's parish constitute the community called Corkery.

Even today, with Corkery's old Rural Routes 1 and 2 postal service long gone and the percentage of Catholic Irish families in the area sadly depleted, the only way Corkery can maintain its existence as a distinct place is to do so within the spiritual fringes of St. Michael's parish.

As long as St. Michael's looks out across West Huntley Valley, then Corkery and all it stands for has a chance of surviving and keeping its place in the sun.

Charlie

Sing from the boreens, you Gaelic hearts
In the vales let the fiddles fly
It's Charlie calling us all once more
To dance a square on heaven's floor.

Reflections of Youth

A person of the country is more attuned to nature than his counterpart in the city.

Living in an environment free from urban contaminations, he appreciates better the sensual wonders around him. He becomes a student of the universe and a part of each season that unfolds before him. He and nature become one.

As a child in the country, I became enticed by nature's fascinations. I remember coming home from Almonte on Saturday nights and standing in the front yard by the farmhouse under an awesome canopy of stars. Somehow they then seemed closer and brighter than today. It was as if each sun and planet really did come out to play. For a young boy, it was magic time.

Soon I learned to read nature's lessons. Rain often followed the bold low sweep of the barn swallows or the bothersome bites of houseflies. The movement of early fog often predicted the day's weather as did the tell-tale signs around moon or setting sun. The unusual eating habits of farm animals were as good or better than any barometer.

While all seasons had their own charm, certainly autumn in the country was my favourite. In West Huntley, the boreens and knocks took on softer warmth and richer hues. On the bushy side roads, the tall elms and broad maples blushed more radiantly with each cold night. Evergreens grew darker in the nocturnal shades. Bare fields opened to the wind. Nature was preparing to die with its customary majesty.

In the late Thirties, harvest time was enchanting. The whole valley was a garden of produce. Farmers had to cultivate more land then to feed the cows and horses and pigs so necessary for survival in an era of depressed economy. Women raised more geese, ducks and hens. Vegetable gardens grew near each farmhouse. Golden crops of wheat and barley and oats gave to the land a delicate balance of colour not seen today and probably never to be seen again.

Near Maurice Mantil's house on the Mantil Side Road near Panmure, the fields swept downhill from the Eleventh Line like the basin of a dry quarter moon. Bland sticks of oats lay between honey-heads of wheat and farther west near the town line a haze rolled along the horizon.

Another spot of visual treasure started at the corner of the Vaughan Side Road and the Eleventh Line near the poor croft of the saintly Johnny Kennedy. A flood of pastel ran east from the top of Martin Ryan's farm down over the flat fields of Edmund Newton's into Jimmy Vaughan's. Crops of buckwheat, flax and clover spread blends of ochre and sepia across the land. Even today this parcel of the country seems special to me as it emits its friendly glow.

Then, as now, autumn was a time of rejoicing for the farmer. After all, the farmer is a businessman and, like all businessmen, he enjoys his successes as exemplified in his abundant crops. The fruits of his labours are indeed sweet!

And what labours they were in the Thirties! Nothing was easy! Especially putting in those crops. I remember walking behind the single ploughshare, the horse reins round my waist, my fists fastened to the big handles, my feet in and out of the furrows, my eyes and mouth full of dust. A good day's cultivating in those times put little brown in a twenty-acre field. Turf was turned over as a leaf in a book, one unit at a time.

The next phase of cropping was disking. The farmer sat slightly ahead of double rows of metal disks on a seat shaped like a question mark to which he tied old granary bags to help cushion the jolts to his posterior. The sharp disks knifed into the turf at forty-five degree angles cutting up the grassy furrows into readiness for the drag harrowing that was to follow.

The drag harrow resembled the front view of a crossword puzzle that had been divided into several sections. Each section was joined to another by short chains with the whole unit attached to and pulled by a ten-foot-wide crossbar connected to whippletrees. The underside of the sections was covered with four-inch-deep spikes that dug into soil with the forward motion of the team. As in disking, the farmer had to harrow the field twice in different directions to make sure the ground was entirely covered. If the soil was particularly dry and the wind unusually strong, the harrower found himself walking through a considerable amount of swirling dust. He had to learn to let the wind work for him whenever possible; nature can be helpful if you let it.

So it was with the actual planting of the crops. The farmer had to choose the right day and the most suitable conditions. The piece of machinery that he used was called a seeder. The farmer poured loose grain into a long thin box that rested on top of funnels similar to those of a pipe organ. Most farmers chose to walk behind the seeder box where they had better control over the amount of seed flowing from the bottom of the funnels. After seeding, the fields were again harrowed in opposite directions to protect the seeds from the elements and the birds. If heavy rains flooded the newly sewn field too soon after the planting, then the whole process of harrowing, planting and harrowing had to be repeated at considerable expense and labour to the farmer.

The cutting of the crops was more satisfying. The harvesting machinery was in readiness. The fruits of his work were at hand. The hay, tall and brown; the grain, bent and golden.

The smell of new-mown hay still conjures up images of my uncle riding his bucking mower up and down the knolls. I hear the noisy slashing of the knives above the abrupt commands to his team: "Come on, Queenie!"; "Babe, do something!" or "What good are you two!" Some days everything would go wrong; his hat would fly off, knives would break, or a gear unmesh. Several times he had to get off his iron seat to pull out the hay jammed between teeth and knives.

A binder and seed drill enjoy
well-earned retirement on the Williams' farm.

Such problems were all part of the game. When it came to machinery, the farmer knew that every day brought its special problems and that no amount of careful maintenance would assure trouble-free miles in the field. Such a philosophy was particularly true when it came to the operation of the binder, a machine that for my money was true to its name.

The binder by 1940 had been around to harvest grain crops for one hundred and ten years. Three horses and one man could harvest fifteen acres per day, while a good reaper could only cut about an acre. Farmers were also able to plant bigger crops since the danger of spoilage as under more primitive conditions was eliminated.

When you actually saw the machine in action in 1940, you wondered how it worked at all, especially back in the early 1800's. Here was a machine that had been perfected down the years to the point where it was, to my way of thinking, nothing but a bag of bolts held together by prayer and the farmer's determination.

To say that it was "ornery" was an understatement in kindness. It looked like an iron cube standing on one corner. It moved through the field like an engine block being dragged in mud. It took twelve hoofs pounding away full out to get it on a roll. And on a good day, it could shred the sanity of a cigar-store Indian.

The design of this engineless Edsel was simple enough. A double set of knives cut down the grain in such a way that the shafts fell uniformly on a moving canvas. Other canvas then brought the cuttings into a position where they were bundled, tied and popped free by the thrust of a revolving fork. The power for running all the gears and chains and canvas came from the centre wheel armed with a set of teeth for traction.

But handsome is as handsome does. I remember the binder as a necessary evil. On any given day, any number of problems developed. Canvas might jam or tear, gears might unmesh or chains snap. If a broken part was not reparable (often parts came off older binders), then the farmer might have to go to the dealers in town, and harvesting might be delayed several days.

Often, too, binder twine (made from South American plant fibre) could be a problem, particularly during the Second World War when the twine's quality was poor. The twine would often snap or unravel as it was pulled from its spool. Other times the tying mechanism would fail and sheaves might be tied twice, or loosely, or not at all. Any loose cuttings had to be gathered up and recycled. The farmer had much to watch out for. No wonder most rode the binder with one foot on the binder itself and the other dangling along near or on the ground for a fast getaway.

Two of the more exasperating situations involved the centre wheel. When it hit mud, it would spin hopelessly until the farmer could negotiate the team onto better ground. If the situation required the farmer to back up the binder, the task was a formidable one since a three-horse team doesn't back up that easily. Nor did the horses relish trying to pull a binder's main wheel from a ground hog's deep burrow. Fits of rage were not uncommon among the gentlest of men. To my way of thinking any farmer who could put up with this pile of nuts and levers known as the binder was already on the road to sainthood.

After the binding came the stooking. The farmer walked up and down a field collecting several sheaves into a stook. The sheaves in the stook were placed so as to lean forward for support on one another's tops like the poles of a wigwam. An open space was left at each end for the drying west wind. Some farmers took real pride in their symmetrical arrangements of stooks as can be seen in the many harvest scenes displayed on old calendars, etc. With the coming of the combines, the beauty of a stooked field was no more!

But then everything changes!

Take threshing machines. Not many around now. That's a pity! Threshings were fun times in the country. Men and women came to one another's homes for the happy purpose of "bringing in the sheaves". In the fields and kitchens good neighbourliness prevailed. The providence of God and the ingenuity of man, not to forget the toil of the dumb beasts of burden, had once again worked together to prove that every seed's corruption brings a miracle of rebirth. Indeed, a time for "rejoicing"!

And an exciting time for a young city boy! Wagons coming and going. The men's humour, the bantering, the spirited horses, and the slosh of the big threshing machine like a huge gravyboat, handle and all, devouring the sheaves. As mesmerizing as anything you'd see at a circus!

The men seemed to work to the beat of the machine. Grates swished back and forth. The wide *figure-8* leather strap from the motor to the thresher flapped in the centre as it met itself coming and going. And everywhere the wind ... inside, fanning and cleaning and winnowing ... outside, whirling and spewing the straw from the spout onto the stack. At the side of the machine, fat elbows of tin guided the threshed grain into burlap bags which were stood up straight, tied at the necks with twine and carried to the granary. Every so often, the owner of the machine would poke here and there around its girth, monitoring its performance as it flailed, shook, rattled and rolled into the memory of a little fella lucky enough to be there.

Being a small boy of unsound working abilities, I didn't do much around threshings except stay out of the way and wait for the dinners. Could anyone forget those pies and cakes and cookies — all capable of making eyes bigger than stomachs? I practised the philosophy then that they too serve who stand and watch and eat. It's not easy, but somebody had to do it.

When I grew older, I attended some threshings in a working capacity. I remember the threshings at Bob Mantil's farm on the Twelfth Line. Everyone was kind and friendly. I remember Jimmy Flynn, Des Grace, Jimmy Forrest, Eddie Grace, Mohr O'Brien, Sylvester Finner, Ignatius O'Brien and the Mantils, Ray, Jackie, Bobby and of course Bob himself.

Now there was a lovable man! His main farm backed on my grandfather's place and one day back in May, 1934, Bob was ploughing a nearby field when he heard that my grandfather had died. Bob immediately stopped working and put his team away in deference to his good friend and neighbour. Such was the quality of this man whose ancestors were among the first to take roots in West Huntley Valley.

Since Bob had most of his crops planted on his Twelfth Line farm, he had to make his way up there on the days when the weather was fine. And so it was that he passed by grandmother's house on his two-mile journeys. He sat on the raised bench of his little milk wagon with his el-

Bob Mantil
1924

bows on his knees, his head lowered and the reins dangling limply over the front apron. As they might say in Huntley, "Neither he nor the horse were in any tear to go anywhere!"

Most times you could hear Bob and his wagon before you saw them because he had the habit of singing to pass the time. The airs of his mellifluous melodies still haunt my memory as they rose and fell on the breeze. Like strange blendings of joy and anguish that blew from beyond the seven seas! Like a wail that wasn't! Tuneful lyrics of yesteryear learned at his mother's knee? Laments? Odes? Incantations? Ballads? Like

an Indian Chief by the fireside or a cantor in a synagogue or a gypsy in repose.

His songs seemed to release the stored-up past of the Irish people: the wanton cry of a dying peasant, the misty oration of a Druid priest, the persecutions, the partings, the secret joys of family love. Bob, your singing shall never be forgotten! I still see you and your horse and wagon and hear your call. It meant much to me.

Another threshing I remember was at John O'Keefe's. John assigned me to duty on the straw stack. We were threshing peas and it was my job to spread the straw as it shot in wild fury from the long dinosaur neck of the great machine. Although the day was sunny, it was twilight on the stack. I could easily have been in a prairie duststorm. I was completely enveloped in dirt, mould, dust, matted grass, unmatted grass, fertilizer, flaked mud, unflaked mud, green clover and stray peas. It was a matter of survival!

John, of course, had great fun watching my antics and casting impish remarks my way. Later on in the threshing, he relieved me from my misery by putting me on the granary detail where I soon learned that a bag of peas can have a mind of its own.

Getting a bag of peas from ground to shoulder is not easy. Bagged peas have a way of settling that places their centre of gravity halfway to Hades. Once you get the bag on the shoulder, the gravity splits, half the load fore and the other aft, and it takes a fair amount of balancing to carry it what with each pea rolling on another, and the whole load moving like porridge. I don't ever remember going back to John's threshings again, since my next summers were spent working on construction jobs in Ottawa. But if I had, I can hear him yet, "Gar, have I got a challenge for you; it'll make a man of you!" And being already pea-brained, I probably would have done whatever he asked.

In the early Forties, where the Carroll Side Road meets the Tenth Line, lived Jimmy O'Connell and his wife, Anna, in the old Pat Manion house. Jimmy was having a threshing one summer and since my Uncle Nash had a sore back, he asked me to take his place.

I was happy to go because Jimmy was a good guy, as hardworking and freewheeling as Anna was good-natured and affable. You couldn't ask for finer people.

The weather was great; the crop plentiful. I was given the opportunity to pitch to the wagons and on several occasions the responsibility of throwing the sheaves into the thresher. All this was big time for me!

In my books, the threshing was a success, especially the dinner. The men had worked all out and their appetites were sharp. There was rich gravy, fresh beef and potatoes, pies and cakes, steaming green tea and cold milk.

I still remember the weathered faces around the big rectangular tables: Jimmy and Gerry Vaughan, Lorne Charlebois, Edmund Newton, Gerald and Angus Carroll, Clarence Williams, James Brown, Roy Clarke, Frank Scott, Angus Killeen ... the young and old, shy and bold, each with a funny story to unfold.

About two years ago, I heard that Anna Brown O'Connell had died. And my mind went back to that threshing and the last time I met her at the home of her daughter, Donna, wife of the late fondly remembered Grant Murphy.

Anna said to me that day, "I am sorry I can't see you, Gary. I have been blind for several years. But I remember you!"

And her face broke into a beaming smile as she continued, "You're the young man who told me at one of our threshing dinners that you were crazy about my pickles."

"But that was thirty-five years ago!" I countered in surprise.

"Yes, I know," she said, "but I have never forgotten you!"

Marriage Knot For Him

A prosperous and eligible farmer of West Huntley had been courting a widow for a period of time considered to be well beyond propriety. With no marriage in the offing, a younger neighbour asked his father one day why the couple hadn't tied the knot. The father replied, "My son, there's an old Irish saying: 'You don't buy a cow if you're getting the milk free!'"

An Irish Farewell

May the good angels watch over thee,
May your heart beat strong and free,
May the wind blow safely to your lee,
May you see age four score and three.

May memories soften each day,
May your cares dissolve like the dew,
May part of your heart here stay
And some of ours go away with you.

An Old Irish Toast

Here's health and life to you,
The man or woman of choice to you,
Land without rent to you,
And death in Ireland.

Anonymous

A Rendezvous

They strolled down the lane together.
The sky was sprinkled with stars.
They reached the gates in silence.
And he lifted up the bars.

She neither smiled nor thanked him.
For indeed she knew not how,
For he was just a farmer boy
And she but a Jersey cow.

Anonymous

Smelling the Roses

You learn the value of time while sitting on the back rack of a wagon going nowhere in no hurry. Even a shopper on an escalator can run up the steps at a faster pace and a parachutist can change his downward velocity to his liking. But on a wagon behind two horsepower, you learn to go with the flow.

On the farm you learn to sit back with a waving strand of timothy crossways in your teeth and let the rest of the world go by. Neither man, beast nor nature itself, will be pushed beyond its limit. Nothing can be harvested before its

Maurie Williams
at age seventy-five with his
nephews Frank and Arnold
Prudhomme.

time. No thrust of energy will challenge the set biological patterns of animals and vegetables.

The Irish farmer of West Huntley, at least up to the middle of the Twentieth Century, was a servant of nature's whims. His inner rhythms complied with the beats of nature's drums. His very genes cried out for a sensible approach to the passing of life's cycles. His Celtic nature threw aside the shackles of the clock. By being gentle with time's passing and patient with nature, he was a man at peace with himself.

This Irish farmer that I knew in the Thirties, Forties and Fifties was not a clock-puncher. He worked at his leisure and brought leisure to his work. His hours could be long or short depending on nature, his humour, and the importance of the job at hand. He tended to respond to the pressures of immediacy with practised tenacity. He was in a sense, a child of nature. The cow chewed her cud, the cricket measured his call, the mare "in time" dropped her foal, the sap could not be hurried, and the Huntley farmer was his own man.

He always seemed to have a spell to chat over fence, by road, or down a lane. A "take ten" in the morning work could easily stretch to twenty. A snooze after lunch was as mandatory as lunch itself. Seldom in a hurry, everything was nevertheless still done on time within a framework of that time. By never challenging time, the Irish farmer became its master. And life became savoured moment by moment, a delicacy of immeasurable contentment in a timewarp.

The longevity of my uncle, Maurice Williams, over ninety-five at his death, was in large part due to his respect for time. It was as if his biological rhythms were in perfect sync with the undulations of nature.

He was up with the birds and to bed with the chickens. In between, his daily chores were completed with the devotion of a monk. Even though a man of considerable emotion, he seldom wore his heart on his sleeve; life was there to be lived with a quiet courage. Verbal amplification sometimes released exasperation but only for a short time and in controlled tones. Once, the Archbishop of Ottawa unexpectedly came to visit Maurie's mother who lived with him for some years. When Maurie looked up in his kitchen and beheld the majestic red image framed in the door, he reverently cooed: "Sweet Jesus, it's the Archbishop!"

In 1941, I was ten and my uncle was fifty-six. Slightly round-shouldered, he was still a handsome man, face wrinkle-free, a touch of charcoal-grey hair, and a lean, lithe bearing. His voice was so soft it was almost inaudible; his personality of a gentle persuasion. After his usual quickly eaten dinner, he would settle in his favourite rocking chair and send Raleigh smoke rings adrift in the old kitchen. My cousins and I had great sport trying to catch them while he listened to Frank Ryan's farm broadcast on the little G.E. radio in the window alcove.

On some days, we sat and listened to his reminiscences. He enjoyed narrating anecdotes which he always introduced by the same phrase "I mind the time". Most stories ended with a chuckle on his part and all of us would join in appreciation whether or not we understood what had been said. After the evening chores he sometimes retired to the parlour at the end of the house to play his fiddle. His son Clarence accompanied him on guitar while I banged on piano. Old favourites flowed from his hand: "The Little Burnt Potato", "Big John McNeil", "Turkey in the Straw" and "Down Yonder". In his later years a few popular old-time fiddlers would visit for jam sessions. The opportunity to play with people like Ward Allen gave him great happiness. Another favourite "after supper frolic" for him was to run his hand down and over my face, plucking my nose from its mooring and putting said snozzle in his pocket. He never tired of this trick and I never did either.

As a neighbour, he tended to his own knitting. His message was clear for man and God: take me as I am or let me be! Although he seldom visited a neighbour's home in his later years, he welcomed everyone graciously to his. Only necessity took him into towns or crowds. A man of few words, men were careful what they said to him.

His unassuming manner, his hushed voice, and his measured pace of working marked him as a man at peace with himself and neighbours, a man for whom earth's treasures had little meaning. His animals and crops were the custodians of his time. By never rushing at anything, the ravages of time seldom left any imprints on his body or mind. He lived in a sort of eternal presence which no doubt made his transition into eternal life an easy one.

My Uncle Maurie was known to me for some forty-six years. Often, in my working days, I would drive alone to his farm, sit with him in his kitchen and soak up the saneness of his being. While there, the pressures of the games people play and the ping-pong politics of the working world would pale into insignificance before this old man's marvellous philosophy of life.

As a young boy, my uncle had many occasions to be angry with me as I supposedly worked around his farm. Often I would spill milk while milking or separating. Then there was the day his son Allan and I ate fourteen eggs for lunch. And the time I spooked the hens and they broke some of the hennery windows. He usually said little: a few grumbles and a stare that would move clouds.

However, there was one miscue that did test his temper. I was about ten and I was sitting across from him at dinner. I had poured hot, hot tea almost to the very top of a big, big glass, and while he mumbled a warning about the danger of such a feat, I began to stir in the milk with great flourish. To emphasize my success I drew out the spoon and gave the lip of the glass a sharp hit of satisfaction. As the glass shattered and hot tea ran across the table and down his pant leg I heard a very strong condemnatory oath cast in my direction ... something about somebody being a total idiot, I think!

Black Oak

For three hundred and fifty years the Irish owned neither house nor land. They rented both. Their furniture, utensils and farm animals, however, were their own; all were hard to come by, especially the furniture. Dressers, chairs, benches, and chicken coops had to be made by local carpenters from black oak logs dug out of seven feet of bog.

The quest for the logs began early in the morning before the white frost had gone. Local men looked for the complete outline of a log on the turf, since frost is always less over buried wood. An iron bar was spiked into one end of the outline until it hit the log. A second bar was then driven into the other end until contact was again made. A tester then placed the exposed end of the second bar against his teeth while another worker tapped the exposed end of the first bar. If the tester felt vibrations, the log was considered solid and in one piece.

With the discovery of a suitable log, the men quickly removed the top sod and cut out the turf layer by layer. Slowly the trench filled with water and the log floated up. A horse then pulled it home for drying. Later a whipsaw cut the log into planks and boards.

At this point, the carpenters were hired. So good were they at their craft that foreclosing landlords always made sure the furniture was "confiscated" before the houses were burned. The peasants' houses were no more, but the furniture lived on.

Chicken coops, by the way, were kept inside the kitchen. In fact outbuildings were scarce since the rent went up according to the number of buildings on the property. That's why a cow often bunked in the lean-to.

11

Making Do

*Ignatius O'Keefe
with his father Tom,
around 1925. Ignatius is
about eighteen and his
father about sixty-five.*

On rainy days, my Uncle Nash sat on his porch and hammered out crooked, rusty nails as old as the Crucifixion. Such a practice was an example of the "waste not, want not" philosophy of the early Corkery people.

They developed this frugal way of life because of the great economic hardships they endured. The wolf was seldom far from their doors and even though they wasted nothing they still were in want. Many just made ends meet; others didn't.

Poverty is a difficult term to define and even more difficult to defend if applied to a certain group. Many subjective and relative variables must be carefully examined before definite conclusions are reached.

One also hesitates calling anyone poor. Poverty can imply a lack of dignity or industry and there's a stigma attached to poverty even though the people involved do the best they can in almost impossible conditions.

I can't really speak reliably for the Irish people in Corkery before the 1930's. But, I can speak for the years after. And it is my opinion that the majority of the people I knew were poor. And if they were poor, it is reasonable to assume that most of their ancestors in the first hundred years were also.

The depression of the Thirties was the straw that broke the Irish back. Following war and severe epidemics, it challenged the physical and emotional grit of mothers and fathers already well beyond their prime of life. At the very time when pastures of retirement were within sight, the economic landslide changed everything. Many could take no more; many died; some moved away; others lost their farms in bankruptcy. Many farms were sold for the price of the taxes. The ranks thinned out.

Fortunately, a strong core rode out the storm. They did so by continuing to live lives of complete austerity. Without being niggardly or parsimonious, they scraped and saved and recycled. They made the best of everything they had. Their homes were neat and tidy. Their dress was adequate. Their meals nourishing. Their deportment exemplary. They gave up much in their lifestyle so that everybody could enjoy a little. They proved that poverty cannot destroy character or take away dignity. And that man can still be rich in spite of being poor.

As a young boy I watched them eke out a living. I saw them patch milk pails with rags and reinforce smocks and skirts and trousers at the elbows and knees. I saw holes in barns covered by fragments of old spruce boards and tears in screens plugged with cloth. Old pieces of leather were grafted for harness in need of repair. Broken handles from forks and shovels were taken out of their heads, shortened, reshaped, and reinserted. A slightly chipped cup might stay in circulation for years. The oilcloth on tables, shelves and floors was used far beyond its time of obsolescence. Tape supported cracks in windowpanes. Pieces of cardboard filled the space of a broken window.

During meals, my grandmother often cautioned us on our over-consumption of butter. Cream was not always as available as green tea. Dishes came from different sets and cutlery seldom matched. Drinking glasses were of all shapes, colours and sizes. Many of her beautiful antique platters bore the wrinkles of old age.

The big red Imperial Oil battery-radio in the living room was played as low and infrequently as possible. With my ear almost stuck to the speaker, I would listen to the Grand Old Opry from WWVA, Wheeling, West Virginia, or from Brooklyn tune in on the Dodger broadcasts of Red Barber, his voice fading in and out on the radio waves. Even before the rooster crowed, I often stole downstairs to pick up the farm advertisements and songs from the Midwest United States. Over the years I can't recall any mechanical or electrical object that gave me more fun than that radio: Minnie Pearl's call of "Howdy" ... the Duke of Padooka who always went back to his wagon because his shoes were killing him ... Red Foley and Ernie Tubb ... Jackie Robinson ready to steal second!

It is difficult for young people today to comprehend fully a world without electrical and electronic gadgets and all the luxuries of convenience, a world where raw physical labour was the only means to survival. One can't expect them to understand because they were not there to experience it. You had to be an integral part of it, live it, feel it, taste it, to even understand it a little.

I remember reading yesterday's newspapers (they always came one day late) by coal oil lamps with the wicks turned down low for conservation. I remember using those same papers in an outhouse built some fifty yards from the house, a long walk over packed snow in the dead of night. I saw big rusty barrels full of soft rain water for washing. I saw clotheslines held up by

The O'Keefe Homestead
at O'Keefe's Corners.

13

rough poles with mouths cut in their ends.

I remember the buttermilk saved from the churning. And the turnip and potato skins kept for the pigs. I watched the skimping and felt the ache of doing all the farm chores by hand. I saw the day in and day out sweat and strain. And I knew why the colour had gone from my grandmother's cheeks and the sheen from her hair.

Actual money in the hand in those days came only from livestock and cream. This cash bought such food items as spices, raisins, sugar, tea, yeast, baking powder, chocolate, certo, salt, vinegar, pepper, etc. Some clothing such as scarves, gloves, socks, dresses and blouses could be made on the Singer; others like shoes, suits, shirts, ties, coats and underwear had to be purchased.

Many other responsibilities could only be met with cash. The parish priest and church had to be supported. Doctors and veterinarians and undertakers had to be paid. Parts for broken-down farm machinery had to be bought, roofs needed resheeting, new stovepipes had to be installed, new wells required drilling, and farm animals needed to be replaced.

True, a dollar went a long way, but then people had to go a long way to catch one.

Everything was more valued in those days. Each item was important in the way of things. Even those tapered, rectangular-headed nails that Nash was straightening were resurrected for another day.

Their whole life was like that.

Time-Arunning

In the early Twenties, not all people in West Huntley owned a watch. The time in a farmhouse was kept by the family's mantle clock. If this clock stopped, (since not everyone had a radio), the time had to be fetched from a neighbour.

Bob Mantil and his wife Rose Grace once lived at O'Keefe's Corners in a house previously owned by John O'Keefe and wife Mary Sheehan who had gone to reside in Almonte.

Grace Mantil, Bob's daughter, reminisced one day about the occasions she and her brother Jackie used to scamper over to their neighbours, Dave O'Keefe and his sister Katherine, to bring back the time.

The distance was only five hundred skips and jumps, but for little memories (Jackie was about five and Grace four), it was a long way to remember anything, let alone the time.

After Kate's cookies and milk, Grace and Jackie would take off for home all the while shouting aloud over and over the correct time so neither would forget.

Back at the house, Rose would reset the clock and add a few minutes for "travelling time".

A Brief History of Ireland up to 1600

In the Ninth Millennium, just after the last ice age, the first Irish had already settled in what are now the Western counties of Sligo, Derry and Offaly. They came from the Far East, probably India, by way of France, Spain and Portugal over the natural ice fields that then connected with Ireland.

During the Stone Ages from 9000 B.C. to 3500 B.C., these Irish immigrants lived largely by gathering plants and nuts, hunting deer, boar, hare, grouse and pigeon, and by fishing for salmon, cockles, mussels and oysters.

By the Bronze Age in 3500 B.C., most inhabitants were farmers. Agricultural races from the Middle East had started arriving by boat in the Fourth Millennium by way of Brittany, Spain and Portugal. They had brought with them seed and livestock and polished-stone tools for planting and tilling. They cleared the lands, stocked the mountains with sheep and goats, and ran cattle over the downs scraped clean by the sweating glaciers.

By the time the oceans had finished rising around the British Isles and Europe, Ireland was an island 302 miles long and 171 miles from East to West at its widest. Its West Coast was warmed by the Gulf Stream that began its journey in the warm waters of the South Atlantic. Its shoreline ran for three thousand miles and eight hundred lakes and rivers were placed as if by design among limestone mountains and forests and verdant vegetation of breathless beauty.

The real sculpturing of Ireland's face, however, went further back some seventy million years during which time volcanic eruptions, floods, gales, and ice all left their individual markings.

From the Thirty-First Millennium, archaeological findings in Ireland show that deer and elephants romped with hyenas, foxes and wolves and continued to do so undisturbed by *Homo sapiens* for twenty-one thousand years. For the last eleven thousand years man and beast have shared one of the most naturally beautiful islands in the world, an island whose very isolation has kept it from radical biological and cultural changes and thereby helped preserve for posterity one of the most pristine civilizations ever unearthed by modern man.

It was in the Iron Age, 900 B.C. to 100 B.C., that the Celtic people first came to Ireland. Ireland has never been the same since. The Celts had started as a race sometime about the beginning of the Bronze Age in lands beyond the eight-hundred-mile-long Carpathian Mountains that run to the Black Sea between Czechoslovakia and Poland. By 900 B.C., they controlled all the land between the North Sea and Mediterranean and the Atlantic Ocean and Black Sea. Over the next six hundred years, they drove their chariots with their wicker sides and iron wheels into the rhino's nose of Turkey, the uneven fingers of Southern Greece, the bird's head of Denmark and even down into Italy's boot. Some tribes went as far as Egypt, Scandinavia, Portugal and Central Spain. By 500 B.C., one large contingent called the Belgae had sailed to Britain from Northern Gaul (now Belgium and part of the Netherlands and the area around Dieppe in France) while another group known as the Gaels moved by sea to Ireland and the West of Scotland from Western Gaul (France and part of Spain).

Generally speaking, the Celtic people were a loose federation of tribes held together by a common tongue, culture and religion. They had no written language and no political nationhood. They were excellent farmers, brave warriors, and talented artisans. They traded iron, copper, salt, tin and slaves, principally for flagons of wine. They invented mechanical harvesting and perfected methods of fertilizing and rotating crops. They worshipped over four hundred gods, road naked into battle, sacrificed humans, cut off the heads of their vanquished, and gave equal rights to their women. They seemed to take the best of the Bronze and Iron Ages and apply their own unique creativity to its perfection.

The personality of the Celts is documented, albeit "with bias", by the Roman and Greek historians. The Romans, who were being constantly nipped in the flanks by marauding Celtic war parties, thought the Celts to be highly emotional barbarians ready to fight at the drop of a helmet. They saw an intelligent people with innate ability to learn, who never wrote anything down, who spoke sparingly and then only by way of riddles and hints, in a sound reminiscent of baaing sheep. The Greeks too found them to be as naturally evasive in communication as they were tactlessly straightforward in war.

The Greeks in general, were a bit kinder. They wrote of a race known for its courage, especially in battle, where the warriors, both men and women, fought side by side in a brainless but nevertheless fearless manner. They tell of a people who, while not intrinsically evil, could easily be provoked into a frenzy when the safety of all was in jeopardy, a people who often threw their javelins first and asked questions later. A warrior might enter battle supported by raw courage alone. With no overall game plan to follow, his survival depended upon his own ingenuity. He was free to run forward in any direction, even for causes that were nonexistent. How you fought counted ... winning was secondary!

These same writers, the Greek ones, Herodotus, 5th Century B.C., Aristotle, 4th Century B.C., and Plutarch, 1st Century A.D., and the Roman ones, Caesar and Siculus, 1st Century B.C., and Tacitus, 1st Century A.D., provide us with a few but precious facts on the Celts' physical attributes: they saw them as a tall blue-eyed blond or reddish-haired race whose voices were harsh and deep and whose appearance was intimidating especially when under the influence. Some sported moustachios.

Aristotle in 350 B.C. called Ireland, "Iernia" while Plutarch referred to it as "Ogyia". To others, it was the "sacred island". The modern name of Eire evolved from the sun goddess, Eriu, who was worshipped by the Gaelic Celts who came to Ireland from Western Gaul.

About the time of Christ, Ireland was known as Scotia and its people Scots or Scoti. In 506 A.D., three sons of a chieftain named Erc crossed by sea to Scotland (then known as Alba) which was of course already Gaelic. They settled on territory now called Argyllshire meaning in Gaelic, "arregate" or "territory of the Gael". To distinguish the two Gaelic countries, they called the present Scotland, Scotia Minor, and the present Ireland, Scotia Major. Such names continued until the Eleventh Century when Scotia Minor became Scotland, and Scotia Major, Ireland from Eriu.

In a strict sense, the name Gael and Celtic are not interchangeable. Celtic is the general term given to all the Celtic tribes who as we have seen were in Eire by the 900-800 Centuries B.C. These first tribes settled mainly in part of Connaught province. They were followed by other Celts known as the Laginians who took over Leinster as well as all of Connaught. Another faction called the Ulaid set up the kingdom of Ulster.

The Goidels or Gaels were the last group of Celts to come and they went to Munster, the only area left. It was these Gaels from Western Gaul who were part of the late European Gaelic culture. It was these Gaels who continued to fight the Roman Eagle in France until retreat to Eire was the only recourse. It was these Gaels who brought with them to Ireland that particular Celtic tongue which became the basis of the modern Gaelic still spoken by over two million people.

If we do use the terms Gael and Celtic interchangeably today, it is probably due to the fact that the Gael's particular brand of culture, religion and art eventually dominated all of Celtic Ireland and much of the Northern, Central and Western sections of Scotland. The Celts were divided into major groups called tribes and naturally some tribes tended to come to the top in the way of things. Apparently, the Gaels did.

After the arrival of the Celts in 900 B.C., no other hostile nation was to set foot on Ireland for 1800 years. In 837 A.D., the Vikings from Norway, Sweden and Denmark, the real barbarians of their times, sailed their small oar-driven ships up the Liffey River and ravaged the area later to be called Dublin.

For reasons unknown, the Roman Legions, camped on the shores of Wales in 82 A.D., never turned on Ireland. It was not a case of discretion over valour since the Romans had already driven the Celts of Europe and Britain into mass graves, total subjugation, or onto waiting ships. Not even the fact "Ireland was there" was sufficient reason. Maybe Agricola, the Roman General, saw nothing of value in Ireland. Or maybe Ireland owed its deliverance to divine providence which would not allow the savages of Rome to desecrate two cradles of Christianity, the one in Jerusalem and the second yet to come in Ireland.

So Ireland missed all the "civilization" of Roman domination. Law and order remained among the leaders of the Gaelic-Celtic tribes. No great roads and bridges ran among cisterns and bathhouses. There were no villas on hillsides, no brothels, no forts, no forums, no great cities, no taxes for the Caesars of Rome, and above all, no domination by the Latin language. Gaelic would remain basically free for another 1500 years until the English would try to eradicate it completely.

Strangely enough, much of the more popular history of the Roman Empire that we studied as students took place long before the Eagle landed on the chalk cliffs of Dover.

Sulla had already replaced the five-hundred-year-old Roman Republic with its first dictatorship. Pompey and Julius Caesar had clashed in civil war, with the former being murdered in 48 B.C. Caesar's own dictatorship ended with his elimination in 44 B.C. followed two years later by the murders of Brutus and Cassius. Marc Antony had married Cleopatra for her dowry of Egypt only to lose everything by 31 B.C. to Caesar Octavius. The year 27 B.C. saw this same Octavius as the divine emperor of Rome and all her dominions.

An event of not much apparent significance took place in the twenty-eighth year of Augustus Octavius's reign. A Jewish boy was born in Bethlehem. He grew up in Galilee, a province of ancient Palestine under the governorship of the Roman, Herod Antipas. Unlike Cyrus, Sophocles, or Alexander, he carried neither pen nor sword. His ideals were simple; yet unique. He was condemned as a rebel and executed.

Yet within a few centuries of His death the Roman Empire was to be called Holy. The myriad gods worshipped by the Greeks, Romans, Egyptians and Celts would be put away in deference to this "hippy's message" whose kingdom was beyond this world and whose name would one day be synonymous with all that was good on earth. How His message survived was a miracle! It should have died for all intents and purposes with His crucifixion on Calvary. But it didn't. And although many moons came and went before Christianity took hold in Europe, the seeds were planted; the reaping would have to wait.

Meanwhile, the Roman conquests continued. One year after Christ's death, Tiberius the Emperor himself died and six years later, the Celts in Britain were under attack. The year was 43 A.D.

By the end of the First Century, the Roman General Agricola had subjugated Britain as far as Ayrshire in Scotland. In the Second Century the Emperor Hadrian built a spite-wall across southern Scotland to keep out the northern Celtic Picta, thereby allowing the Roman governors the freedom to "latinize" England as they wished. The governors instituted City States, marblized the temples and forums, and put walls around the city cores. Tax collectors went door to door to suck up coins from the poor as homage to Rome.

But the Celts of Ireland went free. Their society grew up in civilized hierarchial layers. At the top were the aristocrats: the members of royalty, clergy, warriors, judges, poets, historians and special advisers. In the middle were the freemen, mostly merchants and farmers. At the bottom were the slaves, those men and women and boys and girls who had been captured from the Roman holdings in Spain, Germany, France and Britain by Celtic warring parties. Even St. Patrick was a slave, a Roman citizen, taken from the west coast of England (near Bristol) and placed as a swineherd on the hills of Antrim in Ulster.

The Celts did not live in cities. It was not in their nature to build great meeting places for business, worship and pleasure. Their ancestral ties were instinctively tribal and family centred.

Everyone, then, of these truly first Irish had come at different stages from either the Near, Middle or Far East, from historical mists beyond Europe, Russia and the Caspian Sea. At first glance, they appeared historically to be a *potpourri* of the Stone, Bronze and Celtic Iron Ages, but in archaeological retrospect they were indeed one massive group cut from the same cloth, a people of intelligence, artistry and passion who fought hard, played harder, lived for the moment, loved nature intensely, and cherished their own with a tenacious loyalty.

In every society, certain families end up with all the wealth and power. Ireland was no exception. It had its strong families ruled by chiefs and kings. Naturally some of these chiefs and kings became in time more powerful than others. And as to be expected, some even tried to be "King of All Ireland", a title not easily won, or kept, or lost.

These Irish chieftains and kings ruled parts of Ireland from the Stone Age to the Fourteenth Century A.D. Even up to the Seventeenth Century, families like the O'Connors, O'Connells and O'Neills fought to keep the Celtic strain free of foreign contamination. The Viking, Norman and Tudor armies often felt the cold steel of these Irish families.

One family in particular was potent: they were the O'Neills. King Niall defeated the Picts of Scotland in the Fifth Century and later helped drive out the Romans from Britain. With the Romans gone by 407 A.D., his Celtic descendants joined up in the Sixth Century with other Celtic clans to conquer Wales and a large part of Western Britain, thereby re-establishing the Celtic presence in Britain. In Ireland, the O'Neills ruled the northeast and northwest for over a thousand years. In Tudor times, Hugh O'Neil, the clan head, fought the last major Irish battle against Elizabeth 1's armies at Kinsale in 1601. His loss on Christmas Eve marked the beginning of the end for Gaelic Ireland. It would be another three hundred years before the Irish could mount a recovery.

Queen Elizabeth, already in power in Britain in 1558, was considered by the Anglo-Saxons, Normans, and by more than a few Irish to be the Queen of Ireland, a title she inherited from her excommunicated father, Henry VIII. Henry had declared himself King of all Ireland in 1541 and a different kind of kingship cast its shadow over the Irish. In 1603, a persevering O'Neil finally surrendered officially to the British forces. The date was March 23 and the next day Elizabeth died. The last great clan leader fled to France. The Saxon net was pulled tighter around the Irish.

The age of Celtic power was gone. Cromwell, William of Orange, and the Famine were yet to come.

The Rushend

(In Irish, the word "Currach" means racecourse. Thirty miles from Dublin in county Kildare is the five-thousand-acre, two-thousand-year-old racecourse known as the "Curragh", home to the Irish Derby.

I attended the running of the Oakes in July of 1968 and watched the famous rider Piggott guide his mount Santa Tina to victory. The general admission seats were nothing more than cement steps and reminded one of the rushend in the old Ottawa Auditorium.)

The House that T.P. Gorman built
Was a bathtub with seats round the sides
And the cries of the fans do linger there
Though the arena itself has died.

There were red seats and green and some in between
For the people who had the means,
But the best seats, my friends,
Were the ones for the poor
In the grey, cemented rushend.

From our caged vantage point
The game would unfold
And our cheers were a melodious blend
For none knew the game as well as we did
In the grey, cemented rushend.

"Go, get him, Bobby! Take her all the way, Ray!"
We'd shout to our deft defence pair,
And then "Legs" would pull off another great save
With both feet split high in the air.

And "Butch" would hit Lude
With a stiffening pass
As "Wiener" Green would cut for the net,
And before you could say "a hole in the tack"
The goal had a bulge high in its back.

The grey, cemented rushend has gone with our youth
But its memories are still our own
When our roars were enough to put a tilt
On the House that T.P. Gorman built.

Conditions in Nineteenth-Century Ireland

Back in Ireland, life for the Irish had gone from bad to worse to disastrous. In 1801, when Ireland was absorbed politically into the British Empire, Ireland had a debt of $85,000,000. One major reason for the economic crisis was Ireland's one-eighth contribution to the total cost of the Napoleonic wars: in fact, it was the second largest amount of money given to those wars from any country in the Empire.

Between 1830 and 1850, there was no industry in Ireland. Ninety per cent of the nearly ten million population depended on casual farm work. Many, of course, joined the British army or navy. In fact, the Irish were the majority force in the British campaigns. A noted historian of the Nineteenth Century called the Irish privates the finest of soldiers. They joined the Iron Duke of Wellington, himself a Dubliner, to defeat Napoleon at Waterloo; they fought at Crimea in Russia and in every part of the world where the British flag challenged or was challenged ... all for a shilling a day!

Yet a paltry shilling was more than most of the Irish were making back home. Unemployment was seventy-five per cent and even those who did work saw no money. The twenty-five cents earned for a fifteen-hour day had to be given to the "gombeen man", a moneylender. It was he who loaned the Irish worker money (at twenty-five per cent) to buy food from the English landlord in the late spring. The food was needed to get families through the summer "meal" months, since the potatoes stored for the winter never survived much beyond April. The head of the family always found himself borrowing on his future earnings because landlords only accepted cash for "meal".

The potato failures which many early Irish immigrants to Canada had lived through in Munster and Connaught in 1800, 1807, 1821, and 1822, became more frequent and severe as the Nineteenth Century unravelled. The vulnerable spud failed again in 1830 and 1831 at Mayo, Donegal and Galway. In 1832, 1833, 1834 and 1836, certain areas of Ireland were hit with dry rot and curl. Ulster was the victim in 1835 followed by failures throughout all Ireland in 1836, 1837, 1839 and 1844.

The summer of 1845 at first gave every indication of providing a bumper potato yield. But by August, all hopes were dashed with the arrival of the pestilence known as the blight. This uncommon disease was as mysterious in its nature as it was deadly in its potency. No amount of scientific and agricultural research brought results. By late October, this infection had travelled by air to reek devastation in England, Scotland, Belgium, Wales, Holland, and France as well as Ireland.

In Ireland, it was as if the gates of hell had opened. Being entirely reliant on the potato for sustenance and being almost totally deprived of land and employment for decades, the poor people were literally "sitting ducks". Further failures of potato crops in 1846, 1847, and 1849 added to the devastation and by mid-century, starvation, fever, and emigration had lowered the Irish population by three and a half million souls.

In a real sense, the famine was the "last nail in the coffin", the ultimate culmination of a hundred years of national suffering. Evil men had been planning Irish eradication for centuries. Hiroshima was over in minutes and the burning of Israel in some five years. But the annihilation of the Irish was torturously dragged out over several centuries. The incineration of the Japanese would be blamed on the self-defence of war and that of the Jews on the insidious hatred of a madman. But the elimination of the Irish had no explanation or excuse. It was systematically arranged by men of supposedly good breeding, men who "killed at arm's length" in order to subjugate a nation considered to be populated at best by a bunch of "upstarts".

Slowly and carefully over the years, the Irish had been stripped of their minerals, produce, and forests. By diabolical plans, unjust laws, broken treaties, and unreasonable punishments, these descendants of saints, scholars, and kings were spiritually, emotionally and mentally driven into the ground. First came the Normans, then the Tudors and Cromwellians and finally the parliamentary marionettes of the Germanic Kings. At one time or another, the Irish had no schools, no language, no books, no vote, no freedom of speech or religion, and no right to own land or anything of value. The dastardly implications of those years will never be truly known except by those who were there.

And so it was that the Irish still able to walk sought refuge in other lands. The majority went to Great Britain, Glasgow and South Wales. Others sailed for North America on the coffin ships. In the middle 1840's so many were buying passage out of Ireland that travel brokers were established in all the major ports.

The shipping companies welcomed the opportunity to fill their two thousand ships, particularly on the North American run. Hitherto, the outbound ships sailed with empty holds to the West and returned home with full cargoes of forestry products. The human ballast on the western swing filled the coffers with a new-found treasure.

The passenger business was not only lucrative but also competitive. Shipping lines were forced to undercut one another in fare structure, particularly on the runs to Quebec and St. John. Most passengers wanted to avoid the British Colonies of North America. The United States being quite free of British dominance became the popular choice and the flow to Canada turned to a trickle. To attract business on the Quebec route, some tickets went on sale for as little as two or three pounds.

British officials at home were also very concerned over the influx of too many unskilled, penniless refugees into a Great Britain already economically deprived and heavily populated. Better for them that the Irish went to British North America where the population was but a million. So they allowed the brokers to run their own show and every small town in Ireland had its mini-broker who bought up blocks of "space" on boats destined for Quebec, and then sold them at the lowest prices.

Hoping to go to the United States (supply and demand being what it was), passengers were confronted with fares as high as twenty-one pounds. To avoid this monetary obstacle as well as the tough American immigration standards, the poorer Irish bought passage to Quebec, accepted the "sometimes offered free passage" put up by the British for the trip up to Montreal, and then silently and illegally crossed the border into the "Land of the Free". In 1844, three-quarters of the sixty-eight thousand who sailed for British North America turned their backs on the Union Jack. In 1843, less than two per cent of twenty-one thousand stayed in Canada. Even though these Irish knew the Anglo-Saxon United States wanted only strong, healthy, legal immigrants of the Protestant persuasion, they also were aware that they and the Americans had one common bond: they both mistrusted the British.

By nature, the Irish are not nomadic, so that any severance from home, family, or locality, places severe emotional stress upon them. Listen to the songs written about Ireland by her children on distant shores and feel the deep love reaching across the waters for roots. Only unrelenting forces like famine and typhus fever could have shaken them into the reality that escape was the only way to survive.

With three-quarters of the people reduced to walking skeletons, the decision to accept the sanctuary of other lands was more easily made. And so began the ceaseless wanderings of Irishmen into every part of the civilized world, even into the small niche called West Huntley. The poor sparrows were on the wing to find any nest in the West.

Not Your Ordinary Grandmother

A West Huntley woman named O____ was happy to become a grandmother, but would have nothing to do with being addressed by any title remotely associated with the honour.

"What shall we call you then?" asked a granddaughter. "If you're not a 'grannie', or 'grandma' or 'nana', what are you?"

"Call me anything you like, but forget that granny stuff!" she replied.

"Okay," said the granddaughter, "then we'll call you what we've always called you!"

"What's that?"

"The old b____," said the granddaughter. "It suits you to a tee!"

"I love it!" hummed the grandmother. "I love it. The old b____ it is!"

And so it was. And still is. I met her the other day, the sweetest old b____ of a grandmother you'd ever want to meet!

6

Monica

A scratchy voice said, "Come in!" and I did and there was Monica Flynn sitting by the window enjoying one of those views for which Fairview Manor in Almonte is so aptly named.

"And who might ya be?" she said. And I told her I was Eva O'Keefe's son and she remembered and quickly warmed up to my intrusion and began to chat.

At one point I said, "Monica, do you remember as a little girl walking three miles to Saturday Catechism classes and stopping on the way at my Grandaunt Kate's for a visit and sometimes sitting with her beside the spring, combing out her long, long hair?"

"Ah, I do remember it well, now that you mention it! She was a fine woman and good-humoured too and always kind enough to sit me down to a cup of tea! And she had a brother, Dave, who lived there too, a quiet decent man so he was, always wearing a straw hat as I remember! And, then, I'd be on my way to Catechism. And it was hard, too. Father Stanton was there and you wouldn't dare not know your work!"

She then paused and seemed to be thinking through what she had said. She began again, "They say they were the good old days! I wonder if they were! Do you think they were?"

"I think in some ways they were!"

Suddenly, her face took on a softness and her voice dropped a shade as she said, "I guess they were good, good for the soul, helped us to better save it and get to heaven and that's good, don't you think?"

Shortly after, two friends dropped by and I got up to go. And I remember thinking of some people in Corkery and others round the world, myself included, who had acquired more worldly goods than poor Monica, who had been more places and given more orders and read more books, and yet in their hearts would trade everything to feel the peace enjoyed by Monica in this room by the window where she viewed life in her special way.

For many of us, it is already too late. We have stored up the wrong kind of treasure!

"Do come again!" she said sincerely. "I shall, Monica, I shall. Say a prayer for me!" "Oh, I will! I will!" she said with her swollen fingers wrapped in mine.

Somehow I knew she would.

You see, Monica in a sense had always remained the innocent barefooted little girl that Father Stanton knew and, as such, her prayers were powerful enough to demand the full attention of that loving Father near whose throne she had faithfully lived out her whole life.

7

Timmy

Cursory examination of West Huntley's history shows some clans took harder knocks than others. One such clan was the Scotts.

The Scotts go back a long way around Corkery. In the 1830's Michael Scott and Julia Banks settled in the pines and cedars between the Seventh and Eighth Lines. They had five sons. Three, Patrick, James and John married three Carroll sisters from South March: Mary Ann, Catherine and Sarah. Another son named Michael, married Mary Jane Kennedy of Corkery, daughter of Pat Kennedy (son of John, the first settler) and Mary Ann Horan. The fifth son, Tim, married Emma Hayes, also of Corkery. Their son John Leo survives. He's ninety-four.

I have known many descendants of these five marriages. Their fine mettle is largely due to the many tragedies which have plagued their lives ... their characters have been forged in the fire of suffering.

I remember the time Matt Scott lost two children in a fire. I remember Kathleen Scott losing her husband Archie at a young age and the severe burning incurred by her son John. I remember Walter Scott's loss of his dear wife and his courage in raising six children alone and how John Leo Scott had ten to care for after his wife Jessie's untimely death. Cecilia Scott Carroll buried her daughter Theresa (only thirty) and Susan Gosson Scott buried her seventeen-year-old daughter Rita and her thirty-nine-year-old husband John Matthew. Then, there was the accidental death of Michael at age four (son of John Scott and Sarah Carroll) and the death of Mary Ann Carroll Scott (wife of Patrick Scott) at age twenty-eight.

Another Scott family that has had more than its share of trouble is the family of Edmund and Lois. They have buried four children. I never knew the first three, one of whom, a ten-year-old girl, was killed by a car in front of their home. But I did know the fourth, a son, who just may have been one of the finest Scotts of all. He died a year ago this writing. He was but thirty-nine. He left Donna and two children, Colleen and John. His name was Tim.

I first met Timmy in 1971, around the time I bought my grand-mother's farm and some twenty head of cattle from her son, Ignatius O'Keefe. Timmy was then living with his parents, and as I often called upon Edmund to help me in my arm's length operation of the farm, I came to know a bit of Timmy: a low-key, obliging young gentleman with a natural love for farming, hunting and nature. He soon became a valued employee of an elevator company, married, and built himself a cosy home on the back of his parents' farm on the Tenth Line. In 1981, he relocated: he purchased the lower fifty acres of my old O'Keefe farm and in time began construction of his dreamhouse there, just off the Carroll Side Road.

Timmy was his father's son. He had his dad's habit of taking one step at a time, of thinking things through, and letting a plan unfold after ample consideration of all possibilities. He also brought a freshness to the challenge of farming, enjoyed tinkering with the machinery, and took pride in his accomplishments. As a man of the soil, he saw agriculture as an art and in his chatty discussions about farming showed a wisdom beyond his years.

Father and son had a strong bond. They shared a mutual respect. They worked, travelled, and hunted together. One the king, the other his prince. The prince learned well at his father's knee and at times even became the teacher. The openness of their relationship led to heated discussions, but I could never imagine Timmy speaking too uncivilly to either of his parents.

Over the next seventeen years, Timmy and I developed a quiet friendship. I have no idea what he saw in me, but, in him I saw a natural goodness, untainted by worldly ambitions. When I heard he was dying, it took me some time to decide if he would want to see me.

To be honest, I have never found it easy to visit the terminally ill. Deep hidden streams of conflicting emotions overflow into one's consciousness: to find the correct words; to bring cheer without bravado, compassion without pity, and tenderness without sentiment. Often no words come: just the silence of antiseptic walls ... two friends alone sharing thoughts and feelings ... two souls touching on a plane beyond time.

Such moments with the dying are awesome ... both visitor and patient aware of powerful forces of peace, hope, courage, love, and great energy at work far beyond human understanding.

A lady once touched Jesus's cloak. She was healed. Jesus asked who had been responsible for the energy leaving His spirit. It was a singular moment of great grace! A miracle had taken place as easily as electricity runs a wire. So it is with our visits to the dying. Latent forces of spiritual healing are present. Like Christ, the visitor gives something to the patient; like the woman with her sickness, the visitor receives special blessings from the one marked for paradise.

This field of power surrounding the dying was clearly demonstrated by a young mother whom I once visited in the Palliative Care Centre of the old Ottawa General Hospital. I passed along cavernous halls of grey, green and purple into a large dreary room and saw in one corner my friend Anne Hinton lying as a white rose on a wasted moor.

We talked for an hour, her keen mind dissecting ideas like a surgeon's scalpel. Attractive, well-educated, an accomplished pianist and mother of four, she spoke as one already grappling with the wonderment of her new journey. What strength she showed! Poise! Dignity! *Savoir-faire!* All her thoughts expressed in terms of endearment. The exact nature of our discussion has escaped me. But one of Anne's statement has not, "Gary, I can literally feel in my heart the power of the prayers being said for me and over my bed I often see a small white cloud which I take to be a sign of the prayers being offered for me in heaven and on earth!"

That night I took away far more than I left. Her brother asked me to be a pallbearer. I said no! I would be too upset. I hoped Anne understood. I took a seat in the back far corner of the church. The entire Mass was a joyous celebration orchestrated in every detail by Anne herself. A white cloth on the coffin, white flowers, white vestments ... as if a big white cloud from Anne encompassed everyone.

The fifty-acre farm of Tim and Donna, simply put, is postcard-picturesque. All sides slope gently towards a long gully once probably an extension of Coady's Creek. These hills and burns and glens skirting this gorge form a charming vignette. In this valley, a fresh spring was once deep enough for a summer's dip. On a knoll some hundred yards from the Carroll Side Road, once stood the first log house built in the late 1850's and beside it several apple trees and a trusty old well. It was on this same rise of land that Tim strung out his beautiful bungalow in 1982.

As a boy I knew every ground hog hole and bush on this land. Many people have owned it, but only O'Keefes ever worked and lived there. Up until the arrival of the O'Keefes, speculators passed it around: first Cornelius Buckley in 1823, then Pat Nelligan from Ramsey, John Meehan from Corkery and W.G. Wylie, a business tycoon from Lanark County. In 1847, Edward O'Keefe bought the whole one hundred acres for his bride Mary Anne White, the daughter of nearby neighbours James White and Honora Mahoney. Like poor Timmy, Edward died young. The land first went to David his brother, then to another brother Tom, then to Tom's son, William, and finally to John, a widowed brother of Edward. The first three brothers built their home on the upper half of the hundred while John took the lower to continue raising his five children, all of whom came with him from Ireland around 1857. Margaret married a hotel owner named Cox from Pakenham; Betsy married Tom Kennedy and lived where Mary Benny Kennedy now resides; Patrick married Catherine Flynn from Corkery; David married Sara Cavanaugh from Goulbourn and William reached into Pointe Gatineau for a Mary Mc-Nulty.

While some doubt remains about John ever owning the land, certainly his son Patrick and his wife Catherine, daughter of Mike Flynn and Dorothy Ryan, and granddaughter of John Flynn and Elizabeth Kelly, did. Their children, ten at loose count, were all born there commencing delivery in 1874. By 1940, the last of their children, Jim and Agnes, had moved to Almonte and Ignatius O'Keefe bought the land back for the price of unpaid taxes. I knew both Jim and Agnes, particularly Agnes.

Our first meeting around 1936 was unforgettable. I was sitting in the outhouse at my grandmother's farm, going about my own business as it were, when I spotted through the half-open door a fairly large unfamiliar woman approaching from behind the stables. Apparently it was Agnes coming up the back way from the lower farm to visit her cousins. To a

Tim's favourite hobby.

five-year-old boy, she was a ghost. I threw back the door and put skin to the turf. Only I forgot to pull up my pants: every few feet I fell, then scrambled up and fell again, all the while shouting blue murder. Agnes was spooked as well by the sudden evacuation of an obviously very cheeky child and my grandmother never got tired telling the story. I never forgot Agnes. Her apparition still walks in my mind!

So it came about, that forty-one years later Tim and Donna Scott put life back into the lower fifty: bails of hay and machinery in the yards, fields groomed, clothes on the line, little children scampering under the great oak bordering the laneway in front of the large log barn.

As I pulled Rosie, my relic of an Oldsmobile into that familiar farmyard, the bright November sun did little to lighten my heart.

Inside Timmy was dying and I had come to say good-bye.

Timmy was sitting up in bed reading *Rod & Gun* and as we talked, he continued flipping through the pages absent-mindedly.

My big trepidation was that I was intruding on the delicate privacy of a young gentleman too kind to show any offense if he felt my presence unwarranted. This fear was removed when Timmy suddenly looked my way and said softy, "I kinda knew you were going to come!" Timmy's remark immediately explained why I hadn't been able to get him off my mind for over a week and had got up that morning and said to my wife, "I'm going to see Timmy!"

Timmy expressed only two regrets in our chat. He missed his job, saying he would be willing to work for nothing just to get back in harness. And he was also noticeably upset because he had promised to take his son John hunting and felt he wasn't going to be able to make it.

As I was leaving I went over and took his right hand in mine while he remained seated ... I held a Visitation Order Cross containing the relics of three saints on his forehead and together we said the Our Father, Hail Mary and Glory Be ... during the prayers, his eyes of serene fathomless blue never left mine ... I felt he was staring into my own soul ... a cold tear ran down my cheek as I said, "Timmy, I wish to God I had the power to heal you!"

And he said, "I wish you had too!" And he blessed himself.

As I turned Rosie around beneath the big oak, I could hardly find the laneway.

If anyone ever asks me what heaven's like, I can always say, "I really don't know, but I saw a bit of it once in the eyes of my friend, Timmy Scott!"

Mysteries

Michael O'Keefe and his wife Nellie Moran once rented the old Tom Brown log home perched on the eastern ridge. His son Basil recalled that one morning, around the year 1913, his visiting father-in-law awoke in his ground floor bedroom to see a stranger enter the room, cross in front of the bed, and exit by an adjoining pantry door. Since the pantry had no exit but a bolted window, he expected the man to come back out at any time. After a considerable wait, he looked into the room — it was empty. The window was still bolted on the inside. Based on the description given by Mr. Moran, the stranger could have been a farm hand named Huddlestone who had worked for Michael and had subsequently died.

Cecilia Lockhart often talked about the moving lights she and so many others used to see in and around this same Brown house. As a young girl in the Twenties she remembers seeing lights flitting from house to barn at dizzying speeds. One minute an upper window of the house would be aflame and then one by one all the windows. In a flash, the lights would be gone. And so it went. No rhyme nor reason — one light, then hundreds.

During the same period an identical magic-lantern show used to take place at Clarence Williams' farm on the Dwyer Hill Road. Lights up and down the lane — off, on — frenzied and then measured. At times, both houses became raging infernos.

These lights were not seasonal nor predictable. The sun had long gone; cloudy skies or clear made no difference. The residents of both homes were never aware of anything peculiar happening around them. Yet this strange phenomena was witnessed by many people. By 1926, they had disappeared completely. By then, both houses had new owners.

Angus O'Keefe related another matter of wonderment about this Brown farm. It was common knowledge among his relatives that the woodbox at this home of Michael and Nellie O'Keefe, his aunt and uncle, was often found in the mornings to be completely full of wood, even though no one in the family had brought any in or heard anyone else doing so during the previous night. Was it again Mr. Huddlestone?

Never Put Better

In his book, *Life Is An Adventure*, Robert J. Manion, cabinet minister, surgeon, and winner of the Victoria Cross in the First War, paid an exemplary tribute to pioneer women. His mother, Mary Ann O'Brien, a first cousin of my great-grandfather Ed McDermot, was the daughter of Patrick O'Brien and Nanora Dowling of Ramsey. Although R.J. never knew his grandmother (she died two months after his parents' wedding in 1874) he must have heard much about her.

In his book, R.J. never talked much about West Huntley where his father Patrick grew up, the son of Andrew from the Ninth Line and Mary Forrest (from Eganville), both having died before R.J. reached the age of reason. In 1886, Mary Ann, whose mother was a sister of Ed McDermot's mother, Johanna Dowling, took her children to join Patrick in the North, eventually settling in Fort William (now Thunder Bay).

It was there Robert came to know the heart of the women folk. Blessed with an observant eye, he was a shrewd judge of character, an ability not uncommon among the Irish. As a doctor, he met countless souls roughing out a living in tough times. His appreciation of women's role in the pioneer life has never been put better than in the following lines:

"The chief redeeming feature to counteract the example of rough men, most of whom were uneducated, was the influence of good women — my own mother and the mothers of my boy chums. Many of these women were of the very noblest character: patient, kind, generous and good; seeing no evil, telling no evil; ready at all times to sacrifice themselves for the physical comfort, the moral improvement, and the general happiness of their husband and children. Most of them were ladies in the highest sense of that word, for the term ought to refer more to the quality of heart than of head. They might not know (except by gentle instinct) the niceties of polite society in a modern drawing-room, and they might not always use the proper spoon or fork at a society dinner; but the manner of their gracious spirit was impeccable, for their minds were always bent on serving others. Never would they intentionally hurt anyone's feelings; thoughtful of their loved ones, their neighbours also felt the inner warmth of a self-sacrifice that was of the noblest character. By their unselfish actions, they unconsciously inspired their children to better things. During the years that have gone I have had the opportunity of meeting people of all classes, titled and untitled, and I have met few who equalled them. No doubt the women of today would measure up to the old standards of nobility of character; but they are fortunate in not having to develop their virtues by enduring the hardships and denials."

(By permission of the publisher)

8

Expressing the Heart

Everyone experiences life in a different manner.

Not everyone hears the song of a bird in the same way nor has the same appreciation of its beautiful sound.

In the emotional labyrinth of the mind, our reactions to powerful happenings in our lives are unique. Tears over a tragic loss may profusely flow from one family member whose grief may actually be less than another member who sheds none.

Appearances are deceiving. The heart has its reasons the head has never dreamed of. Reading the heart is a Godly gift.

For most of us, these feelings are not easily understood or expressed. Artists are blessed in that they can use pen, brush or knife to create likenesses of inner joy or pain. But we the silent majority must struggle on with our mediocre interpretations and externalizations of feelings, oftentimes never succeeding very well.

What is most important, however, is that we try. For our own sake, and the sake of others. Joy and grief were meant to be shared. By giving witness to our hidden thoughts and feelings to the best of our ability, we indirectly take on one anothers' burdens.

Our interpretations of life, unprofessional and unskilled though they be, may well hold the answers for others who cannot find their own. Doors are opened and hearts healed by our honest analysis of life's mysteries.

Years ago, a man's love for God was a help to me. His way of telling the world how he felt about Love itself was an inspiration.

I was walking one evening after supper with a Cistercian monk at his monastery at Oka, Quebec. Among other things, I asked him what he would do if the Abbot were to unexpectedly ask him to leave the cloister. The tall habitant in his black and white robe looked down on me with the austerity only seventeen years of penance could have developed and said, "I would lie outside the gate until I was dead!"

A few summers back, my wife and I were attending Mass four decks below the Atlantic on the cruise ship *Bermuda Star*. In the movie theatre where we were it was very quiet. Beyond the hull you could faintly hear a strange hollow sound as man's creation challenged the ocean's force.

It was in this hush that a nightingale named Anna McGoldrick from County Monaghan "stole our hearts away". Anna's voice took on an unearthly tone as she sang a hymn in honour of several couples who were celebrating their anniversaries.

The sheer brilliance of it moved all of us, but especially the old Irish priest saying the Mass. On the verge of tears he described his emotion as he said, "Anna, you must be an angel! My dear father would have stood barefoot all day in the snow just to have heard you sing!"

Not long ago, I went to visit a middle-aged man at his century country home. Under the fat branches of a great Manitoba maple we recalled yesterday's shadows. His stately red-brick home baked in the Sunday sun. His border collie sought the breeze by the house's corner. A lovely daughter came with tea. There was no wife.

She had been killed some months ago. And you could tell my host missed her and still saw her everywhere and that her strength was ever with him and the children.

Later, as I was about to leave, I cautiously inquired how he stood the pain of her parting. He said he didn't know how he ever survived the terror of it all. And his talk quickened as images returned. And I caught the intensity of his pain and I hoped to myself I hadn't upset him.

And then among those thoughts he so honestly released I heard a phrase that said it all and shook me with its force, "My sorrow was so great, it was as if my heart was going to stop!"

The Nickname "Jack"

Around the farm, my uncles and cousins had the habit of calling me "Jack":

> "Time to get the cows, Jack! Time to hit the sack, Jack! How are ya doin', Jack?"

I never gave much thought at the time to the significance of this common appellation. After all, there's "Jack and the Beanstalk", "Jack, be nimble, Jack, be quick" and "Jack of all trades". Lately, even my older son Tom calls me "Jack" and gets a great charge out of it.

Last month I accidentally found out the derivation of its use. It goes back many decades and all the way to Ireland.

In a book I was reading, an American tourist in Ireland picked up a young man thumbing a ride.

"Where are you from, my boy?" said the tourist.

The young lad replied, "I'm proud to say I'm a Dubliner Jack!"

"And what's a Dubliner Jack?" asked the tourist.

"A Dubliner Jack is any young man from Dublin."

So there you have it. My uncles were probably called the same by their uncles and so on, back God knows how many generations.

Now that my son knows he's calling me a young man, he probably will withdraw the complimentary term "Jack" and stick to his other name for me, "Big Guy"!

9

West Huntley's Early Settlers

Unlike the Tudors who came later to Ireland in the Sixteenth Century, the Norman invaders of the Twelfth Century were Catholics. As such, various Religious Orders came in their wake. One Order known as the Cistercians was given a site for an abbey on the River Barrow in Kilkenny County. It was to be called De Valle Santi Salvatoris. As the first monks stood on a hill above the valley, many wept at the view: "a place of horror," they said, "a vast solitude ... darkened with wood and shrub!" A valley waited to be tamed, and even disciplined monks shuddered at the challenge.

The first settlers in West Huntley, the Mordys, Kennedys and Manions must have felt similar disillusionment as they looked upon their new lands. The year was 1821. Around them, before them, and below them stretched hectares and hectares of forest and vegetation wrapped in that same darkness and silence as Kilkenny's Valley of Holy Salvation.

Just getting to West Huntley was a battle: no roads nor bridges, no escape from the humidity of the forest floor with its stagnant swamps and marsh plugged by rotting trees and brush. And everywhere the spreading mantle of nature's massive sentinels forever guarding the brooding darkness from the sun.

A lonely, desolate place! The home of the wolf, fox, bear, porcupine, weasel, mosquito and snake. Here, swarms of blackflies swirling in the breathless air. There, flocks of birds banking out of darkness into blue, running the crest of the valley's great treetops, racing into sunlight and cotton clouds and then disappearing up and beyond the black valley wall.

The sight of that primitive valley bordered by its great pines on limestone ridges must indeed have salted the eye of these first white settlers.

Before any clearing of the land was begun, a pioneer had to know where the best soil lay. For this information he turned to the trees. They knew, for example, that elm, white oak, red oak and white ash grew in the best soil of organic matter, clay and sand. The presence of chestnut, maple, hickory, birch and butternut also meant good loam. Sandy areas mainly nourished pine, yellow birch and spruce, while growths of red and white cedar signified swampy terrain. Dark clay was found under the soft maple and black ash, and white clay beneath the small poplar and white birch. Knowing where to begin was vital to saving time and energy.

As these first 1821 West Huntley settlers were "bushing off" the four-mile Eastern Ridge from the site of the present Catholic Church of St. Michael's to the end of what is now called Manion's Road, they were joined in 1823 and 1825 by the Irish immigrants brought over by the British government. The man in charge was a Scot named Peter Robinson. He was commissioned in 1822 to select from the southwestern part of Ireland some five-hundred Irish peasants for settlement in an area of Canada not too close to the United States Border. The Dukes of Wellington, Kingston and Bathurst in England joined with the Dukes of Ireland such as Devonshire, Doneraile and Kilkenny to give Robinson their fullest support. And what a fine job he did!

These two groups of Robinson's Irish had their fares paid from embarkation at Cobh, Cork, to arrival at their assigned lots. Food, clothing and certain basic implements were also provided. All males over eighteen were given seventy acres plus another thirty which had to be purchased for fifty dollars within a fixed time. Those settlers slated for West Huntley settled on the Western Ridge towards Panmure or in the valley itself mostly north of present Highway 44.

Their names are synonymous with West Huntley's growth: Meehans, O'Keefes, Whites, Currans, Ryans, Manseles, Nagles, O'Connells, Forrests, Sullivans, Buckleys, Cronins, McGraths, Walshs and Roachs. These were the families who along with the Mordys, Manions and Kennedys won each square foot of clearance at great individual sacrifice. By 1825, they numbered thirty-four families and although the white puffs from their crude shanties were few and far between, they had come a long way from the wretched squalor of Ireland. They were coping! They were making a living! They were breaking the trails which we have followed over the decades. They were writing history with their accomplishments.

According to Robinson's rules, each settler was expected to first clear a thirty-three-square-yard opening for his home.

It was a demanding process! Before a tree could be felled, surrounding brush had to be uprooted and smaller stones carried away. With each great tree on its side, all its branches had to be trimmed and piled with the brush for burning. Only then were the logs cut into required lengths, usually twelve feet.

The choosing of a tree was important. Each tree had its own special use and the best size was eighteen inches in diameter and eighty feet in height. The first cut was made on the leaning side some three feet from the base. The fat part, above the stump and below the section suitable for logs, was cut up for shingles or cut out for troughs and buckets. Logs not suitable for buildings were used in fences, roads, bridges, or as rough boards for overlapping roofs. Crevices in the shanty logs used for the buildings were covered over with planks (usually oak with bark) or often with the plain oak bark itself. With the removal of trees, the forest floor began to dry in the shafts of welcome sunlight.

The major difficulty in clearing, however, was the stump. Stumps had to rot before they could be pulled free and stacked for burning, and most stumps took from ten to fifteen years to oblige. Some trees, like the virgin white pines, were protected by their own special resin and they required a waiting period of twenty summers. Only after the stumps were gone could a piece of land be labelled as "cleared" and no longer "under cultivation".

34

While waiting for the stumps to decay, settlers had no choice but to plant their potatoes, Indian corn, wheat and vegetables around those stubborn remnants of other millenniums.

Believe it or not, swamp areas cleared the easiest. By draining water from around the already collapsed beaver-toothed trees, the result was a small grassy area known as a Beaver Meadow. The grass was stringy and tough and very low in nutrients, but it did provide some summer grazing and made excellent bedding for stock in winter. Some country lads were wont to use the folded diameter of beaver blade to whistle out a shrill tune, often slitting open a ruby lip on its sharp edges.

By the 1860's, the white puffs as seen from Finner's Hill, (now Corkery Woods) were a little closer. An influx of new settlers came in 1830, '36, '47, '51 and '54. Some were directly from Ireland. Others were old Robinson settlers from neighbouring townships. A few were "experienced" immigrants from New Brunswick, Nova Scotia and the United States. To the Twelfth Line came the Graces, Mahoneys, O'Briens, Hogans, Morrisseys, Hickeys, Currans, Macdonalds, Kellys, Larkins, Foleys, O'Learys, Leahys, Flynns, and Curtins. Into the valley came the Vaughans, Newtons, Delaneys, Clancys, Malones, Doyles, Killeens, Corcorans, Finners, Murphys, O'Connells, Browns, Carters, O'Briens, Egans, and O'Keefes. On the Ninth Line, the new families included Carrolls, Gallaghers, Egans and Forrests. To the Eighth and Seventh Lines came the Langfords, Bassetts, Caseys, Hayes, Corbetts, Egans, Clarks, Scotts, Horans and Kennedys. West Huntley's development was slowly edging along.

The Irish were proving they could be good managers if given half a chance. Their many insecurities deeply engrained by poverty, illiteracy and slavery were being neutralized. They were gaining confidence in themselves, not just living by the sweat of the brow, but also by the cool calculation of their wits.

Soon vegetable gardens flourished where stumps once rooted. Fruit trees were tenderly nursed along. Among the wild flowers were placed boxes for honey bees. From the ashes of yesterday's trunk, came lye for soap. (It took an acre of hardwood to make one barrel of potash.) They churned their own butter, baked their own bread, and preserved wild berries. And from the maples, they tapped and boiled nature's sweetest nectar.

They learned to cap cool spring water. They dug holes for wells, lined them with stone, and filled the bottoms with slate. They fashioned barrels from slats and caught soft water for washing. They stacked axed piles of maple, ash, oak and cedar to dry in the southwest winds. They built cedar and spruce sheds for flocks of geese, ducks and hens. Small flagstones formed paths through mud; bigger ones acted as doorsteps at house and stable.

Wines came from the dandelion and the chokecherry. Pork was salted down and cold storage set up for keeping milk and baked goods cool and fresh. They canned apples and plums and developed proper facilities for keeping potatoes, carrots and turnips over fall and winter.

To survive in the bush, they developed "bush sense". They avoided swamps considered too dense. They learned how to read the signs of nature, especially when travelling. Every settler knew that moss forms on the north side of trees and that tree branches, particularly the birch's are always longest on the south and southeast sides. Following a creek was a sure way home, and if it was dry, the grass and roots peculiar to its bottom always pointed to the outlet of the stream. Even its stones were cleaner on the side near the source. Coming across cattle was another escape from being lost: chase them and follow them home. To appease hunger, if lost, a knowledge of berries and nuts was mandatory information. Everyone knew how to recognize the green snakeroot herb: shaped like a colt's foot and running horizontally underground, thick like a pipe and bitter like lemon peel. In fact, many immigrants made tea from this herb with a touch of added sugar.

By the summer of 1870, the Irish had been in West Huntley for nearly half a century. By then each farm had a few small outbuildings and bits of land in wheat, potatoes, Indian corn, turnips and pasture. The first log church, built in 1837 within the grounds of the present cemetery, had been replaced with a new church across the road in 1864. It even had a tabernacle and seats. In 1853, a stone house for a resident priest was constructed.

The Irish had considered themselves lucky to have itinerant priests like McNamara, O'Connell and Smith for their first thirty years. Now they had the unheard-of luxury of their own resident priest!

By 1870, education (with four school locations) was rather well developed. Politically, West Huntley was represented by a councillor and deputy-reeve at the Huntley Government Centre in Carp. Catholic families numbered over a hundred and twenty and more than a few good Presbyterian homes added their Scottish stability to West Huntley's progress.

The progress had been slow. But the evidence of these pioneers' efforts was there. The Irish had one foot in the door. It was up to the second and third generations to open it all the way and walk into the next century with pride and distinction.

Paddy

"Paddy, this drinkin' has gotta cease, d'ya hear?" said the judge. "I hate to do this to ya, but it's five hundred dollars or a month in jail!"

"Thank ya, your Honour," said Paddy. "But if ya don't mind, with all the troubles I've had lately, I just as soon take the five hundred this time. I need the money!"

*Statue of the Virgin, at St. Michael's Church,
dedicated to all the Corkery pioneers and their
descendants. It overlooks St. Michael's
graveyard.*

The Burnt Lands

My sun was always golden
In those green, green years of yore,
When the burnt lands held all the dreams
A little heart could store.

Its meadows did meander
To a haze of lightening blue
Where the amber clouds of morning
Met the melting silver dew.

On those burnt lands of fresh delight
My spirit still runs free
Over hills and dales and hidden trails
Known secretly to me.

Lovely Gougane Barra

(I visited Gougane Barra, the Sixth-Century home of St. Finn Barra. He had a hermitage on the edge of a lake high in the mountains of West Cork. Monks prayed there in stone cells for six hundred years. It became a place of pilgrimage and still is to this day. It's a lovely, mystical, sensuous setting. Robert Gibbons, a Protestant biologist and writer, often visited there. He called it the holiest place he had ever known.)

Round deep lagoons   *Where sighs did rise*
Wild flowers bloom   *Up limestone sides*
In lonely Gougane Barra,   *Of dark-eyed Gougane Barra,*
Where hermits longed   *Where rains run down*
In prayer and song   *Without a sound*
Like Knights   *Round the crown*
Under moons of Tara   *Of St. Finn Barra*

Here the Lee breaks free
Down to the sea
From its womb in Gougane Barra,
And ferns do creep
Round hermits' sleep
As herons are awinging,
And somewhere near
For only God to hear
The nightingales are singing.

Ireland, July, 1987

The Burnt Lands, Upper Mahoney Road, 1989.

Gougane Barra, Cork, with Cronin Hotel on the left, 1987.

The Little Artist

(On O'Connell's Bridge in downtown Dublin, I saw a little girl drawing pictures on the pavement with coloured chalk. Old newspapers served as her mat. I chatted briefly with her as people dropped coins on the paper.)

As she sat upon her paper rug
Her soul so cold and bare
The faceless throngs did pass along
A few to stop and share.

What sorrow had her wee heart borne
And she but only seven
This little bird of Dublin Town
With one foot set in heaven.

Upon the bridge, she traced her work
With a silent stare of need
Parnell fought for such a one
Against the men of greed.

Now often when I feel depressed
By a lack of this world's leaven
My mind runs back to that paper rug
And that sweet colleen of seven.

Ireland, March, 1968

Another artist on O'Connell Street, 1988.

10

The Way It Was

When the first Irish came into Upper and Lower Canada, they were well aware they would be under British rule just as they had been at home. In government, commerce, justice, education, and religion, white Anglo-Saxon Protestants would be in firm control.

With one major difference: the Irish knew they would be basically free to live without the fear of foreclosures, famines and religious restraints. They also knew the English had not eliminated the cultural identity of Canada's original inhabitants, the Indian and the French.

Back home, race, religion, suffrage, ownership, culture and even language, had been virtually eradicated under Elizabeth, Cromwell, the James boys, Anne and the Four Georges. The Act of Union in 1801 had placed Ireland and Great Britain under the title "The United Kingdom of Great Britain and Ireland". The great Grattan spoke eloquently to his fellow Anglo-Irish parliamentarians urging them not to accept the British bribes (allowance pay) in return for their votes to dissolve the Irish government. Just before 1800, Wolfe Tone gave it his best shot only to witness the disaster of the French-supported West Coast rebellion of 1798. Even Robert Emmet's insurrection in 1803 went for nothing. The British brought his lover, Sarah Curran, down to the Dublin jail by carriage and with a flick of its window blind, she saw his head spiked on an outside post. Ireland had virtually ceased as a nation. What had been a foregone conclusion for centuries was made official by the Act of Union.

True, Ireland had a hundred voices at Westminster. But they were seldom heard. Four and a half million Irish "British" citizens had no say in the operation of their country. Landlords subdivided the land into smaller and smaller plots, forcing the Irish peasant to grow the cheapest crop, potatoes. The taxes and the rents increased, import protection disappeared, and the recession after the Napoleonic Wars brought little value for produce.

O'Connell set out to win emancipation. In those days Catholics could go to Westminster providing they took an oath declaring the chief doctrine of the Catholic Church was false. Since no one would take the oath, no Catholics went to London. Eventually, by peaceful trickery, O'-Connell and Fitzgerald found a way to contravene the emancipation law. Ultimately faced with either civil war or emancipation, the Duke of Wellington and Sir Robert Peel reluctantly allowed the Emancipation Act of 1819 to be passed. In 1831, a National School System was set up allowing religious instruction by the clergy of different faiths. Unfortunately such concessions didn't help feed the impoverished millions. By 1835, poverty had made heavy inroads into Ireland.

The Irish were poor long before they were hungry. O'Connell cried out: give us legislative independence and the distress of Ireland will lessen. Thirty meetings of O'Connell's believers were held in 1843; one at

Tara's Hill had 250,000 present. They called for a repeal of the Act of Union; they never got it. O'Connell died a broken man in 1847, the same year the "Black Forty-Seven Famine" hit all of Ireland. Two million would die of hunger and disease. Some luckily took to the seas long before the big famines arrived. By 1835, sixty thousand per year were leaving. In 1854, the number going to the United States was nearly half a million. All together four million left Ireland for better or for worse.

Here in Canada, as a whole, the immigrants, like the original inhabitants, fared better. In fact the survival of the French Canadian gave some confidence to the incoming Irish. They saw that, in spite of constant raids along the seaboard by the New Englanders, in spite of the loss of Port Royal (Annapolis) in 1710 and Louisbourg and Quebec in 1757, in spite of the 1713 Treaty of Utrecht which gave the English, Cape Breton and Acadia (made up of Nova Scotia, P.E.I., New Brunswick, Labrador and Newfoundland), in spite of the deportation of thousands of Acadian French in 1755 to make room for thirty thousand Anglo-Saxon refugees from the mutinous Thirteen Colonies, in spite of all these factors, the French had stayed culturally intact.

By 1812, the three hundred thousand mostly French population of Lower Canada had received many governmental goodies from the Empire's first two English governors of Upper and Lower Canada: James Murray, Earl of Dalhousie, and Sir Guy Carleton, the Baron of Dorchester. Murray's kindness was such that he was replaced after only five years (1763-1768) because of his unsympathetic treatment of Quebec's Protestant merchants who just happened to be outnumbered in population, sixteen to one. His replacement, Sir Guy (1778-96), brought in to tighten the noose round the French, all too soon discovered, as Murray did, that English greed was behind many sanctions imposed (especially in Upper Canada) by the Legislative Ruling Class. He did his utmost to settle unfair practices and redress injustices. Eventually, he was shipped out as well, not back home, but to India. Ironically, both these good men were Gaels: Murray, Scottish, and Carleton, Irish from County Tyrone. Pre-Confederation Canada had many such Gaelic leaders guiding the colonies or provinces to Dominion Status.

Although the French did receive some favours, the situation wasn't all rosy. The 1763 Treaty of Paris gave all New France to the British. The French Motherland as much as disowned its children. Many French, in fact, sixty thousand, did what the Irish Earls and Wild Geese had done in Ireland when faced with similar restraints from the British: they got out of the country. To remain, meant enslavement to a culture, government and religion foreign to the French-Catholic seigniorial system, to land dealings ruled by Clergy and Crown, to trade and commercial enterprises reserved almost exclusively for British entrepreneurs, to a system of education extended only to the Upper classes, and to a judicial and legislative administration entirely in the hands of the Establishment.

With the French of Canada on the ropes in the late Eighteenth Century, why not the knockout punch? As far as numbers went, the French population was small compared to the numbers in Ireland. Their absorption and suffocation could have been swift.

Why did the English tolerate the French presence?

The answer is simple: the British needed the French in case of attack from the Thirteen Colonies. The Colonies, it is true, had worked for decades with the British to squeeze the French from the Atlantic seashores and provinces. But, now the winds blew differently. The Colonies were revolting against the heavy burden of taxes imposed by the British. Independence was soon to come!

When it did, the British military need for French and Indian support became ever more vital. The possibility of the United States invading Canada was great. France had already helped the Americans during the Revolution since it didn't want an "All-British North America". In turn, the British, if they lost the French Canadian military assistance, might end up with North America being all American. Such a situation would have been economically disastrous for the British, since their treasury was already bankrupt after the Napoleonic Wars (even though they had bled Ireland of men, horses and cash).

So it was that as long as the American menace loomed, the British could never and would never completely stamp out the French Canadian. In fact, without the Frenchman's presence and his strong pluck for independence, and without the American threat on the horizon, Canada could have easily become part of the United Kingdom of Great Britain, Ireland and India. In addition, without the French, Catholicism, Presbyterianism, Methodism, and indeed all minority religions in Canada would most likely have been completely destroyed. And, as it turned out, without the French help in the war of 1812, Canada might easily now be part of the U.S.A.

As a result of concessions to the French, Guy Carleton could boast he had 60,000 Frenchmen ready to take up British arms. Indeed, when war did come with the Colonies, the British did receive their promised help from the French who also convinced their allies the Abenaki Indians to join the British side. After initial losses, the British team rallied and given the back-up of forces fresh from Napoleonic victories, the war soon ended in 1814 with several North American boundaries being expanded in favour of British holdings.

But as so often happens, once the circumstances in the political amphitheatre change, certain sides decide to revise the rules of the game in their own favour. Once the Americans had been removed as a danger, the British began to turn the screws on the French.

In Lower Canada, the Protestant merchants this time successfully renewed their demands for control. The result was the Rebellion of 1837 and the rise and fall of French heroes like Chenier, Chevalier, Prieux and

Papineau. In 1841, the British "united and conquered" by dissolving Upper and Lower Canada into one Province. The French thus lost the legislative protection promised in 1774 and with it the freedom of language and religion. Soon the seigniorial system would be gone forever.

In actuality, the neutralization of the French majority had been started many years before the Quebec rebellions. The plan was to allow into Canada as many immigrants as possible of non-French, non-Catholic persuasion. The process went on for some hundred and thirty years, even long after the American war. Streams of Loyalists continued to come from the Colonies, and mercenaries from Germany, Switzerland and Holland (all Germanic countries) were welcomed into military service during the two wars, and in return were given, as were the British veterans, choice acreage in both Upper and Lower Canada. Well into the mid-Nineteenth Century, the WASPS poured into Quebec, Montreal, London, Waterloo, Guelph, and York picking up the best that patronage could offer. The Orange Irish and Scottish Presbyterians came too as did Negroes, Quakers and Mennonites. Many a Germanic immigration boat sailed by the quarantined coffin ships of the Irish (anchored at Grosse Isle below Quebec city), carrying healthy, well-fed singing passengers upstream to the waiting arms of the British authorities.

When the Canadian ports finally opened to Presbyterians and Catholic-Scottish weavers and Irish-Catholic peasants, the main reason for the British decision was not entirely philanthropic. After all, even though they were Gaels, they were also British subjects. They were also good workers and very fertile. The British took little risk. They knew some Gaels would intermarry with the French, that the chosen settlements for the most part were on lands far from the trouble spots, and that the immigrants of 1819, 1820, 1823 and 1825 had been hand-picked by loyal British administrators (teachers, pastors and magistrates) back in Ireland.

The immigrants of 1823 and 1825 to Carleton and Peterboro then were on the face of it, mostly peace-loving, hardworking, supposedly loyal Royals. Naturally many faked support for the British just to get out of Ireland. But it is a fact that had they not shown in Ireland a general respect for the British way, they would never have been chosen. The idea that the British paid good money to set up peasants at odds with the Crown holds little veracity. It's true, troublemakers were moved out, but usually to such places as the sugar-cane fields of Bermuda and the mines of New South Wales.

The Ballygiblins of Ramsey, part of the 1823 Robinson settlement, were an exception. They may have been a different lot. They were branded as a rough-and-ready crowd of hotheads, not typical of the average law-abiding Robinson settler. They got into a skirmish at a tavern near Carleton Place with some Scottish-Orange soldier-settlers. The Scots replied by attacking the home of an Irishman named Roche in Almonte. It was a Sunday and the Ballygiblins were at Mass there. An

44

Irishman was killed and Roche's house burnt. As a result of these clashes, the Ballygiblins were never popular in Ramsey. Some were no more welcome in Irish homes than Scottish ones.

The Ballygiblins were apparently named after the parish in Ireland from which they emigrated. Since Ireland's parish limits often crossed county borders, the Ballygiblins were probably from an area overlapping Tipperary, Cork, and Limerick counties. The quickness of some fellow immigrants to acknowledge their disdain for them, would suggest they were known back in Ireland as not being the best British citizens. The British may well indeed have sent them over to get rid of them.

The truth of this Scottish-Irish encounter is that an impartial inspection of the court cases that followed the troubles, revealed the Ballygiblins had been unjustly treated by the presiding judge in Perth. After all it was Scottish country. And the witnesses from Almonte were all influential Scots who, as they say in the West, "owned the town".

The fact that the Ballygiblins never fared well in Ramsey after the court cases was unfortunate. After all, they merely reacted to the banterings of a few soldiers: remember they were still Catholic, still Irish, and just as free as the next settler. Being slightly off-Tory-blue didn't matter; their fight was with their fellow Gaels, the Scots, not the English. They made it clear they weren't in Canada to be insulted. Perhaps their stance left its mark!

Revenge runs deep in the wilds. The Donnelly murders in Western Ontario showed how deep. The Donnellys were hated because they had sided with the British in Ireland. The Ballygiblins were disliked because they probably were cool to the British ways and didn't quite fit into the Scottish milieu. Both the Scots and Irish have long memories.

The names of the Ballygiblins have never been entirely recorded. As result of those two battles in April, 1824, nearly all the Ballygiblins left Ramsey. Many went to West Huntley; some left the country; some were murdered or disappeared mysteriously.

John Curran was shot in the attack in Almonte. John French and Bat Murphy both drowned (?). Patrick Lahey died unsuspectedly in 1825 in West Huntley. John Sullivan and John Roche were murdered in West Huntley around 1828. Con O'Keefe, John Ryan and James McGrath moved away. Patrick O'Keefe's son, Tom, died in 1831 in West Huntley; he was in his late twenties. Pat Sullivan went to Montreal. John Coughlin in 1826 mysteriously left his wife and family in West Huntley, never to return. Bill Roche, of course, lost his house and his brother John. Bill Brown went rafting and never came back. Not a good record by any means. The Ballygiblin affair was an insidious sore that took over a decade to heal.

As already mentioned, further Irish immigration into West Huntley followed in 1830, '36, '47, '51, '54. As they settled and busied themselves just surviving, the fight for freedoms raged on, especially in Upper Canada. From 1820 to 1851, men like Gourlay, MacKenzie, Lount, Duncombe, Matthews, Rolph and Anderson challenged the ivory towers of Sir Francis Bond Head, Powell, Fitzgibbon, MacNab, Attorney General John Beverley Robinson (brother to Peter), the British Governor, Sir Peregrine Maitland - the Governor of Upper Canada, John Simcoe, Bishop John Strachan and others like Ryerson, Jarvis, Bolton and Hickory. In 1790, only one-tenth of Upper Canada was Anglican, yet nearly all control of church and state rested in the hands of Anglican gentry.

As the years unfolded, the various revolts paid off. In addition, the Scottish Presbyterians and Yankee Methodists, Baptists, and Congregationalists helped weaken the Family Compact. Soon the Loyalists were outnumbered in Upper Canada despite the increased immigration of German, Black, Indian, and Orangeman. By 1851, the Establishment was crumbling under its own weight. The Independence of Canada was not far off.

Canadians owe much to these reformers. Without their nettlings Canada would be different today. The school history texts written for years by teacher-historians steeped in Loyalist ties and chosen for the schools by educational ministers with strong Saxon roots, never gave much credence to these radicals. They were branded as instigators of bloodshed, lootings, burnings and executions. But Riel, MacKenzie and Papineau and men of their mould were not all emotionally warped buffoons. Because of them, the Canadian man in the street had the vote long before the lower and middle classes of Britain.

Nevertheless, after 1867, Canada, of course, was to remain still very much a British stronghold. The wealth of the old Anglo-Saxon families naturally continued to rule the parliaments and market places. Patronage persisted: "who you were" taking precedence over "what you were". To give truth its due, however, most of Canada's fine structural organization can be traced largely to the excellent orderliness and intelligence of these Anglo-Saxon minds.

The average early West Huntley citizen probably had only fragmentary knowledge of these political struggles. His historical awareness would have been quite limited. He would know that Carleton County had been once part of Bathurst District (named after the Secretary of State for the Colonies) and that in 1838 it shifted to the District of Dalhousie (named after the Earl of Dalhousie, Governor in 1820).

Some may have known Huntley was named after the estate in Northern Scotland of the then present Governor, the Duke of Richmond, and that Carleton was named after Sir Guy Carleton, once Governor of the Colonies. Some might have heard that Carleton County was formed in 1792 and that the Townships of March, Huntley, and Ramsey (named after James Ramsey, a Colonial Administrator) were established in 1821, a year after George IV came to the throne. Of course, nearly everyone would have known the seat of local justice had been switched in 1838 from Perth to Bytown and that West Huntley had official representation on the Huntley Administrative Board by 1851.

West Huntley's position, far from the borders of discontent, helped it get on with the business of living. The people worked in the relative peace they deserved.

They had had their fill of unrest on other days in another land where wins and losses on battlefields, roadsides, and oceans were often greedily reversed in the drawing rooms and bedrooms of the mighty, where kings and queens and barons played games of intrigue to protect their castles, where bishops and knights, to get the edge on opponents, often coldly sacrificed their unknown subjects as pawns.

Better the peace of the valley! And the work of the day and the rest at eventide!

Limericks

A lady named Margaret's verbosity
Was exceeded only by her velocity
In confession her sound
Drove the people around
To completely empty the sacristy

•

There was an old man named Sheehan,
Who came home as high as the ceilin'
Upon hitchin' his horse
To his house's front porch
He pulled it away with great feeling

•

There was an old lady named Scott
Who to confession went more than she ought
When once in the bin
It was sin after sin
'Til the priest's holy dickens she caught

•

A man named Joe found his sister a bore
In fact, he didn't like her much any more
So he took up his axe
To settle their match
And buried it deep in her locked kitchen door

(Based on true stories in West Huntley)

11

A Man Named John

My wife and I came upon the Catholic Church in Rathmore quite by chance. We had been hopscotching around the back roads of Kerry, Ireland in our scarlet Cortina in hopes of finding a Mass we could attend since it was August 15 and the Feast of the Assumption. I say hopscotching with tongue in cheek since a foreigner tends to do nothing fancy in a car that has the steering and shifting equipment on the right side.

In Ireland, this Feast of the Blessed Virgin is a Holy Day, a day when the Catholic faithful are required to attend Mass. Since many people were entering the church, we presumed that a Mass was about to begin.

Inside, the church was tastefully designed and decorated. It was ablaze with light. Vigil candles burned everywhere and a strong summer sun animated the church's stained-glass windows.

Except for the very front and the very back of the church, the place was packed. The tendency to leave the front pews empty is a common practice in most churches. But the large empty space at the back between the entrance and the last pews was a bit of a mystery. What could this area be for?

The answer soon came. Just before Monsignor O'Dougherty stepped out on the altar, a great body of men swished silently into the church filling up the back. It was the standing-room section. No pompish heraldry for them. They were the perfect examples of Christ's admonition that the last shall be first, or was it, the last *in* shall be the first *out*?

Shortly after their arrival, as if on cue, the priest entered the sanctuary and Mass began. It was as if he wouldn't start without them. During the Mass they knelt on the marble floor, hats in hand, answering all the prayers by rote. I felt I was watching the heart of Ireland at prayer.

After the final blessing, the same precise swiftness shown at the start of Mass was repeated. Before the priest's tender tootsies hit the sacristy, the whole group had left as stealthily as it had entered.

Of course, no one would dare misconstrue the rapid coming-and-going of these good men as a lack of devotion. It's just that most rural Irishmen don't go in much for broadcasting their piety. Ostentation and ritual are not part of their religious practice.

Perhaps, these Irish came by this habit good and honestly. Religious persecutions may have hammered into them this custom of hiding their religious beliefs so as to keep their religion alive. It was only yesterday that sentries guarded the caverns and barns where Masses were offered. Failure to raise the alarm could mean death for everyone. Each Mass participant carried a crucifix in his great coat or sweater with the cross's arms cut off to escape detection. They were careful people in matters of their faith. Spies were everywhere. Flame, sword and gun swept the land. They hid their Mass Stones with care. Perhaps they learned to hide their religious feelings, too.

In West Huntley, the spirit of faith as practised by those of Eire was also prevalent. My memory recalls those late Thirties and early Forties when the hayburners still brought the families to church. Of course, many like Eddie Grace, Hugh Kennedy, Alex Grace, and Dinny O'Brien had turned in harness for horns, but a good number still used buggy and cutter as standard modes of conveyance over the washboard or snow-packed roads.

Before Mass, the men always gathered under the log portals of the horse stalls to exchange barbs and news. The Irish wit is particularly keen among its own. Everyone seemed to delay his entry to the church as long as he could. Suddenly the church bell would give its five-minute warning. Last puffs and chews would be taken. And then, just like the men of Rathmore, they would hit the entrance with unrestrained gusto.

My cousin, John O'Keefe, was a members of this "last-minute club". With the aura of a man on a vital mission, he headed directly for a position in the loft. With that arm-swinging canted swagger of his he would ascend the twisting stairs two or three steps at a time, bow to the ladies' choir perched before the rose window and without breaking stride, slide into a wooden pew, his rosary beads already out and slipping through calloused fingers.

Everyone liked John. He was the same with all he met: the nervous smile, a bit of blarney, and a warm hand in greeting. He fell easily into the category of a ruggedly handsome Irish gentleman.

John and Margaret O'Keefe's Family
Back: Stephen, Joe, Kenny, John, Gerald, Terry, Carroll
Front: Pat, Noreen and Ray

John and his wife Margaret Carroll had bought the old Curtin farm from John's uncle, the neighbourly Nash O'Brien. This nostalgic home had a beautiful setting in a valley just off the Twelfth Line. A half-mile lane fell gently to their front yard.

On a summer's eve, from a vantage point on the north side of the Twelfth Line, the sweep of colour would steal any heart: crops running with the breeze, chestnut mares and Durhams on the green, mature elms splitting the big setting sun, and grey and white outbuildings beside the old home, its red brick a fiery hue.

My wife and I often visited John, Margaret, and their ten children. We would all settle around their sprawling Findlay stove and enjoy tea, cookies and pleasantries. How Margaret ever had any cookies with ten children on the prowl was always a mystery. While short of most worldly possessions, no one in this home wanted for necessities, especially love. I always felt comfortable in their home and appreciative of the hospitality so gladly given to all who visited.

John O'Keefe loved his God, family and neighbours. He was his own man. Like most Irish men he had a private side no one would ever see. His faith in God was carefully based on the rock-bed tenet that Divine Providence guided his life. Like the other men of Corkery and Rathmore, his faith was not flauntingly paraded, but kept in quiet reserve as the cornerstone of life's trials. One had the suspicion that if John O'Keefe was ever called upon to defend this faith, he would bring his fist to the mouth of any man who would disparage it.

After Mass, John and others like him would gather quickly around the old church well. As the single tin cup moved about the group, I can still see the faces of so many good men since gone for our midst: Jack Killeen, Tim and Frank Scott, James Vaughan, Tom Kelly, Lorne Charlebois, Eddie Grace, Jim Carroll, Mohr O'Brien, Alphonse Meehan, Jimmy Flynn, Martin Ryan, Jackie Mantil, Lawrence Kennedy, Jimmy Kennedy, Bob Mantil, Jack Curtin, Benny and Mike Kennedy, Allan Williams, Ignatius O'Brien, Ignatius O'Keefe, Jackie and Raymond Mantil, Alex Grace, Jimmy Forrest and Sylvester Finner ... men who hid much of their faith from public view, yet were the heart of this country's Catholic Church, men whose religious ties reached beyond the sea to their brothers on the west coast of Eire.

For me, John O'Keefe will always epitomize the brash, jocular, devil-may-care Irish Christian of his time.

I last saw him as he lay unconscious in hospital. His great heart was soon to stop. I wished him the reward of his Faith and left.

He was only fifty-three.

All Corkery mourned his passing, especially his faithful Margaret, his charming daughter, and nine of the finest boys any man ever brought into this world.

Paddy Brady of Cork

In his book, *Sweet Cork of Thee*, Robert Gibbings tells the story of Paddy Brady's first visit to a hospital. This is the way he heard it from Paddy himself at an August sheep dipping in Gougane Barra shortly after Paddy came out of hospital:

"Well," he said, "I never put down such a day in my life as that day I went in. I was in Cork before noon and 'twasn't till six o'clock in the evening that I could face up to it. The wife took me to the pictures and what was it but fellows dying in the snow. 'For the love of God, come out of this,' I said. So then we went to get a cup of tea and I couldn't drink it — 'twas that weak, 'twas like water. 'We'll go for a walk down by the Mardyke, have a look at the river,' says my wife. Would you believe it, before we got to the first seat it was raining. At six o'clock she left me at the gate, and who did I meet coming out but Paddy Byrne. 'What ails you?' he says. 'An ulcer,' I told him. 'Oh my God,' he said, 'there's poor Jackie Shea inside and he after being operated on for the same thing, and he'll never recover.'

"I tell you," said Pat, "if a nurse hadn't caught a hold of me at that moment, I'd have bolted like a rabbit. 'Go through the door at the end there,' she says, 'and they'll look after you.' Well I could hardly walk with the fear that was on me. Me own sweat was tripping me. 'Get into bed now,' says another nurse. 'I'll put the screens around you while you undress,' she said. And in all the beds around me there wasn't a face that I knew. I sat down on the bed to take off me boots — they'll never go on me again, I thought, I wonder who'll wear them after I'm gone. And the new pants on me, too. 'Twould have been better maybe if I'd come in the old ones; maybe the family would never get them back. And when I undid me collar the button came off. Small matter, I thought.

"And then, while I was bending down, didn't a voice say over the screen: 'How's yourself, Pat?' And when I looked up, wasn't it Tom Cooney, from Ardtully. Well, 'twas as if I'd hooked a two pound trout. 'Yerra, man, 'tis grand in here,' says he. 'Jack Keogh is after going out yesterday, loose as a hare and I'll be going out meself next week.' Before I was five minutes in bed the nurse was in with a tray full of tea and sure from then on I was like a horse in his own stable."

Friendship?

Any enemy of MacCarthy was Rafferty's friend. "MacCarthy," says Rafferty, "they were discussin' ya at Noonan's the other night, and some said you're not fit to sleep with pigs." Asked MacCarthy, "Ah, ha, and what said my friends to that aspurgement?" Says Rafferty, "Sure ya would ha' been proud of dem. To a man, they said you were!"

Pebbles, Boats, Eggs and Shoes

On the West Coast of Ireland in the Islands, men abandon boats that have lost a man to the sea.

A good boatbuilder in Ireland can feel the bad luck surrounding a boat he is repairing. White stones in a boat are unlucky. And not just in boats! White pebbles were placed near the burial urns in the Bronze Age and ever since, the Gaels have associated them with death.

In Galway, hens are not always a blessing. Their white eggs buried in a neighbour's field are thought to bring misfortune on the owner. Hens are never transported in a car unless to the market. Hatching hens are never taken from their habitat. And it all stems from the fact hens lay white eggs.

Burying the Dead

In old Ireland, a grave would never be opened on Monday. Only close friends or relatives of the dead man's family could dig the grave. The dead were laid out with pennies on their eyelids, prayer books under the jaws and rosary beads round the fingers. The clock of the house was stopped at the moment of death and mirrors turned to the wall. If a man owned bees, the bees were told the news and a crepe hung over the hive. Many corpses were washed and dressed by the same women who had helped at their births. The coffin was carried to the graveyard by friends who always took the longest route. The coffin was sealed with wing-nuts. After the coffin was in the grave it was time for someone to go down, unloosen the wing-nuts and place them on top of the coffin (for the resurrection). If a person's family could not afford a coffin, the body was carried to the cemetery on a front door. A light sheet covered the deceased.

Making A Shoe Fit

The breaking in of new boots or shoes has caused many a man considerable grief. The Irish remedy for those "in a pinch" was to walk through the bog and allow its water to seep in over top. A person was to keep wearing the boots until the leather had softened and completely dried out thereby making a mould of the feet. On next fitting, the boots would be comfortable.

12

Mick Joe

The day they buried Mick Joe Flynn, even nature mourned. It rained so violently only the pallbearers made it to the interment across from St. Michael's. The backhoe operator couldn't come and Bobby Charlebois closed the grave. Bobby is like that ... always around when needed.

Mick Joe Flynn
1924

Mike Flynn had been an antique dealer. And a good one! He didn't make much money, but he had made a living. A little wheeling and dealing! A little badgering, buttering and bantering! Spinning tales, weaving yarns and visiting all the major auctions and sales around the Ottawa Valley. Never taking his work or himself too seriously. Enjoying life to the fullest.

He probably was the best-known West Huntley character of his time. The CBC once did a documentary on him and over the years several newspapers carried his picture with write-ups.

His heart was as big as his fist and his spirit as colourful as his radish complexion and carrot hair. Just a country lad who learned to live with himself and with just about anybody else who chanced to come his way.

Mike and I first met in 1942 when the Eleventh Line was still two paths divided by an isthmus of grass. I was steaming along between potholes on my red CCM bicycle going no particular place fast when I came upon Mike trudging home from the Almonte train. I was twelve and he was in his mid-thirties. My boyish curiosity soon discovered Mike had been with the Jesuit Brothers in Guelph, Ontario, for seventeen years, had decided to return to the world, and this summer day was his first one home. We chatted about the Jesuits, the war, his disappointments and his dreams. And then we went our ways, each, in a sense, beginning his life.

Not long after, Mike built himself a small home and business exactly in front of the stop where we had first met. Only instead of living over the store, Mike lived right in it ... a nest just made for one. If he had ever married, somebody would have had to sleep out. He had an oil stove for heat and no insulation. His inner walls were just big enough to hold up a few personal treasures: old sayings in oak frames, pictures and clocks for which time stood still, knickknacks and knackknicks of all sizes and flavours. Like all of us, Mike kept little mementoes to fill the gaps in yesterday.

Mike's house was a large Fibber McGee's closet, only he lived in it. As the odds and ends slowly stockpiled, Mike was always in danger of one day disappearing into a maze of shoes, lanterns, kettles, chains, harness and "what-cha-ma-call-its". To take inventory was to risk irreversible physical and mental burnout.

Expansion was the only answer. And expand he did! First a huge storage shed and then over the years several appendages to the sides and back of the house. A final touch was the locking into time of a spent schoolbus which he dropped out back and filled with every "you name it, I've got it" item. A bit like Noah's bus, two of all the "doodads" ever made.

His front yard resembled the aftermath of a yearly one-day sale in the lingerie section of Moscow's only department store. Various relics were strewn about like the monuments at Gettysburg.

It was a handy man's paradise but a woman's nightmare: a wheel with no barrow, a birdhouse with entrances big enough for ducks, huge cement flower urns, washed-up washtubs, spindles with no legs and legs with no spindles, each item a conversation piece the character of which enticed countless bargain hunters to his doorstep from all around the neighbouring townships.

But not everyone came to shop. Some came to "shoot the breeze"! Especially, on Sunday afternoons when the seating capacity of his flat was overtaxed by visitors like Herman O'Keefe, the railroader, Harry, the chef, Kelly, the farmer, and Muldoon, the insurance salesman. Mike would shuffle about the kitchen, his rounded shoulders and braces leading the way, his raspy voice idly letting slip a bit of lore about the country with the added punctuation of a whistle, chuckle or gentle slap on his good knee. What a fascinating, engaging character! ... a link with the past, yes, but also a vibrant part of all that was new and fresh around Corkery. A walk down memory lane with Mike was always enjoyable.

The last time I visited him he offered me as usual his best chair, the one identical to a favourite of my mother. Once again I picked his memory. And his face lightened as he stroked familiar names and faces, and his voice would dip to a whisper (even though we were alone) to make an outlandish comment... his hospitality so typical of the Irish ... tea, cookies, fresh fruit, an offer to dinner ... always on the move, puttering, gesticulating, clearing the table, peeling potatoes, moving objects here and there.

Those last forty-five years since we had met had been good to Mike and me. He had been happy in the valley. He had helped make it a better place by his presence. Besides, the Jesuits would never have let him operate a flea market.

When I was leaving, he offered me some fat, red tomatoes and I refused politely saying he probably needed them more than I. Later my wife told me I probably insulted him. I think she was right. I should have taken them. Forgive me, Mike! He had followed me that day to the door as was his custom, and watched as I backed away, his hand slightly raised in farewell.

At the church, Mike must have been pleased. Many friends had come: Pat Egan, Harry Grace, Joe Carroll, Mary Mantil Carroll, Joe Carter, Marguerite O'Keefe Murphy, Basil O'Keefe, Carmel O'Keefe Murphy, her sisters Viola and Inez O'Keefe Beach, and many others I didn't know.

Today, I can't help thinking that Mike must have surely got together in heaven with Almonte's genial Ben Baker, himself a dealer in yesterday's goods. They must spend hours and hours recounting their deals ... Ben in his thick Jewish accent and Mike in his racy Irish brogue. If we could just cop their secrets of selling, we could all be millionaires. If we could learn their secrets of living, we wouldn't bother much about the money.

Elsie's Chest

Nellie was looking through Elsie's trousseau. From the depths of the cedar chest, she lifted out a lovely silk blouse the neck of which was quite shredded.

"Elsie, my dear, what ever happened to this blouse that it is torn so?"

"Ah, Nellie, sweet, I keep it as a reminder of love gone wrong! Do ya mind the time Doodles Maher had my heart aflutter? Well, in case he had any inkling to marry, I casually mentioned to him one day I had a fair-sized trousseau on hand. He never batted an eye!"

"Ah, indeed, I remember Doodles well. As handsome a lad as ever was this side of the Carp. But I never knew why you went off him so quickly."

"Sure the blouse says it all, Nellie. I was sporting it one lazy Sunday afternoon as he and I were sparking on a walk through Flynn's beaver meadow."

"What happened?"

"Well, the poor crature lost all control of himself! And I soon found out Doodles was more interested in my torso than my trousseau and that's why my blouse is tore so!"

Sticks and Stones

Competition is healthy. And school boys have ways of stirring things up. Like the lads from the Twelfth Line who composed this poem about their neighbours in the valley:

> *"Cakes and pies for the Twelfth-Line byes,*
> *Hay and oats for the Eleventh-Line goats!"*

Words guaranteed to add ginger to the next ball game!

55

13

The White Knight of Lahinch

Mrs. O'Brien's easy gaze over the golden strands of Lahinch Bay, County Clare, suddenly turned to terror. There, right under her very eyes was a figure galloping across the beach clad only in a white sheet and a scapular. Her eyes were straining to identify the sex of the apparition, when the sheet blew out to sea and the scapular with a man streaked down the main drag into a pub.

Her friend, a Miss O'Hara, a spinster, and one totally unaccustomed to such sights, had passed the man, head to head as it were, and had become noticeably shaken, her cheeks chalky, and her eyes like cue balls. Mrs. O'Brien calmed her down and together they decided it was not a spirit but young Tommy T_____ in the flesh.

It turned out Tommy had a serious drinking problem. His poor mother was determined to stop him: prayers, fasting, haranguing, threats, and blessed candles burning day and night. This one Sunday morning she had taken a desperate measure and confiscated Tommy's booze and clothes after he had come home sloshed the night before.

Tommy awakened early that Sunday with a woeful thirst, his tongue like glue, his head like a beachball, and the ticks of his clock like rifle cracks in a phone booth.

He went out of control. He made a run for the nearest pub, wrapped in a bedsheet. After one or two, he calmed down, borrowed the owner's coat and walked home, not without shame.

This sad spectacle was re-enacted for several Sundays. It got so when Tommy was dressed nobody knew him. Mothers kept their children indoors; dogs sat in wait; men made bets on his best time from house to pub. The whole town was talking about the T_____'s boy. Tommy had brought colour and dash to the sleepy seaside of Lahinch.

Then suddenly one day Mrs. T_____'s prayers were answered and none to soon, since she had run out of bedclothes. Tommy had come home loaded one dark night, mistook the root cellar for his front door and had free-fallen into the rock basement.

It was to be four months for his broken leg to heal. So a bunch of his drinking buddies passed the hat and sent him off to the Cistercian monks at Mount Melleray near Cappoquin, Waterford, where they ran a small clinic for weaning a man from the bottle.

Tommy's first week there was a wallbanger. His cries could be heard as far as Clogheen, Tipperary. In time he was cured. But he never went home. He stayed on at Melleray as a laybrother and died there in the odour of sanctity.

Back at Lahinch, they were happy for Tommy. But they missed those Sundays when that white-clad knight appeared from behind the break-water hills and raced unabashed into the morning sun. Miss O'Hara continued to talk about it for years after, saying she had never seen anything like it before or since.

Words of Comfort

Some people have the innate ability of saying the wrong thing at the wrong time. Like the time a few friends were gathered around the sickbed of Andy Roach (1870-1947). Andy was lamenting the fact he couldn't remember the places he had buried money on his old homestead (on the south side of Highway 44 at the bottom of Finner's Hill).

Andy had little faith in commercial banks. His grandfather, John, had been murdered around 1829 on the same farm and no doubt Andy's father, William, had drummed into him the philosophy of "never being too careful with money".

As poor Andy was bewailing his situation, one neighbour piped up with the encouraging words, "Never mind, Andy, where you're goin', you won't need money!"

•

And then there's the story surrounding Tom Flannigan's death in a mining accident. The remains were brought home to Aylmer and Kelly and Murphy had the sad task of breaking the news to Mrs. Flannigan.

They knew the street, but weren't sure of the house. By the time Kelly approached the one thought to be Flannigans, his whole body was twitching. He knocked. A lady finally answered.

Kelly was beside himself. He blurted, "Are you the widow Flannigan?"

"Yes," she said, "I'm Mrs. Flannigan, but I'm no widow!"

"That's what you think, Ma'am. Wait 'til ya see what Murphy's got on the wagon!"

•

Neither of the above anecdotes is as cruel as the one told by Oscar Levant. A famous English vaudevillian, George Robey of "The Man Who Broke the Bank of Monte Carlo" fame, commanded a huge attendance at his burial.

Among the mourners was an old-timer barely able to navigate. A bystander asked him how old he was. Shakily the old trouper said, "Ninety-five"!

"Ah," said the other, "it's hardly worth the trouble of going home, is it?"

14

Coffey, Tea, and Sweet Nellie

Herb O'Keefe
1924

For over sixty years Panmure was a thriving stopping place at the cross of the Blakeney-Dunrobin and Dwyer Hill-Arnprior roads. Many pioneer families drove these arteries: families like the Greens, Gallaghans, Cavanaghs, Lunneys, Rowans, Mantils, Moorhouses, Coltons, Hudsons, O'Keefes, Finners, Coadys, Curries and Armstrongs, all of whom had recourse to drop into Panmure for mail and provisions.

But by the Thirties, Panmure and other nearby centres like Antrim and Marathon had lost importance. While many families had stayed on, generally farms grew bigger as the little farmers moved away.

In Panmure, however, one commercial remnant held on: the country store of Nellie O'Hara and her brother Martin. It was typical of many small family stores found even today in Ireland: a nook of a shop out front with living quarters out back and up top. For a small child in the early Forties, Nellie's confectionery on the southwest corner of Panmure was a delight.

"How sweet it is" to have oneself associated with such fond remembrances of childhood. So many adults savour the memory of a dear aunt, uncle or friend who habitually spoiled them with gum, candies and bits of loose change.

Herman O'Keefe who grew up in the Twenties on a Twelfth Line farm recalls the kindness of his Uncle John O'Keefe who used to come out from Almonte to visit his brother. The ritual was the same: tie the mare to the butternut tree, get her some feed, call out to Herman, and then slip him a bag of rock candies before entering the house.

Father Ed Lunney, a product of a Pakenham-area farm, remembers afternoon joy rides in his Uncle Alphonse's new car with the occasional stop at Nellie's for Neilson bars. One time they bought out the last of Nellie's supply of chocolate bars and while Father Ed was of course delighted, other tykes like me, who may have arrived the same day, would have been visibly shaken by this shortage, especially those of us who had pumped a bicycle for three miles against the wind on a hot afternoon with real money in a sweaty palm only to learn that (... @&#%^! ...), just the thought of it!

Nellie must have been a knockout in her youth. Even in her seventies, she still had refined features, baby skin and downy-sheen hair. How many casanovas of the day had had their heads turned by Nellie? And yet there she was a spinster, selling chocolate bars to children, saying the right word, smiling with kindness and giving us all something to remember her by. Sweet Nellie, we do remember!

Nellie, of course, never married and neither did her brother and therein lies an "intro". On the same farm many years before, another brother and sister did marry. They married each other. They were the adopted children of "Long" Tom O'Keefe and Catherine Foley.

Tom was the son of John O'Keefe and Mary Duffy from the Twelfth Line of West Huntley. The nick in his name implied the existence of another Tom O'Keefe who walked faster to cover the same distance, just as the name "Black" Jack Finner meant there was a red one, and a "Big" Jack Mantil, a "Little" Jack, and so on.

None of which has much to do with the romance of Herbie O'Keefe and Mary Cecilia around 1915 except that Tom adopted both, gave them a good home where they eventually fell in love and married. They remained on that farm, had a family, and later sold the farm to Nellie's father.

The neighbouring kids got a charge out of Herbert and Cecilia's affair. They used to tease them with the rhyme, "Cely Coffee loves Herbie Tea" sung to the melody of the song, "I love coffee, I love tea, I love the girls and the girls love me!" Coffey was her real name.

All fun aside, it is indeed a quaint love story: these two young people finding each other. I've met their fine son and watched the grandson of Herbie and Cely play hockey with my own boys.

Next time you pass Panmure perhaps you'll think of those two orphans who found happiness and sweet Nellie Grey who never did. Or did she?

A Matter of Honour

"Turkey Tom" of Huntley was into turkeys in a big way. One day he heard a neighbour had accused him of being a turkey-taker.

Now being a tough bird, "Turkey Tom" all but flew over to his neighbour's yard. With his nervous accuser under wing, "Turkey Tom" rolled up his sleeves and talked turkey:

"I hear you've been calling me a turkey thief, ya yellow weasel! How would ya like to repeat it to my face?"

"Now, Tom, I didn't call you a thief in so many words!"

"Don't pussyfoot with me, you lout! What did ya really say?"

"Well, what I said was — and I know ya have a good sense of humour, Tom — what I said was — as a joke really — was something like, 'If I was a turkey, and you were around, I'd be sure to roost awful high'!"

"Turkey Tom" was not amused. He "totalled" him! It didn't pay to ruffle the feathers of "Turkey Tom"!

A Father's Tear

In Dublin Airport, I stood in line to show my Boarding Pass. Beside me stood a small family. The father had a face of swarthy graciousness. He was old, too old to be standing with cap in hand saying farewell to his precious daughter going to Chicago for work. Neither the girl nor mother was tearful, but the old man would not be denied his moment of hurt. This was not the first to leave, he said, but she was the youngest. The loss of each one left an emptiness.

The Irish have great affection for their children. I had been talking earlier that week with a porter named Shea at the Waterville Hotel. His wife and children used to come to pick him up from work and the children would take turns dashing into the hotel lobby to fetch him. This particular night a young son hit the doors full force and butterflied his way to his father's side. "Boy," I said, "he must be a handful!" "Ah, sure he is," said the nice Mr. Shea, "but what else are we put here for?"

At the airport, I reached out for the old man's hand. I don't know why I did. Maybe to share his pain? To distract his sorrow? I blurted she would be all right and soon be home on holidays. How did I know? But my heart ached at this sight and I had to say something even if it was for my own good.

By then she was gone! And his wife quietly led him home. Over her shoulder, she gave me a faint smile. And you knew as long as she was around, the old man would be okay and the family intact. And I said good-bye to Ireland for the last time. And I felt like the old man did!

Not Quite, George

John O'Keefe and Margaret Carroll decided to invite bachelor George Stone to their wedding. George was delighted. He was telling my uncle about it — (being a home boy, George had little education):

"Nash, I've an invite to John Keefe's marriage! And not only that, but after the church I'll be goin' to their wedding conception!"

Abigail and Winnifred

Two senior citizens Abigail Beecham and Winnifred Wampole had been very apprehensive about their first trip to Ireland. Their friends had warned them of the many *troubles* there and had put them both pretty much on the edge.

Abigail had thought it wise to bring a "mickey" of courage just in case, little knowing how soon it would be needed.

On their second day in Ireland, they were seated in a Dublin Railway Station within earshot of four tourists discussing their previous week's travelling. To the ladies, they could have been the IRA.

One lad gave Winnifred a start by saying, "I for one certainly enjoyed Gorey and Hook Head in Wexford! But what really intrigued me was to see Lisburn in Antrim and Bloody Ridge in Down."

Abigail passed the mickey over to Winnie who turned a paler green when a second lad said, "I missed Five Fingers in Donegal, but I sure got a kick out of that Crusheen of Clare; what a sight! And that incident in Castlemartyr and the big bash in Crookstown where Johnny popped his cork!" And they all laughed!

By this time, the mickey had made several rounds and Winnie became a basket-case when a third gentleman said his biggest thrill of the week was seeing Devil's Glen and the Priest's Leap in Kerry.

Fortunately, both girls were already in shock and loaded when the last lad said he had been over to Kilconnell in Kerry after getting through a big crowd at Knock Shrine in Mayo to Kilkelly.

When they all agreed to head out next day to Kilmore, Abigail, thinking she was now part of them, stood up and raising her arms bellowed, "Count Winnie and me in, boys! We're with you all the way!"

Winnie couldn't disagree. She was a heap on the floor.

Bossie Bossie

A cow is usually seen as a four-legged tranquillizer with the I.Q. of a raspberry. Even her blank stare, similar to a penguin's looking out to sea, suggests a peanut-sized brain completely programmed by biological selection. Most see her as a walking dairy fountain easily whipped this way or that by man's whims, nothing but a huge Dodo bird totally and willingly submissive to an unappreciative society.

But hoolie, hoolie, wait a wee! Is the cow really porridge-brained? Or is that gentle demeanour but a front for a devious, calculating mind? Does this swaggering mass of contentment really carry more upstairs than is realized? Let's take the adventure of milking, for instance.

Usually, this chore of easing a cow's physical discomfort is fairly humdrum. After all, since man and beast are doing each other a favour, the whole experience should be a co-operative one. And, in most cases, given the proper facilities and environment, such as an enclosed cowbar with a stall and iron collar and feed, milking a cow is usually routine.

Unfortunately, not all farmers could afford the luxury of indoor parking for their cows. At my grandmother's, the milking was done in a clearing in front of and just below the house where once deer, antelope and now cows were free to roam. By the very nature of the situation, the success of the milking was in jeopardy. Man no longer had the upper hand — the simple beast and the milker were on equal footing. For once, *Homo sapiens* had to deal straight on with the grey cells of the cow.

Faced with such a laissez-faire situation it isn't long before man learns that, if a cow is unduly provoked, the stage is set for a duel quite capable of shredding the best of nerves. That little clearing becomes a battlefield where the cow can prove beyond a doubt that her intellectual ranking should be considerably higher among the barnyard hierarchy.

The untied cow must be approached with cautious respect. If she is reclining, a gentle brush of toe usually gets the proper response. If the cow sees fit not to rise, then the pressure can be increased within reason. Excessive actions like hitting her with the butt of the pail or pulling on ear or tail may break that gentle strand of mutual understanding so necessary for success.

After the cow has risen, a few moments should be allowed for her to compose herself. Indeed, some cows may still be somewhat embarrassed by the whole situation and need time to psyche themselves up.

Location can be a problem. It is best to milk out of the direct sunlight and in line of any cooling breeze. If the animal is standing too near a "fellow" cow of nasty temper, then it is wise to move the whole operation to a more suitable area.

Another challenge is getting the cow into her proper standing position so that her left foot is ahead of her right. The reason for this is simple: cows are usually left-footed. If the humour is on her to remove a bullfly from under her steerage or to lash out at the milker in response to an overly rough squeeze, any attempt to do so with her left leg would result in a position similar to the RCA Victor dog. Unfortunately, some cows are "ambipederous" and can let a person have it with either leg. Such ornery critters are given a particularly wide birth and unless their milk production is extremely high, soon find themselves in the great glue factory in the sky.

A tried and true way to make a cow put her "proper foot" forward is to approach her nonchalantly from the right side, all the while whispering sweet nothings in your best bovine dialect. As the soothing words find their mark, the milker then places his free hand on the rear flank and pushes, forcing the cow to shift her weight. Failing this, the milker's left shoulder can be affixed solidly up against said area and a gentle but firm bunting initiated in the desired direction. The milker now positions his posterior on his portable seat in such a manner as not to injure himself. Seats were often nothing but chunks of trees cut flat on the bottom and slanted on the top. Jagged edges and slivers could be a menace to the unwary — any quick movement might be calamitous.

Next, the milk pail is unobtrusively swung under the cow and positioned on the ground between the milker's legs, more toward the milker than directly under the udder. The right leg of the milker is fixed for balance while the left leg is planted so as to provide thrust for a quick bail out. The handle of the pail should be readily within reach — spilt milk cannot be replaced.

The actual milking can now begin — slowly and gently at first, but always with confidence. Any timidity can be as dangerous as roughness; either can trigger regressive behaviour by the cow, such as: turning her head and staring at the milker in contemptuous disbelief, sashaying her body to the left just out of finger reach or to the right to subtly push the milker on his back, or whipping the milker's face with her long matted filthy tail. Such deplorable behaviour demands strict self-control by the milker. Little emotion should be displayed, especially when those Bambi orbs turn to examine your reactions.

Another offence mechanism and one particularly demeaning to the milker is the use by the cow of the old answering-the-call-of-nature trick. Great restraint is required especially if the cow persists on a regular basis in ridiculing the same milker in the same way. It is advisable for several reasons to retreat in such circumstances and find greener terrain to begin again. The show must go on and the milk must come down.

It's a long road that doesn't have a bend and there are times when even saints are tempted beyond their strength. Every barnyard milker has experienced it. The moment when self-restraint is totally wiped out. It can come as the result of a culmination of many repeated insurrections, but more than likely occurs after the cow has shifted weight, raised her left leg, waved it in a conical orbit, and driven pail and milk to kingdom come. The loss of the milk, the waste of labour, and the general hopelessness of the situation can cause otherwise sound men to strike out with hand or foot, throw pails and blocks of wood, pull tails, twist ears and utter oaths foul enough to shy the devil.

The scene is humiliating: the distraught milker in an emotional funk; the cow basking in her triumph; pail, seat and hat resting in a puddle of white; and the cow's barnyard friends, pigs, kittens, and hens staring at him, vicariously enjoying his defeat, all waiting for a chance to drink up the nutritional benefits of this latest *cow de grass*.

Cows, stupid! Not from where I sat!!

Miscellaneous Irish Superstitions

- Red is the colour of magic in every country: fairies and magicians always wear red. Red-headed people are considered to possess magical powers.

- Fire, even in a smoking pipe, could not be taken from a house in Ireland during the mornings of May. During churning, the same custom prevailed. The churning was done weekly and everyone dropping in was obliged to help out.

- A man never cut his hair on Monday. In fact, any work on a Monday was considered to bring poor luck. Hair from any cutting was buried outside in a hole and never, never thrown in the fire.

- The seventh son of the seventh son was said to have curative powers over people and animals.

- It was generally believed that disease was the result of evil. The best solution was to pass the disease to a neighbour. If a calf had died from a disease, it was buried in the neighbour's field.

- The owner of a tavern was thought never to have any good luck in his life.

- Years ago in Ireland, roosters were thought to have the power of prophecy. Crowing at certain places on certain times (except dawn) foretold a visitor was expected or someone was to die in the townland.

- Cows going dry and similar misfortunes used to be considered the work of a witch.

- Putting a hat on a bed meant a person wouldn't be married that day.

- Showing a baby its image in a mirror before its first birthday could mean ill health or death for the child.

- It was believed a child who became a favourite of a group of Sisters for an extended period would be taken by God at an early age.

- It was considered good luck for a home if the first visitor on New Year's Day was a male.

18

The Little Saint of Sample's Creek

The moment Rita Sarah died, Kathleen knew that the strange knocks she and Rita had heard a few months earlier had been a warning. Kathleen had told her family about them. But Rita showed no concern.

The strange occurrence took place on the previous November 1, the Feast of All Saints, a Holy Day in the Catholic Church, and one held in reverence for several millenniums by many races.

Kathleen and Rita had just returned to Kathleen's home. The children were resting. Afternoon tea was welcome. Suddenly both heard heavy footsteps echoing from the limestone walk at the side of the house. Someone, presumably a man, was coming to the back door. They waited rather nervously. The door was bolted. A pause. Then three raps ... measured, strong and consistent. Kathleen called out. No answer. Slowly she pulled the door open. No one! She rebolted the door. A long silence. Three more knocks, the same as before. Again Kathleen asked who was there. Again no answer. She opened the door. Nothing but the wind. They resumed their conversation. Three more knocks. Kathleen stayed where she sat. She didn't go again because she knew there would be no one.

Kathleen had always felt that November 1 did hold special significance. The Feast of All Saints is the one day in the year when the Catholic Church officially remembers its dead. And not just the haloed ones of Rome, but all the hewers of wood and drawers of water who had fought the good fight for their faith and are remembered more in people's hearts than in archives and books. It is the one day in the liturgical year when the living and the dead remember one another through the extraterrestrial medium of prayer ... a day when thoughts of love reunite friends, lovers, ancestors ... a day of spiritually sharing ... a day whose meaning requires no explanation for those who believe and has no possible one for those who don't.

The Irish, in particular, had attached importance to this day, long before the coming of Christianity. In fact, this Christian Feast Day is based on an old pagan festival in ancient Ireland called the Festival of Samhain. On that day, the mortals made peace with the spirit world. The High King of Ireland at Tara used this day to celebrate his ritual (divine?) marriage with Goddess Earth, asking her for continued intercession on his behalf. The evening celebrations were full of hauntings and hysteria with spirits coming from earth to taunt and destroy and the mortals trying to drive them back into the darkness. The antics of Halloween somewhat reflect this pagan festival.

It is not surprising then that many ghost stories surround this day. Gaelic Scotland in recent centuries had some parishioners in country kirks who were empowered to receive warnings of future deaths. By merely standing outside in the shadows of a kirk's portals between eleven and twelve on the eve of All Saints, they could watch the images of those slated for death in the parish that year parade out one after the other through the front door. One poor soul saddled with such a gift watched these mournful processions of the living dead for many years until one evening he saw an image he knew all too well, his own.

Rita died on March 15, 1937, and was buried on March 18. Kathleen has often wondered why her death was forewarned ... was Rita special? Was it a way of preparing the family?

Rita was no goody-goody. With her free-spirited attitude towards life, she was about as close to a tomboy as you could get. In her early days she kept her mother and father on their toes. She and brother Matt once got in a fight at school and it took Jackie Mantil a good while to get them separated. In addition, not many people dared tell Father Gorman, the Parish Priest, that he was behaving like a bear. Rita did and Father Gorman never minded a bit. Let's see why not.

Rita Sarah was the fifth child of eight. She lived with her father John Matthew (died in 1929) and her mother Susan on a small farm on the Eighth Line of Huntley, two miles east of Corkery Church. Everyone liked her, because like good crystal, she rang true: no airs about her, a happy-go-lucky lass with lots of dash and a touch of sass. Father Gerald Gorman had taken a liking to her and had given her the job of starting the school stove during the winter. For Rita it was a sentence of death!

One morning in early March long before break of day, the seventeen-year-old Rita set out for her ten-dollar-a-month job at the school. She was a strong young lady used to the rigours of winter and she approached her work with the same zealous reliability so evident in everything she did. To save time, she cut across Sample's Creek behind the home of Jim Sample and his wife Annie Gallagher. In the middle of the swamp, she fell through the ice and soaked herself to the skin. She continued on to the school and finished her work. By nightfall, she was in bed with tonsillitis. The next day the tonsillitis progressed into quinsy and within two more, she had the dreaded pneumonia.

Dr. Dunn came out from Almonte. That same Dr. Dunn who had tended so many young people during the flu epidemic of 1919 and 1920. And now he had to tell the widow Susan that her daughter might not make it. That same Dr. Dunn who many Corkery Irish thought was "the greatest man who ever lived" could only wait and pray like the others for nature to run its course. He had tapped her lung and confined her to bed. In nine days, the pneumonia would break or triumph. It was in God's hands.

Father Gorman came every day. He brought her fresh pears and oranges. He prayed with her, gave her encouragement, even arranged for the Cloistered Sisters of the Precious Blood in Ottawa to pray for her. But it was not to be. There were no antibiotics then and Rita had to cough up the phlegm, but didn't have the strength. She began to sink.

Then it happened. Maybe it was guilt. One day Rita turned to the visiting Father Gorman and said, "Father, one night last year at the parish dance I was watching you through the window of the Church Hall as you went from car to buggy looking for drinkers and I turned to Pat Egan and said, 'There goes that old bear Father Gorman snooping around everywhere!!' Well, I just thought I'd tell you about it! Wasn't I a naughty girl to say that?" And she smiled nervously.

Surely such sweet repentance must have almost floored the good priest. No one knows for sure what took place. But chances are the fifty-year-old Father Gorman, quite accustomed to severe emotional crises, was deeply, deeply moved by his little friend's confession. To think that one so innocent in the eyes of God could be concerned at a time like that about a stray remark made in jest and probably half-true anyway, must have moved his great heart to a crushing silence. He probably held her sweaty hand in his and mumbled something neither he nor Rita understood.

Rita knew she was forgiven. His tears told her so.

The dark-haired, blue-eyed Rita, they say, always had a heavenly aura about her. A kind of "not made for this world something". Astute neighbours saw it. Her family experienced it. Father Gorman felt it. A natural goodness that touched others.

From her bed in an upstairs room she watched her last sunset. It was a Sunday evening after a supper nobody ate. Father Gorman had come and given her the Last Rites and said good-bye.

Her sister Kathleen held her churning body. Once she jolted and turned to her sister Tessie with the words, "Tomorrow morning, Tessie, you and I are going to go to Mass!" Knowing the hopelessness of it all, Tessie broke down, and little Rita quickly apologized for upsetting her saying, "It's okay, Tess, I was only fooling!"

And Kathleen held her tighter that last evening. And soon John Matthew had his daughter with him again.

And "the old bear" said the funeral Mass for his spiritual child and behaved more like a lamb. And some other person was hired to start the school fires who probably never did it to the liking of Father Gorman who had been spoiled like so many others, don't you see, by the charisma of the little Saint of Sample's Creek, Rita Sarah Scott.

Just A Matter of Time

The hounds of Lord Carberry in southwest Cork whisked by, leading horses and riders over downs alive with the colours of white, green and orange and the cries of beasts, bugles and hunters. As soon as they were out of sight, one baneer (old Irish lady) said to the other, "Ah! 'ta oor la aguiv-se 'sa saol-seo, acht, beig aar la aguinne 'sa sao'l eile!"

Which means, "Ah, you have your day in this world; but we'll have our day in the next!"

19

The Teasing of Theresa

It's been said that some Irish, particularly certain natives of Cork, are born with a tendency to tease, much to the chagrin of Kerryites and Dubliners who take little shine to their fast quips, puns and jokes. I found the sons of Mike O'Keefe great fun in this regard and many a dig I took from Basil, John, Allan and Herman.

It's a jocularity similar to the kind often found in team sport and the military. It's not everybody's cup of tea, but then some people have little humour, especially at the expense of themselves.

Another earlier family around West Huntley known for its good-natured banter was the Sullivans, made up of brothers Charlie, Tom and Willie who lived back the Tenth Line in the days when it was open between Highway 44 and the Old Almonte Road. Yet, another bunch of friendly jabbers were the Curries who weren't from Cork or Huntley, except for Archie who lived for some married years in West Huntley. Originally he came from the Currie homestead nestled beneath the flatrock ridge on the Fourth Line of Fitzroy. Terrence Currie, Archie's nephew, his wife, and his four fine children are there now.

Now Archie and his brothers Lennie, John, Eddie and Tommy were all about the same build. And to someone like their friendly neighbour Theresa Finner whose eyesight had dimmed with the years, the boys all looked the same; almost that is.

Once in a while, on a good day, Theresa would slip over to visit the Curries, especially father John and wife Mary. As soon as Theresa was comfortably settled in her favourite chair, the boys went into their act.

Because the big red-brick house (built by grandfather Pat after the great fire) had several entrances, the boys were able to take turns passing Theresa from different directions all the while engaging her in conversation.

Theresa could see well enough to allow the boys to have their fun, but never enough to know what was going on.

The teasing might have gone like this:
Enter Lennie from outside.
"G'day, Theresa! And how are ya?"
"Is that you, Lennie?"
"No, it's Eddie!"
"Landsakes, Eddie, you look every bit like Lennie!"
Enter Eddie from outside.
"Theresa, my love! I'm happy to see ya!"
"Ah, Eddie, You're a sight for sore eyes, so you are!"
"It's me, Tommy, Theresa! And how are ya?"
"Tommy, your the spitting image of Eddie and Lennie!"
"See you later, Theresa, I've chores to do!"

Enter Archie from the opposite direction.

"Good to see you Theresa!"

"Archie, I'd know that voice anywhere!"

"It's Lennie, Theresa. I have a cold. Well, I'm off to the barn!"

Enter Tommy from another direction inside.

"This has to be Archie!"

"It's Eddie again, Theresa! Have you seen Archie? I've been to the barn and he's not there!"

Says Theresa, "I could have swore he left for there just now, but it was Lennie!"

Enter Archie from outside.

"Theresa, have you seen Papa John?"

"To tell the truth, lad, I don't know who I've seen! Is there something wrong, whoever you are?"

"Yes, I need Papa. I can't get that damn Archie out of bed!"

An Even Greater Feat

A certain old farmer in Ireland had a prize bull whose achievements became legendary across Ireland.

So many people wanted to see the bull that the farmer began to charge a shilling for the privilege. It wasn't the money; he just had better things to do all day than show off a bull.

One day a stranger to Kerry asked to see the animal. Being the father of seventeen children he had little money.

He told the farmer about his large family with its many cares and asked him if he would accept only sixpence in payment.

The farmer chuckled and said, "Keep your hands in your pocket, my lad, and stay right where you are. I'm goin' to go and get the bull and bring him out to meet you!"

True Friendship

It's not easy to outdo Corkery people in generosity. Even among themselves. Like the time two locals named Jim Carroll and Jimmy Carter were not feeling any pain after a fun-evening at a mutual friend's.

The weather being very inclement as they made ready to go home, Jim Carroll said to his friend, "Jimmy, it might be best if I were to accompany you to your home!"

To which Jimmy kindly said, "Sure that'd be right decent of you, Jim! And after we get there, I'd be more than happy to walk you home to yours!"

20

A Wee Postie Remembers

Years ago, a few old West Huntley male parishioners occasionally had "fallings out" with their pastors and showed their disdain by refusing to attend or support the Church for prolonged periods.

Some clashes were strictly chemical, but others grew out of actual disagreements over pastoral policies.

Particularly upsetting to these farmers was what they considered to be a pastor's excessive and repeated appeals for parishional support. Rectories, schools, and churches don't run on love and some priests of old usually didn't hesitate, especially in tough times, to ask vociferously for wood, coal, labour, and cash. A few farmers naturally thought they were being pushed too hard and Irishmen as a rule don't "push" too easily, especially hot-tempered ones.

As the records testify, the majority of St. Michael's parishioners, regardless of their opinion of the pastor, always gave what they could and then some. The women too were a great help: cleaning the church, looking after linens, candles and laundry, and (what was even more important), keeping the pastors' pantries and tables laden with fresh fowl and beef, salt pork, canned fruits, vegetables, bread, pies, cakes, cookies and the best preserves this side of the Ottawa.

A story was told me recently of one Irish wife with a Brink's-truck for a husband and how she refused to be intimidated by his weasel-minded outlook on their pastor's needs.

One winter's afternoon, she decided to send a freshly dressed fowl to the pastor by way of the mailman. She watched for his cutter and horses and then called out for him to drive up to the house.

Now the postmaster was used to such requests. His home was down past the rectory and he often delivered articles back and forth on his fifty-family-long route. This day he had his ten-year-old son with him and he sent him in to see what the lady wanted.

As the lad stood talking to the Mrs. as she wrapped the bird for delivery, a bigger bird sitting in the inner dining room got wind of the goings-on in the kitchen. Looking directly on line with the wee postie he bellowed, "Little boy! Go tell the man who does the begging to come and seek his own alms!"

Naturally, the lad didn't understand the full meaning of the remark until years later. But he knew enough from the tone that the chicken for the priest wasn't going anywhere.

But lo and behold, the lady of the house would not be put down by her bully-husband. And soon the boy was on his way with gift under wing and a cookie or two in his jacket.

He was happy of course for the priest, but even more so for the sweet white-haired lady who had stood up to her husband. Even today, some sixty-five years later, he remembers that day so long ago when goodness triumphed over meanness.

Bobbie and Emily

When Bobbie Brown's wife Emily died, he had, much to his regret, no money to purchase a suitable marker for her grave.

After days of anguish, Bobbie thought of a solution he knew would be pleasing to Emily.

Outside their summer road-side croft was a large stone. Its design was such that for years Emily used to sit comfortably on it while reading, knitting, or just chatting with passers-by.

With the help of neighbours, Bobbie moved the great stone down into the valley to the head of Mary's grave... and at least once a week, he would come there of an evening and sit where Emily sat... sometimes he even felt Emily's presence beside him sharing his thoughts of their good times together... and the older he grew, the longer he stayed... until one day he came, and never left!

To this day in this section of the Ottawa valley, people still talk of Emily's stone and her husband Bobbie who rolled it there as a token of his love.

An Opening on Love

Around 1908, a boy from the west tip of Cork, where the mountains roller-coast to the sea, was arraigned in Cork City for getting a young girl back home in the family way. He had already lost his job as a barefoot messenger boy and it looked as if the worst was yet to come.

As the hearing progressed, surprisingly the old judge suddenly began to soften. He became overwhelmed by the couple's love. The result was: he married them in the presence of their families, paid for the license and arranged for the rehiring of the boy. What caused the judge's sudden change?

During the trial, the defence read portions of love letters from the boy to his girl back in the mountains. One paragraph moved the judge to tears. It said: "Far away from where I am, there's a little gap in the field and beyond it the sea; and 'tis there I do be looking the whole day long, for it's the nearest thing to yourself that I can see!"

No Allowances Made

"Father, that woman ya hitched me to three years ago is drivin' me crazy for money. Money, money, always money!"

"Clancy," said the Father, "my heart goes out to ya! What's she been doin' with it?"

"Nothing! I haven't givin' her any yet!"

21

Howard Crosses the Line

Howard Williams was a respected gentleman around West Huntley. A confirmed bachelor, he had less money than imagined and far more than he admitted. He was a good listener and an even better storyteller. He was welcome in everybody's home.

Howard had worked "out" from March Township as a young man, "boered" the Dutch in South Africa and on his return worked "out" again, this time in West Huntley. He was a millwright by trade. During the Depression, he started a berry farm on the old Lynch property purchased from his brother Maurice. In the late Forties he built himself a framed hermit's cottage set well back from the road in the shade of weathered oaks where he lived in semi-retirement until his death in the Sixties.

However, in the years before he moved there, he had the good fortune to live with his brother Maurice and his wife Annie O'Keefe. There, he had all the comforts of life. Annie was not only a great cook and housewife, she was also extremely hospitable to her guests, especially relatives. She had taken in one of Maurie's nieces and raised her; she had welcomed her mother-in-law as a permanent resident; and she had given employment to her brother-in-law, Alex Prudhomme, and her brother, Angus, during the Depression. And now she was providing a good home for her husband's wandering brother who had decided to settle down.

The little story that follows is better appreciated if Howard's attitude towards women and marriage can be reasonably understood. Brought up in the Victorian Age when a man's home was his castle and a woman his vassal, it is not too far off the mark to assume Howard's definition of a woman's role in society differed considerably from the one held by the Margaret Atwoods of our day. Although his treatment of the fair sex was always above reproach, like most Irish men of his time, he probably wouldn't have looked twice at a woman carrying a rolling pin in one hand, a milk pail in the other, and a diaper in her teeth. That is, until the day he almost met his Maker at the hands of a hysterical housewife who took exception to Howard's interference in marital bliss.

Not far from Howard's snug little flat at his brother's, Archie and Kathleen Scott Currie lived in a log house rented from Basil O'Keefe for two dollars a month. That the house was on its last legs was proven by a visit one afternoon of my grandmother who almost lost one of her own. Kathleen was in labour and Archie had gone for Dr. Dunn in Almonte. The main bedroom, as in most log homes of this period, was on the first floor which had floor boards in an advanced stage of decay. As my heavy-set grandmother made her way from the front door to the backroom Kathleen cautioned her to avoid the boards which tended to dip and dive. Too late — one of grandmother's legs went through towards the cellar and right up to her thigh. Grandma somehow finally got out and both women could never recall the incident without getting giddy. That was one day when Grannie put her foot down and down and down!

Anyhow, Archie, Kathleen and their children somehow got by in those lean depression years. Kathleen worked off one dollar of the two-dollar rent by running Basil's sheep and Basil always forgot to collect the other. Archie had a summer job starting the fire at the road-department plant and during the winter the whole family cut about two hundred long thin fencing poles worth a dollar each.

It was a happy home and I enjoyed visiting there as a boy. Kathleen was attractive, intelligent, and dynamic, with a mind of her own. She had worked too hard as a youngster on the Scott homestead after her father died to put up with shenanigans and tomfoolery. A heart of gold, mind you, but as fiery as they come. Kathleen told me just lately that she remembered my visits to her house. "A bit of an imp, you were," she said, "whom I often had to tell to mind!" And then she wondered out

Howard Williams, Lyla Moran O'Brien, Annie O'Keefe Williams.
In front, Inez O'Keefe Beach and Marguerite O'Keefe Murphy, around 1918.

loud if I had held it against her. "Naw," I said, "you never hit me, did you?" (Just kidding!) "Lord, no!" she said. As I said, a sergeant-major type, with a heart of gold. I always liked her and still do!

Archie was a character. Like most of the Fitzroy Curries he was a practical joker — and quite capable of teasing a person like Kathleen to the breaking point. Everybody took to Archie's style: bashful, friendly and always playfully sincere. If a man didn't like Archie Currie, that man had something wrong with him.

Archie and his bosom pal Alex Grace had played the field before settling down ... two sheiks to the wind as it were who took pains to spread their charms à la Valentino among West Huntley's *femmes fatales*. My mother was one of them; so I can't question their standards.

But to the story! One March day Archie and Howard Williams decided to go to Arnprior on business. Howard had a sleek Reo slung out in his garage with running boards, spare tires on each side under nickel covers, and headlights the size of a train's. But for some reason, the two went in Archie's just-purchased Model A Ford whose age was betrayed by its price tag of $20.00. Neither the car nor Archie had a license. The twenty-two-year-old Kathleen expected Archie back by nightfall.

Upon completion of their business in Arnprior, Archie and Howard dropped in for a few at a tavern. As the shadows lengthened, one drink led to another and only after they had reached a level of anaesthetization did the two set out for home. Outside of town they rammed a fruit truck sending the driver into a rage as well as a pile of jam. The police weren't too happy either ... no licenses, extensive damage, and a couple of unruly Irishmen feeling their bottled courage.

Next morning, Archie and Howard woke up behind bars in the Arnprior jail. Kathleen had received no word from Archie. She hadn't slept! She was approaching the stage of "blast off".

Meanwhile Archie had taken over. West Huntley had just two phones: the one at the vicarage, the other at the country post office. No time for a religious harangue thought Archie; so he called the post office. Soon his chum Pat Egan was on his way to Alex Grace's who set out the fifteen miles to retrieve his buddy.

Until the three men casually arrived at her door that afternoon, the young Kathleen had presumed the worst. At first came elation and tears and then the aftershock ... the burning realization of it all ... no one contacting her, the wasted twenty dollars, the car demolished, the disgrace of jail, the drinking, the fines and the nonchalant manner of the three men before her. Her Irish was up and the air was blushing pink. In the midst of her sally, she gave Archie a decided push. At this point, Howard stepped into the breach. After all, he had come along only to give Archie moral support. Turning to Archie he put a hand on his shoulder and said, "A man is not a man if he allows any woman to shove him around like that!"

Right away, Howard knew he had made a tactical error.

Kathleen's guns swung round! She thought to herself: here's a sixty-year-old man who should know better and who is most likely the organizer of this whole mess. And here he is telling her husband how to treat her and himself nothing but a bachelor whose total knowledge of marriage could be put on the head of a pin. Kathleen came up firing! The Boer War had been nothing like this! Howard closed up like a turtle. Kathleen's finishing words ran like this, "If you don't mind your own business, Howard Williams, I'll take that axe over there and break it over your swollen head!"

Howard and Kathleen remained good friends. But somehow Howard's patented view of the male's right to dominance in the home had been shattered. From that day forward, he spoke with even greater politeness to his sister-in-law, Annie. He realized then why Maurie, her husband, never said anything about the running of his house.

The Stranger

In the latter part of the last century, a certain farmer from the Twelfth Line was crossing the Burnt Lands. As he drew near Mahoney's Hotel, he became deathly ill and some friends carried him into the hotel. The man asked for a priest and the word went out for Father Lavin of Pakenham since the Corkery priest was away.

As the priest was coming along the Eleventh Line toward the Mahoney Side Road on his way to the sick call, he was approached by a stranger walking towards him. The stranger told the priest it was not necessary to continue since the man had already died. Something, however, urged the priest to finish his seven-mile journey.

Upon his arrival at the hotel, he found the farmer still alive and conscious, but dying. After confession and Holy Viaticum, he succumbed. When the priest told his story about the stranger, no one knew who would do such an evil thing. It was decided by all that the stranger was the devil himself.

So Long, Archie

Archie Currie and his wife Kathleen, whom we have just met, lived in the 1930's in a log house at O'Keefe's Corners. One Sunday morning with Kathleen away at Mass, Archie was doing his best to change his son John's diapers. Suddenly, two knocks sounded on the kitchen door. Archie shouted to the person to wait until he finished with the baby. Another two more knocks! Another shout! And two more knocks.

Finally Archie made it over and opened the unlocked door. There was no one there. Archie was sure the party, no doubt a stranger, had gone until he looked down at the big flat-stone doorstep. Although a light January snow had been falling, the step bore no imprints.

Later that morning, Archie learned of the death of his good neighbour, William O'Keefe, an eighty-six-year-old saint. The time of death coincided with the knocking. William had come to say good-bye to his friend Archie who had been kind to William over the years.

22

Almonte, The Friendly Town

The town of Almonte has always played a significant part in the development of West Huntley. Its many industrial mills provided employment. Its businesses answered the shopping needs of the family. Its doctors and veterinarians travelled to West Huntley in rain, shine, snow or mud. Even the social life of the area was enlivened by entertainment at the Almonte Town Hall, Fairgrounds, and dance halls.

Almonte has gone by many aliases since 1815. The first was Sheppard's Falls or Mills, probably the prettiest names of all. Up until 1856, it was also called Ballygiblin, Victoriaville, Waterford (the Mississippi river had no bridges and boats moved the people to and fro), Ramseyville, Shipman's Falls (after the town's chief industrialist), and finally Almonte (after a Mexican General, of all people). It has always been known as a pretty town made up of friendly folk.

Almonte traces its Gaelic roots to Western Scotland and Southwest Ireland. The first Irish came in 1823 and 1825 under the direction of Peter Robinson who chose his passengers from Northeast Cork and Southwest Tipperary. He was commissioned to pick not only famine-stricken souls from these areas, but also, as we have seen, a small number of insurrectionists who had been thorns in the side of England.

Some Anglo-Irish Lords of Doneraile, Buttevant, Mallow, Mitchelstown, and Clonmel were quite willing to defray the travelling expenses of good tenants provided some of their districts' disturbers were forcibly shipped out as well. As such, Sir Robert Peel, the British Prime Minister, known as "Orange Peel" by some detractors, did not authorize the expensive Irish migration out of sheer kindness of heart. Compromise has its price in any day! In fact, not only was Britannia able to populate its vacant lands in Canada with loyal Irish and rid itself of some unwanted characters, it was also given an opportunity, as already noted, to fill up its boats which hitherto had sailed empty to the North American lumber markets.

The Scots of course had preceded the Irish into Ramsey. They came better prepared having mastered technical skills under a feudal system which allowed more freedom of development. But, they, too, had come on hard times back in Scotland. In the late 1700's, the weaving trades, upon which so many depended, fell into a depressed state and a defiant Scot sought help from the Government. Soon, lands in this part of Canada were opened for immigration and in the summers of 1820 and 1821 three thousand left Glasgow, Stirling, Paisley and Lanark. Here in Canada they settled mainly by the Tay, Clyde and Mississippi Rivers. Towns and villages synonymous with the Scots are Perth, Lanark, Fitzroy, Appleton, Rosebank, Arnprior, Carleton Place, and of course, Almonte.

An earlier immigration of Scots in 1816 and 1818 to the above-mentioned areas is particularly worthy of esteem. These men and women opened the way for those to follow. They surveyed the land, cleared it, and then built "holdover shelters" for families forced to postpone their settlements on assigned properties due to the ravages of winter. In the spring, they took the immigrants to their lands and then helped them get started. Without these early Scots, no settler would have survived in the unforgiving winter climate.

As the years went by, Scot, Irishman, Presbyterian, Anglican, and Roman Catholic lived in exemplary accord (except for the Ballygiblin affair). Much of this peaceful coexistence is recorded in *The Almonte Gazette*. First published every Friday morning at the cost of a dollar, this little newspaper has helped unify the people of this district for a hundred and twenty-five years.

Its first publication in the middle 1860's came at a time when Almonte was in a state of growth. The Baltimore and Oriole train went South every morning at 8:53 and North every evening at 7:40. The small businessman and woman were everywhere. A carpet-weaving store was at the rear of the train depot. On Bridge Street, R.K. Cole ran the Mississippi Hotel; D.C. Stone was a photographer with his shop in Mrs. Rose's Hall next to the Almonte House. On Mill Street, a hairdressing salon provided "shaving, hairdressing, hair oils and perfumery" while, across the street, a Mr. Crawford supplied bread.

For some strange reason, Henderson's Bookstore also sold oranges, lemons and apples. At the same time, J.C. McKinnon, a dealer in groceries and provisions, also sold liquor. A Mr. McEwen was a tailor and clothier while the town auctioneer was W. Gilmour. If your watch gave you trouble you went to D. Northgraves; if it was your teeth, a T.W. Raines guaranteed "no pain extraction".

The Almonte Foundry was run by R. Driscoll who sold parlour stoves, ploughs, coalers, kettles, ploughpoints, threshing machines and reapers. D.C. Lockead sold coal and oil. In the window of his shop, Noble Bennett advertised for a "stout, able boy, 17 or 18" to learn the blacksmith trade.

On the human side, the *Gazette* reported in 1892 that twenty-nine dollars was stolen from the Station House. That Christmas, a thousand pounds of Christmas pudding were sent to the inmates of the Kingston Penitentiary. In Brockville, a cow swallowed an eighteen-inch snake, while right in Almonte, a Miss Cane was thrown from her buggy. The death of Elizabeth Kennedy, formerly an O'Keefe and a cousin of mine from West Huntley, was announced as taking place on December 2, 1891. On the sport's scene, Almonte and Arnprior were scheduled to meet in a curling match: the Old Country Players against the Old Canadians.

Prices in the Nineteenth Century were interesting. Parlour furniture suites cost twenty-nine to seventy-five dollars at L.W. Shipman's on Mill Street. In 1894, H.H. Cole sold groceries: Japanese Tea at twenty-five cents per pound and Black Tea at fifty. A gallon tin of apples was ten cents while a two-gallon tin of syrup was a dollar. Raisins and sugar were five cents per pound. W. Wylie would buy your wheat at the "highest prices" and sell you in return either Family or Baker's Flour. Wylie even had a direct connection by phone from his posh office to the Almonte Roller Mills.

At Kelly House, Madame Green told fortunes, twenty-five cents for women and fifty cents for men. At the Town Hall on Monday, March 26, 1894, you could hear the famous violinist, H.B. Telgman: general seats, twenty-five cents, and reserved, thirty-five, available at Henderson's Bookstore.

Each succeeding generation saw many changes in the Almonte scene. Shopkeepers came and went. Dusty streets gave way to gravel or cobblestones or the black grass called asphalt. Model T's and then Model A's stood where hitching posts had been. Electrical wires and posts etched the sky. Buggies and cutters, sleighs and wagons faded into a landscape of mechanical progress. Cement sidewalks kept long dresses and shoes dry.

In the Forties, the Superior Restaurant was popular while Barr's Snack Bar and Rooney's Poolroom also attracted a fair number. Peterson's Ice Cream became famous in the valley, especially those chocolate ice cream sticks made personally by the jovial Archie Lockhart. Archie's brother Mel opened a small grocery and gasbar on the eastern edge of town. A Mr. Graham dispensed drugs at his pharmacy. Charlie Finner played at the Cedars on Highway 29 every Saturday night.

A new Co-op store opened on the site of Father Fraser's China Foreign Mission House. Producers' Dairy from Ottawa bought the Almonte Dairy. O'Brien's Theatre came and went. Black Jack Finner took down his blacksmith's shingle. The Woolen Mills closed down in face of synthetics and foreign competition. Trains were more frequent, faster and slicker, and then less frequent and less comfortable. The old CPR Station was saved from demolition. Almonte's bootleggers were put out of business by the "wetters". Lindsay's International Tractor Agency came and stayed.

An artificial ice rink was built. Fairview Manor, the Almonte Nursing Home, and the Almonte Hospital became known for service with a personal touch. Taxis delivered your favourite "poteen" right to the door. Wayne and Gwen Lockhart ran a small barber shop and beauty parlor. And life went on, constantly changing the face of comely Almonte, mostly for the good.

The people of West Huntley and Almonte have walked together for nearly two centuries. And although the industrial features of the area may have changed, the people are still the same: good neighbours living by the side of the road and helping the known and unknown who pass their way.

23

Driving the Old Almonte Road   *(See map on page 349)*

The distance from the Carp Road to Almonte by the Old Almonte Road is about fourteen miles or twenty-three kilometres. The route covers ten concessions of old Huntley Township and three of Ramsey. The Sunday driver should watch for many geographical divisions: valleys, ridges, swamps, stands of trees, and beautiful vistas of arable land which anticipate a guest's arrival.

After a fifteen-mile drive on Highway 7 from Ottawa to the outskirts of Stittsville, turn right (just past the Flea Market) onto the Carp Road (the old Third Line of Huntley). Proceed to the Richardson Side Road now highlighted by the Cheshire Cat, a friendly roadside tavern, converted from an old stone schoolhouse once named Mulligan (the previous school burnt in the Great Fire of 1870). Turn left and continue over William Mooney Drive (Fourth Line) and then very carefully across Highway 17—1.4 kilometres ahead is the David Manchester Way (Fifth Line). Turn right, and after 2.6 kilometres turn left onto the Old Almonte Road. Here the dirt road curls into Mordy's gorge and up through heavy brush.

Spruce Ridge Road (the Sixth Line) is next with more bush and then the road rises 1.4 kilometres to cross the Beavertail Road (the Seventh Line).

The next 1.7 kilometres of asphalt are picturesque. The land about is rugged but open. Two farms on the right are particularly indicative of yesteryear. They come at a great S in the road: first the farm of George Bassett with his little white metal-over-frame-over-log house at the road's edge, and right next to it, the quaint holdings of Allan Howie.

At the Howie Road (the Eighth Line), a newly paved road begins to rise to where breezes always blow. On the right is the West Huntley Fire Department (the site of the first school built in West Huntley in 1841). Just before the Corkery Road (Ninth Line), in on the left, is the second school (now closed) made of stone and sporting a green roof and trim. This Corkery and Old Almonte crossroad marks the first major settlement in West Huntley — it was called Manion's Corners.

The road now falls quickly. The topography changes! The next 2.7 kilometres to the Dwyer Hill Road (Eleventh Line) passes in and out of the largest swamp area in Huntley. The McDonald brothers, residents of West Huntley, labouriously laid the road's foundation. Drive slowly and savour the moods of this long swamp — the cedars and decay and marsh, a solitude where nature seems dead. After the Dwyer Hill Road, the road continues to climb the Western Ridge of West Huntley. Just before the crest of John Kennedy Way (Twelfth Line) in on the right is the Little Red School (now white) first opened about 1863. This is Meehan and Kennedy territory, two of the oldest names in all Huntley.

The next crossroad is the Town Line between Huntley and Ramsey. It's called the Golden Line. Turn right and about a mile down turn left back on to the Old Almonte Road. This area is now Ramsey Township in Lanark County. On the immediate right of the Old Almonte and Golden Line cross is the homestead of the Madden family. It's appropriately named Tara Farm. Its finely preserved stone house and well-kept buildings introduce some of the finest and prettiest land in all Ramsey.

The road here begins a three-mile gentle descent to the Mississippi River. It undulates down past several heritage brick and stone houses to the Twelfth Line and then rises with two sharp cranks to the Eleventh. After a slight drift south, the road turns with the late afternoon sun towards Almonte. Another mile finds Highway 44 and the familiar water tower of friendly Almonte Town.

At the Smithy's

With the potbellied stoves of the old general stores extinct and the twisting candy-cane poles of barber shops fewer, Almonte's old cronies still found companionship round the forge in Jack Finner's blacksmith shop at the cross of Martin and Ottawa Streets.

One afternoon Jack lifted a small but intriguing piece of wrought iron from the furnace and placed it to one side for cooling. As the redness gave way to black, a farmer from Corkery dropped in to kill some time. He noticed this interesting creation of Jack's puddling and decided to take a closer look. No sooner had he grabbed the piece than he dropped it on the floor to the accompaniment of several snickers from the Hot Forge Gallery. Burying his pain in his pocket, he cast a knowing glance around the Smithy's as he glibly said, "It doesn't take *me* all day to examine a piece of iron!"

Time to Bluff

No one likes to lose face, especially an Irishman. Like the time Barney Kavanagh inherited a gold watch from his Uncle Walter in America. One Sunday after Mass, Barney's neighbour, Dimpey Garvey, spotted the watch. He knew Barney couldn't tell the time; so in front of their friends, Dimpey calmly asked, "Barney, 'tis a grand new watch ya be sportin' thar! A real beaut! What time a day do it be showin'?"

Without batting an eye, Barney sauntered up to Dimpey and in one sweeping motion pulled out the watch, flicked open the face, looked at the dial, and idly shoved it (albeit upside-down) under Dimpey's nose saying, "Thar ya have it, Dimpey! Almost time for lunch!"

Momentarily foiled, since he couldn't read a watch either, Dimpey quickly parried Barney's thrust by coolly adding, "By Gar! So it is, so it is!"

24

The Mounted Priest

Reverend J.L. Gourlay, a contemporary of Father Terrence Smith, described him as a man of "gigantic stature" who "when mounted on a splendid charge with a long whip, or even on foot ... was a terror to evildoers!" He remembered seeing this Lone Ranger from County Cavan, Ireland, charging "through on horseback to the Balligibblines in Huntley and like young Lord Lockinvar that came out of the west, in all the wide border his steed was the best!"

And what a border he had! From his little wooden church in Richmond built in 1822, he rode the ranges of Ramsey, Goulbourn, Pakenham, Darling and Fitzroy. If an imaginary point of a compass was placed at Bell's Corners and a semicircle drawn from Richmond to Ashton, Clayton, Middleville, Pakenham and Fitzroy, the sweep of Father Smith's parochial duties can be appreciated. By whatever method he came, horseback, cutter, sleigh or buggy, he would first say Masses and administer sacraments in the mission churches and then proceed to the various "stations" chosen across the townships. At each station, he settled in for a few days.

Around Ramsey and Huntley, such families as the Meehans, Kennedys, Manions, Forrests, Corkerys, O'Keefes, Maddens, Dowlings, Tierneys, Pattersons, O'Briens and McDermots were blessed with his visits. At each stop, babies were brought for baptism, couples came to be wed, and Masses were offered for the nearby neighbours. By the time he left each house, the poor mistress no doubt was exhausted what with meals, linen, her family, visitors coming and going, and of course, the all-pervading presence of Father Terrence.

For Smith could be irascible. As Gourlay said, "he ruled" his flocks. If a baptism was delayed too long for his liking as happened in the case of John Currie's of Fitzroy in 1846, he blasted the parents for their tardiness. And John Currie's father, Pat, being a hard-nosed two-fisted self-made hombre from County Fermanagh, wasn't the kind to let himself be blasted by any man. But he took it from Father Smith. He didn't like it and never forgot it, but he took it just the same. He respected the man and the priest!

Father Smith's pictures bear out his reputation. He stares assuredly into the camera with big, black cannonball eyes; no smile creases the tight, thin lips of a wide turned-down mouth; and below a deep dimple in his chin is the rigid projection of a resolute jaw. He didn't even take off his "grannie" glasses or his biretta for the occasion. Maybe he was bald and near-sighted or stubborn and intolerant ... or maybe all four.

He was indeed, his own man, as well as God's. That he worked himself into an early grave at age fifty-three is not surprising. From 1836 to 1851 (less two years rest in Ireland), he helped establish mission churches all over his mini-diocese. The first churches of St. Clare in Dwyer Hill, the Holy Name of Mary in Almonte, and St. Michael's in Fitzroy were built under his guidance. In West Huntley, he helped construct its first church in 1837 and brought to the Irish there a warm sense of spiritual comfort and communal unity.

Gourlay described him as always "having both hands full!" That's the way he lived and died: full out, on the edge, all business, as testy as his favourite horse. In 1851, he went to Smiths Falls, stayed eight years and died with his boots on. They buried him in St. Francis de Sales'

Church, built in memory of a Bishop from Annecy, France, who also died early (age 55) from burnout.

Terrence and Francis: both Saints, only one officially ... Terrence, the John the Baptist type, Francis, more like a St. Joseph ... the one, dressed in the colourful finery of French nobility, the other, in mud-spattered soutane and manured boots ... both so different ... but each an instrument of God ... with the same heavenly goals ... both to die exhausted in their Master's arms!

Better to Say Nothing

A certain parishioner was attending Sunday Mass at St. Michael's many, many years ago. A child in arms persisted in crying during the parish priest's sermon. Finally, the priest suggested that either the child or he would have to remain quiet. The father of the child took offense, stood up in front of the congregation and told the priest that he for one would sooner listen to the child. He took the child out.

Shortly after, an older child of the same parishioner, suddenly became "not quite right" and as the years went by became progressively worse. Some people blamed the sickness on the public vehemence shown the priest that day by the father.

Not Even a Last Waltz

Back in the Twenties a certain farm labourer of West Huntley made it known that he was very upset with his parish priest's ultimatum that there was to be no dancing by his flock during Lent. In front of a large gathering, the lad said, "No priest is going to stop me from dancing!"

A short time later, in the harvesting season, some men were working a corn blower. Suddenly a rod jammed, and the same farm lad jumped up to repair it. As he stood beside the running blower, he lost his balance and the blades severed one of his feet at the ankle. And he never danced again.

In the Drink

It chanced one day that a Corkery man came upon his parish priest in the compromising situation of having thrown back too many. In the face of other parishioners, the man spoke unkindly to the priest about his weakness for too much drink. The priest was crushed! He said quietly to the man, "Before the day is out, you too shall have more than you can drink!" On his way home, the parishioner drowned.

25

Can Anything Good Come Out of Mayo?   (See John 1:46)

The spiritual comfort given West Huntley's immigrants by its first four native priests from Ireland was providential. Like the Four Horsemen of Notre Dame's Fighting Irish, Fathers Smith, O'Connell, Vaughan and O'Malley kept the people on their feet. From 1837 to 1884, they led their parish teams.

The old parish record books at St. Michael's and Richmond's St. Philip's tell their story. Written in straight pen with weak ink under pale light, hundreds upon hundreds of carefully registered baptisms, confirmations, marriages, and burials provide posterity with the only proof in some cases of a person's existence. The writing styles of these priests examined over a number of years show the gradual deterioration of their health. These ministers of the Word, often raised in a social milieu above the average and therefore accustomed perhaps to roasted pheasant and downy mattress, must have keenly felt the cultural shock of Canadian Life.

But they dug in! They knew their responsibilities! They knew their own: their moods and mentalities. They knew how much their flocks depended on them for inspiration and solace. They understood firsthand how much they all had left behind. They even understood what it meant to be persecuted.

Two of these priests came from County Mayo, one of Ireland's poorest areas. They were Fathers Vaughan and O'Malley. Altogether, they gave thirty-four years of service, not just to Huntley but also to the surrounding townships of Ramsey, Pakenham, Fitzroy and even parts of Goulbourn.

Poor Mayo! The most northerly county in the Republic! Part of a province totally shunned by the English victors who considered it at best a dumping ground for human refuge! In 1565, an English General at the bidding of the Stuarts carved up Connaught into the Counties of Clare, Sligo, Leitrim, Longford, Roscommon, Galway and Mayo. "To Connaught or Hell," cried the Lord Protector Oliver Cromwell in 1649 as he went about Ireland in behalf of the English Parliament revenging the humiliating losses inflicted by O'Moore of County Leix and Roe O'Neil of Tyrone in the great uprisings of 1641. Fortified by infantry, cavalry, artillery, and twenty thousand pounds in coin, he and his mindless sons-in-law, Ireton and Fleetwood, burnt and pillaged the major towns of the provinces of Ulster, Leinster and Munster. His massacres at Drogheda and Wexford have never been forgotten. The terror inflicted there caused many other towns to surrender without a whimper.

In order to reward his officers, Cromwell in 1652 confiscated all the lands of the Presbyterians and Catholics. In Ulster, he drove the Scot north to the hinterlands of Derry and Antrim, and from the southern provinces of Leinster and Munster he filled the roads to Connaught with

Irish refugees of all faiths but the Established Church of England. With the consent of the Commonwealth English Parliament (minus the Head of Charles I) he gave all landowners (some very rich indeed) until 1664 to withdraw beyond the Shannon River. No one could settle within four miles of sea or town, or within two miles of the Shannon.

Connaught became one huge concentration camp! Remote, barren and mountainous, an outback for outcasts! Any strays caught outside the enclosure faced immediate execution. Cromwell even put a bounty on them just as he did for wolves: five pounds for the head of either. The mad and their victims belong to all ages and races!

The Province of Connaught was another Highlands of Scotland; so wild even the greed and vindictiveness of Cromwell found it worthless. Connaught's County Mayo didn't help much! While Mayo has a few areas of rugged beauty along the Southwest Atlantic Ranges near Westport and Clew Bay, for the most part, second to Connemara, it is probably the bleakest county in Ireland. Grim, forbidding coastlines stretch Northwest, and in the East, nothing but dull and barren uplands. A county so inaccessible and unappealing to strangers that it still retains some of the purest Irish culture; so poor, that even in 1952 many people lived on the starvation line; so wretched that the Virgin Mary appeared at a little church at Knock in 1879 to show her compassion for Mayo's sufferings, especially during the great famines.

Is there a correlation between a people's suffering and the quality of their religious faith? The meaning of suffering has been debated for centuries. Some believe it appeases God when offered up in atonement for sin; others see it as only a necessary evil. That Mayo has been strongly associated for centuries with a strong Catholic faith is a fact. That it has produced many religious vocations is unquestionable! That it has borne its share of suffering is irrefutable! Whether suffering and religious fervour are mutually connected must remain a matter of personal faith.

In this regard, at Ballintober Castle which lies equidistant from Croagh Patrick near Westport and Knock Shrine in the East, the celebration of Mass has gone on without a break for seven hundred and seventy-five years. It's the only church in the English-speaking world to make this claim. Twice burned, then proscribed and suppressed, the faithful have even come, albeit secretly, to kneel on damp slabs under an open roof to take part in the re-enactment of Calvary.

St. Patrick saw good in Mayo. A great mountain called Croagh Patrick was named in his honour. From its 2,510 foot summit he chased all the reptiles from Ireland by ringing his fourteen-inch-high cowbell and throwing it down after each departing horde, only to have some ministering angel bring it back up so the process could be repeated for the next lot.

Pilgrims still commemorate this event by climbing the mountain as a penance. At the top they hear Mass on a small plateau. Garland Sunday on the last weekend in July brings thousands of climbers. Many struggle

St. Michael's Rectory, 1991

Church and Rectory from a postcard mailed December 22, 1914 and received December 24. The rectory was then six years old; the church, fifty. Father Cavanagh built the rectory.

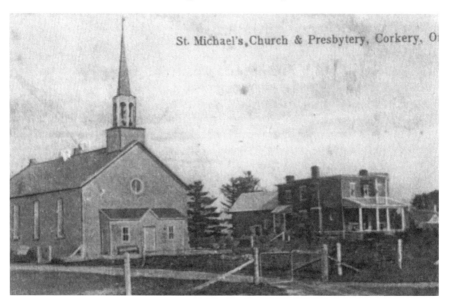

throughout the night passing one another's shadows in the blackness. They go up on their knees sliding around on the slippery pebbles. Once a lovely koala-eyed colleen working in the Tourist Bureau on O'Connell Street told me she had just returned from climbing the mountain but, "Never again," she shuddered. I almost said I'd help her next time! What a beauty! She'd turn the head of the Pope!

The mountain's ascent can be started from an Abbey founded by the O'Malleys. The O'Malleys, O'Flahertys and O'Connors ruled these coasts of Ireland with pike and sword long before the Normans. The last native King of All Ireland, Roderick O'Connor, died in Mayo in 1198. As you would expect, he died in an abbey.

Some ten miles west of Patrick's Hill is Clare Island, the home of the notorious sea piratess, Grace O'Malley. A courageous Amazonian Queen of that Island, she married first into the O'Flahertys' clan, once the terror of the Western and Northern Coasts. Later she married Sir Richard Burke with the proviso that either party could end the arrangement in one year. During that time, Grace secretly took over every Burke castle and on the last day of the agreement promptly ended the marriage by literally slamming a castle door in Sir Richard's face. Grace, naturally, was on the inside!

Grace once met Queen Bess and made sure the Queen had to raise her hand higher to shake Grace's.

"I'd like to make you a Countess!" says Liz.

"Oh, but you can't do that!" says Gracie.

"Why can't I?"

"Aren't I a queen the same as yourself?"

The two became friends. Elizabeth even made Grace's son the Earl of Mayo. They must have been alike.

In his 1924 history of St. Michael's parish whose people he loved, Dr. Dunn, who took over Doctor Lynch's practice in 1897, praised the work of Fathers O'Malley and Vaughan. From his patients, many of whom were former parishioners of these two Mayo priests, he heard firsthand the esteem in which they were held. Speaking of Vaughan, Dunn says, "This name is always treasured in Huntley as its first parish priest" whose "eloquent voice was ever heard in upholding the faith" and whose "cheering words of encouragement to the negligent brought many to mercy and repentance!"

Dr. Dunn's use of the word "eloquent" is interesting. Eloquence usually implies a fine speaking voice as well as excellence in style and content. Few speakers have all oratorical blessings.

I remember once speaking on the phone to a female Information Operator at Bell Canada. Her Irish brogue was a tonic in itself:

"Are you long from Ireland?" I said.

"Only two years!" she countered.

"And what part are you from?"

"The garden spot of it all, Mayo, of course!"

"Well you certainly have a clear resonant lilt in your voice!"

"And why wouldn't I? Don't you know Mayo produces the finest singers in all Ireland?"

Of Father O'Malley, the good doctor says, "He loved his religion, and his voice and work were always given in furthering the Kingdom of God ... He was beloved by all who appreciate such qualities. The older ones among us still tell of the cheerful, genial, kindly, witty, pious Father O'Malley!"

The Irish of West Huntley do not remember all their priests with the same affection. The blood-and-thunder ones they recall with reverence, but the kindly mild ones they remember with love. The Gael doesn't take too kindly to being embarrassed or coerced! A bit of the donkey in some of them! Gentleness goes a long way! So does a little wit, a touch of humility, some "quality of mercy", and half a blind eye to alcohol.

Mentioning money is a "no-no". Far better to come into the pulpit with one sleeve out of the surplice or the whiteness of breath on the cold than bring up the subject of money. Better the priest tell them he can't make house calls any longer because he had to butcher his horse for food. They'll get the message! They'll come through as they always have!

Neither of these Mayo men were much for parish organizations. But they were great builders! Penny by penny, log by log, and stone on stone, they raised up the complex on the Ninth Line. Up until 1851, no resident priest had been appointed outside the village of Richmond.

Father Vaughan and his few faithful take the credit for the first rectory built in 1853. Commuting from his log house in Irish Town, Almonte, he supervised the construction of a flat-stone house similar to John Kennedy's just down the road. This sturdy home built among the cedars across the road from the southern part of the graveyard was the priests' abode for fifty-five years, a meeting-house for another nine, and a church hall for another fifty-five. In 1972, it burned.

My son Tommy and I were driving past the area that spring day. We saw the black smoke and licks of deep red and we drove to Carp to get the Fire Department. From a garage I was directed to someone's home, etc., etc. In those days the Administrations of the two townships were wrangling over "limits of responsibility". Anyway, the reels from both Almonte and Carp arrived together just in time to bid farewell to this fine one hundred and nineteen year old monument. In my backyard, I have a birdbath made from its stones.

As mentioned, Father Vaughan also built the stone church in 1864. He called it St. Michael's. These were difficult times for him! His health had become precarious in the late Fifties. His parish duties demanded his saying Mass at Mission Churches and family "stations" throughout Pakenham, Darling, and Lavant. The constant travelling and worrying wore him out. He went back to Mayo (probably in the year of his twenty-fifth anniversary, 1861). He resigned his position sometime after his return (about 1865) and sought the dry climate of the Midwest. After working a short time in Osgoode, he retired permanently in 1869 to the peace of a monastery at Tracadie, New Brunswick, and died there at age sixty-nine in 1882. Only pious men remain in monasteries and he did for thirteen years!

Father O'Malley wasn't young when he came to Corkery from Eastern Ontario and Northwestern Quebec. But he was more robust than Father Vaughan. Fortunately he didn't have to do the same amount of travelling. Almonte got its own resident pastor in 1872, but not before O'Malley helped the parish build its first stone church, (ninety by fifty-five feet), with a tower and pews and wood-burning heaters and a bell.

How lucky Almonte was: its own Father O'Malley who just happened to be "going their way" from Mayo to help the people build a new church to the memory of the Holy Name of Mary. Dowling drew stone for it; Gleason, sand; Madden mortgaged his farm to get the project going. Sleighs and horses were loaned to the workers. Statford and Reilly sought and received the willing support of area Protestants and someone went to Ottawa to beg, borrow, but not steal from Parliamentarians and other dignitaries. In 1869, the church had its first Mass. Old Father O'Malley was a mover and a shaker.

About this time the economy changed. To add to the recession, the Great Fire of 1870 drove many Catholic families from West Huntley. The sheds of St. Michael's were burnt. O'Malley's income dropped to one dollar per family per year. He struggled on: built new sheds for $400.00, put a veranda on the church, bought a bell for the tower in 1877, and purchased a new organ for St. Michael's first choir. In 1876 his income was only $264.00. He often dug into his own savings to keep going! In 1884, after sixteen years of service to countless souls, this dignified servant of God retired to the Mayo for which he had never stopped pining. He was well on in his seventies.

The pioneer families of West Huntley deserve much credit. Under the guidance of Irish priests like O'Malley, Vaughan and Smith they built, (this side of South March, Arnprior, Richmond, Almonte, Clayton, Dwyer Hill and Fitzroy Harbour), the first Catholic missionary church, the first residence for a priest, and the first stone church.

The financial support for a resident priest in Corkery was particularly significant in that his presence opened up channels of grace for a vast number of Catholics spread over a great expanse of territory beyond Corkery's parish limits.

Such accomplishments show the true mettle of the Corkery people. Neighbouring townships should forever be in their debt.

Some afternoon when grey clouds hover above the valley and the stillness of the country is on the breeze, come stand on Finner's Hill and see the gaunt Smith on his steed riding in and out of the great pines on his way to the McGraths or Whites ... at John Kennedy's flat-stone home, see the great bulk of McNamara leading a few faithful into the barn for Mass ... see the huddled form of Vaughan making his way from the presbytery to the damp log chapel in the graveyard and hear his golden tones leading his flock in the rosary.

I look at the little birdbath in my garden and in its stones I see the frail old O'Malley rocking on a winter's night with only the howlings of wind and wolf for company, dreaming of the brooks and dells in Mayo and his running across the downs towards the aproned beauty of his mother ... he hugs her again at the knees and feels her hand in his hair and her strength.

I see him later disembarking at Cobh, taking the steamer to Cork and then the train to Westport. He had come home ... nothing much left there ... most friends gone ... the people still struggling for bread.

But he had his beloved Mayo again and the breeze from Clew Bay and the mists on the moors and the soft Gaelic sounds of Ireland.

I see him by his mother's grave where part of his heart had always been and where not too long away he would lie near her. And he asks himself: has it been a dream? ... so many years ... where have they gone? ... was it worth the pain? ... did we do any good, Eddie and I, by leaving Mayo for the mission fields of Canada?

And the inner voice of his mother whispers, "Can nightingales sing, my son?"

Alex's Ecumenism

It was raining buckets, so it was, as three ladies on their way to their Good Friday afternoon Presbyterian Service were forced to seek shelter inside Father O'Hare's little church.

As the kindly old cleric was vesting in the sacristy, he spied the three standing sheepishly at the back. Turning to his faithful white-haired sexton, he whispered:

"Alex, my boy, would ya mind givin' three chairs to those Protestant ladies thar at the rear!"

Alex shuffled away.

As the good Father mounted the altar steps, the solemnity of Good Friday was shattered by Alex's raspy voice. He was addressing the congregation:

"Folks, could I 'ave yer tension for a bit?"

As the wide-eyed priest turned, he saw Alex inside the communion rail. He saw him raise his cap on high and heard him shout:

"Now let's all give three rousin' chairs for the Orange ladies at the back! Hip-hip _____; ___ ___ _____; ___ ___ _____!"

26

A Home Boy

When George Stone died, his soul must have taken a direct sighting on heaven. For in all his eighty years, he never harmed anyone.

George was one of the Home Boys who came to Canada from England around the turn of the century. His first home placement was a disaster. After much suffering, he was withdrawn from there and placed with the Harrold family who lived on the Eleventh Line of Huntley. As the second son of this fine couple, (they lost their first in 1911), he found acceptance and peace.

When I first met George, his parents had already died and the Depression had given way to the Second World War. How George scraped out a living on the small farm he inherited is a credit to God's mercy. Jobs were scarce and George was illiterate. Yet survive he did. He had a few animals, some pasture and a little crop. He never complained. He was usually jovial. And my grandmother liked him!

From my grandmother's veranda, you could see George coming down the line in the early evening dusk. You could tell it was George by his stride and swagger. His heavy half-tied working boots moved with powerful precision. His centre of gravity was low. His body suggested a stability in keeping with his name.

Even those who would make George the butt of a prank (like at Halloween when they moved his outhouse to the top of the pigshed) were careful not to stray beyond the danger level of George's good nature. His handshake was a test in pain and his laugh as big as his heart. He lived on porridge, potatoes, green bacon, salt pork, vegetables, cheese, tea, bread and butter. No one ever imagined George being ill.

By the time George reached my grandmother's, all the chores were done. The cows had gone to pasture, the horses had been watered and bedded down, and separator parts, milk pails and supper dishes washed.

Evening was a mellow time, a collection of priceless moments when nature and human nature came to rest. A certain contentment filled the air. Grannie rocked on the veranda in time to light conversation about weather, ghosts, crops, etc. The men rolled their own or chewed their favourite. Young ones sat and listened.

All too soon, the fireflies cast shadows on the woodpile. Cheerful crickets chirped the temperature. And from his lofty perch in the bush across the road, the whippoorwill announced the edge of darkness. Any noise, imaginary or otherwise, sent little hearts in the rookery all aflutter. Spring piglets squealed and snorted as they stacked themselves in a corner to ward off the cold. The call of a neighbour's dog told us we were not alone.

Soon, everyone moved inside. Coal oil lamps were aglow. The fire in the big Findlay stove was given a sound shaking. Everything was set up for the ten o'clock news which came on at nine o'clock because Grannie refused to recognize *fast* time. If the night was cool, the battery-powered Rogers seemed to work better. More than often, the news was sad — many brave hearts were dying for freedom on foreign shores.

After the news, George and other guests followed their lanterns home and soon the last pins of light on the roads were swallowed by the night. Often George was the recipient of a fresh loaf of bread from Grannie's barrel with the cream-coloured lid. She liked him.

A few years later, George found employment with the Ottawa Road Department. At this stage, he met his second family where he found new love.

At his wake, this new family came to mourn, the parents and their children who had grown up with George, and they all spoke of him as one of their own, one for whom they had genuine affection.

His last years were at the Fairview Manor in Almonte. I found him there one day sitting in the main lobby — his voice more crackled, his smile as contagious, and his handgrasp the size of Smokey the Bear's.

He said he hadn't been walking downtown much, since he had taken a bit of a "turn" on his last outing.

His face still had its strength and a quiet resignation. Here was a man who had met poverty and adversity and solitude with extreme courage. Indeed, his favourite expression, in his best cockney, for anyone poking fun at him was, "Lad, if you'd went fru, what I went fru, you'd be dead!" And of course, he was right.

At the Manor, he was ostensibly and deservedly happy. I marvelled how gracious he was and how gentlemanly his words. As I shook his hand for the last time, I wished I had told him how much I admired him. Maybe he could tell.

His monument in the Corkery Cemetery is one of the finest there. George is with another family now. I am sure my grandmother was happy to see him. She liked him. The little Home Boy has gone home!

We All Do It

We're all guilty of using words that only resemble the sound of the correct ones. One person may use "incinerating" for "insinuating" and another describe a worker as being "laxative" on the job. Like the little lad who always enjoyed one particular hymn every Sunday because it gave him a chance to sing about "Gladly, the cross-eyed bear".

Back in the days when motorcars first came to West Huntley, a middle-aged lady from the Ninth Line was describing for her friends some features of her husband's new car:

"Yes, 'tis a grand machine! It has four baboon tires, real electric lights, and its own self-commencer!"

27

A Pair of Jacks

Since 1823, West Huntley has had at least six John or Jack Mantils (also spelled Mantle, Mantel and even Mansel by two very early brothers named Martin and Lawrence).

I have known two. One was Jack Mantil (1880-1970) married to Bridget Loretta Killeen (1892-1989), daughter of John and Margaret Grace. (John was born at sea.)

I first met Jack outside his front door on the Tenth Line. I had called on him for help to get my car out of the April mud. He brought out his team and in no time I was on my way — the other way. He was eighty then, agile, alert, and ever so mild in disposition. He told me we were related and, of course, I had no idea how. I later met his son Angus, named after Bridget's brother. He worked at the *Almonte Gazette* until his untimely death just a few years ago. I understand his other son Greg is every bit as fine as Angus.

Two braw sons by a man who never married until he was fifty-two. He was respected by everyone and even today his neighbours never mention his name without commenting on his goodness of character. He was called Big Jack and he was big in so many ways.

Big Jack Mantil
1924

Jack Mantil
1988

The second Jack Mantil was the son of Bob Mantil and Rose Grace. He married Marian Greenfield in April, 1958. They had three boys and a daughter. This Jack was named after his grandparent, John, husband of Mary Gallaghan. He and Big Jack and I shared the same ancestor, John, the initial Mantil settler back in the Pakenham-Panmure area.

Jackie Mantil was the oldest of eight children, the one all his brothers and sisters looked up to. Like Big Jack, he was extremely kind and unpretentious with a sharp wit and a flashing smile. He talked quickly and decisively as do the people of Cork. When a neighbour needed assistance, he was the first to go. He helped me once when I was but ten: he pulled me from ten feet of water at the Appleton Dam; I was going down for the third time.

As his devoted wife so aptly puts it, "Jackie had friends everywhere!"

Jackie died on July 8, 1990. He had been sick for only a few weeks and he suffered much. I went to see him in hospital a few times up until the end. I met two of his boys, Barry and Mike, and his wife. I told him one day his daughter Rosemary was one of the prettiest girls in Huntley (she is) and he smiled with a great pride. When I mentioned that Clarence Williams called him the best neighbour he ever had, he smiled again.

He never complained. As he slipped in and out of sleep, he would look round at his two sons, Barry and Mike, each of whom held a hand. He was comforted by their presence and his pain became more bearable as he gazed up at each one. Seldom have I felt such love between father and sons as I saw in those moments at the Queensway-Carleton Hospital.

Jackie Mantil was a good Catholic, a good neighbour, a good husband, and a good father. He was also a gentleman. A decent man.

His children and I have one common bond. Without Jack, none of us would be here.

I was talking to my good friend Mary Basil about the singular love Jackie's children and wife had for him. And I said, "Do you think our children will be with us so lovingly at the end?" And Mary said, "They will, if we deserve it!"

Jackie deserved it! Mary will deserve it! About myself, I'm not so sure!

On my second-last visit with Jackie, we were alone. I had given him Communion. We chatted. I said I must be going. He took my waiting hand in his. He always had great strength. It was still there! He squeezed tightly, longer than usual. He raised himself slightly off his pillow. His eyes found mine. They brightened. He said, "Gary, thanks for everything! I'll never forget ya! Catch ya later!"

About a week later he died. See ya sooner, Jack!

Her Father's Girl

A sixteen-year-old Irish girl in the year 1830 was digging potatoes in a far pasture. Her father and a stranger approached.

"Catherine," said her father, "this is Mr. T____ W____, your future husband. You'll wed him within a year and go to Chicago!"

And she did and she went.

After a hard but happy life, Catherine lay deathly ill one morning. She awoke to see a white dove enter the room and hover over her bed. She told her little grandson, one of two to become priests, "Tommy, I am going home today. My father has sent the Holy Ghost to take me!"

And that evening, Catherine again obediently arose and went with Him to meet her father!

28

Rose

In her sunny rose garden,
None shone so fair
As sweet Rose Mantil
Whose heart it did share.

As often happens, I have been down with
the flu at the very time a friend in Corkery
was very ill. It was like that the time Cecilia
Carroll died and the same upon the loss of
my dear friend Rose Mantil.

She had been sick nearly all the summer
of 1980. She took a turn for the worse in
November. Unable to visit her, I wrote her a
letter. It almost arrived too late. It was delivered to her house the day she died, Nov-

Rose Mantil
with grandson Barry,
1960

ember 23, and someone read it to her in the Almonte Hospital with all
her family gathered round. Her daughter Mary said Rose was pleased.
And that made me happy. Rose was a rose! And the fragrance of her
memory lives on.

Every time I pass her old now-vacant home on Highway 44, (the last
house on the right before the Dwyer Hill Road on the way to Almonte),
I can still see her tending her garden, her little face peeking from a bower
of colour. She used to talk to the flowers, she said. They must have liked
what they heard, because, from her veranda to the road fence, hundreds
of happy blooms blushed contentment.

This garden and her little framed log home meant the world to her.
She and her husband Bob had lived in several areas of West Huntley:
back at Sunnyside in Panmure, in the old John O'Keefe house at
O'Keefe's Corners and in the brick home of Ned Forrest on the Twelfth
Line. They settled down around 1930 in this old McGrath-built home.

After the McGraths left, Lawrence Curtin and Ellen Clancy lived
there for some forty years. Nine children were born to Ellen in the wee
downstairs bedroom. Ellen, daughter of Tom Clancy (1818-1883) and
Mary Lormasney (1821-?) from Cork, my grandmother's grandparents,
was born on the Dwyer Hill Road. My great-grandmother, Mary, born in
Ireland in 1846, was Ellen's sister. In fact, the Clancy family first lived
with my great-grandfather Tom O'Keefe at O'Keefe's Corners. Mary's
daughter, Genevieve, was to later marry my grandfather, Tom.

I mention Ellen, whom I remember, not so much because she was a
relative and a "grand old lady", but because she was truly a Lady of Sorrows. She buried her husband, parents, all eight brothers and sisters, and
at least six of her children (three young men to the killer-flu, one boy to

appendicitis, one girl to a heart condition and another to a blood disease). Only one girl survived her, Kate, named after Ellen's sister. She married Jerry Mantil, and their only child, Mary, now has her own lovely family in Brockville, Ontario. Mary married the affable Ed Enright from Ottawa. Even as a child, Ellen bore a terrible shock. She lost her twenty-year-old brother, Tom Clancy, to a falling tree.

Bob and Rose, thank goodness, met with better luck. Their eight children (six born in the McGrath house) had good health and all lived to shower Rose with deserved affection. Her son, Billy, a successful businessman in California, even built her a custom home adjacent to the old house. The southwest corner of the new bungalow has several windows obviously designed for Rose's new indoor garden. Rose loved it there, but her heart remained at the old place. It had been her Garden of Eden for forty years.

Rose was christened Loretta Rose Grace. She lived on Lot 24, Concession 12, on the west side of the Burnt Lands' Road. She was the third last child of Peter and Ellen Hickey. From 1877 on, fourteen children were born in a house no bigger than a small cabin. Downstairs had half as a kitchen and the other half divided into parlour and bedroom. The upstairs had two bedrooms. Of the children, all but two infants grew into old age. Peter and Ellen gave their family roots, wings, love, and great dispositions for having a good time. It was a happy home. Ask anybody who went there. Grace Mantil O'Keefe, Rose's first daughter, says it was a fun-home with always a crowd hanging around. For Ellen, it meant bake, bake, bake, and bake some more. In between bakings, she had fun too.

That's how I remember Rose — a fun-person, a twinkle-eyed fast-quipping mischievous tease capable of laughing herself to tears.

She was a thoroughbred: mercurial, impetuous, high-strung, but, oh, ever so kind and friendly. I can't imagine anyone in West Huntley not liking her. She touched them all at one time or another with her charm.

She was the perfect example of the old adage that the best presents come in small packages. Like four of her brothers and sisters whom I knew personally, Eddie, Amanda, Lollie and Maude, she was small-framed, petite, even delicate looking. But she was anything but a cream-puff: resilient, wiry and energetic, and quite capable of working herself to a frazzle.

My Granduncle Michael O'Keefe was like that. He too was of medium build. But according to a neighbour Jim Ryan who often sawed wood at the O'Keefe home, pound for pound, Michael O'Keefe could work any man into the ground. I never knew Uncle Mick, but I knew his sons and they could work as fast and as long as any man in the country. Jim Ryan used to call him "the great little man". Such titles are not easily thrown about by the Irish.

In my estimation, Rose was a "great little woman". She could start a party in a morgue. In an intimate crowd, she was in her element. She had a zany side to her as if she was programmed for fun. Apparently her brothers William and Jack in Renfrew had this same streak of buoyancy; her brother Lollie certainly had, as did Amanda, her sister.

Amanda Grace O'Connell — now there was a bundle of joy. In old pictures with her chums, the cameras captured her pixie smile, her trim figure, her wavy auburn hair, and that wholesome country image of the girl who "married dear old Dad". The youngest of the fourteen, they called her "Baba" or "Babe". She never lost her looks nor her good humour. Like Rose, she held up no barriers of sophistication. A bit of a cutup, she couldn't have been more spontaneous and refreshing — a good friend and I miss her.

Nowhere did Rose's effervescence show up better than in a game of cards. She thrived on competition. With adrenalin flowing, she became a whippet at the post. Her strategy was simple: attack, attack, attack and play every hand as if it were the last. For her the game mattered, not winning. Defeat, in spite of her whelps of dismay, really meant nothing.

Although Euchre always remained the popular card game in Corkery, an old game called "Burn" enjoyed a return to favour in the Fifties. Not everyone liked it, but certain families like the O'Keefes, Charlebois, Mantils, and Carrolls seldom turned down an opportunity to participate.

Up to seventeen could play, but usually about eight formed a nucleus. Each player received three cards followed by a declaration of trump. The object of the game was to win as many of three possible tricks. A player had to state his intention to "stay" or "fold" before the beginning of play. If he decided to stay and failed to win a trick, that player "burned". The penalty for burning required the deposit in the pot of an amount of money equal to the total pot upon completion of each hand.

Some pots could grow very large. For example, with eight players and five staying, the number of possible burns could be anywhere from two to four and the pot would rise accordingly. Let's say player one deals: he first puts eighty cents in the pot as an ante, ten cents for each player. Player two stays and wins all the tricks. Four burn. Each burner then must put eighty cents in the pot after the winner has removed the original eighty cents.

The pot is then worth $4.00 including the eighty cents from the new dealer. In the next round, if three burn, the pot is $12.80. So it went, with bigger pots and stiffer penalties.

Dropouts increased according to the level of risk. Rose, of course, seldom cried "Uncle". Her never-say-die optimistic spirit kept her in most games. She operated on the premise that the best defence was a good offence. She bluffed with good hands and bad.

She had a bag of tricks: moaning profusely with a "mitt full"; whooping it up when she had nothing; declaring her intention to stay deliberately "out of order", thereby pressuring later declarers to drop out; searching for matches and cigarettes, asking for water, rummaging through her purse, or commenting constantly on the play with carefully placed barbs. Rose lost more than she won, and she stirred everybody up in doing it. She was there to have fun and make sure everybody else did too.

I never felt more at home than at Rose Mantil's. She and her family were most cordial hosts. In the summer, in the big backyard with its circular drive, old pump, trough and vegetable garden, we'd often sit for a chinwag. The car motor wouldn't be turned off before she'd hit the door to greet you.

In the winter, the big Brock stove provided boiling water for tea, and out of the big pine-frame cupboard came a tin of homemade oatmeal cookies. As I prepared to leave she'd say, "What's your hurry?" and at the car her last words were always, "Come again soon!"

Rose was a sweetheart ... she had a folksy down-home way of talking as if she was sharing a secret with you ... she had that knack of being on the same wavelength as her guests ... even when I was but a child, she lifted me up to her level ... after all, she was thirty-four years older than I ... yet I was always accepted ... we understood each other ... we were friends.

The warmth of her personal attention to visitors never changed over the years ... even amidst all her suffering, the sparks of love for her children and friends never died ... she was always the same Rose ... radiating goodness and kindness every day of her life ... none of her flowers was ever her equal.

The song asks, "Where have all the flowers gone?"

I know where one Rose went!

Now You Don't See It, Now You Do

Father Cavanagh, parish priest at St. Michael's from 1906 to 1913, asked a parishioner, Cornelius Curtin, to go out into an adjoining bush and cut down a base for a new statue of St. Michael. The priest carefully described the kind he wanted, one cut from a tree with three branches extended like the trinity. Con made it known that such a tree would be impossible to locate. But to please the priest, he set out.

As Con expected, he trudged through the bush and found nothing suitable. He headed home. But just as he was leaving the bush, there on the perimeter stood the exact tree described by the priest. To the end of his days, Con maintained the tree was not there when he entered the bush. Shortly after, the new statue was placed on its miraculous stand near the altar of St. Michael's Church to the joy of everyone and the consternation of Con.

29

Spring Memories

For over a hundred years, the Egan log house at O'Keefe's Corners was a familiar sight. Under a canopy of cedar, at the base of the rock-ridge, its ashen-grey, white-chinked logs, and Irish-green doors and windows overlooked the Mahoney Road but a few yards away. Across the road, just inside the log fence, was a spring, which like its sister-spring on the south side of the house, was fed from the hills that eyebrowed the west side of West Huntley Valley. These watering holes, then as they do now, offered cool refreshment to man and beast. Unlike wells in the area, they seldom gave in to drought conditions and even withstood the dusty Thirties.

During real dry spells when tree frogs sing and barn fowl open their beaks to breathe, my grandmother would send me to fetch water from one of these springs. The clear silvery-blue waters mimicked my boyish moves until my pail scooped up about as much as an eight-year-old could carry. The dog Teddy would lap up his fill, I would have one for the road, replace the old cover, and head on home to relieve grandmother's thirst.

The spring by the house has had many visitors over the last two centuries. Pat and Bridget Egan and son Dennis first lived beside it. And later Katherine, Dave, Margaret and William O'Keefe. Archie Currie and his wife Kathleen Scott and four children were there in the Thirties followed by Basil O'Keefe in the Forties and the Angus Carroll family ever since.

Mary Mantil Carroll recalled one day that Monica Flynn once told her she often stopped there on her way from the Twelfth Line to Saturday Catechism classes. Katherine O'Keefe lived there then. The middle-aged Katherine had long brown tresses that fell below her waist, and it was little ten-year-old Monica's pleasant chore to comb and brush out Katherine's hair as she sat on a kitchen chair by the spring.

Just recently I met my cousin Margaret Muldoon from Arnprior whose mother Annie Rowan was a niece of Katherine O'Keefe. As a young girl, Margaret often visited her grandaunt at O'Keefe's Corners.

As we were talking about old times, Margaret suddenly asked me if the old spring was still there. When I said it was, her eyes brightened as she leaned forward and said excitedly, "Do you think I would be permitted by the present owners to go and see it?" I said, "Certainly," and she added, "I'll ask Ed [her husband] to take me." I didn't inquire as to what sweet memories the spring held for her, but it was obvious she associated many happy moments of childhood with its presence.

Not long ago, Kathleen Currie remembered my visits to her home and its spring. I told her I remembered her place as a happy one; (isn't it strange how as children we size up people and places and carry these impressions all our lives)? As we talked of Archie, her husband, I told her

I remembered him as a happy, content man who loved to "kid" and make people smile. And she said, "That was my Archie!" (He died some ten years later.) And then she went on to discuss those hard, hard times in the Depression — no work anywhere, no income, her four children, the harshness of it all.

And then she spoke in glowing terms about how my grandmother sent over five pints of milk morning and evening all year round for many years and how my grandmother said that a certain productive cow had stopped giving milk the year (1939) that Archie and his wife and children moved to another part of West Huntley. Such was grandma's faith!

And she spoke of the fire in 1952 that took two of her brother's children, and how her own son John spent months in hospital recovering from his burns and how Doctor Dunn did so much to help him recover his health. How the people during those times shared their troubles, and always gave when they had so little.

It was all there welled up inside her — so many sorrows and laughs — so many days when people who had nothing, still wanted for nothing — so many nights when eyes filled from joy and heartbreak.

And here we were forty-nine years later sharing our memories of half a century when I was a pup and she but a new bride.

And the old spring is still there where it all began waiting for Margaret Muldoon and other friends to return for a visit.

How many reflections does it hold?

A Compliment for Connie

Being as St. Michael's was having a mission, a certain hired man who hadn't been to church for a good many years decided it was time to go to confession. Not knowing the parish priest from the Watkin's man, he took a seat upstairs.

The rosary was being said. Usually Mary Ann Grace Curtin led the congregation, but on this particular Sunday her husband Connie did the honours. Connie was a good man for the job, a fine-living parishioner who not only looked holy, but was! After the rosary came confessions and then the Mass.

At home that evening, his employers asked the hired man if he had made it to confession.

In actual fact, he had "chickened out". But, as he didn't want to lose face, he said he had gone. Since several priests hear confessions at missions, his inquisitors asked; "What priest did you choose, then?"

"Ah, he was a good one indeed, so he was! Sure it was the little priest who said the rosary before the Mass!"

And nobody let on they knew!

30

Evelyn

Irish skies are changeful
But Irish hearts are true
And tender is the lovelight
In Irish eyes of blue

As the years passed and I grew a little wiser, I came to realize the riches possessed by mother, Evelyn (Eva) O'Keefe. The above words of Eva Brennan help best describe her — a woman bonded together by fierce loyalty and fathomless love, a woman of great complexity who kept about her a wispy veil of sophistication that not only set her apart but also helped hide her depths. Those that saw beyond the veil became her friends.

On the surface she was a pleasant, uncomplicated woman. Her smile was warm but reserved; her conversation careful but engaging. She loved a good joke at her expense, yet never dared to poke fun at another. She put herself down by apologizing for the uncleanliness of her immaculate home or the unsavoury quality of her deliciously cooked dinners. She made little of her new clothes or coiffures and fended off compliments with mild embarrassment. Opinions she might have held on controversial subjects were kept to herself in deference to the views of her guests. Is it any wonder I had difficulty in fully appreciating her!

My mother was the third oldest child, the one perhaps most like my grandmother. She was the first daughter to lose her husband to death and the first to die.

Her initial job was in Ottawa as a clerk until her marriage in 1930. During the war she worked for the government in one of those "permanent-temporary" buildings so prevalent at the time. In 1953, after her husband's death, she became a postmistress for

Tom Ogilvie and his wife Evelyn (Eva) O'Keefe — about 1930

some seventeen years, first in Westboro, then at Carlingwood in Ottawa and finally at Murphy Gamble's Department Store on Sparks Street in downtown Ottawa.

I often took the children to visit her at Murphy's up on the mezzanine near one of the best snack bars in Ottawa. I admired her quietly from the distance as she greeted customer after customer with the same disciplined courtesy: "And where are you sending this twenty-nine cent money order, my dear?" ... "Did you say two five-cent stamps or five two-cent ones?" ... "But, madame, packages for Christmas delivery should have gone four weeks ago!" Never a grimace would she show ... never a verbal slap to the overbearing and rude.

After her retirement, she continued to live alone for another twelve years in the white bungalow built by her husband in Westboro in 1934. She died in December, 1977. I found her on the bedroom floor just where she had fallen. A beautiful smile graced her lips and I knew she had not died alone. Yet I wish I had been there too, for I never had a chance to say good-bye. I held her, kissed her, told her of my love, and left.

Her life had always been one of service to her family, and to her, family was everything. If any of us needed assistance, she was there. If prayers were required, she would storm heaven for a solution. Her devotion to Christ's Mother knew no bounds. She attended Our Lady of Perpetual Help devotions every Wednesday for thirty-five years. I remember going with her in the mid-Thirties to the old Assumption Church in Eastview, a distance of twelve miles from Westboro. The trip required over an hour of travelling time and three streetcar changes each way. Later the devotions were shifted to a centretown church which was still some six miles from her home.

Her favourite prayer was the rosary. And it was during its recitation that she told her brother that she was dying. And a couple of hours later she did. No doubt it was Our Lady's presence that put the smile on her lips. She had come for her!

Her loyalty was tenacious. She spent many summer holidays helping out at the homestead at O'Keefe's Corners, cleaning cupboards, washing floors, putting up curtains, etc. When her brothers Ignatius and Edward were recovering from surgery they stayed at her home. Later, after Ignatius's death, Edward stayed with her until her own passing. She was absolutely devoted to the care of my father, me, her parents, and all her brothers and sisters. Mel Lockhart, her brother-in-law, told me once (and by that time, he had stood over the graves of his parents, brother and a grandchild) that he only cried once at any funeral and that was at my mother's. She had that kind of goodness about her.

In many ways, she was her mother's child. She had that Irish mystique so difficult to understand. On one hand she would dance and laugh with the best of them — on the other she quietly withdrew into shy repose. True and tender, but wistfully changeable too — so much like the Irish skies — shifting from mood to mood according to her nature's whims. If she did allow herself to worry, fuss, or fume, she nearly always maintained her graceful dignity. And if a great fury did sweep across her soul, she usually kept it hidden behind many externalized defences.

Everything she believed in or held dear was coloured by her faith in God. And as she grew older, her resignation to God's providence became even deeper. From this concentration on religion, she developed a code of values which helped her get by in life. She developed a wisdom beyond her years. She came to know the hearts of men and could read those hearts as easily as she read tea leaves in a cup. She had no time for braggarts and frauds, and hypocrites raised her hackles. In time, I came to realize how exact her judgement of people really was. She looked unconsciously for the truth of Christ in men and if it wasn't there, she went her way and they went theirs.

With the years, her shoulders grew round and her frame grew smaller. Her eyes dulled somewhat and her hands were cooler. She took on an almost doll-like fragility and her delicate veneer of gentility seemed even more pronounced.

She used to tell me she was going on a long trip and wouldn't come back. At the time I didn't know what she meant. Some months after her death, I realized the true significance of her warning. She must have known.

Her mysticism continued after her passing. Favourite red shoes she had kept in remembrance of her dancing days in the Twenties disappeared completely. Small individual miniature pictures of her grandchildren that hung from a portrait-tree disappeared from the living room sofa where I had put them. And there were many other occurrences too numerous to mention and too mysterious to understand. She was indeed a woman whose love seemed to reach from even beyond the grave into the lives of those who meant much to her.

I never had a chance to say good-bye! Maybe someday I shall have the chance to say hello and thank her for everything. She was the best friend a fella ever had!

Cheeser

On the evening of October 6, 1917, Michael O'Keefe and Nellie Moran gathered their family around them in the parlour to pray the rosary. It had been a sad day: the parish of St. Michael's had buried little nine-year-old Albert Curtin, affectionately known as "Cheeser" to his school friends.

The pallbearers that Saturday morning had been his school chums. They all wore white gloves for the occasion. Ignatius O'Keefe, his first cousin, and Basil O'Keefe, son of Michael O'-Keefe and Nellie, were two of those pallbearers. It was Basil that told this story.

Before the rosary started, Basil remembers a family member suggesting they offer up the rosary for Albert. Michael chuckled that Albert was too innocent to require any prayers

for his soul. Suddenly outside the parlour window a wild
screech terrified the family. Each looked at the other. Then
Michael said, "We'll say this rosary for 'Cheeser'!"

Remember

Remember those days of love
And friends you held so dear.
Remember good times by-and-by
And you'll never shed a tear.

Count your blessings one by one
How goodness came your way
When moments were so full of joy
And happiness filled your day.

A Call

Come, my sweet
Your life is almost o'er
'Tis time again for us to meet
And share our love once more.

Do not linger, my sweet,
The best is yet to be
'Tis time to leave your distant vale
And rest forever here with me.

Come, my love
To the far side of the moon
Where in the garden of my heart
You have never failed to bloom.

A Friend

That old country pump
Still sits on its well
A kind and trusted old friend.
How often I wish that I could return
To its wonderful world again.

That old country pump
Still sits and stares
A true friend of a country lad
Who dreams he could once more return
To those wonderful days he once had.

31

Bells and Belles

The Belles of Munster are sweet and fair
Like St. Ann's Bells on the summer air

Just off Shandon Street in the hilly northwest part of Cork City called Shandon (old fort) is a small church with a big steeple and the sweetest sounding bells in all Ireland. It's called St. Ann's. Built in 1722 by the Church of England, it has been immortalized by one of its pastors, Francis Mahoney (1804-1866) in a poem, part of which goes:

The Bells of Shandon
That sound so grand on
The pleasant waters
Of the River Lee

In 1970, I climbed up to a room above the entrance of this church by a narrow limestone passage. I had heard that tourists were allowed to play the bells. My wife and mother waited in a taxi outside the church in absolute terror of what they might hear. Sure enough, on the wall overlooking Church Street were eight ropes connected to the bells some hundred and twenty feet above. The ropes were numbered and beside them were musical scores for several appropriate songs. I chose "The Bells of St. Mary's". I pulled and I played and I sent across the River Lee and its fourteen bridges a flawless rendition of the song made famous by Bing Crosby. It was a marvellous experience! After all, how many people get a chance to play for a city on two hundred and twenty-year-old bells?

The church steeple is shaped like a pepper castor. It has three tiers and four sides, two of white limestone and two of red. Each side has a clock and each clock has a slight variation in time, the result being that the steeple of good St. Ann's has been christened (no doubt by Catholics) as "the four-faced liar". In spite of this aspersion, St. Ann's is still a gem, its Gloucestershire-cast bells forever sending their cheerfulness across the most Irish of all Ireland's cities, the patriotic city of Cork.

In the shadow of St. Ann's, in fact, almost adjacent to it, is another landmark of Cork. One that goes beyond even the Eighteenth Century. It's the old Cork Butter Market, once considered by many as the biggest of its kind in the world.

The butter once came here from all over Munster in big tub-like containers called firkins. Since a firkin was usually too large for one family to fill, three or four usually pooled their produce. Each week a different house was used for the firkin preparation.

Barefoot young women did the work. After twice washing the individual outputs in pure spring water, they blended the butter on the kitchen table with big butter spades. Since each farmer's butter had a different shade due to the amount of clover in it, the blending gave the butter one solid colour. Adding a bit of salt for zest and some saffron for colouring, they then packed the firkin, covered it with muslin, and fastened the lid with hoops.

Any butter left over after each family's needs were satisfied, was shaped into small bricks and marked with a flower design outlined on the face of the butter spade. These bricks were then wrapped in fresh cabbage leaves and given to families with no cows.

Before roads, the butter was shipped by family members on horseback; later, after roads, on carts filled to a horse's endurance. Some journeys were long, often requiring overnight rests for man and beast. These forced stops gave the men a chance to enjoy one another's company and stories.

At Cork, the market formed a circle. The merchants came in droves since the butter business was lucrative. Their purchases depended on the judgements of professional, impartial butter-tasters who went about from farmer to farmer burying their auger-like testers into the firkins and running the long shafts of butter across their noses as they tasted their quality from top to bottom.

After the market, the sellers set out for home with cash or merchandise to await the next week's shipment from the buttermaids. When, once again, barefoot maidens would whip the butter to the cadence of song and chatter ... standing on the damp turf ... their black and strawberry locks impishly askew ... their sea-hazel eyes alluringly afire ... full of beans and malarkey ... the cream of Ireland's pulchritude.

And it was the same in those days whenever and wherever such colleens worked ... full of fancies and fun, whether collecting dulse on the beach, loading hay, baking, milking, plucking fowl or blending butter ... always that same wild freshness of spirit, that same *joie de vivre* ... that same flush of delight as felt when eating with fingers ... cupping cool spring water to drink from hands ... running through the surf ... shouting echoes from a cliff ... or removing shirts to the run of the breeze.

Even today, Ireland has the resonant call of Shandon's bells and, best of all, still has the sweet songs of its Erin belles — earthy, unpredictable, brooding, electrifying, passionate, deep and vexing, and oh, oh, so brimful of a natural harmony and rascality unsurpassed anywhere else in the world. I know; I married one.

Red-Circled

A German war prisoner who worked on Martin Manion's West Huntley farm for two years was easily identified by the large red circle sewn on the back of his jacket.

The Cliffs of Moher and O'Brien Castle, County Clare, in 1987.

The grey south shore of the River Lee just on the western fringe of Cobh, the last view for the emigrants of the spire of St. Colman's in the distance, 1968.

A lonely jaunting car on the blue rim of Lough Leane, the largest and lowest lake of the Lakes of Killarney, 1970.

Cobh harbour, 1987. At the pier, bottom centre, the emigrants embarked after attending mass at St. Colman's, rebuilt in 1868. The new church was constructed around an older church which was dismantled after the new walls and roof were up. It has been called the "Church of Tears"! The Titanic made its first and last call, anywhere, here in 1912.

A jaunting car near Muckross Abbey, Kerry, 1970: Horse Charlie, driver John, the author's mother, Sister Margaret Power, and the author's wife. John called us Mrs., Mrs., Mr., and Sister.

A pony express on the golden sands of Lahinch, Clare County.

White stone pebbles symbolize death in Ireland. The top picture is of a hermit's cell at St. Finn Barr's Retreat at Gougane Barra, Cork, still a place of pilgrimage. The bottom picture shows the grave of Mary Carey, 11 years old, 1844, of Ballybride, Cork. The grave site is near Knockmourne, Cork.

In Connemara, 1970, I asked a peat worker if I could take his picture. Without looking up from his work, the Irishman said, "No!" Apparently, many are superstitious about having their pictures taken. These pictures show the cutting and piling of peat, 1970, in Connemara , without the worker.

Lake Currane — Waterville — Ring of Kerry, 1987.

Marilyn on stairwell in Barry's Castle, Cork County, in 1987.

32

The Entertainer

Lollie Grace could make a groundhog laugh. So remembers Herman O'Keefe who listened as a young boy to Lollie's colourful stories. Lollie lived on the Burnt Lands' Road about a mile north of the O'Keefes and manys the evening strolled back to Mick and Nellie's to while away the time. With the young O'Keefes at his knee around the warm hearth of a great lion's-paw stove, he spun yarns culled from his father Peter, and old-time neighbours like Con Curtin, Dinny O'Brien, Ned Forrest, Tom Morrissey, Andy Forrest, Tom White and John Delaney. His speciality was ghost stories.

Lollie Grace
1924

As Lollie grew up, times got harder. He saw his mother Ellen Hickey forced to raise turkeys (no easy task) in the early Depression to avoid foreclosure on her little eighty-four-acre farm. He remembers his father's brother, Michael, being forced to sell, and the financial squeeze felt by his other closest neighbour, Dinny O'Brien. Being in debt in the Depression was hazardous to one's wealth. Often relatives could be as merciless as strangers in their insistence on full reimbursement from mortgages and wills. Lollie quickly came to appreciate the value of a dollar and realized that the only way to fight poverty was to go to work.

Lollie worked "out" in West Huntley, the surrounding townships, and up the Ottawa Valley. He could turn his hand to anything. He was a good worker. He toiled in quarries, mills and shanties. Often he hired on with local road gangs on a "come day, go day" basis, shovelling and spreading gravel with exceptional ease. He lived by his wits and survived by the seat of his pants, all the while storing away images and details of funny characters and situations. Blessed with an astute mind, a blotter-memory, and a Midas touch for blarney, he easily became one of the top storytellers in West Huntley. He was in fact an entertainer!

As a natural charmer with a gift for persuasion, Lollie eventually slipped into the selling business. He could sell rosaries to a Masonic Lodge and sun lamps to the Arabs. He went from farm to farm with such items as Wolfe River Apples (tough and dry) and old hens for hatching (tough and lean). In his later days, he owned a small gas station on Martin Street in Almonte. He died alone there in 1963. He was seventy.

Until his marriage to Violet Hall from Lachute, Lollie lived on the homestead with his brother Eddie and sister Katie. Vi and Lollie only had about a decade together before Lollie's passing. But they made the most of it. They bought a house in Almonte. They enjoyed each other's fun. They had good times.

Vi had her work cut out for her. She knew that confirmed bachelors and spinsters can be very set in their ways. And she realized full well that her red-haired, freckled-faced Lollie had marked traces of black-sheep syndrome. Fortunately she was equal to the task of reining in Lollie whenever he became too immersed in poker and horse racing. They never had a dull moment! Vi and Ellen Grace may well have been very much alike. Doesn't every Irish boy worth his salt marry someone like his mother?

Lollie's escapades are myriad. One story tells of his working in a lumber camp near Pembroke. To make extra money, he set up a barbering business. Whether he ever cut hair before remains doubtful; then again he may have learned the trade from a neighbour "Johnny the Barber" Mantil. Anyhow, Lollie bought handclippers, scissors, comb, razor and strap and commissioned the camp cook to build a barber's chair. The chair's size prompted Lollie to tell everyone it had five hundred feet of lumber in it. Such trivia attracted customers.

One evening a green French lad from the Quebec side made a bad decision. He agreed to a haircut and shave. The haircut was hitchless and before long Lollie had the thick lather brushed on for the shave. As Lollie sharpened the straight razor on the black leather, his tone with the young man grew solemn. Suspecting some devilment, a small crowd gathered.

As Lollie put the cold steel to the hot throat he stammered, "Now, see that you sit still, young fella. The other evening my razor slipped and put a gash in a customer's throat. Naturally, I've been a little shaky since; so don't do more than breathe!" Well, the poor lad began to tremble and was soon on the verge of terror as Lollie kept mumbling away about the accident. Eventually, the lad ran off into the night feeling around his face and throat for blood. That was Lollie!

Another time Lollie played a practical joke on his usually even-tempered brother-in-law, Bob Mantil. Bob needed a horse and Lollie said he could borrow one of the ones he kept back at the rented stables of Jimmy Lynch, the cheese maker. After a considerable hike back to Lynch's, Bob found two old horses, one almost dead and the other lame. They say it took Bob half a day to calm down. That was Lollie!

Once, Lollie approached a farmer on a Huntley Line to inquire if he had any cattle for sale. The farmer said he had one calf he would let go. It looked good said the farmer but in fact wasn't a "doer", as old Jack Mantil would say. Lollie bought it and after a few hundred yards up the line pulled into a farm owned by a close cousin of the calf's original owner. Lollie set a healthy price based on the animal's "purebred lines", and the cousin bought it.

Not long after, the two cousins met over euchre. The second cousin invited the other over to see his new purchase supposedly from the Story farm back at Fitzroy. Which farmer had the biggest shock was never revealed. They knew Lollie had taken them for a ride and probably didn't know whether to laugh or cry. That was Lollie! He had struck again. Was it for the money or the fun?

All things considered, Lollie was generally honest in his dealings. If a calf turned sour after a deal, Lollie picked it up. Satisfaction was guaranteed. Like Professor Harold Hill in the *Music Man*, he knew the territory, his merchandise, and his customers. But unlike Hill, he couldn't leave town for the next stop. Lollie had to stay among his own, wheeling and dealing with farmers who knew the score as well as anybody. Like the "Man in the Grey Flannel Suit", Lollie knew his reputation had to be unblemished to survive in a small community. Cheat one and you cheat them all. Lollie's longevity as a salesman reflects his acceptance in the community as a fair businessman. Naturally he had to be shrewd! He wasn't playing with amateurs!

Occasionally, Lollie was on the receiving end of practical jokes. At a friend's farm in the Pakenham area, Lollie was invited to make an offer on a calf. In the dusk, the farmer told him to wait alongside the barn while he went to fetch the animal.

Now Lollie had imbibed, back at the house, enough to somewhat impair his usually keen powers of observation. The shouting of his friend soon attracted him to the back of the barn where Lollie, with the poor light and his unsure vision, could vaguely see his pal and the calf wrestling on top of a manure pile. "This calf is frisky, Lollie; I doubt if I can bring him in!"

Impressed by the healthy strength of a beast he couldn't really see, Lollie told the farmer to throw him into the back of the truck. He'd buy him! On the way home, Lollie wondered how he was going to manage such a spirited brute. When he got down from the cab, he was ready for anything. But the calf made no resistance! It just lay there. It was dead. It had been on its last legs from the start.

The same friend, H_____ was his name, had another favourite victim, the good-natured poor-sighted Tom M_____. Tom had the habit of jingling change in his pockets (my father had the same habit). Even at church, Tom sat there jingling away. One Sunday, H_____ took his seat behind Tom and at a moment of reverie in the service dropped some loose change on the wooden floor. Tom naturally thought his pocket had sprung a leak and dove down on all fours trying to retrieve his money. His eyesight didn't help matters any and he went about groping for some time. The same H_____ later spray-painted Tom's dog a different colour and poor Tom kicked his own dog off his front veranda every day for two weeks 'til someone put him wise.

Basil O'Keefe, my dear friend, knew Lollie in his prime. Some fifteen years younger, he remembered Lollie as a great lad. He saw him as a good neighbour ready to pitch in and lend a hand come sun or sleet. If a farmer needed a part for machinery, Lollie would hunt one down. Said Basil, "Everybody liked him. Nobody coming into a yard was more welcome than Lollie Grace!"

With the humour on him, Lollie was a funny man. Such people are blessed by fate with the often burdensome talent of making people happy. Always on stage, at home or on the road, bringing sunshine into someone's heart. Like Harold Hill. "Always leave them laughing," said a famous Hollywood comedian. That was Lollie's lot! And only men and women with sensitivity to life's sorrows and pain know the true value of humour. Humour helps them fend off life's blows and gives them the healing satisfaction of knowing another's cares and worries are lessened by their merry hearts. Some days, being funny comes naturally; on others, the show goes on in spite of personal problems. Often these difficult performances are the best and most fruitful. Every clown cries alone! Without the tears, he could never make anyone laugh!

Lollie, the entertainer, has joined his compatriots in fun: his brother Eddie and sisters Maude, Rose, and Amanda, (all products of the happy house of Peter and Ellen on the Burnt Lands' Road), as well as his good friends Alex Grace, Archie Currie, Arty Morrissey, Mary Meehan, Loretta Forrest, Maggie Hunt, and Maggie and Mary O'Brien.

No doubt they're reliving the parties at the Grace's and Delaney's and laughing about the cutter rides under bearskins and the good times at picnics and socials and local dances, remembering those roaring Twenties when a nickel was a nickel and a lady was a broad, and flappers holding a garter in one hand and champagne in the other wiggled the Charleston to a scratchy gramophone record.

Lollie often came to my grandmother's for cards. I played euchre and some poker with him. I was thirteen; he was fifty-one. But I remember how the old green kitchen took on a glow when Lollie got on a roll.

Everybody grew younger in his presence! Even my grandmother of sixty-five. At cards her face would flush, her eyes would flash, and her fist hit the table with renewed vigour. She and Lollie were a matched pair and dear friends. I truly believe Genevieve O'Keefe took the place of Lollie's departed mother.

I can imagine the day when Lollie arrived in the great beyond (only eight years after my grandmother's death):

"Lollie, what are you doing up here? I thought you were afraid of spirits and heights!" (both true)

"Vive, my angel, I had to come! You were here! Although, after all your cheating at cards, I'm surprised you made it yourself!"

"Shush, you old imp! Let's have less talk! I've got the cards; you shuffle. And don't wear the spots off them. And I want to cut them. Then I'll show you, Mr. Lollie, where the bear got in the buckwheat!"

D'ya Sea

An old Irish sailor once said, "A man who is not afraid of the sea will soon be drowned; but we do be afraid of the sea and we do only be drowned now and again!"

33

Seamus and Colm

Ireland's geographical centre is a few miles from Mullingar, a Westmeath (pron. Westmeed) county town somewhat north of the cities of Galway and Dublin and about halfway in between.

The country round is lavish with woods and waterways, and many fine houses attest to Mullingar's importance over the centuries as an agricultural centre of some repute. The local farmers are experienced breeders of quality horses and cows, the latter having won national renown for their girth. So much so that all of Ireland has come to use the term "Mullingar heifer" to refer good-naturedly to a woman overly endowed in size.

Sean the Shoe told this story about Mullingar and its beefy bovines.

Seamus the Fireman called down from the fourth-floor window of a burning hotel that a female guest was stuck in her bathtub, one of the old-fashioned narrow ones, I believe.

His partner, Colm, shouted up from the ground, "How big is she?"

Seamus shouted back, "All beef to the heels!"

"Like a Mullingar heifer?" asks Colm.

"Bigger!" says Seamus.

"Glory be to God," says Colm, "may the Saints preserve us! Can we get her down in one load, d'ya think?" says Seamus. "Not less I can put handles on her! She's heavier than the tub!"

Well, Colm climbed the ladder to join Seamus and after throwin' a sheet round her, they started tuggin' as best modesty would allow. But the poor creature was beside herself with terror and embarrassment and her face was ruby red and her eyes bulged, and her screams shrill enough to shatter glass.

Says Colm, himself a bit shaken, "If I had a harpoon, I'd soon put her out of her misery." And the woman shrieked like a stuck pig!

Says Seamus, "What she needs is a tranquillizer shot!"

Says Colm, "Now d'ya have to go mentionin' a shot at a time like dis!" his mouth just about stuck tight with the "drouth" that was on him.

Then Seamus calls down for two ropes so as to lower tub and all to the ground. And Colm, accident-like, lets his elbow fly to quiet the poor woman. And then the great white tub with its great white cargo was slowly lowered. Seamus and Colm were on the verge of expiration when Colm says, "We could launch the *Queen Mary* a lot easier than this!" And that set Seamus to laughing and he lost his strength and the rope gave way on one side and the good woman was thrown out like a white whale on top of a local wag named Willie Cumback who never did because he couldn't and said he wouldn't if he could.

Later on that week the lads gave Seamus and Colm the Mullingar award for bravery in the face of fire. And since that day to this the sayin' that "Ya can't get far wid a lady from Mullingar" has never been forgotten around "them" parts.

Words of Wisdom

Irishmen can get pretty worked up about getting married. By the time they reach the church some don't know their own names and others barely remember the service. The experience is bad enough when everything runs smoothly. But if something goes wrong, the nerve endings can become downright raw.

That's the cue for the best man to earn his gift. Calming the victims down. Restoring confidence. Keeping them conscious. Helping them find the church and altar, even the bride.

On his wedding day, Frank Scott was fortunate to have his older brother Tim as best man. Tim had been through it all. Married to Mary Margaret Delaney, the older sister of Hannah, Frank's future wife, he had stood in this same Delaney farmyard just a few years earlier. He considered himself an experienced hand at the marriage game. The romantic starbursts had faded and the grim reality of raising a family had made him a wiser man.

So far everything had gone without a slip that Saturday morning. Frank was "steady as he goes" and Tim bounced around emitting his contagious ease. Three cars were to be used by the wedding party. Martin Ryan and Erskine Johnstone already had their Model T's parked for the getaway and the third car loaned by an Edser Shaw was due at any moment.

But they waited and waited. And no Edser! As it turned out, Edser had had a flat somewhere between Pakenham and Delaney's. An hour went by! Frank began to wither. He began pacing faster and talking faster. He was working himself into a lather!

Tim to the rescue! The "old married" brother took charge. He walked over to Frank, stared down at him (Tim was taller), firmly gripped one padded shoulder, and uttered, only half in jest, those immortal words that have already survived seventy-five years:

"Frank, my lad, pull yourself together. You'll be married to her long enough; so stop your fretting and enjoy what little time ya have left!"

Not To be Greedy

Most Irishmen doing business like to set the price to suit themselves and then give in a bit on the terms. As one Irishman put it, "When we get a deal, 'tis only fair we should give back a little of it!"

34

Sticking Together

The Irish are never happier than in the company of family and friends. It's their Celtic nature to form deep attachments. They view their home, their children, their animals, community, and even nature with the Romanticist's eye.

Such sentiments are not easily discernible. The Irish don't usually wear their hearts on their sleeves! As the late Leo Hogan of March Township once told his children, "Never, never, tell anybody your troubles!"

After the Civil War in the United States, Robert Lee, the Irish leader of the Confederate Army and perhaps the most brilliant mind ever to pass through West Point, was appointed President of a Washington University. Naturally, reporters, students and historians tried to pick his memory for anecdotes and reminiscences of the war. In his best southern civility, he answered questions about the battles, often meticulously reviewing some major occurrence. But not once, did he ever share his heart with anyone.

Naturally, with provocation, an Irish fist may fly out at an insult brought to family name or honour. But for the most part, the Irishman hides his emotions. In my association with Corkery's Irish, few ever discussed their personal feelings. Few could ever be accused of bragging or "bellyaching".

Rather than seek sympathy or praise, the Irish are usually content with the support received from their own. Even in difficulties, they stick together. Amid the prejudicial attitudes of big-city life in America, Australia, Great Britain, South Africa, and Canada, they survived by helping one another. Business windows from Boston to Melbourne carried advertisements like: "Men and Women Wanted - Irish Need Not Apply". The ruling class called them "the peasants from the bogs". Along with the Blacks, Poles, Italians and Chinese, they were the doormats of the New World. But they stuck together and gathered strength from unity.

In time, as the Industrial Revolution expanded in the United States, cheap labour was required by the upper and middle classes. Irish women worked the sweat shops of the garment industry. Every Piedmont and Morgan had Biddys in their kitchens and Paddys in their stables. Irish women took in laundry or went out to clean and scrub.

Irish men, five thousand strong, laid half the track of the Union Pacific to the West. Thousands worked in the bush and on the rivers. Thousands fought in the War of Independence, the four-year Canadian-American conflict and the American Civil War. They loaded barges, freed rivers of silt, dug tunnels and canals. In the coal mines, Irish lads, as little as ten years old, rode elevators to the eternal blackness. There, they helped set off the explosives for which their "gutsy" compatriots had wagoned in the nitroglycerin.

But, regardless of the hardships, after work, the Irish always returned to their slums, ghettos, cabins, and boarding rooms where they derived nourishment from the culture of their own people.

Recently I met a rather cool young Irish bellhop in a fairly fashionable London hotel. With the cost of living at an outlandish level in England, I asked him where he stayed. "Oh, no problem, there," he said with practised disinterest, "I stay in an Irish community in Wimbledon" (a suburb of London). Within this social framework of Irish loyalty and hospitality, he maintained his sense of identity and put on a cover of security which enabled him to meet daily challenges with a measure of buoyancy.

By turning to the warmth of Irish friends and family in time of tribulation, the Irishman bears the pains of life. His tendency to react with violence or bottomless melancholia is more than often redirected by the companionship of his community. Problems become smaller; morose thoughts are tossed back as easy as a dram of good cheer. A clenched fist and a closed heart lead but to guilt and sorrow. An open hand to strangers and an open heart to friends: "that's the ticket"!

Outside Father Flannigan's "Boys' Town" in Nebraska is a statue of a young boy carrying another boy on his shoulders. The plaque reads: "He's not heavy; he's my brother!"

It was like that in West Huntley. They depended on one another. They shared the losses; they pulled as a team. A family without firewood, no problem. A barn to be raised, lots of help. Money needed for an operation, collections taken up. Bread and milk always given to those in need. Sandwiches ready for wandering destitutes. A mother down with sickness, cooks and maids fill her kitchen. A farmer unable to work, no chore too big for his friends. They mourned and laughed and struggled together. They shared the weight of the entire community's cares on their shoulders from the cradle to the grave.

And that's how West Huntley was built.

Working Within Yourself

Edward O'Keefe worked at his own speed. Even as a young man, he paced himself. One summer in the Thirties, Joe Lee his uncle from Toronto, was visiting Edward's mother, Genevieve, sister of Joe's beautiful wife, Laura.

One afternoon, Joe was down at Jim Carroll's and he and Jim were watching Edward forking hay in an adjoining field. Now the astute Joe Lee always called them as he saw them, a straight shooter who told it like it was. Jim said to Joe casually, "That Ned lad sure ain't short on strength!" To which Joe replied, "He shouldn't be; he's twenty years old and hasn't used any of it yet!"

35

The First Shelters of West Huntley (See map on page 350)

Many present day immigrants from communist countries cannot survive in the large American cities. They miss the State's control and protection. In America, democracy gives them its four freedoms and then casts them adrift to make it on their own. The responsibilities of making all their own decisions and their own livings often swamp their initiatives and they go back home better resigned to the domination of non-capitalistic regimes — freedom has its price and every right, its duty.

Irish immigrants also came from a country where they were little more than strangers in their own land. With no ownership, suffrage, or religious freedom they were entirely at the mercy of the State's puppets of power. But unlike the immigrants from socialistic-communistic countries, in the Americas they readily embraced the four freedoms as well as all the civic responsibilities and duties that come with rights and privileges.

The Irish in West Huntley also withstood the test. They vindicated the faith placed in them by the British administrators in Canada, England, and Ireland. They showed that, given half a chance, they were capable of upholding the enterprising nature of the Celtic race. They became good British subjects in a British colony, worked hard at even the most demeaning jobs, bore arms for the British in the Crimean, Finean and Boer conflicts, as well as the Great War, and by their successes eventually convinced British and Canadian Port Authorities to open their doors wider to the Irish. The phrase, "luck of the Irish", has been bantered about as an explanation for Irish good fortune. Luck, my foot! History never shows luck helping the Irish. Maybe "pluck", but certainly not "luck"!

I have often wondered what the proudest moment must have been for these Gaelic immigrants. Knowing their deep Celtic affection for home and family, my guess it was the day they first crossed the thresholds of their new Canadian homes. What dark recesses in these unlettered romantics were stirred by the first possessions of their own houses? Surely it made all the sufferings worth while! Surely these were their finest hours!

Granted these first homes weren't much to look at! The majority were just shacks! Even in 1851, the census-taker making his way along the trails of West Huntley recorded in his journal a preponderance of these humble quarters. Of seven shelters listed on one page, five were shanties and two, log houses, one of which held two families. A shanty was usually a one-storey, flat-roofed shelter made of any combination of logs, poles, brush, boards, twigs, etc.

By 1860, most shelters were log houses a few of which are still seen here and there in the valley. Their sizes varied: 20'x30', 22'x32', 24'x36', even 28'x38' and 30'x40'. Their foundations were flat stones piled six feet high and some twenty inches wide. Logs were cedar rather than pine because they better resisted rot.

Between the logs, often shaped on four sides, was placed a mortar of lime, sand and water. Two-by-fours were then strung out vertically for the nailing on of closely spaced wooden laths. These laths were then covered with a plaster of lime, sand, sawdust and water. The pure slaked lime came as a hard powder made from the calcination of limestone, which had been mixed with water into a gritty white lard-like substance in an old half-barrel or iron cooler. Sometimes horse hair and paper were first stuck between the laths and logs for insulation.

The inside walls could be left as plaster, but most farmers in later times chose to finish the ceiling and walls with different sizes of thin tongue-and-groove pine. Sometimes, especially in bedrooms, walls were brightened with very flowery wallpaper. Every few years, a new roll of colour was stuck over the old until eventually some homes had several layers of paper scenery. Each scene went a few more years back in time!

The floors were of tongue-and-groove pine or spruce or in some cases, planks of thick ash or maple. Pine trim was used on windows, cupboards and door jambs. Roofs were supported by rounded, straight tamarack or spruce poles called rafters, spaced every two feet across each side of the roof. The tamarack grew in great abundance in the swampy areas of West Huntley. It was also choice fuel for industrial ovens because it burnt slowly and with great intensity. It was used for roofing because it was tough and durable and, being a member of the deciduous pine family, quite resistant to rot. The bottom ends of the poles were cemented into the wall by mortar and the tops of the poles joined together by oaken pins driven into holes twisted out by wood augers. The rafters were then covered over by horizontally placed rough pine boards anywhere from eight to twelve inches wide to which were added cedar shingles, a double row of which was used as extended edging along the bottom of each side.

Two coats of whitewash made up of pure crumbly slaked lime, (slake being the heat generated by pouring water on pure lime), were then applied liberally to the walls. Window frames and doors were painted, usually green.

Most homes originally had only one brick chimney. When framed country kitchens were added on in later years, another chimney was needed for summer cooking. Most farmers also had only one big stove. When the kitchen was closed up for the winter, the stove had to be moved inside. In this way, each chimney was used only half a year. During the Fifties, electric stoves were put in some living rooms for cooking in the winter, the big stoves stayed in the kitchen, and small oil furnaces provided the heat. Some furnaces were in the basement; others were floor models placed under the living room chimney.

At first glance, few log houses remain around West Huntley. But in actual fact, more exist than meet the eye. Many have been hidden under wood, brick, and vinyl or aluminum siding. Frame modernization probably first came sometime after 1870, followed by brick, and later by the aluminum and vinyl siding. When it comes to buying one of these "spruced up" log houses, obviously what the buyer sees is not really what he gets!

Four log houses, all in the valley, deserve mentioning. Three are occupied. All look pretty much as they were one hundred and thirty years ago. All were built by pre-1850 settlers.

One log house is on the southwest corner of Robinson Road and Highway 44. It was built by the McGraths. Simon McGrath and his wife Ann lived there in 1851 with Simon's elderly parents, Michael and Ellen. Just a half-mile west and well set off Highway 44, was the home of Simon's brother Michael and his wife Julia Manion. Both houses are now owned by Leonard Killeen. Michael's house is abandoned. Leonard lives in Simon's. For the interest of historians, the McGraths also built the old Lorne Charlebois house across the road from Michael's home. It's now demolished. John McGrath, son of Michael and his wife Margaret Mahoney, once lived there as did Willy Delaney (1881-1975) and his wife Nora Sullivan (1878-1973). Somewhere along the way, the Killeens and the McGraths must have intermarried. John Killeen and his wife Margaret Grace lived almost across the road from Simon McGrath's. Jack Killeen, John's son, later lived at Michael's place while another son Alf took over Simon's house. In 1851, an Ellen Killeen (37) lived with Simon and

Not as easy as it looks, but two horses helped.

125

his wife. Perhaps Simon was married to Ellen's sister, Ann. The Killeens and McGraths were both Tipperary.

This little corner from Highway 44 to the south end of Robinson Way was once the nucleus of Corkery's 1917 baseball team. On the south side of Simon's were Tim Scott and wife Mary Delaney living in a frame house built by Parker Kennedy and Elizabeth O'Keefe, (recently burnt). Across from Tim's was John Killeen's log homestead with sons Alf, Jack, Angus and Herbie. And next to John Killeen's (subsequently the married home of son Angus) were the Sullivan clan, three of whom took to the field, Charlie, Tom and Willie. All were sons of Lawrence and Mary Coughlan. Other players included Tim's brothers Frank and Ed, Jim Carroll, Pat Kennedy and Bill Egan. Eight players came from this small section of West Huntley.

The Sullivan boys never married. But the McGraths married into the O'Brien, Mahoney and Manion clans, to name a few. The country is now thankfully full of Killeens since Angus and Carmel Carroll had seven boys. The Carrolls are still present, thanks to Jim and Cecilia Scott, as are the grandsons of "Big" Will Egan and Tim Scott.

The Vaughan log house on the Vaughan Side Road between Dwyer Hill and Robinson Roads has natural weather-beaten logs. It was moved to its present location on rollers or skids around 1900 by Edward Vaughan whose father James and wife Catherine Ann had probably bought it years before from a James Whalen as part of a land purchase. Ed Vaughan married twice: to Julia Grace and a Francis Devine from up above Renfrew. His son Jimmy married Gertrude Curtin, daughter of Cornelius Curtin (1845-33) and Mary Ann Grace (1856-21). Jimmy had a large family, mostly boys, one of whom, Gerald, married to Bertha Carroll, now farms not far from the old homestead. Gerald's son, Lorne, lives in the old house.

The first resident pastor of St. Michael's in 1853, Father Edward Vaughan, was probably a relative of James who had already settled on his property in 1851. James' son Edward was no doubt named after the priest. The Vaughans came from Sligo County which is above Connemara and below Donegal. I have known nearly all Jimmy's family — good farmers, good workers and good neighbours. The old house has been well cared for. James and Catherine Ann would be proud.

My grandmother's whitewashed log house on the southeast corner of the Dwyer Hill-Carroll Cross also deserves a look. It was probably built in the early 1850's, (replacing an 1847 shanty), by Tom and David O'Keefe, brothers from Conna, Cork. David inherited the property or bought it from his brother Edward's wife, Mary White, after Ed died in 1848. Seventeen children were born in the little 7'x 10' first-floor master bedroom. At least five adults died in the house: my grandparents, my great-grandfather Tom, his brother, David, and Tom's son, William.

As owner of the farm and its hundred acres in 1973, I tore down the summer kitchen built around 1902 by my grandfather Tom and his wife

Abandoned McGrath home on Highway 44.

On the Robinson Way, another McGrath home, now occupied by a Killeen.

The ruins of Paddy Carter' home on the abandoned section of Robinson Way.

Coady's creek was not always a creek as seen by this gorge adjacent to the Morgan O'Brien homestead.

The spring-fed swimming hole a few yards from the Mahoney Hotel.

The Mahoney Road looking east. The picture was taken from directly in front of the Mahoney Hotel site. Little has changed in this desolate area, 1990.

Well off the Twelfth Line is the restored home of Morgan O'Brien and his wife, Sarah Lynch, c. 1855. Many new owners have made similar attractive additions and improvements to old log houses, 1991.

The Vaughan Homestead on the Vaughan Side Road, originally built by the Whalens around 1855 — moved to this site probably by James Vaughan, father of Ed, 1991.

Small stable on the old Tom Montgomery Homestead — Highway 44, 1989.

Sheep on the old Ryan Homestead — Robinson Way Road, 1991.

Genevieve McDermot. The present house is almost just as it was in the 1850's except the windows are new, the roof is of asphalt shingles, and the foundation has been reinforced with cement. About fifty cedar logs were used! An addition has recently been added.

The downstairs had a bedroom, living room, kitchen, pantry and parlour; the upstairs had three individual slant-roofed bedrooms, one of which measured about 4'x6'. A fourth bedroom, affording no privacy, was just off the stairway. (Most log houses had their own individual layouts.) Outside the front door was a wide cement veranda facing the northwest. I sold the farm by 1981. (See map on page 353).

Unfortunately many log houses are now gone as are their owners: the Listons, Lynches, Graces, Morrisseys, Hogans, Forrests, Oakleys, Harrolds, Sullivans, Finners, O'Briens, Delaneys, O'Keefes, Whites, Corcorans, Roches. The country is dotted everywhere with old log-house ruins, sad reminders of the past.

The Man Who's Square

(Maurie Williams kept a scrapbook for about fifty years (1928-1978) and filled it with colourful clippings about local, national and international events. Occasionally he copied out a poem reinforcing his views on morality. The following poem illustrates Maurie's belief in honesty of character. It also shows how the meanings of certain words change, unfortunately not always for the good. This author is anonymous.)

> *There's something in the twinkle*
> *Of an honest fellow's eye*
> *That can never be mistaken*
> *And can never be passed by;*
> *Be his station high or lowly,*
> *There's that doubtless, upright air,*
> *That convinces all beholders*
> *That the man they see is square.*
>
> *Heaven gives such men influence*
> *Over those they daily meet;*
> *If they see a fallen Brother,*
> *They will help him on his feet.*
> *Makes the sneaks a bit uneasy,*
> *Makes the false act kind of fair,*
> *For the greatest rogue on record*
> *Will respect the man who's square.*

Early Stone Houses on the Ninth Line (See map on page 350)

The oldest stone house in West Huntley is John Kennedy's homestead on the Manion Road. Constructed of flat stones and mortar, it reflects simplicity and order. Some call it Adamesque style. John Kennedy (1798-1877) built it sometime after 1840. His wife was Margaret Manion (1798-?), probably a sister of John Manion (1794-1872), who came with John Kennedy from Richmond in 1821. John Kennedy's family was large and in 1851 included his wife's mother, Mary (1772-185?). His son Andrew (1832-1913) took over the farm and married Sarah O'-Leary (1842-1906). Locally, two sons, Ed and Hughie, married Carrolls. A daughter Margaret married Bill Egan. Onaugh married Frank Forrest.

After Andrew's death, a bachelor son Joe carried on the farm by taking out a mortgage with the China Mission College of Almonte. Unable to pay off the mortgage, Joe lost the farm and James Carter bought it for back-taxes. James and his wife Rose Brown gave it to son Joe Carter. It's now for sale.

Further along the Manion Road, past the Old Almonte-Stittsville Road, are three other stone houses. The first was built by John Manion and his wife Mary. John Manion served on the Huntley Council from 1854-1872 and was once a Deputy-Reeve. Their house is the second oldest stone house in West Huntley. Built of cut stones, it is much larger, better constructed, and more stylish than Kennedy's; yet it retains the simplicity and practicality of the homes built in Ramsey, Huntley and Fitzroy during that early period (1850-1870). In later years, John's son, John (b.1830), married Bridget Tierney in 1870, and their daughter Susan later married James Forrest, son of Cornelius of the Twelfth Line. John also became a Deputy-Reeve of West Huntley as his father had been and continued to operate a Tavern-Store-Post Office complex at Manion's Corners. Eventually, the homestead fell to John's grandparents the Sherlocks, which connection suggests that John Senior's wife may have been a Sherlock. Bachelor Paddy Sherlock (about 80 in 1925) later lost the farm for failure to pay the taxes. Times were getting tougher!

The Manion farm had a reputation for being haunted. Harness thrown over horses in the stable were pulled off from the other side by an unknown force. Joe Manion, a great-great-grandson of John Senior, told me phantom buggies have been heard turning in the yard at night. Neighbours Pat Egan and Jimmy Carter give little credence to such stories. But Joe is not so sure. John Senior was killed in 1872 on his way to Almonte. Apparently his horse bolted. Details are sketchy. Was he on horseback? In a buggy? A sleigh? In those days, deaths on wagon trails were common: horses were spooked by bears or trains; there were collisions with other drivers; bridges gave way and axles broke or a horse's equipment snapped. Was John's death due to someone's carelessness in harnessing his horse? Is there really a ghost in that stable showing its irritation at someone's stupidity ???

Both the Kennedy and Manion homes overlook the valley. Even today the barren, rustic flat-stone Kennedy house looks perfectly at ease, even though a little worse for wear. The Manion home has been artfully refurbished by its present owners. It has carried its age and memories well.

Unlike the John Kennedy strain, the Manions are now scarce around West Huntley. Many ultimately moved away and many men died young. But for a period of hundred and twenty-five years they had land and kin. They farmed most of the highlands on the Corkery-Manion Road and many of their forty-plus offspring stayed on to marry Forrests, Egans, McGraths, Kennedys, Meehans, Sullivans and Oakleys, all members of West Huntley's pioneer families. The four Manion brothers, John, James, Andrew and Martin, who came to Corkery with John Kennedy, together formed the backbone of early West Huntley. Another Manion, Patrick, son of Andrew Manion and Mary Forrest (from Eganville) who lived across from St. Michael's Church, became a successful hotel owner in Fort William in 1886 and had a son Robert who became a Federal Cabinet Minister, writer, surgeon and winner of the Military Cross in the First War.

It's a long way from Tipperary, but Corkery should be proud of the Ninth-Line Manions and Kennedys who, with the Egans, O'Learys and Mordys, decided to emigrate to Canada and did much for the economic, social, educational and religious development of West Huntley. The Corkery-Manion Road should be called Tipperary Way!

The other two stone houses near the Manion House were built by the Mordys. Tom Mordy (1806-1877), (English-Anglican), and Sheaby his wife (1814-?), (Irish-Anglican), had raised a large family of seven boys by 1851. They had come to Huntley with John Kennedy and John Manion.

The first home is just off the road. Surrounded by mature trees, its black peaks and flecked-grey stones blend with the haze of the valley below. The stones were cut from a quarry just south of the house by the Jones brothers of Almonte who built the house probably between 1875-85. Jimmy Carter, the present owner, praises the ability of stone masons to judge the quality of the best limestone blocks by reading the seams. Jimmy inherited the farm from his father James (1865-1948) and his mother Rose Brown (1874-1929). James had bought it from George Mordy, Tom's son, around 1895. It is now up for sale.

The second Mordy house, built for son Brock Mordy, is down in the valley some five hundred paces from the road. The lane is private. It's identical to Tom's house. It's very close to Coady's Creek which begins to form in this area. (A check of West Huntley's stone houses shows almost all their construction was near Coady's Creek.) This home was later bought from Brock Mordy by Bill Grace, son of Michael Grace and Ellen Foley. He never married. In the Thirties he sold it to Maurice Williams and Annie O'Keefe who left it to their son Allan who left it to his brother Clarence and Barbara Ballard. New owners have given this old house a well-earned lease on life.

37

The Four Stone Houses of P.J. Manion (See map on page 350)

Four other stone houses of West Huntley were built by Patrick J. Manion and his wife Catherine Lindsay. Patrick was the son of John Manion, the original pioneer on the Ninth Line. Patrick Manion married Catherine about 1846 and probably first lived for some years along the present Highway 44 in the 10th Concession. By 1861, he had moved over to the northwest corner of the Carroll Side Road and the Tenth Line (Robinson Way). Here he set up his homestead. Sometime in the next few years he built himself a stone house very similar to his father John's on the Ninth Line. It was a handsome place under pines and cedars and right next to Coady's Creek which in those days was more like a river.

Unfortunately, Patrick's house was bulldozed into the creek in the Seventies, but not before it had given shelter to four families. In 1885, his son Joseph and Joseph's bride Christine Anne Ryan were ostensibly given the house with the understanding that Pat and Catherine could live on there. Patrick passed away in 1907 and Catherine in 1913 and Joe and Anne died tragically in a car-train crash near Carleton Place in 1919. The new owners were Joe's son Martin and his wife Esther Sullivan who sold to Jim O'Connell and Anne Brown in the mid-Forties. In the Sixties, the O'Connells moved to town and the fate of the grand old home was sealed.

Patrick Manion's fatherly interest in his sons' welfare was typically Gaelic. In fact, he was somewhat of a sugar daddy. Joseph got Pat's house and each of his three other sons received four hundred dollars to buy land and construct his own stone house. Each son then was to carry his bride over a limestone threshold of a mini-mansion every bit as comfortable as similar homes of the gentry in Ireland.

These three houses of the Manion boys were the last stone houses built in West Huntley. They were also the finest! And still stand today.

Basically identical, they show architectural flair, stability, practicality, and a controlled spaciousness. The use of many gable roofs allows the luxury of extra windows once so vital in a world dependent for light on sun, kerosene lamp and candle. The houses' stability stems from walls made of hundreds of twenty-two-inch-wide stone blocks, and cornerstones some sixteen inches in height.

Every room was given a solid hardwood door with matching mechanically operated transom. Window sills ran two feet deep. All floors were of natural pine except the kitchen's which was strengthened by one-and-a-half-inch-thick maple boards.

Each house had three stoves and three chimneys. Heat rose from stoves in the kitchen, parlour, and dining room to five upstairs bedrooms, all of which had at least two windows. Some master bedrooms, often positioned on the southwest corner for maximum light and warmth, had three windows.

The storage upstairs was usually two closets, and downstairs, one or two closets plus a pantry off the kitchen. In one home I frequented, a four-foot-wide mahogany staircase was brightened by coloured glass panels over and along the sides of the front door. And in the kitchen, another stairs went up along the north wall. Dressed white pine decorated all doorway, window and floor mouldings.

Outside, a trapdoor opened onto stairs leading down to a three-quarter stand-up basement. Verandas were of cement, and roofs were cedar shingles. Each house had two entrances, even three in some cases, with thresholds of one-piece sculptured limestone slabs.

All in all, these houses are indeed beautiful. And many of the new owners over the years have added their own touches of improvement. Today, they still command attention: resolute, durable, harmonious, a perfect dovetailing of the pragmatic and artistic; as quietly gracious and unpretentious as their first owners.

Patrick J. Manion must have been delighted to be able to see all three sons' stone houses from his own living room window. Southwest was the home of Patrick F. and his wife Elizabeth Tierney known as Patsy and Lisa. Patrick J. had bought the land from the Robinson settler, Michael Meehan, in 1855, and probably built the stone house around 1883 in time for Patsy and Lisa's wedding; Michael Meehan was married to Esther Manion, Patrick J.'s aunt.

Michael Meehan probably got the hundred acres from William White, son of James White and Nora Mahoney, who by 1836 had cleared much of the land assigned him by Robinson in 1823. By 1842, William had married Johanna Forrest and moved up to the Twelfth Line. There, his father, James, had a farm just across the road which was taken over by James's other son, James, who first married Alice Lindsay, probably a sister of Catherine Lindsay, wife of Patrick J.

At age sixty-nine, in 1925, Patsy had a fatal accident in his barn and soon the land and house were purchased by Jim Carroll and wife Cecilia Scott who had lost their own stone house on the Old Almonte Road to fire. Jim was the son of Tom and Mary Rowan and grandson of Paddy Carroll and Jane O'Leary. Cecilia was the daughter of Mike Scott and Mary Anne Kennedy and a granddaughter of Mike Scott and Julia Banks. On the maternal side, Jim was a grandson of Patrick Rowan and Bridget, and Cecilia, the granddaughter of Patrick Kennedy and Mary Anne Horan. Cecilia's great-grandparents were John Kennedy and Margaret Manion, the early settlers in Corkery in 1821.

Patsy and Lisa had five children: Homer (drowned), and Leo, Bill, Jimmy and Stella, all of whom died young except Jimmy. Jim Carroll and Cecilia had nine: Carmel, Mary, Bertha, Joe, Emmett, Angus, Theresa, Gerald and Edgar. In 1959, Gerald Carrol and his wife Betty Mantil bought the farm, and in 1970 sold to Bill Pick, the present owner, who has also done much to restore this fine home.

This stone house holds many happy memories. I remember its three large verandas, the spacious front lawn, the large indoor kitchen, the carefully furnished parlour, and on the west side of the house the spreading beaver meadow with its creek where games of shinny helped fill the Christmas holidays. Across the back of the house stretched a summer kitchen always well-ventilated by a balmy western breeze.

The Carrolls were a good-natured lot. "Pa" Carroll, as the boys called him, enjoyed playing "Fish" with me. Gerald and Angus were my swimming companions and dear Theresa never tired kibitzing, usually getting the better of any exchanges. Bertha and Mary were always very kind and gentle Joe's steadying influence could always be felt. The dapper Emmett was the most Irish and little Edgar always full of fun. An older daughter Carmel's happy disposition was mirrored in her dancing eyes that probably caught many a man's fancy long before her husband's, Angus Killeen.

In their book on Ireland, Jill and Leon Uris speak of the Aran Islanders' ability to read another's thoughts, (especially a stranger's), with "terse accuracy". I believe Cecilia "Ma" Carroll had that power.

I can still see her watching and reading me. In my day, she was still a young woman as she presided in the summer kitchen over a circus of activity with the coolness of a Vegas dealer. She did it with her eyes.

I once worked with a beginning teacher, a Jane Graham, the daughter of an Almonte pharmacist, who had that same "Ma" Carroll charisma. Not much bigger than a pole and with a voice as gentle as a mourning dove's, she could settle down any class of rowdies as easily as Billy the Kid's entrance could hush a saloon. She just stood her ground at the front of the class and did it all with her eyes.

Stella Kennedy, a contemporary and relative of Cecilia's, now over ninety herself, said Cecilia had the nicest nature of anyone she had ever known. She did indeed! No amount of hurly-burly ever seemed to disturb her inner equilibrium. I'm sure I was in her way many a day, but all I ever received for my botheration was a kind word and that look of understanding and controlling serenity. Cecilia Scott Carroll was one dear lady, a fitting mistress for such a beautiful home.

Patrick's other two sons' houses were on the right side of the Dwyer Hill Road, a kilometre or so north of the Carroll Side Road, directly west of Patrick's home.

Patrick J. Manion purchased the first farm from Mrs. Mary Cooney Hogan in 1885 for six thousand dollars. Pat Cooney and Mary had raised a large family on this land sometime after 1861. In 1871, they still had six children at home, sixteen to three in age, plus Pat's mother-in-law, Margaret Cooney. A Tom Hogan, possibly an older son, attended my great-grandfather Tom O'Keefe's funeral in 1890: Tom O'Keefe had lived on Lot 17 and Tom Hogan on Lot 18.

The Hogan's log house was set back in the middle of the farm, closer to the Carroll Side Road and the Panmure Road which ran across the Brown farm to the east of Patrick Manion's. These side roads locally known as forced roads were the main links between towns, communities, churches, taverns, stores, and post offices. West Huntley's first shanties and log houses were built along their sides. The direction of a log house's front door often gives away a house's age.

Mary and Pat probably didn't build that first log house since Michael and Mary Cronin were the first owners of the land, coming there on Thursday, October 23, 1823. Their farm is the only pioneer's farm in West Huntley for which the exact date of the first settlement is known. The Cronins raised a small family, cleared much of the land, but by 1841 had moved away.

An obviously spirited and sensitive young man, Michael wrote his mother three days after his arrival to tell her the news. They had left Cobh, Cork, on July 8, 1823, on the *Hebe*, and set foot on their Robinson claim one hundred and eight days later. Today, the same trip in the opposite direction, by car to Ottawa from Corkery, by plane from Ottawa to London, and then on to Cork by air, can be done in fourteen hours.

Other local immigrants of interest on that same ship, most of whom settled in the Corkery area, were James White, John and Michael Meehan, Richard Forrest, whose grandchild one day would purchase this Cronin farm, and David Dowling and wife Mary Mahoney, my great-great-great-grandparents whose entourage included seven children, one being my great-great-grandmother, Johanna. The Dowlings settled on the town line of Ramsey and Huntley.

Michael and Mary Cronin were from a small town called Mitchelstown situated in the northeastern part of Cork County. Mitchelstown, named after a Norman family, was the ancestral home of the Fitzgeralds, powerful Norman knights who joined the English Parliament in Dublin against the Irish chiefs in return for the title, Earl of Desmond. From 1330 to the early Sixteenth Century, Norman families like the Fitzgeralds held on to power in Munster and South Leinster but only at the expense of constant enmity with both Irish and English. The Norman elite, like the Driscolls, Barrymores, Clares, de Burghs, de Courceys and de Laceys married into the great old-Irish septs such as the O'-Sullivans, MacCarthys, O'Donovans, O'Learys and O'Carrolls of Cork, the O'Donoghues of Kerry, the O'Briens of Clare and the MacDonnells of Limerick, just to name a few. The names of the towns near Mitchelstown also bear out the French-Norman insemination in this small section of Cork: Buttevant (seat of the Barrys), Charlesville, Doneraile, and Castletownroche (named after the de Roches). One happy sequel to all these bedroom treaties was the ability of the resulting children to speak bilingually in French and Gaelic, a situation the Anglo-Saxons tried to remedy for many decades.

It was Mitcheltown's First Earl of Kingston, the marital heir of the Desmond legacy through the O'Connors, who reluctantly helped choose the Cronins and others from his territory for resettlement by Peter Robinson in 1823. Kingston's time was largely taken up that year building himself a new mansion with cheap Irish labour. Unfortunately, a hundred years later, in 1922, Irish sympathizers burnt it down and sold the stones to Cistercian monks from France who constructed the magnificient monastery of Mount Melleray in Waterford, thereby adding further insult to the memory of Lord Kingston, a strong devotee of the Established Church of England.

The Patrick J. Manion stone house ("the House of Lights") was built on this old Cronin property around 1895 for John James Manion (1865-1912) and his wife Mary Jane McKenna (1873-1901). They had four children, John and Mary who died in infancy, and Tom and Josephine. The latter two inherited the farm and with the help of their nearby Uncle Joe Manion and his sons Martin and John operated the farm for a few years. In 1922, the farm was sold to Michael Forrest (1843-1924) and his wife Bridget Gleeson (1847-1926). Michael's father was Cornelius and his mother Ellen Kennedy. Cornelius's father, Tim Forrest, was a Robinson settler, just as the grandfather of John James Manion had been, John Manion.

In 1926, two of the unmarried Forrest children, Joe and Theresa, sold to Maurice Williams (1883-1981) from March Township. In 1928, Maurie married Annie O'Keefe (1903-1983), my aunt. By 1983, the sole heir to the farm was their second son, Allan, my first cousin. Weighed down by the deaths of both his parents within eighteen months of each other and all the ensuing legal pressure he had to handle, Allan himself died suddenly of heart-arrest in 1984 just nineteen months after his mother.

Just fifty-three, his loss was keenly felt by his brother Clarence who considered Allan his best friend. Allan never asked much from life. He was content with his lot. He was humble, humorous, and innocent of malice. I can never remember even coming close to quarrelling with him. Clarence recently showed me an old picture of himself, Allan, and their dog. The boys were about seven or eight. Allan had that same docile, apologetic look about him and I realized even more how friendly and likeable he had been. I looked at Clarence and he was crying.

Within three years, Clarence had buried his mother, father and brother. In 1984, he and sister Shirly inherited everything. Today, the farm has new owners. An end of an era!

During the 1920's, before the arrival of the Williamses, strange lights were often seen at this house. My Uncle Nash and my Aunt Cecilia Lockhart who both grew up across from the house told me about them. All night long, windows in the house would light up one by one and then in unison. These peculiar lights flashed with amazing speed up and down the lane and around the outbuildings. When the Williamses came in 1926, the lights stopped. One old-timer told me that ghosts seem to follow the Forrests — even to their graves!

This Williams' house, hidden by leafy awnings over a half-sunken laneway, and shaded comfortably by century-old trees, contrasts with Mary Blackburn's nearby stone house which stands appropriately adorned with a few well-positioned cedars.

Built around 1892 for Lawrence E. Manion (1857-1908) and his wife Hannah Agnes Devine (1864-1946), it has been carefully restored by Ms. Blackburn. Its architectural lines are balanced and uniform, its stones as clean and fresh as a hundred years ago. It's the perfect example in West Huntley of the creative and technical finesse of the old masons. The house and grounds are especially striking in the late evening light — a blush of misty colour.

This land in 1823 belonged to Robinson-settler James McGrath whose brother Luke had the hundred acres across the road. By 1825, John Kennedy and wife Margaret with their three children had taken over James's place. John was the brother of Tim Kennedy who married Patrick O'Keefe's daughter, Mary, from the Twelfth Line, after his first wife Joanna Forrest, daughter of Richard Forrest, died, probably in childbirth. Richard, Patrick and Tim, as mentioned earlier, were all from Cork and all Robinson settlers.

In 1846, John's daughter, Mary, wife of Con Mahoney, died at age 27. In 1848, at age 52, John was killed by a falling tree, followed in death by his daughter, Ellen, wife of Cornelius Forrest, in 1849 at age 32.

Allan Williams and his brother Clarence, with Pup, about 1937.

139

In his will, John divided the farm — the North section to a son-in-law named Sullivan and the South section (the Blackburn farm) to Con Mahoney, his other son-in-law. By 1879, the owner of the latter farm was Con Mahoney Junior.

Lawrence Manion lived about sixteen years in his new home. He died at age 51, one year after his dad, P.J. — Lawrence buried two baby children. His other son, Patrick, died in 1912 at age 17, a year before his grandmother, Catherine Lindsay Manion. (Catherine herself buried three grown sons, a twenty-six-year-old daughter, and her husband).

Shortly after, the farm was bought by Ned Kennedy, (1861-1927) and his wife Catherine Carroll (1871-1930). Ned was the son of Andrew Kennedy and his wife Sarah O'Leary, and Catherine, the daughter of Tom Carroll and Mary Rowan. Ned's grandmother was a Manion and a grand-aunt of Lawrence. (Land was usually kept in families). Jimmy Kennedy, Ned's son, lived there until his death in the Forties. The house lay empty for some time, but the farmland was rented. The coming of Ms. Blackburn gave the house a new life. What had been a "House of Tears", has become a joyous reflection of happy country living. (Recently, the house has been sold).

Two Irish Friends

I went to see an old Irish priest in his hospital confinement and he told the visiting religious sisters already there that I was his best friend and I felt humbled.

Then he cupped my hand in his and rubbed it in caress and said he was happy I came ... and his round, clear, sad eyes showed the isolation of his suffering, and his memory jumped around in the past.

Then, as I went to leave, he asked me to bless him and say a Hail Mary over him with my hand on his brow ... and I did so falteringly thinking he must have taken me for some other priest ... and he thanked me and asked me to come again... "Promise!" he said ... And I said, "Of course!" ...As I turned out the door, I heard him say to the others, "He's my best friend!"

And I wept as I went to my car!

•

Bagpipes add a regal touch to memorable gatherings. Particularly moments of final parting. In Greenock, Scotland, their drones enveloped the misty-eyed Highlanders as their emigrant ships slipped into the unknown. So it was the day we bid farewell to Basil O'Keefe. During his final illness he told his pastor of his love for the pipes. And Father William Penney didn't forget. It was February 11, 1992. As Basil's body was eased out the portals of St. Michael's, a piper's lament expressed our sorrow for the departure of a true son of Corkery.

And I cried like the rain.

38

Other Heritage Homes in West Huntley

A son of George Mordy, named Joseph, brother to Tom, built himself a stone home on the Dwyer Hill Road near Alonzo Kelly's red-brick house. A bachelor, Joe later sold out to the Crawfords whose son Eddie and his wife, Myrtle Morrow, inherited it. They in turn sold to the Kropps and they to the Rowneys. Part of the Rowney's restoration was a new addition. The effect is impressive — a fine country estate. Unfortunately, the house, with its well-kept original log outbuildings, is a good piece off the road. (See map on page 350 as you follow this chapter).

Alonzo Kelly's henna-brick home near the Hamilton Side Road is just one of six such houses built by Jeremiah O'Brien and wife Catherine Foley (1828-1889). Jeremiah (1820-1890) was a son of Tim O'Brien and Katherine O'Leary of Ramsey (East 1/2, Lot 8, Conc. 7) whose children married other settlers like the Dowlings, Maddens and Foleys. The O'-Briens and Foleys came from County Cork. Both families did well financially in Canada.

Jeremiah O'Brien built his brick homes for his sons. With so much intermarriage in that area among Kellys, O'Briens, Carters, Kennedys, Carrolls, and O'Learys it's very difficult to form any historically accurate list of original owners. One home was bought by Michael Lowe and Ellen Kennedy on the Twelfth Line (demolished by fire); Paddy Carter and Elizabeth Kelly had one on the Tenth Line (burnt in 1925); Hugh Kennedy and his wife Henrietta Carroll bought one on the Eleventh Line (still lived in); Mike Kennedy, son of Hugh Kennedy and grandson of pioneer John Kennedy, bought out the O'Brien homestead on the Hamilton Side Road (now covered with siding); and Paddy Carroll purchased Alonzo Kelly's present house from Jeremiah's son, Richard. Joe Kelly and Mary Mears later settled there and Alonzo got the farm from his father, Joe. The O'Briens certainly did their share for West Huntley's architecture.

The O'Connell stone house on the McArton Side Road was built in 1873 by Richard O'Connell and Esther Meehan. It has been in the family ever since. The present owner, Helen Smith O'Connell, has this farmhouse in mint condition. Her fine husband, sad to say, died in the late fall of 1991. The stonework is exceptional with small limestones of soft grey intermixed at the corners with larger, darker ones. The house has two gables flowing in different directions making it quite unlike any other stone house of that period in West Huntley. The white trim on windows and doors and the silver-coloured roof highlight the light grey stone giving the home an ambience of cheerfulness. The outbuildings of log are as good as on their day of completion. Indeed the whole complex presents itself as one of the tidiest and prettiest farms in all West Huntley. The first settlers on this land in 1825, the great-grandparents of Peter, William O'Connell and Margaret Flynn, would be pleased at the outcome.

Another stone home of this earlier period is on the Burnt Lands' Road. It was built to house the ten children of John Flynn (1824-1897) and his wife Elizabeth Kelly (1827-1900). The land was purchased from Dick Forrest. The stone was drawn from near Foxes' Hill out of a quarry owned by the Ryans. Michael Flynn, a son, stayed on the farm and married Dorothy Ryan. They had at least seven children, one being Michael Joe Flynn, the antique dealer. Not one of their children married. The farm has since been inherited from Agnes Flynn by Dominic Ryan's son, Jimmy.

The simple design of the house suggests it was built before 1870. John Flynn was from Limerick and his wife from County Carlow. Patrick O'-Keefe, my grandfather O'Keefe's first cousin, married Catherine Flynn, John's daughter, and lived on the East 1/2 of the West 1/2 of my grandfather's farm on the Dwyer Hill Road. The Flynns known to me were mild-mannered, unassuming folk. Several still live around West Huntley. And more than one have red hair and ruddy complexions in keeping with the meaning of the word "Flynn" in Irish.

Past the Vaughan Side Road on the Burnt Lands' Road (see map) are three brick homes. The first on the east side was built by Ned Forrest. Ned was a son of Cornelius Forrest and Ellen Conlan. Cornelius was the son of Robinson settlers Richard and Nel Harran. Cornelius lived in a log house on the same land as Ned and raised fourteen children, seven by Ellen Kennedy, daughter of John Kennedy who lived on Mary Blackburn's Dwyer Hill property. (Ellen died a year after her father in 1849). Cornelius had his other seven by Ellen Curran. Ellen had been a servant at the Hudson's home in Panmure. In 1861, Ellen and Con had twelve children at home, age two to twenty. A fair number, it's true, but not as many as James Bonsfield who lived back the Twelfth Line near Panmure. He had twenty-two, eighteen of whom were singers, dancers or musicians. One became a doctor in Ottawa.

Ned Forrest (1863-1921) married an Annie McGuire from Campbell's Bay. Apparently they met on a train-pilgrimage to St. Anne de Beaupré in Quebec. St. Anne has always held magical powers for finding marriage partners. "Good St. Anne, find me a man" was once a popular prayer. Ned and Annie later both admitted going to that shrine by the St. Lawrence River for the purposes of praying for a matrimonial mate. My wife once made a nine-day novena and on the ninth day, for better or worse, I called her for the first time. Her greatest mistake she says, was answering that call.

Annie was later widowed and married Sylvester Finner. Basil O'-Keefe and his wife Mary Carroll later bought the farm from Annie. The present owners are Basil's son David and his wife, the pretty Wendy Gruer. The well-preserved home is fronted by manicured lawns and neatly surrounded by fenced fields. Many a happy hour I spent talking with Basil and Mary in their comfortable sunny kitchen. No people were any better to me in West Huntley than Basil and Mary. I also remember

Mrs. Finner and Sylvester. Syl was a quiet man: as his wife said often, "He loved to stand around and think." Annie McGuire was lots of fun and extremely well-liked by all her neighbours. Even in her older years, she was a fine looking woman.

The second brick home on the west side of the Burnt Lands' Road was built by Ned Forrest's brother, Andy. His wife was Margaret Carberry from Ferguson Falls. The Carberry name runs deep into southwest Cork. O'Donovan Rossa (1831 to 1913), a freedom-fighter against the British and a man respected even by his enemies, in his book, *Rossa's Recollections* (printed in 1898), recalls his birthplace as being Ross Carberry, a holy place of learning. The Carberrys were big landowners in this area and Rossa remembers the Lord of Carberry chasing hounds over miles of his own land. I found the book in my grandmother's deserted house. It had been borrowed from the Corkery Public Library: P.F. Manion, Chairman; W.E. Cavanagh, Sec-Tres; Librarians, John A. Killeen, John Carter and John H. Kennedy.

The presence of such a book in a country library shows some people in Corkery were well aware of the Fenian movement in the 1860's and sympathetic to the cause for an Irish Republic. Rossa's death in Ireland in 1913 was mourned by true Irishmen everywhere. His heroic life, dedicated to Irish freedom, indirectly led to more volunteers in the Irish Free Army and eventually to the Easter-Sunday Riots in Dublin in 1916. His funeral in Dublin was one of the biggest ever held in that city.

Jimmy Forrest who lived on in the Andy-Margaret brick home after his Uncle Dick had it, was a descendant of these same Lords of Carberry whom Rossa described as Protestant but "just" landowners. Jimmy married Anita Donohue from Renfrew. I always found Jimmy very friendly and his wife a personable, refined lady. The house and farm now belong to Barry and Pauline Mantil. The land has many memories since the time Richard Forrest, the pioneer, built his first home there. His four sons, Cornelius, James, Timothy and Richard did much of the clearing in this section of the Burnt Lands. Timothy's and Cornelius's descendants are still very much alive in West Huntley.

Down on the west plateau behind the Richard Forrest homestead-site is another fine brick home built in 1906 by Cornelius Curtin and his wife Mary Ann Grace. Cornelius's father, Cornelius (1808-94), first settled there with his wife Margaret Casey (1818-1896). Mary Ann Grace (1856-1921) was the daughter of Michael Grace and Ellen Foley who lived on the Eleventh Concession near Pat Kelly on the south side of Highway 44. Michael's daughter, Margaret, married John A. Killeen. Ellen Foley was a daughter of the Foleys from Ramsey and later from Huntley. The Foleys were very well off.

This farmhouse has had many owners. Jack Curtin, Cornelius the Elder's son, a harness maker, lived there as did Jimmy Curtin, the son of Cornelius II. Jimmy was a close friend of my mother. He married a Kelly from Osgoode. They sold out to Ignatius O'Brien and Lyla Moran and moved to South March and then into Ottawa. After his wife's death, Jimmy became the caretaker in the late 1940's and early '50's for Father Bambrick at St. George's Church. He lived under the church in a room where I took Grades One and Two in St. George's Elementary School.

Jimmy Curtin was a winsome man as was his father Cornelius. In a pensive way, he was extremely pious and exceedingly humble. He always praised my mother (he took her out once or twice). I once met Jimmy's niece. I have never forgotten her beauty: jet-black hair, cobalt-blue eyes, and the complexion of a baby. One of Jimmy's sons studied to be a Brother. Jimmy's own brother, Leo, was a priest in India. Cornelius Curtin, their father, had the respect of all West Huntley.

After Lyla O'Brien's death, John O'Keefe bought the house and farm from Ignatius O'Brien. He and Margaret Carroll had ten children. John's son Ray later lived there. The house has new owners now, the Whites. It is somewhat older than the Forrest homes — even the brick is a darker shade.

At the northeast corner of Ray O'Keefe's and Barry Mantil's homes, at the edge of the Burnt Lands' Road, a clump of trees can be seen. Cornelius and Margaret buried some of their sons and daughters there in unmarked graves, a practice quite common among the early settlers.

One of the prettiest stone houses in West Huntley is farther north on the Dwyer Hill Road. For setting and design, it leaves little to be desired. It was built by Tim Forrest after 1879 and probably before his marriage to Catherine Delaney around 1890. Coady's Creek runs behind the house and then across the Dwyer Hill Road. Tim was the son of Cornelius Forrest and his second wife, Ellen Conlan. He was raised on the property now owned, as already mentioned, by David O'Keefe on the Twelfth Line.

Catherine Delaney was the daughter of John Delaney (1847-1942) and Mary Jane MacDonald (1857-1924). John lived on his father's property straight across from Tim's stone house. William Delaney (1805-1862?), originally from Wexford, had come to Canada sometime before 1839. His wife was Elizabeth Hendricks. The Hendricks were from Perth where the five Hendrick sisters took several prizes in local beauty contests.

Originally, the Forrest farm was owned by Robinson settlers, Tim O'Brien and Mary. Tim died in 1828 but his widow kept everything going. In 1840, she was still there. Eventually, a son Tim took over by 1863 and another son Denis had the adjacent property straight over to the Vaughan Side Road.

This Denis was the father of a popular Twelfth-Line raconteur, Dinny O'Brien, who, according to his confreres, had the mind of a "Philadelphia lawyer". On one occasion, a neighbour took Dinny to court. The appeal case was heard in Ottawa with Dinny acting as his own defence lawyer. His classic home-spun erudition easily convinced the judge of his innocence and Dinny returned somewhat of a hero. He was also one of the finest figure skaters in all West Huntley, (so he claimed), and played some violin. Hidden behind all Dinny's outrageous stories were bits of wisdom usually only ascertainable by those attuned to his philosophy of living. Dinny O'Brien was like the Irish poets of old who entertained their neighbours with "guileless wisdom". As for charity, many a vagrant received nourishment and shelter at Dinny's door during harsh winters. I have never met a West Huntley person who didn't love him and cherish his memory.

Dinny's father moved to Douglas while Dinny stayed on and married a Mary White, daughter of James White Jr. — James Jr., as mentioned, married Alice Lindsay and after her early death, Catherine Sheehan. Dinny's grandson lives in Renfrew, son of Norman. Norman worked around Corkery for many years. I always enjoyed meeting him.

Across the road from Dinny O'Brien on Allan O'Keefe's property lived Tom White, son of William White and Johanna Forrest. William was a brother of James Jr. — William Sr. or his son, William, apparently lived for a while on the lot immediately north of Tom's where Des Grace now resides.

Another child of Tim and Mary O'Brien, Margaret, may well have been the wife of James Mantil, grandfather of Bob Mantil and great grandfather of Bobby and Margaret Mantil of Highway 44. James lived at Panmure and left his farm to his son John who married Mary Gallaghan.

The intermarriage of Whites and O'Briens and Mantils and O'Keefes has continued for over a hundred years. They were all Robinson settlers and darn good ones.

It was Tim O'Brien then who sold out to Cornelius Forrest, but by 1879, Cornelius' widow, Ellen, had the property. Ellen gave the property to her son, Tim, for one dollar and love. Around 1879, the old house, presumably the one of Tim O'Brien, was on the far side of the creek and placed well back near the eastern ridge base. Tim Forrest built his stone house nearer the road.

Tim Forrest had a tragic death. While skinning a cow whose loss had upset him terribly, he cut himself and eventually contracted lockjaw. His death was excruciatingly painful.

Catherine, Tim's wife, later remarried and moved into Ottawa. John and Mary Jane Delaney who had already moved in with Catherine after their house burnt down soon became the sole tenants of the Forrest home.

In old age, John and Mary continued to live there with their sons Jack and Louis. A sister Annie (b. 1898) also returned from Perth during the early Depression to raise a large family there with her husband Tom Murphy (1892-1965). I remember their sons Anthony and Grant and a few of their daughters, especially Theresa and Rita. Annie and her brothers Jack and Louis were also known to me as well as her husband Tom. They were very friendly people!

Catherine Delaney Forrest's sister, Mary, (b. 1888) married Tim Scott (1882-1967). They lived on the Tenth Line in Parker Kennedy's old house, (recently burnt). Tim and Mary had a large family and, like the Murphys, left their mark on the history of West Huntley. Edmund Scott, Mary and Tim's son, recalled for me the day his grandfather John told him how the Delaney family back in the late 1850's took the corpse of William Delaney on a wagon across the ridge road to the cemetery of St. Michael's. A long, lonely ride for Catherine and her young family! And I thought of the old popular song which says, "The night that Luke Delaney died, I went out behind the barn and cried." Young John probably did too.

Annie Delaney sold the farm to Art Hitchins in the 1960's. It was Art and his wife who restored the house. Art gave me a tour of it in the early 1970's. I still remember the shiny hardwood floors, the polished banisters of the central staircase, the delicacy of the beautiful wallpapering, everything so fastidiously finished — a clean and comfortable country home in every way. And outside, a setting perfectly suited to this silver and grey home — the tree-lined creek at its back, the little knolls about the house, and in the distance, the sombre blue of Foxes' Hill.

Edmund Scott once told me his mother, Mary, was an excellent midwife. He recalls her going to Cecilia Carroll's on the Carroll Side Road to help out. The midwife usually stayed on a few days in the new mother's home until reasonable order was restored. I mention this side-line career of Mary Delaney Scott to call attention to the many West Huntley women who were trained as apprentices in this nursing science by their mothers, relatives or even neighbours.

Ignatius O'Brien, grandson of Morgan O'Brien and Mary Lynch, said his grandmother was known miles around for her midwife skills. His father, Paddy, once told him of a man coming by horseback from South March to seek Mary's help. He brought with him an extra horse saddled for the occasion. And Mary went with him and was gone for more than a week. Interestingly enough, Mary Lynch (1837-1879), lived on the Twelfth Line not far from the back of Delaney's farm. Did Mary Lynch O'Brien teach Mary McDonald Delaney the secrets of midwifery and had Mary passed them along to her own daughter?

Mary Lynch must have been a very special person. I wish I had known her! She lived as a child on the present Highway 44 in Ramsey between the Eleventh and Twelfth Lines. A Tony Hickey lives on the property now, and it turns out Tony is a great-great-grandson of Mary and her husband Morgan O'Brien. Tony's mother, Rita, wife of Bernard Hickey, is a great-granddaughter by reason of her father John being a son of Paddy O'Brien, Mary's son. John O'Brien married Annie Mantil, daughter of John Mantil (1850-1930) and Catherine Whalen. John Mantil's father was Robert and his mother Ann Finuken. John married twice. His first wife Catherine (1849-1885) died as a result of a kick from

Two old Mordy Homes — Corkery Road.

The John Manion Homestead — Corkery Road.

The O'Connell Homestead — McArton Side Road.

The old P.F. Manion Home on the Carroll Side Road.

The old George Mordy Home on the Dwyer Hill Road.

The old Lawrence Manion Home on the Dwyer Hill Road.

The oldest stone house in West Huntley — John Kennedy's on the Ninth Line, (Manion Road)

The old John Manion Home — Dwyer Hill Road.

The John Flynn Homestead — Burnt Lands' Road.

The old Tim Forrest Home — Dwyer Hill Road.

The Ryan Homestead — Robinson Way.

a cow. His second wife was Mary Anne Foley. Ignatius O'Brien, who died in December, 1991, at age 95, was a brother of the aforementioned John O'Brien and was best man at his wedding in 1921. Rita O'Brien and Mary O'Brien, John's daughters, both reside in or near Almonte. Mary married a Francis Ryan.

Rita, Mary, Joe, and their mother Annie once lived on Scott Street in Ottawa. My mother was a close friend of Annie and the children. Rita remembers particularly my mother's dulcet voice and pretty smile. Rita and Mary were great company as young people and neither has ever lost that youthful spirit. Many a happy hour I spent at the O'Briens as a young man. And I thank the two O'Brien girls and their mother for their kindnesses.

Mary and Morgan O'Brien (no relation to Dinny) built their log house (see map) around 1855. The present owners, the Masons, have kept the log house intact and restored it faithfully. The house, in the middle of rolling terrain and halfway between the Twelfth and Eleventh Lines, can barely be seen from the road.

The first building put up by Mary Lynch and Morgan was actually the stable and their first son was born there. Mary died at age forty-two, probably as a result of childbirth, and Morgan lived on until one hundred and five. His son, Paddy, stayed on the farm and married Hannah White (d. 1921) daughter of Tom White (1828-1911) and Honora McNamara (1844-1891). Paddy's son, Ignatius, married Lyla Moran from South March, and another son, Morgan, married Frank Colton's daughter, Jane.

Morgan and Jane's daughter, Sarah, married Jack Mantil and they lived in the Colton house (see map) where Maurice Mantil, Jack's son, now lives. Jack was a brother of Bob Mantil and their parents were John Mantil (1831-1886) and Mary Gallaghan (d. 1904).

After John's death, Mary married Edward O'Keefe (1851-1935). Before Paddy's death, a son Mohr and his wife, a Forrest, lived on the O'Brien property. Mohr was a sincere, mannerly gentleman and a great friend of neighbour Eddie Grace. He was the last O'Brien to live there.

Over a stretch of a few months in 1972-1973, a sad occurrence took place: four neighbours on the Twelfth Line, all of whom were friends since childhood, died. They were Jimmy Forrest (1906-72), John O'Keefe (1919-72), Eddie Grace and his pal Mohr O'Brien. All were sorely missed! Two widows and two empty houses in a matter of months!

Are there such things as geographic-patterns and time-cycles for death in some families? Leo Kennedy, son of Mike Kennedy and Margaret Legree, says nearly all his descendants have died in September. A friend, Sister Margaret Power, from Sydney, N.S., recently told me of a discovery made by her in relation to her immediate family. Her father, sister and three brothers all died between 6 a.m. and 6:30 a.m. while her mother and another brother died in the morning close to 8 a.m. (the exact time not being known at this writing). Recently, she was sitting with her brother Bill who was also dying. The time was 5 a.m. The nurse urged her to go home for some rest. Sister said she would wait until 6:30 since she felt Bill would die between 6 and 6:30. And he did!

Directly behind the old Forrest farm were the hundred acres of Martin Ryan (1818-1915) and his wife Elizabeth Herrick (1828-1922) from Fitzroy Township. In 1880, he and a son James built a stone house beside the old Panmure - St. Michael's Church Ridge Road. The house cannot be seen from the present Tenth Line.

A Mordy from the Ninth Line helped in the building as did a Bill Hunt and Bill Garland. The stone came from just behind the house. To help with the building, they constructed a fifty-foot sloping ramp to the highest point of the house. Severe work never killed anybody, especially Martin who lived to be ninety-seven and James who died in 1950 at age ninety-eight.

In 1896, James Ryan, then forty-four, married Annie Sullivan, age eighteen from Sheenboro, Quebec (across from Pembroke). In 1937, son Dominic married Rita Stanton from just outside Pakenham and raised a large family at the Ryan homestead while continuing to look after his mother and father. In 1980, Dominic and Rita moved to Ottawa. A friendly person named Mrs. Wilkes now owns the stone house and property.

Martin and James also had large families. They must have raised service-conscious children, for a large number became Royal Canadian Mounted Policemen and teachers. James Ryan had a portable sawmill which took him into most of the barnyards of West Huntley. He also went to the shanties every winter off and on for some forty years.

Rita Ryan's sister, Sister Mary Stanton, once taught my wife at Corpus Christi Separate School in Ottawa and her brother Pat, was a popular worker for St. Puis X High School's Development Drives. One of Dominic Ryan's sisters, Veronica (1907-1958), later Sister St. Dominic, taught in many schools across the Ontario Northland. Four of Dom and Rita's children are teachers.

The descendants of Martin Ryan and Elizabeth Herrick are numerous. The Ryans have married into the old families in West Huntley like the Graces, Caseys, Browns, Manions, Flynns, Kennedys and the Coltons. The old house has indeed been the scene of the coming and the going of many Ryans: it can be proudly called the "homestead of the Tipperary West Huntley Ryans"!

An Irish Halo

St. Patrick was never canonized by the Roman Catholic Church. It was the Irish people who put the halo round his head.

The Lady with the Massey-Harris Parts

A borrower soon gets a name for himself. Especially, if he never returns the article! One day, a certain professional sponger met his match. As he crossed the field, his neighbour's wife saw him coming. Since he seldom called socially, she knew he'd soon be at the door with his hand out. Being as her husband was a pushover for everybody with troubles, she told her husband to stay put. She herself would handle the visitor.

"Well, g'day to ya, Mrs. O_____. A fine bright afternoon, to be sure! Is your husband home?"

"That he is! But wouldn't ya know, he's taking a nap. Can I help with anything?"

"Good of ya to ask, Mrs. O_____. I be needing a part for my binder and I see ya has just the ticket on an old model out behind your stable."

Fixing a glare on him that would have frozen a walrus, the old lady dismissed him with this curt but ambiguous reply, "Excuse my saying so, Mr. D_____, but when I need my new parts, I go to the Massey-Harris man! G'day to ya, now!"

The sponger went home miffed, but apparently got even by telling the whole country about the woman made out of Massey-Harris parts.

Two Potato Stories

Bob Gallagher told this story on himself. One afternoon, he picked up a very young Raymond Mantil on his way to Almonte. To make conversation, he asked Ray how the potato-picking was going. Ray answered, "Not too good, Mr. Gallagher. I often find only one here and none there!"

Not a bad answer for a young lad!

•

One day an old-timer approached a neighbour in the back-breaking process of planting potatoes. Perhaps enamoured by the neighbour's good luck with previous potato crops, the old-timer asked, "And what kind of potatoes are ya puttin' down this year, Angus?"

Angus looked up painfully and replied, "Same as last year, Bill. Raw ones!"

A Wish

As my wife's Aunt Minnie Fleming Black approached her hundredth year, she became more disenchanted with life. One evening she lamented, "You know, tomorrow morning, I wish I could wake up dead!"

39

Architectural Ramblings

Gables became very popular in West Huntley after the fire of 1870. They are mainly vertical triangular ends of a building. A gable roof has a gable at each end; some homes have four or more gables.

Not all gables are triangular. Some roofs are curb or gambrel in that the roof ends have double slopes, the upper slope being less steep than the one underneath. Each such gable is pentagonal. The Mordy homes on the Ninth Line have this feature.

Gable ends are Gothic in nature. The more romantic, neo-classic, or Gothic a house's style becomes, the less classical are its features. Classic styles come from Greek and Roman architecture. Many modern homes of today combine mixtures of the classic and Gothic.

Along the gables and the eaves, architects often added gingerbread or bargeboard trims. These were playful pretzel-like wood or plaster carvings. Such fanciful decorations are romantic variations found in Gothic architecture and tend to the whimsical by combining the sublime with the offbeat in direct variance with the classical forms of early stone houses which were simple, practical, ho-hum, correct, proportional and formal. Naturally such architectural etchings cost more money and their use depended on economic endowment. No matter what the era, every frill has its price.

On the top of gable points, especially on larger more expensive houses and churches, the crowns were often adorned with ornamentals called finials. As an integral part of the Gothic design, they were very much Teutonic-Germanic in origin. Since Canada's later population was mainly comprised of this culture, it is not surprising that the architecture of Victorian times followed Gothic lines. Gothic implies a lightness and freedom of expressive form quite different from the restraint and heaviness of the Romanesque styles. Also, the Roman and classical had smaller windows while the Gothic opted for larger windows permitting more natural light into bedrooms, kitchens, parlours, choirs and sanctuaries.

Transoms and sidelights were used in the early stone houses of West Huntley. They are not Gothic in origin. Transoms were windows, often coloured, placed over main entrances, while sidelights were windows built along the sides of front doors. Some doors had only one sidelight. These windows not only added an aesthetic touch but also gave light to the hallways.

The 1850-1870 Huntley stone houses were classic in nature: symmetrical, practical and balanced. They didn't have many original intricacies of stone or wood. They belonged to the Georgian era (1710-1830). The façade or front was on one of the long sides of a rectangular-shaped building. The main entrance was usually but not always in the middle of the façade with a window on each side. Over this entrance, on the roof, was a small gable with a window. A central hall ran from the front door to the back of the house and gave access to all the downstairs rooms.

The use of arches, perfected by the Romans, became more prevalent in the later stone and brick houses of West Huntley. The church of St. Michael's has a few examples of arches in its ten large windows and three main entrances. Arches are best described as curved toppings over doorways, windows and open entrances. Bricks or stones are fanned at angles across the curved opening, giving support to one another and thereby holding up the weight above the arch. The windows and doorways of St. Michael's are slightly curved in a form called basket-handled.

Other churches in Huntley have windows and doors coming to a pointed arch called the lancet style. Architects, most of whom were stone masons, had many unique variations of brick and stone over these openings and entrances. Even rectangular windows had some embellishments.

Another feature of the later homes, churches, and even schools were small circular windows with the outside bricks or stones fanning outwards round the circumference. These rose windows, as we call them now, added a graceful boldness to the architecture. Corkery Church has three. These "portholes" were usually placed on the façade of churches in the gable end below the steeple.

Not all trappings were confined to the brick and stone houses. Framed houses began to be built around 1850 at a time when mills were available to saw logs into lumber. Although basically simple in construction and appearance, many had gables, verandas, eaves and angles enlivened by trims known as treillage or latticework.

Fluted columns on porches and at front doors give a Grecian beauty to some homes. Some had intricately lathed designs very much in keeping with classic homes. The use of gingerbread had apparently given way to these fluted supports. Two and four-column types under a small gable-pointed roof lend elegance to main entrances. They also keep off the rain. Many modern homes and a good number of funeral parlours have recently adopted fluted columns for their façades. The old Forrest home on the Dwyer Hill Road uses fluted columns with simplicity and restraint.

The arrangement of keystones at the corners of brick and stone buildings is known as quoining. A quoin is the wedge-like stone itself. Masons had the ability to join these quoins in imaginative symmetry without sacrificing the safety of the edifice. The centre stone in an arch is also called a quoin because the support of the whole arch depends on its size and position. Masons with special flair could quoin sandstone, granite, and limestones of various colour and size into very appealing forms of art. The O'Connell house is a good example.

40

Pinch Hill

I didn't know it then, but I do now, that Armer Howie of the Eighth Line of Huntley was "putting me on"!

It was a sticky afternoon. I had pulled up my merry Olds, Rosie, in front of a sleepy century-old beauty of a farm on the Old Almonte Road. I had seen a surveyor working just inside the fence and I wanted to ask him if he had ever heard of a spot called Pinch Hill.

I had been researching the great fire of 1870 and according to the fine little book "March Past" the fire had flared up again at Pinch Hill. It was Edmund Scott of Huntley who suggested it was to be found in this area.

The surveyor, an obliging fellow named Ron Cavanagh from Fitzroy's Fourth Line, had never heard of Pinch Hill, but he was good enough to call over the owner of the farm, one Bill Howie, who was working nearby. Bill didn't know either, but recommended I see George Bassett, his neighbour, who went back more years than the rest of us put together, almost.

Just then, a pickup pulled alongside Rosie. The driver introduced himself as Armer Howie, brother to Bill. Dressed in Sunday togs on a Wednesday, he was every bit a country gentleman. He said he had just come from taking his mother to a doctor's appointment. He had an easy pleasant manner about him and, as I was soon to learn, a special brand of humour.

We got to talking about the fire of 1870 and Armer minded his grandfather telling him about a John Huston and his men sweating out days and nights in the Seventh-Line Pinery trying to extinguish the huge smouldering branchless white pines, the green resin of which persistently resisted the flames. In fact, later on, these same pines "from the trunk up" were cut into logs and used around those parts to build barns and stables. The trunks themselves were dissected into blocks and taken to sawmills to be cut into shingles. Surplus trees were left to rot, were axed down, were crosscut or burnt.

I asked Armer about the house fire in 1925 at Tom Carroll's farm just up the road. Mrs. Julia Scott O'Reilly had told me she was there that evening and that the fire was ignited by a live ember on the roof shingles. She remembered the house could have been saved except the men were afraid of heights.

This reminded Armer of another house fire on the Tenth Line of Huntley. A certain Irish farmer noticed his house's roof ablaze and instead of grabbing a water pail, went into his kitchen and danced an Irish jig. His wife blithely asked him why he was dancing, especially at that time of day, and he sang, "Because the house is on fire." No one recorded what the wife said or how much her husband had consumed. The house was reduced to ashes.

Armer obviously had a storybook mind. But he knew nothing about Pinch Hill. George Bassett might know. "Why don't you ask him yourself right now? He's over there working in the field across from his house."

I looked over to see a straw hat with a head moving along the top of a brae. I decided, however, the day was too humid for walking that far (perhaps for nothing) and that I would come another day to see George.

I was anxious just the same to see the Seventh-Concession Pinery on the south side of the Eighth Line now called the Howie Side Road. The road begins at Highway 44 and three miles later meets the Almonte Side Road where as far as I knew it stopped. However, Armer assured me that the road ran another five miles to Highway 7.

So I wheeled two ton, eleven-year-old Rosie around and drove back to the Eighth-Line Cross.

The road was there all right, but not having a machete or guide, I thought better of asking the impossible of an overweight Rosie. I returned to the group at Bill Howie's place which, by the way, is the geographical centre of Stittsville, Carp, Almonte and Carleton Place.

"Armer," I said, "That road looks like a trail. Are you sure it's open all the way?"

"Ah, but it is! But not for the like of that car! A jeep is what you need!"

"A fine time to tell me! You wouldn't be putting on a boy from the city, would you?"

He just laughed. As I drove away he added, "Be sure to see George Bassett about Pinch Hill. He'd love to talk to you," as he smiled wryly under sunny eyes.

The following week I called at George's. His little home is close to the road. An aroma of home-cooking drifted out through the screen door followed by a white-haired man with rosy cheeks and boyish grin whose steely handshake conveyed all was right in his world.

If contentment is a measure of a man's worth, then George Bassett is a rich man. Here was a gentleman satisfied with his lot and appreciative of his blessings, a man who could sit down to the meal being prepared in his wife's kitchen without wondering how hard he worked for it, what it cost and where his next one was coming from.

Silver linings, ladder tops, and green pastures held no attraction. In the door frame of his red croft was the picture of a happy man. It reminded me of a painting of a senior Walter Scott, both typifying the spirit of men at peace with themselves and other men.

George Bassett and I talked about mutual acquaintances in West Huntley. And we remembered with nostalgia the Produce Wagon (truck) of a Mr. Green. Back in the Thirties, Mr. Green used to call once a week around Huntley with canned food and fresh produce. George used to work out at a garage across from Mr. Green's Hotel in Stittsville and got to know the Green family quite well. We agreed he was a good man with a nose almost as large as his heart.

I remember the scene like it was yesterday. Mr. Green's truck in my grandmother's yard. After the big people had made their purchases, the kindly Mr. Green would reach behind his cab-seat for a six-quart basket laden with goodies — peanuts, crackerjacks, chocolate bars, and three flavours of gum, Spearmint, Doublemint and Tutti-Frutti. My dollar a week allowance was usually "shot" that day.

Mr. Green died soon after, and his grandson Mr. Watchhorn took over the route. Before long, believe it or not, as if by magic, Mr. Watchhorn's nose grew almost to the size of his granddad's. More important, however, was that Mr. Watchhorn also had his granddad's disposition and everybody liked him just as much. He's still alive today, George said, somewhere up around Pembroke.

That truck from Stittsville was a welcome sight for the lonely eyes of a wee lad — much like a Sally Ann Wagon must have been at the Front for a soldier.

Finally, I told George why I was there keeping him from his supper. Armer Howie said he would know the whereabouts of Pinch Hill.

"That's not hard to come up with. We're standing on it!"

"Your kidding; there's no hill here!"

"Yes, there is! Not much of a one, mind you, but a hill just the same. It runs for a good many acres around here."

"Where did the name come from?"

"Don't know! But it had something to do with a big wedding one weekend back at the Cox farm on the Fifth Concession. We're not sure exactly what happened but ever since then this area has been called Pinch Hill!"

Before going, we talked about the old days, the hardships of the past and the economy of the present. We discussed the O'Keefes, the Egans, and the Carters, one of whom had recently died and the other so very sick. He spoke as a man with great love for the country and its people and one who felt the pain of another's difficulty. I found Pinch Hill that day, but I also met a fine citizen.

Once home, I realized that Armer Howie knew all along that George was sitting on Pinch Hill. That's why he wanted me to go over that day; so he could enjoy watching George tell me all about it. Armer set me up. Twice!

But what about Pinch Hill? What event took place to warrant such a bewitching name? Did the police raid the premises? Did boys get rowdy and girls' derrieres black and blue? Were there bottles of Pinch's Haig and Haig there that day?

One thing for sure; it wasn't an afternoon tea at the Ritz.

Perhaps it's best the explanation remain a mystery. Let imagination do the rest! Vinegar Hill, San Juan Hill, Blueberry Hill; now Pinch Hill. Somehow it fits.

What a party it must have been!

Mick the Nail

No one knows the final outcome of Mick the Nail's first confession in twenty years. A hard-working carpenter known for his fairness and ability, he was nevertheless a rough and ready character with few refinements.

Before entering the box where the Ear of God awaited, he spent some trying moments putting together a summary of his sins. The longer he spent, the more he remembered and the more nervous he became.

By the time the priest pulled back the grill between them, Mick's shirt was drenched and his tongue like grist.

"How long has it been since your last confession?" said the priest, tired waiting for Mick to start up.

"Fi-ff- fifteen ye-ye-years!" stammered Mick.

"Glory to be God," said the priest, "what all have ya done wrong in that length of time?"

At this point, Mick's memory failed him altogether and after a great pause for air and strength, he summed it all up as best he could. He blurted, "Every G__ d__ sin, Father, but suicide!"

God's Problem

The parish priest thought twice about approaching "tightwad Andy" for a donation to the "lightning rod" fund, but he decided to have a go anyway.

"Andy, we need new lightning rods for the church. How much can I put you down for?"

"I beg your indulgence, Father, and, no offence intended, but I won't be givin' a penny!"

"But surely, Andy, you realize the danger and the terrible loss if the church should be hit!"

"Indeed I do, Father! Indeed I do! But the way I looks at it is this: it's God's house, and if He wants to blast her, He can blast her!"

Taking Over

"Did ya say it was fifty years since you last confessed?"

"Aye, Faather," said Dooley.

"In that case, so's we won't be here all night, I'll ask all the questions and you just answer 'Yes' or 'No'!"

41

Eddie

Eddie Grace
1924

Eddie Dennis Grace lived all his eighty years on the Peter Grace homestead on the Twelfth Line. His mother Ellen named him after her brother Dennis Hickey who drowned at age thirty (b. 1853). Eddie lived with his sister Catherine until she died some fifteen years before him. Until his own death in 1973, Eddie and his faithful dog, Timmy, kept the home fires burning. His tiny five-room log house is gone now, but down behind the Grace farm, great pines still lean from the wide banks of Coady's gorge.

Eddie was everybody's friend. His smile was as true as his word. His disposition: mild and courteous. He spoke almost apologetically. Underneath, I felt Eddie was wistful and melancholic; yet his manner always shone with unpretentious good humour.

He never complained nor maligned. He practised to the letter the old Irish practise of never contradicting anyone's incorrect statement. He enjoyed a joke, often indulging in a quip or two. Never a recluse, he attended dances and socials. His pleasant nature helped him fit in anywhere.

Eddie could have been a leprechaun. His stature was small; his features delicately refined. Like most Irishmen, he had a mind of his own. He knew what he was about and kept to his own knitting. Always thinking, he seldom gave way his thoughts or feelings. He had about him an air of secrecy. Eddie was a "good guy"!

Eddie never left the farm. Neither did his sister Catherine. They made a living. Eddie had a good eye for cattle and Kate kept turkeys and geese. Eddie and Kate were on friendly but reserved terms. I often remember seeing Kate working around the house and stables. She wore black and showed her years in her pace and stooped frame. Eddie always wore running shoes in his latter years because, unlike Kate, he moved quickly. He never seemed to grow old. He was like his brother William from Renfrew. They took William to an old-age retirement home in Renfrew for a trial run. He refused to stay because the people at the home were too old. He was ninety at the time. He died years later at his own house.

Neither Kate nor Eddie spent much money on themselves. Whatever money Eddie had, he put in the bank. But not so with Kate.

As it turned out, she buried her savings of some fifty years in the flower and vegetable garden. No one, not even Eddie, knew of her secret treasure. If he did know, he never let on. Every month she tucked more and more away — always bills stuffed into preserve sealers.

Just before she died, Kate told her nephew Jackie Mantil that he was her heir and she gave him the locations in the garden. Her will officially named Jackie.

Not long after her funeral, the sealers were dug up. Jackie invited a few brothers and sisters to the unearthing. Imagine the surprise, especially for Eddie. To quote one witness, "There were hundreds and hundreds of dollars and far more." *Flabbergasted* describes everyone's reaction.

Eddie probably got a charge out of the caper. He likely chuckled about the treasure being right under his nose. Just like Kate, he'd say. He'd be only too happy to see Jackie receive the inheritance. Jackie deserved it. He liked Jackie. Besides Eddie didn't put much store in money. His kind of happiness didn't come from monetary measure.

I went to see Eddie in the Almonte Hospital about four days before he died. He had cancer of the bone. He still looked young, like a little boy. His short black-grey wispy hair he patted down with his right hand. His left hand rested behind his head. His knees bent with pain. He had no blankets over him. He lay on the bed fully dressed. I stayed about ten minutes.

When you talked to Eddie, he always made you feel he was imposing on your time. Eddie was still the perfect host. Upon leaving, I shook his hand with my two and then rested one on his little forehead as I muttered a prayerful good-bye. At the door I looked back as I am wont to do. Eddie was watching me.

A few days later, knowing the end was near, he turned his body to the wall and died. Even in death, he kept his privacy. But unlike the desert flower, Eddie's "sweetness" was never wasted.

Not Just a Matter of Horse Sense

A city-turned-country boy in West Huntley tried unsuccessfully for several weeks to break in a horse.

During heated training sessions, the easily rattled lad subjected the poor beast to so many interjections, expletives and tyrannical ravings, the horse didn't know his own stable.

A neighbour better disposed by disposition and experience to such matters offered to take the horse home for a time to see what could be done to harness its energy.

Three months later, he brought back a horse that geed and hawed with the best of them.

"How did you do it?" asked the owner.

Before the neighbour could answer, the owner's father, who knew his son well, interjected, "Like I've been telling you all along; if you're going to train a horse, you've got to start out knowing *more* than he does!"

42

Richard

Tucked under the local news section of the *Perth Courier* in its weekly edition of Friday, October 3, 1890, was a brief notice announcing the death of a nineteen-year-old boy named Richard. The lad had died apparently of consumption on the previous Friday, September 26. No wake or funeral was mentioned, but a burial had taken place in Huntley, County Carleton. The editor concluded by extending sincere condolences to the family.

The appearance of such a personal offering of sympathy by the local paper would suggest that Richard's family held more than a little prominence in the community. Naturally such families are in the public eye and more susceptible to censure. No doubt, then, the sudden and expedient dispatch of poor Richard without so much as a wake or solemn religious observance set many neighbours' tongues wagging. And many wondered out loud why Richard was buried at the Catholic Cemetery in West Huntley and not in the family plot at Perth's St. John's Cemetery where Richard's father and sister already lay.

The rumours would have multiplied if anyone had bothered to follow the camouflaged wagon on its ten-hour, thirty-mile journey by way of Lanark and Ramsey Townships to West Huntley. When the "hearse" got to Almonte, instead of directing the team out to St. Michael's Parish Cemetery, the drivers left Almonte by way of Ottawa Street, passed St. Mary's Cemetery on the edge of Ramsey, turned left across the Burnt Lands, and went down the Twelfth Line to the farm of Tom White and his wife Bridget. There, in the backyard behind the house under a ripening apple tree, the remains of Richard found their first resting place.

But Richard was no stranger to this farm. He had often been there with his parents on summer holidays and shorter visits. His mother, Mary, was a sister of Bridget McNamara who had married his Uncle Tom, sometime in the early Sixties. The two McNamara girls had grown up in West Huntley. Their parents John and Honora Graham had come to West Huntley from the Perth area. John had accepted a teaching position at #8 Section on the northwest corner of the Vaughan Side Road and Dwyer Hill Road. Their log home was on ten acres of land across from the Delaney's.

John McNamara and at least one other brother, Denis, had come into the Perth district from Askeaton Parish in Limerick, Ireland. Denis died in Arnprior (meaning church by the river) where John had moved in retirement after his wife's death in 1863. If monuments in graveyards are any indication of wealth, then the McNamaras must have had some. While John and Honora's tombstone in St. Michael's Cemetery is fairly opulent, certainly the one for Denis and his wife Catherine Brady in the Perth Cemetery is even more elaborate; in fact, perhaps the most expensive one there. The epigram on the stone depicts the quality of the McNamaras. It reads: "He that hath mercy on the poor, lendeth to the Lord, and He will repay in full."

The McNamara girls, Bridget and Mary, had no shortage of play-mates on the Eleventh Line in the 1850's. Among the pioneer families (many of whom came with Robinson in 1823 and '25) were the Kennedys, Graces, O'Briens, Listons, Vaughans and Sullivans. Across the back fences on the 11th and 12th Concessions were three families of Forrests as well as Flynns, Buckleys, Hogans, Morriseys, O'Keefes, Curtins and Whites. The younger girl, Bridget, married Tom, the son of William White and Johanna Forrest. The other sister, Mary, married a Perthite, probably a distant relative of her mother, and settled in the Perth district where Richard was later born.

In later years, Richard also had many friends his own age down on the White farm. John Flynn's younger children, Sarah and Michael, were there, as were Morris Keefe's boys, Dan and John. Other "adopted cousins" back the line were the children of homesteaders John Keefe, Peter and Martin Grace, and Patrick O'Brien. On Tom White's farm he had his real cousins, Michael, Caroline, William, Mary Ann and Hannah. Hannah married a girlhood chum, one Patrick O'Brien. Their son, Ignatius, was held in much esteem by all the people of Corkery. Ignatius and poor Richard would be first cousins once removed.

Richard must have came to love that farm in the 1880's as I did as a boy in the 1940's. My Granduncle Mike O'Keefe owned the farm from the mid-1910's on, and I often spent a few days there during my summer holidays. Richard must have romped through the fields free as a tern on the wind, played games round the buildings and even swung on those same apple-tree branches that were to later shade his grave. He would have joined in the milkings and fed his favourite calf from his favourite pail. He would have watched the horses running in the pasture after a day in harness, fed the chickens and geese, and hunted for eggs, butter-nuts, and birds' nests.

He would have been as happy there as I was. For that farm has something special about it ... a serenity that comes to a place where good people have lived. The lakes around Glendalough, Wexford, in Ireland had it, a breath of joy left by the monks who lived there for six hundred years. I felt it once in the British Art Gallery in an unfinished picture by Constable of a summer's eve in the English countryside; also in the chapel of the Cloistered Visitation Nuns of Partridge Green, Sussex; and in the hospital room of a long-suffering saint. Three families had left their goodness on that farm. Is it any wonder it was unique!

The first settler there was probably William White of Clogheen, Tipperary. He was the son of James White and Honora Mahoney who lived across the road with another son, James. William set his log home and buildings a good piece from the road so as not to use up the acres more suitable for crops. Behind the house was a garden and orchard. In the front, he planted oak trees. On the small slope to the right of the house, he fixed his barn and stable.

Richard and his friends would have played along the wagon trail which ran behind the barn and then sharply down into the valley and over Coady's Creek. They would have run as far as the heavy tree line where the road loses itself in the thick bush. From there, looking back, they could see the little white log house on the ridge, its chimney beckoning them home for supper. And they'd see the orchard, and cows lolling on the slope near the grey barn, and in the middle Aunt Bridget waving them home. Is it any wonder Richard would sadly go back to Perth after his holidays, already counting the days until his return?

But all that was past now. There came that September weekend when Richard's body was brought back to his holiday home. And word spread across West Huntley about his coming and the mystery of it all confounded everyone. His playmates came to weep before his sodded grave in the corner of the apple orchard.

It was Hannah White who told her son Ignatius that her Aunt Mary was hiding her son from the authorities because they had wanted to perform an autopsy on him. They had reason to believe he had died from a disease far more lethal than consumption and wanted to know what it was. But Mary said no and took her son's body from them and hid it. And the whole family took turns guarding it ... Tom, Mary, Bridget, Michael, Caroline, and the rest. Even at night someone sat inside the kitchen window overlooking the grave, the weak glow of a lamp adding some cheer.

Weeks later when the trees were bare, those same silent men returned and took Richard away and reburied him in the parish cemetery with his father and sister by the railroad track outside Perth. And the Corkery people watched him go, no easier about the matter than before. Who or what was the mother afraid of? Was she protecting the family name? Was it the honour of her son? Were the authorities really going to perform an autopsy? Did they ever look for Richard? Did they challenge the mother on her return? Or was the whole episode simply due to the paranoiac imagination of a distraught mother?

Imaginary or not, we do know a mother was moved to take extreme measures. In the face of dilemma, she made a decision and acted on it! Her resolution was that her son's body would never be profaned by the vulgarity of an autopsy and her heart rested easy because of that.

Somehow I feel Richard's spirit would have been happier if his body had remained in that orchard on that farm he and I loved so much ... the great oaks of the Whites are still there ... and the little white home slumbers still at the laneway's end ... and the apple blossoms still brighten the backyard ... and in the corner, where Richard slept under some brush, can be seen the large rusty wrought-iron statue of St. Michael still guarding the site it was asked to protect one hundred years ago by a mother named Mary McNamara G___ from Perth by way of West Huntley.

Two thousand years ago another Mary also protected her Son's body. And like Richard, his first resting place was not to be lasting.

166

43

Lawrence Kennedy's Last Tour of West Huntley

Many a cloud has drifted since Lawrence Kennedy and I first met thirty years ago. It was a hot day in July and I was on my way to Almonte. My car broke down in front of Lawrence's house just after one of my passengers, my Aunt Mary Prudhomme, said she was having a heart attack. I used Lawrence's phone to get help.

In the fall of 1988, I dropped in on Lawrence. I had heard he wasn't well. Three years earlier, within a period of twelve months, he lost his wife, his daughter, his brother, and not surprisingly his health.

Lawrence Kennedy
1924

He missed his wife. She collapsed in front of him one day and his whole world went down with her. Lawrence had been on the mend. He got stronger every day. Living alone was tough, but when things get tough, the tough get going. Friends like Dom Ryan and Pat Egan kept in touch. He got to Mass on Sundays and Tuesdays. And every day he spent an hour and thirty-five minutes in private prayer. He was that kind of a man!

It didn't take long to learn Lawrence loved his home. He lived on the old homestead property of his father Mike and mother, Jenny. He was proud of that! The original farmhouse is the first home on the left after turning onto the Hamilton Side Road coming from Highway 7. Lawrence's thoughts were often there. He was lonely, but memories were company. Over the long haul, comfort and support always came from family, friends, and neighbours.

He worried about his friends — like Jim Carter, Pat Egan, and Ignatius O'Brien who also lived alone. Of those already gone, he eagerly recounted their virtues. He had great compassion especially for those neighbours who had difficulties.

Like all docile men, Lawrence always had to control a red-hot temper, not easily ignited, mind you, but one that required self-control. He learned many years ago that an open hand goes further than a closed one. The temper was still there he said, but it became more of a stubbornness and that was good because it kept him going. It was not surprising the people of Corkery loved this man. My cousin Clarence Williams had admired Lawrence from afar. He says of Lawrence, "Huntley could not boast of a finer man — the salt of the earth!"

As I talked with Lawrence, I realized his many misfortunes, (and he had more than his share), had never been allowed to embitter his life. No cynicism, no wrong turns, no regrets, no missed opportunities. He wouldn't change a thing! He saw God's hand in everything! In our conversation he often repeated these words, "Gary, God has been very, very good to me."

Obviously neither one had ever forgotten the other!

Lawrence Kennedy had an easy charm about him. He was laid-back, but nobody's fool, especially in business. He judged no man, more inclined to fault the sin than the sinner. He put up no walls. He took you as you were. Chatted openly. You'd think you knew him all your life.

Such a warm person was a pleasure to know. Especially for me! I'm not comfortable about invading another man's privacy. Privacy is such a precious thing! A truly great freedom! And since I tend to be intensely private myself, I do try to respect the privacy of others, especially in my work. I have seen too many students cut open by prying counsellors, teachers, and administrators and left to bleed.

So I try to be careful what I say in conversation. Not to enter areas beyond my business. Indeed certain recesses of the mind are better left closed. When a tender area is touched, it's best to let the speaker work his way through the emotion if he wishes and then try to subtly change the subject. Sometimes, an airing of yesterday's sorrows are good; oftentimes it isn't.

As an educator, then, I wasn't much for interfering too closely in another's life. For this reason, the home life of children and parents was a sacred matter. I seldom contacted a home in thirty years of teaching and counselling. I felt parents had enough on their plates without my needlessly disturbing the few hours in a day they could call their own.

If I had something to say about a child, I might send a note home with the student or send a personal letter by mail, or wait for the parents to contact me on Teacher-Parent Nights. Always put the ball in their court as it were, and let them control it from there. If an emergency developed, I even preferred to call the work-place rather than the home.

For me, the home is special — like a church! Another world! Sort of a last frontier! A retreat! An oasis of escape from a bizarre civilization. A hiding place in the woods. A tree hut above the turmoil. A secret place where moments of joy and grief unfold, where a family can be itself, let its hair down, unwind, and recharge. Where civil wars are waged and hearts mended and decisions handed down. A mini-fortress that gives a man and a woman a measure of independence in an otherwise energy-sapping autocratic jungle. To enter one another's home is a privilege! To cross another's threshold without an invitation is an invasion of privacy. Neither Queen nor Bishop nor Prime Minister has such a right. No matter if the home is a hovel or a mansion. A man's home *is* his castle!

That's why calling on homes like Lawrence's has not been easy for me. I feel I am imposing. Who am I to disturb their routines? To question them about the past? To stir the embers? Challenge their fading memories? I come as a stranger opening doors and windows long since sealed. I walk them through the lands of the living and dead. And all for the creation of a book. It is worth it?

Maybe! Time will tell. Perhaps I feel their stories should be told. Their names remembered. Deeds recorded. Tombstones can't tell the tales. And the clock is running. The rare vintages of the golden harvests are almost gone. The vines have already withered.

So I write this commemoration in spite of my natural reluctance to infringe on the privacy of Corkery's good people. And I thank them all for permitting me into their homes, apartments, hospital rooms, and even into their hearts. All this, so that on another day in another time, they shall not be forgotten and their breath always felt on the land.

As a boy I knew little of Lawrence's area, the perimeters of which are the Old Almonte Side Road on the north, the Tenth Line of Huntley on the east, the town line of Ramsey on the west and Goulbourn on the south. (See map on page 348).

It was an area not settled as early as other sections of West Huntley, a situation probably due to a large swampy section between the Eleventh and Tenth Lines and the rocky shelf of the Twelfth Line Crest. Only a few lots near the southwest end were allotted by Peter Robinson in 1823 — Pat Leahy had the West 1/2 of Lot 7, 12th Concession, John Leahy had the West 1/2 of Lot 2, 12th Concession, and a Pat Field was assigned the West 1/2 of Lot 1, 12th Concession. A Jeffrey O'Donahue received the East 1/2 of Lot 15, 11th Concession.

By the middle 1800's, however, Lots 1 to 14 in this southwest corner of West Huntley were very much populated by the Kellys, Foleys, Larkins, O'Learys, Leahys, Galvins, O'Connells, Meehans, Hamiltons, Sullivans, McArtons, Kennedys, McDonalds and O'Briens, many of whom were Robinson settlers who had previously received lots outside Huntley. Only a few of these families remain — the Kellys are there and the Kennedys, O'Connells, McArtons, and Hamiltons. The rest have pulled up stakes.

The O'Learys, for one, left around 1910. But not before they left their mark. O'Leary boys had married Carrolls, Maxwells, Muldoons, O'-Briens and Corbetts. And as far back as the 1830's, O'Leary girls also proved their popularity by marrying into many of West Huntley's grassroots-families: Catherine O'Leary married Tim O'Brien; Jane married Patrick Carroll; Anne, Michael Carroll; Elizabeth, Andrew Foy; Sarah, Andrew Kennedy; Jane, Tom Kelly; Mary, John Ryan; and Julia, John Sullivan. Patrick and Samuel O'Leary were the original settlers.

Stella Kennedy recalled for me the day one of the last of the O'Learys left this section of West Huntley. She was only a mite of a girl, but she never forgot the tearful widow O'Leary loading children and belongings on the wagon for the trip to the Almonte Railway Station and a new home further north. And all the neighbours watching her go. Coming to the gates to wish her well and hugging the children and giving them a coin or two or a keepsake or a bit of clothing or food. Huntley has seen too much of such uprooting. It makes one sad to think about them.

One afternoon, Lawrence showed me his old stomping grounds. Starting at the Hamilton Side Road, we drove along the Dwyer Hill Road toward Goulbourn, as far as the McArton Side Road.

On this small stretch, around 1875, lived farmers John O'Brien, William Lang, William Arthurs, James Sullivan, Tom Kelly (Senior and Junior), Tom O'Leary and brother Dan, and at the corner of the McArton Side Road where we had turned right, Danny Sullivan.

Further up the road on our right Lawrence suggested we pull over. He wanted to show me a beautiful stone farmhouse in front of a backdrop of well-preserved log buildings. Built, as mentioned, in the 1870's by Richard O'Connell (1831-1920) and his wife Esther Meehan (1844-1937), niece of pioneer John Manion of the Ninth Line, it later fell to their son Joe and his sister and then to Richard's grandchild Peter and his wife Helen Smith, Peter being the son of Richard's son, Danny (1879-1956) and Mary Fumerton (1880-1944).

Lawrence praised the O'Connells. He and his father Michael before him found them to be the best of neighbours and one or the other had known or heard of almost all the O'Connells: Richard's father and mother, William O'Connell (died 1871) and Margaret Flynn (1795-1869) of Goulbourn; Richard's older brother William and wife Jane who came into Huntley from Goulbourn around 1850 and were gone by 1863; Kitty O'Connell, Richard's sister, wife of John Meehan; another brother, Michael, and his wife Margaret Meehan; Ellen, another sister, the wife of Patrick Roche; and the rest of Daniel O'Connell's children including Peter's brothers and sisters, two of whom were known to me, Jimmy and Lorne.

Certainly any family capable of maintaining an unblemished reputation over a century and a half must be exemplary. The reader is well advised to take a gander at this Nineteenth-Century farm complex of the O'Connells, the order, cleanliness and cosiness of which indeed suggest good people at its roots.

I learned from Lawrence that the McArton Side Road divides the 12th Concession of Huntley from Goulbourn, and that it was there a few hundred yards further along from O'Connells on the Goulbourn side, that the educational Commissioners of both townships agreed in the 1850's to support the construction and staffing of a Union School. Lawrence pointed out the abandoned frame structure of #9 Huntley-#16 Goulbourn set well in off the side road, the size of the numbers showing the difference in the two townships' populations.

This first public school in this area, like all the other eight schools of Huntley, was log. In 1898, a new frame school was agreed on, a decision indicative of the continued co-operation between the Protestants and

Three Weddings

Above: Margaret Carroll and John O'Keefe. Attended by: Irene Carroll and Herman O'Keefe.

Middle: Katherine Scott and Archie Currie.

Below: Mary Mantil and Angus Carroll with Angus's parents, Cecilia Scott and Jim Carroll and Mary's mother and father, Rose Grace and Bob Mantil.

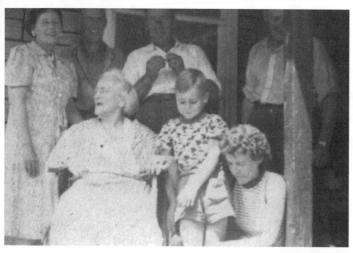

At O'Keefe's Corners, 1950
Back row: Eva O'Keefe Ogilvi[e]
Clarence Williams, Ignatius
O'Keefe, Edward O'Keefe. Fro[nt]
row: Genevieve O'Keefe, Gary
O'Keefe and Rita Kennedy.

Susan Gosson Scott from
the Eighth Concession and
her five Scott sisters-in-law,
sisters of Little Michael.
Front row: Susan,
Mrs. Sarah Sullivan. Back
row: Mrs. Tessie Clarke,
Mrs. Kate Maxwell, Sister
Margaret Alicoque, Mrs.
Bridget Lavell, c. 1944.

Wedding picture of Lucy Veronica
O'Keefe, daughter of William O'Keefe and
Mary Jane McNulty and granddaughter of
John O'Keefe and Mary Corey of Ireland.
William grew up on the lot east of Tom
O'Keefe's at O'Keefe's corners. Her
husband is James McDermot from
Cantley, Quebec, c. 1910.

Edmund
Newton, Sr.

Bill Roach

Barney Grace and Andy Forrest

Maurice Egan and Emmett Forrest

Patrick Meehan and
Pat Liston

James Kennedy

Pat Egan

Michael Grace and Anselym Byrnes

Andy Egan

Lambert Grace, Tom Kennedy, Pious Pat Kennedy, Alphonse O'Brien and William Grace

All the
pictures on
this page
were taken
in 1924.

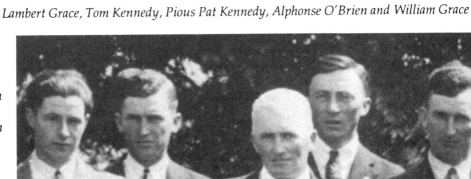

Wedding of Vernon Murphy of South March and Carmel O'Ke with her sisters Viola and Inez and neighbour, Mrs. Syl Finne

Three good friends:

Raymond Mantil, Herman O'Keefe and Emmett Carroll, c. 1945.

Evelyn (Eva) O'Keefe Ogilvie, Alex Prudhomme and his wife, Mary O'Keefe, c. 1925. My mother had the most beautiful hands.

Catholics of both townships. Not until 1938 was the school closed for lack of students.

All told, the two #9's and #16's gave eighty years of service, a run that compares favourably with our modern school life-expectancy of only three or four decades. In fact, this one-room type of education is looking better every day compared to the chaotic conditions created by certain present-day bureaucrats and trustees whose "closed-boundary, no-walls, nobody-fails, dollar-oriented philosophies" have subjected student, teacher, and taxpayer to unwarranted pressures. The numerous outdoor tin shacks, used in some areas today as schoolhouses alongside many main school buildings, and the empty halls of other schools just nearby, clearly indicate a breakdown in co-operation between municipalities and a failure to understand one another's economic and social needs. The pioneers could teach our educational and political leaders of today some lessons in sharing.

By 1863, education, then, was available to some thirteen Presbyterian and Catholic families in this remote corner of West Huntley. Not an easy task without general subsidies from Township coffers: so many expenditures: a teacher's salary of some fifty pounds (about $245.00 in those days); wells to dig; books, pails, brooms, dippers, scribblers, fuel, lights, chalk and brushes to supply; and other furnishings like table, chair, benches and work-areas for teacher and students to be purchased. It was an age of sacrifice for teachers, students, trustees, and parents; a time for compromise; an era of "hand-me-downs-barefoot-o'er-the-fields" education.

No running water then! ... no terrazzo floors! ... no central heating! ... instead, stinking outhouses, woodless floors, and heat from one stove at the back with its long stovepipe running under the ceiling to the chimney up front ... no individual desks, just two long slanted work-tables nailed to the logs and running some twenty feet down each side of the room, and underneath, sitting benches roughly hewn from half logs.

A no frills education! No gimmicks or teaching aids ... just head to head education in its purest form.

Imagine wee tykes such as Merin and Jennet McKinley, Christy and Hughie Aikins, Elizabeth and Catherine Nutterfield ... Mary Sullivan, Tom and Dan Kelly, David, Emma and Jean O'Connell, ... Jean and Ann Clancy, John and Ann Donaldson, and Gregory Langford ... all skipping along mud-packed trails, 'neath towering trees, round rotting trunks ... through beaver grass, by cedar swamp ... amid wild flowers, chipmunks and grass snakes ... so much to see and smell and wonder at ... so much reverie .. the games with friends on the way ... the teasing, pushing, titterings ... and the final arrival at school in complete disarray.

And there waiting for them, the young teacher trying to compose herself for all her duties ... the off and on again of coats in winter ... so many grades to teach ... so many differences in intellectual levels ... so many handicaps besides sight and hearing ... each child so unique in needs ... the leaking roofs, the dirty stovepipes, the stoking of the fires ... the fights at recess, the cuts and bruises and bleeding noses and tears ... the homework to give ... the lessons to prepare ... the cold, the heat ... the sweeping and shovelling ... the stealing, the bullies, the imps ... the trips to the outhouse ... the wood to carry in and the brushes to clean ... all quite enough to drive anyone but a dedicated, trained, and understanding teacher off the deep end. Yet these young teachers persevered and sent out into the world from these little 14' X 28' and 20' X 20' log rooms some of Canada's finest citizens, equipped with ideals and morals of the highest order. Across Canada and the world, these country graduates have gone forth to become priests, nuns, judges, teachers, missionaries, nurses, doctors, harness makers, carpenters, farmers, shoemakers, and good mothers and fathers.

Let the record show the names of these teachers in Corkery, so we won't forget them: Dorothy Maingot, Dennis Egan, Daniel Egan, Jane McGahey, David Leahy, Mary Mantil Carroll, John McNamara and his daughter Bridget, Mrs. Loretta Hogan Madden, Irene Kennedy, Margaret Neville O'Neil, Ethel Golden Scott, Annette Rodier, Bridget Neville, Carmel O'Keefe Murphy, Mary O'Neil, Margaret Mulville Egan, Patrick Foley, Canon Corkery, Father Stanton, Mr. Shanahan and Misses Roger, York, Halfpenny, Nagle, Fife, McDougal, Teskey, Anderson, and Shaw.

The burden of sacrificing for an education was not new to many early Irish-Catholic immigrants (1823-60). Their Ireland of the two previous centuries had banned Catholic education. True, by 1831, a National School System was established, but up to that point in time, all elementary schools were for Protestants only, or such Catholics willing to have their children receive the religious instruction of the Established Church of England (which instruction strongly condemned the Roman Church). Consequently, some Irish parents took their schooling system underground just as they had done with their religious practices. "Centres of learning" became hedge-schools under the guidance of hedge-school-masters. In winter, these classes were held by peat fire, and, in summer, under the shade of hedges and trees.

If an early Catholic Irish West Huntley immigrant wasn't illiterate, he had to have received his education (especially the English language) in one of three ways: private tutoring, hedge-teaching, or at the English Elementary School. My great-grandfather, Tom O'Keefe, and his brother Edward (or Edmund), were illiterate and probably spoke only Gaelic and smatterings of English. Tom signed his Will with an X in 1887 and Edmund made his mark on the "Agreement to Purchase" of the O'Keefe homestead in 1847. Edmund never lived to see his offspring educated. But Tom did. Hearing some of his seven boys and two girls read him the *Almonte Gazette* must have been "music to his old ears".

Next, Lawrence and I and Rosie passed on our right one of the three sections of the old Twelfth Line. It's now called the Lowe Road. The other two sections are John Kennedy Way and the Burnt Lands' Road.

Such divisions in Concession Lines are not uncommon in Townships. Years ago when these Lines were just wagon trails, most were continuous unless they came to a creek or a river. Bridges were too expensive. At present, the only Line in West Huntley that is continuous is the Eleventh Line — now the Dwyer Hill Road. It runs from Arnprior to Dwyer Hill.

Lines were and are mainly used to provide access to the forced roads which were once the main arteries. These forced roads allowed neighbour to reach neighbour more easily and also delineated the Concession-divisions (imaginary or otherwise). The real history of any township is on the Forced Roads, not the Lines.

Lawrence presumed the naming of the second section, John Kennedy Way, was in commemoration of the original pioneer settler, John Kennedy from the Ninth Line. The Ninth Line has two names. At one end, it's the Manion Road; at the other, near Manion's Corners, it's the Corkery Road and both are joined. All quite confusing!

Lawrence's ancestors in West Huntley go back to its beginnings. Lawrence's great-grandparents were pioneers John Kennedy and his wife Margaret Manion, sister of pioneer John Manion. Lawrence's father, Mike (1866-1931) was the son of Hughie Kennedy (1828-1900), the son of John and Margaret. Lawrence wasn't sure of his grandmother's name since grandfather Hughie married three times. In any case, Lawrence has the distinction of being the grandson of two of the three earliest families in Corkery and you can't go back any further than that in West Huntley!

Multiple marriages especially by men were common in the Nineteenth Century. One at a time, of course. Some men who married twice were: Cornelius Forrest, James White, Tim Kennedy, Ed Vaughan, Andrew Manion, John Mantil, Tom White, Tom Rowan, Patrick Hogan, and Ron O'Connell to name a few. The "Mickey Rooney" to beat all, however, was Con Mahoney who married four times, a sure way of begetting heirs and collecting land in the bargain.

Naturally, many women remarried too. In the pioneer world, men needed the help of women and children on the farm as much as the women needed the brawn and financial support of the men.

Except for death, few marriages broke up. Divorces were unheard of, possibly because neither party could afford them. Separations did occur infrequently like the lad named White in Goulbourn who solved his matrimonial difficulties by building his own bachelor-pad at the end of his farm. Certainly a much better solution than another fellow who remained with his wife but never spoke to her except by way of small notes (Imagine the language? And the meals?). Another way out for some was the disappearance trick. Usually the man deserted with only the clothes on his back and a few bucks.

As I read the history of West Huntley and listen to its older citizens, I wonder how many other poor souls escaped their lots in life by choosing self-destruction. Every community experiences such tragedies and our hearts go out to friends and loved ones. Explanations for such violent endings can often be attributed to quirks in certain family histories or/and genetic "foul ups" brought on by marriages too close in bloodlines.

Yet how many of them could attribute such fatal decisions to life itself! They'd had enough! Not just of matrimonial problems, but enough of life's little agonies that chisel away at one's heart and sanity; the loss of children, sometimes two or three in half a month; the death of sisters and brothers, some in the prime of life; so many diseases to face and no defences available; the cold, the heat; the stillbirths, the intense unbelievable pain of labour; those unexplainable imbalances of body and mind often caused by changes in life cycles; the relentless repetition of backbreaking chores; the disasters of crop from wind, rain and drought; the loss of livestock by disease, lightning or accident; the death of parents and spouse; the loneliness of winters; men away at work; the longing for the green fields of Ireland and relatives; bad health. Really, how much was some sensitive, fragile soul expected to endure and for how long?

And then the pain for loved ones to watch the Church bury these tender hearts in fields outside consecrated ground — a final humiliation from a Church going by the book and not its heart. Would it not be merciful and fair and proper to bless this ground where they now lie? A way of saying, we understand and forgive you and leave your fate in God's hands! Isn't it the least that could be done?

The next line crossing the McArton Road after the Lowe Road is not "the High", but obviously one held in high esteem: it's the "Golden Line". There, a left turn takes the traveller to Ashton, a turn right to Highway 44, and, going straight on, to Carleton Place. This cross, as the Irish still call intersections, marks the coming together of four townships — Beckwith and Ramsey on the west of the Golden Line and Goulbourn and Huntley on the east.

A Sunday driver must have patience about this renaming of these old Lines. As mentioned, the Ninth Line off Highway 44 is the Manion Road, but at the other end from the Old Almonte Road, it's the Corkery Road. The Old Almonte Road itself stops at the Golden Line, but begins again under the same designation a mile or so to the north, almost as if the earth had one day shifted. Even the Golden Line has a different name for drivers coming onto it from Highway 44, something like "Borderline". Obviously, "Borderline" was considered by some official as an improvement over the original name "Town Line" which really is what it says it is, except it divides townships not towns. Sounds as if these systems were set up by and for people not overly concerned if they were coming or going.

To add to the confusion, Huntley Township has now become part of "West Carleton Township" which also includes the former townships of Torbolton and Fitzroy. West Carleton Township is naturally part of Carleton County, not necessarily the entire western part of the County, but part of the part, as it were.

Lawrence and I next turned right onto the Golden Line. On our left, the open-groomed fields of old pioneer families like the Kennedys, Teskeys, Tierneys, Armstrongs, Dowlings, and Foleys caterpillar over two concessions of Ramsey to the shores of the Mississippi River, once considered by the early Scottish weavers to be another Clyde. This Golden Line is well-named! It brings rest to the eye! A peaceful panorama at any time of year!

On our right, the more rugged traces of West Huntley's past slipped by. Along this corridor, the pioneers of 1840-1890 included the Atkins, McGregors, Kellys, Foleys, Galvins, Larkins, Hamiltons and Leahys as far as the Old Almonte Side Road, and beyond that, the dwellings of the Drummonds, Wilsons and more Galvins and Kellys.

One old house deserves a mention. Either the deserted home of Tom Foley or more likely Peter Larkin, it's on or near the East 1/2 of the third lot of Concession 12. I first saw it from the end of the Lowe Side Road which according to an old map is the beginning of the former Larkin and Nutterfield properties. Straight to the southwest on a hill, this house boldly rises, a barren windowless shell of a place, its blackened frame a witness to a thousand and one seasons; boldly, for it has not yet run its time and still speaks haughtily to us of dreams and joys. Even as the cold rays of a winter's eve shine round its loneliness, its very hollowness fills our imagination with admiration for those spirits who once lived there.

At this point, another abandoned farm deserves recognition. It's on a deserted section of the Tenth Line, north of the Old Almonte Road. A sign at the entrance says, "Not maintained by the Township" and back in 1850 it wasn't either. Except for the once great forest, it probably looks just as it did then when James Carter and Elizabeth Kelly built their homestead some two kilometres in the road. In those years, the Line opened out to Highway 44 with an offshoot lane running east to the Ninth Line for the convenience of churchgoers and visitors to the Manion area. Families of Killeens, Carrolls, Roches, Sullivans, Scotts, and Kennedys lived along this line which wasn't then as God-forsaken as today. Now the road beyond the Carter's ruins is Jeep country. The present owner of Carter's would like to keep the road private, but the authorities say otherwise.

The approach to this Tenth Line entrance can be made by following the Old Almonte Road past the Ninth Line (Corkery Road) and downhill towards the swampy marshes of West Huntley. Old-timers call this section the Long Swamp Road, the dry, navigable condition of which is due to the MacDonald brothers who, as mentioned earlier, drew hundreds of loads of gravel from their homesite to fill in the roadbed. That's a hundred and forty years ago and still no problems of drainage are apparent, even in the spring.

James and Elizabeth Carter probably married around 1850. James Carter (1824-1894) came to Canada as a young man from the downs of

County Tyrone. His wife Elizabeth Kelly (1830-1900) came as a young girl from the flat agricultural lands of County Carlow. Carlow is sandwiched between Counties Kildare, famous for horses, and Kilkenny, famous for cats. One day in West Huntley the northern lad fell in love with the southern colleen and they settled down among massive trees beyond a great swamp.

James was an enterprising farmer. He worked out at Wylie's Mill in the village of Almonte and by 1880 owned over three hundred acres of high and dry farmland. And he built himself a fine red-brick home just as the Forrests, Kellys, Kennedys, Curtins and others had done in West Huntley during that period. The combination of Tyrone and Carlow was a good one. And the Carter name flourished.

As true Gaels, their children's welfare was of a high priority and they provided them with a good start by giving them their own land and shelter. To their son, Paddy, (1868-1952) they left the homestead where he and Mamie Vaughan, daughter of Ed Vaughan (1860-1945) and Francis Devine (1865-1903), raised a small family. For their older son, James (1865-1948), they bought the original stone house of Tom Mordy on the Ninth Line at Manion's Corners. James was to marry Rosie Marie Brown (1874-1929), probably the daughter of James Brown and Helena Forrest, and before his death shared his father's fervour for generosity by also providing for his own two sons.

He and Rose left the Mordy house to son James, and bought for son Joseph, the stone house of pioneer John Kennedy. Unfortunately, Joe never married and James (later called Jimmy) and his wife Margaret Legree left no heirs. Soon the big stone houses will go to new families and the Carters be just a memory in the back of an old-timer's mind. But that's the way of things!

At the old homestead, on the Tenth Line, nature mourns the passing of the Carters ... the fine brick home, hit by lightning in the Twenties, burnt to the ground ... the once new log house has fallen in ... the outbuildings are lost in wild dark green grass ... a sadness moves round the ruins ... the untravelled road lies like unused track by a deserted station ... the middle of nowhere ... no birds nor flowers nor children ... the woods are closer, taking away the horizon ... nearby, the muffled crack of a .22 ... somewhere in the rubble, a creaking board ... overhead the wispy trails of a jet ... the good has gone from the place with the people it served ... never have I felt such emptiness in West Huntley ... everything changes ... "all is vanity" cry the moors!

Lawrence suggested we turn down the Hamilton Side Road. On our immediate right on the North 1/2 of Lot 6, Concession 17, was the eighty-eight acre homestead of the Hamiltons.

Perhaps a quick word about Lots and Concessions would help at this point. All of Canada's provinces are divided into lots and concessions according to the British method of surveying. Lots and concessions are grouped under townships, townships under counties, counties under districts and districts under provinces.

A township may have any number of concessions and lots. Huntley, presuming it still exists geographically, has twelve concessions of twenty-seven lots each. The total number of lots is therefore three hundred and twenty-four which happens to be spread over eighty-seven point six square meters or fifty-six thousand and sixty acres. The average size of a lot is therefore one hundred and seventy-four acres. If the assumption is made that the township is square (and it isn't), an automobile would travel thirty-seven point four miles to cover its perimeter.

To visualize the structure of Huntley, imagine Concession I near Carp as one large, long orange crate divided by twenty-seven vertical lot lines of varied widths. On top of this first crate pile eleven more similar-sized crates and the result is Huntley. The last crate on top, Concession 12, borders Ramsey Township. The vertical lots of Huntley run left to right from #1, next to Goulbourn Township, to #27, next to Fitzroy.

Lots therefore are the divisions of each concession and always run over one concession to another. The first Scottish surveyors of Huntley had to chain off the lot sizes according to the dictates of nature's terrain. In West Huntley, they tried to cut up areas into exactly two hundred or one hundred and sixty-six acres, but often had to settle for different sizes somewhere between one hundred and sixty and two hundred.

The most difficult aspect of the surveying must have been the step of dividing a lot into parcels, called halves or quarters, etc. Imagine one rectangular lot of two hundred acres covering the full one-mile height of a concession. Imagine the top facing west and the bottom, east. If a survey crew put stakes horizontally across the middle of this lot they created two parcels, one known as the East half of the lot and the other, the West half.

If this same lot positioned in the same way is parcelled by four lines running vertically in a North-South direction, then the four fifty-acre strips become known, from the left, as the North half of the North half, the South half of the North half, the North half of the South half and the South half of the South half. In the case of the Hamiltons, the family in 1880 had the North half of Lot 6, Concession 12, eighty-eight acres, and their neighbours, the Galvins, had the other eighty-eight called the South half. In the last hundred years, further severances to lots have become so numerous, it requires a lawyer to determine some boundaries. But regardless of the number of divisions, it's good to know each lot's main boundaries remain unchanged.

Free enterprise being what it is, even by 1880, some *strong* farmers of West Huntley owned back-to-back two hundred acre lots. Hughie Kennedy, from Lawrence's area, owned four hundred acres on one concession, just in from the Old Almonte Road. His neighbour, John Meehan, also had four hundred acres along the same road running from the start of the Twelve Concession to the end of the Eleventh. Considering their

Irish ancestors owned no land whatsoever in Ireland, such men and others like them, the Manions, O'Keefes, Forrests, Carters and Egans did quite well for themselves. However, it must be borne in mind that not all lots were prime land — many "plantations" included flatrock, cedar swamps, beaver meadows, and bush.

Perhaps, after this brief explanation of lots and parcels, the terminology of land descriptions can now be better understood, and I can safely use the full lot descriptions. On our left on the Hamilton Side Road, Lawrence showed me the old eighty-eight-acre homestead (West 1/2 of Lot 7) of Patrick Leahy (1785-1825) and his wife Johanna Fahey (b. 1789), settlers of 1823 from Conna, Cork. Patrick died in 1825. He was buried on his land. Another pioneer, Sullivan by name, was also buried on his land, the North 1/2 of Concession 10. Only, he had been murdered! George Stone, who inherited the Sullivan farm from John Harrold's wife, (a Sullivan), knew the location of the cairn: somewhere near the road under a large tree and along a fence. He was told not to disturb the site or disclose the area.

Sullivan's murder was never solved. Not surprisingly either! Few murderers were apprehended in those early days. Scores were settled quietly and efficiently. Farmer Richard Langford was killed in his barn on the Eighth Line; a Jeff Parker was done in not far from Mahoney's Hotel; and a hundred or more years ago, somewhere in the cedars between St. Michael's and Carp, a man was murdered by a group, one or two of whom were said to be from West Huntley. According to tradition, a local man once murdered a hired labourer and buried the body in the area of his house. Even today, the occupants of this house are said to be under some sort of curse. Elsewhere in this book I have mentioned a few other murders. In all cases, no one answered to society for these crimes. In fact, some murders were never recorded and some never even discussed.

The Irish, at home in Ireland under British dominance, had learned the necessity of secrecy within a village, community, or parish. Spies were everywhere; always a Judas and some silver. A stray word or look might bring death or imprisonment to a neighbour; priests were hidden in walls, children taught behind doors; a man could be hanged or ostracized for the slightest infraction of the law. Even in Canada, maiming a horse, or stealing, brought maximum penalties, even death. No wonder the Irish learned to say little about murders. "Snitching" here, as in Ireland, was frowned on. Anyone careless with innuendo or gossip might bring dishonour to all. Even today, the people of West Huntley say little to strangers and some say even less to their neighbour about other neighbours. Gossip destroys! Best to live and let live. If a member of their closely-knit community was in trouble, everybody feigned ignorance.

On the next farm, the East 1/2 of Lot 7, was the homestead of the Kellys. Elizabeth Kelly Carter grew up on this hundred acres, the daughter of Tom Kelly (1806-1880) and Mary Mahon (b. 1806), both from

Carlow. Farther down the Golden Line, across from the Madden "Tara" farm, lived another Kelly named Michael (1797-1864) on the West 1/2 of Lot 11. His family, like Tom's, were all born in Ireland and also came out together around 1842. One of Michael's children, Elizabeth (1827-1900), was probably the wife of John Flynn (1824-1897), later to live on the Twelfth Line near the Vaughan Side Road. Michael and Tom were probably brothers, a deduction based on their similar ages, proximity of land in Huntley, and similar county of origin in Ireland. The descendants of Tom Kelly and Mary are still living in the same area today.

Lawrence spoke well of the Kellys. He showed me the house of Lonzo Kelly and Cecilia Scott at the northwest corner of the Dwyer Hill Road and the Hamilton Side Road, once the home of a Joseph Mordy and later Paddy Carroll. Lonzo has two sons living in the area, one son Joseph on the homestead property of Tom, his great-great-grandfather.

Lawrence has known many Kellys. He knew Lonzo's father, Joseph (1892-1947) and his mother Ann Mears (b. 1890) and their three other sons, Louis, Jack and Hilary. He remembered also Joe Kelly's father and mother, Jeremiah (1838-1918) and Hannah Leahy (1849-1919), and the other children John, Elizabeth, Mary Ann, Tom and Richard. Richard inherited his father's land, Lot 5, Concession 12. He never married and, in his later years, boarded with Lawrence and his wife Dorothy Ryan. Dorothy was so good to Richard he left her the whole lot, one hundred and sixty-six acres, a fine tribute to the generosity of both donor and recipient.

Lawrence even remembered Jeremiah's brother, Tom (1843-1910), who married neighbour Jane O'Leary (1842-1934), the daughter of pioneers Samuel O'Leary and Mary Conboy. The O'Leary's had their homestead across the road from the Kelly homestead on the West 1/2 of Lot 7, Concession 11. Incidently, two of Jeremiah's other brothers also married local girls: Martin (b. 1839) married Mary Ann McDermot, probably from Ramsey (b. 1834), and Michael (b. 1836) married Ellen O'Brien (1847-1879) a daughter of Morgan O'Brien and Sarah Lynch. A sister, Elizabeth, as already mentioned, married James Carter. Lonzo Kelly can trace his lineage back to the Robinson settlers, since his grandmother Hannah Leahy was the granddaughter of pioneers Patrick and Johanna Fahey.

Why was it, I asked Lawrence that some families died out so quickly and others like the Kellys, McArtons, O'Connells and Kennedys lived on? A lot of luck was involved, mused Lawrence, but often the longevity of a family was due to the number of sons: the more the better. Certainly the Kennedys had plenty, as did the Kellys. Why the need of so many, I asked? Lawrence pointed out that some sons never married, others died before manhood, some were widowed early as was his father, and some were unable to have children. Also, he said, so many infectious diseases ran rampant through the country, the whole matter of a family's continuity rested on the survival of the fittest and the sheer weight of numbers. The more healthy boys, the better.

We discussed those merciless killers: the diphtheria epidemic of 1884-87, the Spanish flu of 1918-20, the polio viruses in the Twenties and Thirties, and other diseases that settled like dust storms on a neighbourhood: whooping cough, typhoid, small pox, rheumatic fever, German measles and tuberculosis, to name a few. What could medical science do in the Nineteenth Century for diabetes, appendicitis, pneumonia and complicated births? Next to nothing!

Research of church records shows the family havoc caused by disease in West Huntley. If I mention the loss of sons in particular, it's only to prove Lawrence's point about sons being so vital to a family's survival. God knows the loss of any child is the greatest cross any couple can be asked to carry. "God knows" because He lost one Himself. In addition, while certain families have been singled out here as being hit by multiple deaths, it should be remembered that few couples in West Huntley escaped the loss of at least one child during those hundred and twenty years from 1823 to 1943. Even in my own time, I can think of some fourteen and I only knew a few families around the country.

Here are a few examples: in 1883 Pat and Mary Teevens buried three children (two of them boys) within fourteen days; James Brown and Helena Forrest in 1884 lost two boys and a girl within thirteen days; Lawrence Curtin and Ellen Clancy gave up a boy (27) in 1913, two more in 1919 (34 and 21) within three days, and another boy back in 1917 (9). Tim Whyte and Ann Fagan had at least eight children only one of whom lived beyond the age of 8; in fact before Tim himself died in 1911, he had buried all eight children and his wife; Lawrence Manion and Hannah Devine lost three boys; and his brother, John, and Mary McKenna, lost two infant boys in 1893. An O'Kelly family lost four in the winter of '98.

Let's pause a moment to think of them all.

An old Irish adage holds that God always sends more boys in preparation for a coming war. That may well be! But He also knew many would die natural deaths. And He knew many children were needed on a farm. He also wanted the Irish to survive. He wanted their faith to spread across the land. He would not have allowed so many to suffer needlessly in Ireland for His Church and not do something to safeguard their existence here. So He did send many boys to nearly all Corkery's families; in fact, in my time alone He gave some families, boys galore: the Vaughans, the Charlebois, the O'Briens, Mantils, Carrolls, Manions, Kellys, Flynns and Graces had many; Angus Killeen and Carmel Carroll, as mentioned, had seven; Basil O'Keefe and Mary Carroll, five, and John O'Keefe and Margaret Carroll, nine. Obviously one sure way of getting sons was to have healthy males marry Carroll girls. And over the last hundred years, many did.

Lawrence and I also discussed the reluctance by many West Huntley Irish males to marry.

Academics may offer erudite explanations of a biological and psychological nature for such a phenomenon. The world is full of pundits who fire off expert theories on any subject. But Lawrence suggested

Catholic Men's Benevolent Association — 1897. Charter members — nearly all sons of original settlers. Back row: Hugh Corbett, Lawrence Curtin, Hugh Kennedy, John S. Kennedy, Joe Brown. Second Row: Tom O'Keefe, Pat Carter, Ed Vaughan, Francis Herrick. Front Row: Tom Brown, Herbert O'Keefe, John Killeen.

The Ed McDermot family, c. 1895 — His wife Mary Clancy was raised in West Huntley. Ed was the son of Pat and Johanna Dowling and grandson of David Dowling and Mary Mahoney (of Huntley). Back row: Genevieve (married Tom O'Keefe of Huntley), Kate (married Pat Kennedy of Huntley), Tom, Agnes, Nell. Second row: Joe, Minnie, Ed, Mary, David, Jim. Front: Laura.

Jerry Mantil, Jim Sample, Pat O'Brien and Hugh A. Kennedy

All the pictures on this page were taken in 1924.

"Big" Bill Egan

Tom and Joe Kelly

Richard Kelly

"Little" Bill Egan

Jimmy Curtin

John H. Kennedy

Tim Scott

Mike Kennedy

Hugh Kennedy

Mike L. Kennedy

Michael O'Keefe
whose mother was Margaret Finner,
an aunt to brothers Father Finner
and Syl Finner.

Father Charlie Finner (above) was a Holy Cross priest, a missionary to India and a healer. Syl Finner, as seen in the picture on the left, according to his wife, was always thinking. He lived on the Burnt Lands' Road.

The Burnt Lands' Road looking South from Flynn's Hill.

Burial site (1823-50?) on Forrest property near the Burnt Lands' Road.

one simple cause: many young men often came from large, poor families, and lacked the financial resources for marriage.

Usually the older brother inherited the farm and the younger lads had to pull up stakes. Unless of course, they were fortunate enough to win land — lock, stock and barrel, in a dowry. And many did just that in West Huntley, sometimes more than once. Not just royalty marries for love and gain. In any culture and country, it's simply a matter of good *cents*.

The sad truth of the matter, however, is that many boys had no land, skills or education to attract young ladies of means. Colleens from stone houses usually married lads from other stone houses: one seldom ever married beneath one's self. The only escape from bachelorhood for many (and I'm not for a minute disparaging such a vocation) was departure for greener pastures.

Such a move for many a gossoon required a fistful of gumption. Some lacked that! Then, too, parents often convinced their sons to stay on and help out. And before they knew it; it was too late. Life had passed them by!

In addition, many a boy never left the farm because nothing was a-vailable in the cities and towns. In every decade, since the Indians tucked away their teepees, Canada has had its economic slides. Why walk to Ottawa to stand in a breadline half a block long. What was the point! If railroads weren't being built and canals dug and wheat stooked and logs run, it was wise to stay home and put up with the lot the Good Lord seemed to be sending.

Lawrence and I quit the Hamilton Side Road and turned Rosie left on to John Kennedy Way. The first parcel on the right was the O'Learys, and further down, the land of the early Meehans. At the Old Almonte Road, we "hung a right". The farm on the left (400 acres then) once belonged to Lawrence's grandfather Hughie. Just before the road twists down into the lowest part of West Huntley, the little red #7 schoolhouse (now white) caught our attention on a crown of the Kennedy property. Lawrence went there. The first log school was replaced in 1900 by the present frame building. The first school had no floor.

Lawrence talked about his mother. She taught at #7 and also back at #8. She was a Jane McGahey from Kemptville. Not all West Huntley men and women married locally. Some reached out to Arnprior for Legrees, Eganville for Forrests, Manotick for Gleasons, South March for Carrolls, Morans and Williams, and to Perth for Hendricks and Grahams. My own Aunt Mary O'Keefe married Alex Prudhomme from Paris by way of Ottawa and my mother married a Tom Ogilvie from Glasgow. No dowries there; small trousseaus sufficed!

Lawrence said he knew my mother and once took her to a party at Jim Carroll's place (now Pick's) on the Carroll Side Road. The year was 1927. Lawrence sparkled as he spoke of my mother, "One of the best-looking girls in these parts!" I told him she also went with Wilfred Colton and Archie

Currie from Fitzroy Township and Alex Grace from Corkery. I knew each of these men, all sterling lads. My mother had taste! Lawrence was just like them. An old saying has it, "You can always tell a man by the woman he marries!" And to the best of my knowledge, all my mother's West Huntley boyfriends married good women.

As we drove along, Lawrence said the farm on the right was owned in his time by Patrick Meehan, the son of John Meehan and Kitty O'-Connell. Patrick's grandfather was Michael and his grandmother Esther Manion. Patrick was actually raised on the next farm on the right between the Dwyer Hill Road and the Manion Road. John and Kitty had a large family with three of their children marrying Connells from the Mc-Arton Side Road.

Lawrence had known John and Kitty and was particularly fond of Kitty whom he called a great Irish mother. John Meehan, himself, was the son of Mike Meehan and grew up back on the Dwyer Hill Road just before Panmure (on the left heading towards Arnprior). That was the Meehan homestead, East 1/2 of Lot 26.

It was Patrick Meehan who hurried to fetch Father Cunningham on that cold winter evening of Monday, January 6, 1908. Jane Kennedy, mother of three and the apple of husband Michael's eye was dying at age thirty-four. It was a good five miles to St. Michael's. As he and the priest cuttered back across the swamp later that dark evening, Patrick pushed his horse to the limit. Suddenly, Father Cunningham put his hand to Patrick's shoulder and softly said, "Never mind, Pat, ease up, she's already gone!" They continued on to the Kennedy red-brick house on the Hamilton Side Road and sure enough she had already died. Jane had succumbed at the very time Pat was told by Father Cunningham to pull up. Lawrence was only five. His dad never married again.

After a quick visit along the Manion Road and then a look at the proud Kennedy holdings off the Golden Line in Ramsey, I took Lawrence home. I saw him for a minute another day when I dropped off a lemon pie made by my wife. I said, "Lawrence, how are you keeping?" "All right," he said, "I'm getting around." "Lawrence," I said, "you've had such sorrow in your life, there'll be no purgatory for you; you're going to go straight up!" He laughed, "Well Gary, that's doubtful; I've done my share of sinning. But you know, there's one thing I'm mighty proud of. I never took Our Lord's name in vain once in my life!" I told him we had that much in common, for I never had either. We agreed to pray for one another and I began to leave. He followed me out to the car to say good-bye. The last I saw of him, he was standing in the yard stroking his old dog. It was late September.

On January 11, 1990, long after I had finished this chapter, Lawrence died of cancer. All his children were with him. At the funeral there were three priests, and people shoulder to shoulder, upstairs and down. His daughter, Dorothy, gave a farewell address at the end of the service. Her message tore at the insides! She talked of Lawrence's philosophy of life:

running barefoot through the fields ... getting up after falls ... licking obstacles ... carrying crosses with a smile ... eating ice cream ... smelling the roses ... kicking up heels.

Hemingway claimed life eventually breaks everyone. It didn't break Lawrence, although he lost three children, his only granddaughter, his wife, brother, parents, and looked after a handicapped son, Michael, for over fifty years ... he stood tall after it all ... never complained or whined. Chesterton said there were two ways of accepting life: taking it for granted or receiving it with gratitude... Lawrence saw God's will in all things and thanked Him often, regardless of the circumstances.

My tour with Lawrence may well have been his last look at the land he held so dear.

The day he arrived in heaven I can easily imagine the Lord saying to Lawrence who had never used His name frivously, "Lawrence Kennedy, welcome to eternal peace! By the way, you can call me by my first name if you like!"

A Letter from the Farm to Home

(The date of this letter is August, 1939. I was eight years old. It was the end of my third summer on my grandmother's farm. The letter was written in pencil. Carleton Thibideau and Jimmy Statham were chums from Westboro, Nepean. Angus O'Keefe, an uncle was leaving for the harvesting in the West.)

Dear Mother.

Hope you are well and no cold. And daddy is too. And what I am writing for is I would like to know when I started back to school. And hears what to do. Go down to Carleton and asked Carleton when I go to school. I hope Jimmy is well. And everybody is too. Grannie is well and everybody is too. Angus might be going next Saturday. If school started next Monday, write back when you get this letter.

Your Boy

Gary

44

The Mahoney Road

The cellar ruins of Con Mahoney's can still be found in a small gully halfway between the Eleventh and Twelfth Lines on the old Mahoney Road (now Carroll's Side Road). Some of its logs I'm told were sold to the builders of the Mill of Kintail outside Almonte. Shortly after 1823, Con came to West Huntley from Tipperary with his father Patrick and his mother, Margaret. By 1863, their log domain included a store, post office, hotel, tavern and home — a kind of mall as we know it today.

It was a tranquil spot! To the northeast, thick trees cut the wind; to the west, a spring sat on a gentle raise over an old swimming hole; to the north, a rocky hill overlooked the small glen where Patrick first made his home. In the 1940's my uncle rented this land for grazing cattle, and, as it was my job during the summers to fetch and return the cows, I spent a great deal of time there.

The pasture was in the middle of the Burnt Lands, just above Mahoney's Hotel where the land is flat and the devastation of the Great Fire of 1870 most apparent. Today, the area is filling in with heavy growth, but in the early Forties the "pastures" of switch grass were bare of trees. With only a few birch and juniper to stand in its way, the wind fairly whistled across the plateau.

Much of the Mahoney Road which rises gradually out of the valley is made up of smooth limestone swollen into various heights from nature's core. Along its sides, chokecherry and hawthorn trees once grew among the smooth rocks. Inland, towards Highway 44, slow-maturing trees like the butternut, red maple, and oak have already made a start in regaining the stature of their ancestors.

Sparse and rough as it was, these Burnt Lands were a bit of heaven to me ... never had I been so free ... I heard nothing but my own joy in the breeze's call ... no cares, worries or pain ... this was my Tintern Abbey of Wales, my Gray's churchyard of England, my Isle of Iona ... I ran and sang, and ran some more ... I caught the honey strands of twilight in my hair ... I felt the dew between my toes and heard the Killdeers' plaintive "kill-dee" ... my youth had seemingly stopped where time had no meaning!

Now that I know something of the history of that place, I wonder if I was truly alone as I gambolled in its meadows. Many Irish families had made their homes on these Burnt Lands as far back as the early Nineteenth Century. Perhaps they were still there, and in my frolics as a boy they played along. If I had listened, I might have heard the spirited laughter of Patrick Mahoney's grandchildren at play with Michael and Mary Hickey's two sons, Dennis and James. I may have seen William and Catherine Connell passing along that old trail to visit with Tom and Mary Clancy on the Eleventh Line.

Come with me now and stand by this road to Sheppard's Falls! Experience the presence of the past; feel the pulse of good people. There's Dennis Egan returning with the mail ... David O'Keefe on his way for groceries ... Dan Clancy and nephew Tom to hunt for deer ... in and out of the vales they go: Manions, Ryans, Hogans, Cronins, Flynns, Buckleys, Macdonalds, Whites, and Forrests ... this pasture of my dreams still echoes their words and songs and tears and laughter in a land where my days were always green.

Marilyn and Clancy on the Mahoney Road, 1990

A Matter of Cents

On Friday, Duffy walked up to the postmistress in the seaside town of Roselare.

"Give me twenty four-cent stamps, Tess!"

"What would ya be doin' with so many stamps, Duffy? Sure ya hardly write more than a letter a year!"

"Ne'er ya mind, Tess! I've had a stroke of genius. How often can ya take the government for a bob or two? Don't ya know the postage rate's goin' up next week to five cents? That's a saving of twenty cents! Don't ya see the beauty of it, Tess?"

193

45

What Are Friends For!

Huntley had its first taste of self-government in 1850. The voters elected five Councillors, one of whom acted as Reeve. The Councillors then hired the paid help: Township Clerk, three Assessors, one Collector and two Auditors.

Their first meetings were in Public Houses such as Alexander's, Clark's, Dooley's and Newton's. The Councillors had a wide choice of taverns. Huntley in 1851 had an inn or public house for every male in Huntley over twenty. With the population at 2,519, at least four hundred males would be in that category. If the Council met twelve times a year at different locations for each meeting, it would take some thirty-three years to cover them all. That's a fair amount of travelling and a "power" of drinking.

At their meetings the usual concerns of surveying, roads, back-taxes and education filled the agenda. One year, however, the matter of liquor and beer control became top priority. Moonshiners and bootleggers were costing the Township a *staggering* amount in lost revenue. Something had to be done!

So the Councillors soon passed laws for Distillers and Tavern Keepers and backed them up with severe fines and jail terms. And they hired Inspectors with the badges of Marshalls and gave them sets of wheels and horsepower and told them to get out there and destroy all stills, confiscate all poteen and beer, and arrest all culprits.

Some summers later, one of these wardens-of-the-spirits descended on Mahoney's Hotel. Caught unawares, Con had no time to dismantle his illicit equipment and barely enough to escape to his outbuildings.

The Inspector found all the evidence he needed more quickly than he could find Con. The place seemed deserted except for a lone labourer forking manure at the stables. He headed that way.

Con had two factors going for him that day. The Inspector had never met him, and Michael Hickey, Con's neighbour, had been hired to hoe Con's gardens.

Poor Mike, an innocent bystander, a small chunk of a man forced by circumstances to work "out" to feed his family, a docile rustic who deserved better treatment than Con gave him that day. His own trusty neighbour!

Mike had already had his share of tricks played on him. The locals knew his wife Mary Sweeney hated the very smell of liquor. So they used to coax Mike in for a wee dram and with one nip leading to another the poor lad would float home to another verbal lashing by the exasperated Mary. Mike, of course, didn't really mind these escapades. Such "on the house" flings were well worth the price. Con's ruse was far less enjoyable.

By the time the Law reached the stable, Con probably looked every inch a hired man: a bit of grime here and there, ooze up to his shins, tattered overalls, and more than likely a large sweat 'neath the band of a well-tilted straw hat.

"G'day to ya, Sir! I'm lookin' for Con Mahoney. Would you be he?"

"I wish I was, to be sure!" says Con.

"Well then, ya wouldn't happen to know where he's at?" says the Inspector.

"Well, Sir, I do," says Con. "That's himself workin' over dere in the garden."

The Inspector arrested poor Mike on the spot and took him away. No one's sure how long it took him to prove his innocence. And thank God no one ever heard Mary's reaction to Mike's explanation. She must have shook down a few branches.

What is known is that by the time the Inspector returned to Mahoney's, the hotel was closed, and Con was "on the lam".

Con may have escaped the Law, but I'm sure later on, Mary Sweeney had a few choice words for him. After Mary got through with him, Con probably wished he had left with the Inspector.

You've Come A Long Way, Baby

With times so difficult in the old days, honeymoons were often totally eclipsed. On Tuesday, August 22, 1882, Lawrence Curtin married Ellen Clancy, my great-grandmother's sister, at St. Michael's Church in Corkery.

Later that week, Tim Scott, their neighbour, was surprised to meet Lawrence at a threshing. Tim asked:

"Well, Lahr, where did you git to for the honeymoon?"

"Ah, ah," said Lahr quite proudly, "sure me and the Mrs. walked home from church and drew in nine loads of hay before sundown!"

•

Talk about respect for your husband! A sister of Maurie Williams, Rose, married Pat Kennedy, a neighbour of hers in South March. She was sixteen and he considerably older. Throughout the entire marriage, she always referred to her husband in front of others as "Mr. Kennedy". The intimacy of "Pat" was reserved for their times alone.

•

It was once very much a man's world. A birth notice in the Twenties as published in the *Almonte Gazette* often went like this: "Born, August 9, 1921, in Almonte, a boy, son of John H_____ of Corkery." Now, there's a miracle!

46

A Pub in Cork

A heavy mist rolled down St. Joseph's Mount into the basin of Cork City. It was mid-July and the evening soft with a balmy breeze from the sea.

Darkness soon enclosed my rain-coated figure as I strolled along St. Patrick's Quay and across the Brian Boru Bridge onto the Island of Cork City. I was looking for an Irish singing pub.

The streets were almost empty. To my left, a freight for Limerick or Dublin announced its departure from Glanmire Station. Standing on Anderson's Quay, I looked back over the River Lee towards the rear of my hotel. The Metropole's small red neon sign shimmered in the greyness that is so much a part of Cork, even in the day.

Several times I peeked in on inviting taverns. At one, the whole room was full of young people belting out the songs of Broadway. I had never seen such a happier group of youths. It was Ireland at its best! But, I was searching for a pub with a different atmosphere. And, it looked like I was going to be out of luck.

I crossed over the southern arm of the Lee by Parnell Bridge onto Albert Quay. City Hall was on my left and ahead up a steep street called Anglesea was the Blind Asylum and then the Victoria Hospital where an old friend named Murphy worked as a Boiler Engineer.

I had met him and his family two years earlier on the *Inishfallen*. He was going to London for his daughter's marriage. A pleasant, curly-haired, placid man, he shared his sweet tea and sandwiches with my wife and me in the tourist section of the train from Fishguard, Wales, to Victoria Station, London. He had never been out of Ireland before. As I passed the hospital, I wondered if he was on duty. How he was getting on. Even now, twenty years later, I think about him.

Somewhere high above the Lee, I found my pub. It was called The Highwayman, 1798. One look inside and I knew I had been lucky. As the rain began to pelt, I slipped into a room full of the warmth of Irish hospitality. They knew I was a stranger and they took me in.

There were two snug rooms. In the backroom, sat a dozen Irishmen round three oval tables. All were well-dressed: some in suits; others in sweaters and ties; their shoes reflecting the dim light. I was immediately offered a chair and met everyone in the room including a young man named Collins. It turned out they were all miners.

Soon after, a distinguished-looking man called Joe approached the small bar to our right. He wore a dark suit with vest, and a conservative tie which he loosened with one hand as he coddled a tall glass of Guinness with the other. After a healthy swig, he turned to his friends, put his free hand inside his vest, and effortlessly filled the room with mellow song.

Joe sang with the passion of a tenor before the hoity-toity of Covent Gardens. Like Caruso, he gave a hundred and ten per cent. Like John

McCormack of Dublin, he loved to sing with his own people. He was certainly no amateur: everyone listened as if they had never before heard him. He sang the legendary oldies of Kern, Porter, Berlin, those romantic lullabies the likes of which will never be written again. His great chest swelled. Perspiration trickled from his brow. If a song had a chorus, the whole room gave Joe all they had. It was a moment of musical rapture.

After Joe finished, the room seemed quieter. The men were more pensive, alone with their thoughts. After a bit, a man beside me, it was Collins, began to sing. It was the poignant song "Sailor" which up to that time, I had never heard. He was oblivious to the silence around him. Into the amber blackness of his ale, he sang softly about the sea and its men and their romance and sorrow. At the chorus, everyone joined in. And then as easily as he began, Collins's soothing melody ended. And conversation slowly returned.

And so it went around the room ... another voice, another song. Someone asked me to sing. And I did: a shallow rendition of "You Are My Sunshine". I bought a round for our table. The evening slipped away.

Then one by one they made for home. I shook each hand and soon got up to leave before I was alone. I tried not to show any extra warmth for Collins. I have forgotten nearly all their faces, but his I remember, and Joe's.

Collins was singular — spirited, manly, polite, with the freshness of an Irish breeze. He epitomised the spirit of Ireland. In fact, these miners all had something special ... honesty, depth, candour ... a deep strength of character beaten into them by toil beneath the surface in possibly the toughest form of labour ever devised by man.

Outside, a driving rain did little to dampen my spirits.

This past fall I was reminded of Joe and Collins and the rest. I visited the Miners' Museum in Glace Bay, Nova Scotia. In this fine museum, just inside the front door on the left, stands a large coloured 4' x 6' photo of a miner at work. His name was Young. He had died in a mining disaster shortly after its taking.

No pen can do justice to Young. But the camera did: it captured the essence of the Eastern Atlantic. All the distinguished quality of this breed of men radiates from his face. If he walked into a room, he'd fill it with his presence.

Collins was the same.

A Little Backward

Immigrant colleens were pretty "green"! The snobbish, landed gentry referred to them as "fresh young things straight from the bog". One story told of an Irish maid employed at a Boston mansion who descended the house's great winding staircase backwards, because back home the closest invention to stairs she had ever seen was a ladder to the loft.

47

Thorns and Then the Rose

Like his contemporary Walter Scott, Robbie Burns was a Gael. He was therefore a Romanticist, a lover of all nature, and a poetic song writer who told of the little people's lot in a language too simple to be misunderstood and too beautiful to be forgotten. He was the spokesman of every Scot's buried feelings, the keener for every lover's shattered dream.

The son of a tenant farmer, he struggled all his life to make a living. He knew the bitter and the sweet. It was the bitter that enabled him to understand the human heart. An unhappy marriage. A congenital heart ailment. A problem with drink. And worst of all, the loss to tuberculosis of his only true love, Mary Campbell, before they could be wed.

He had loved this dairy maid from Montgomery Castle near Tarbolton with all the devotion a man of his great sensitivity could offer. He spent the remainder of his life trying to find another Mary in other women, friendships, alcohol, and writing. Only in his poems did he touch her spirit. Only in death at thirty-seven did he finally find her. How well he knew the meaning of his line:

"The best-laid schemes o' mice an' men
  Gang aft a-gley"

Twists in fate come to everyone. Life changes in seconds. No explanations are possible. The ways of the Light are not ours. Not easy to understand; even more difficult to accept.

On February 9, 1890, my grandaunt, Mary O'Keefe Rowan, was visiting her mother, Margaret Finner O'Keefe, on the O'Keefe homestead. Margaret had just lost her husband Tom two weeks earlier. Mary had just finished telling her mother how fortunate she was to still have her own husband when word came he had just died. Not long ago, the lovely Kathleen Madden Carroll lost her gentle husband Joe when the car he was repairing fell on him. My cousin Inez O'Keefe Beach found her good husband, Byron, dead in the stable, the victim of a heart attack.

Another grandaunt, Agnes McDermot, while serving overseas as a nurse in the Great War, married an army officer named Poulton only to lose him two weeks later in the French trenches. Years later on Remembrance Day, she laid the wreath at the Memorial Cenotaph on behalf of the Province of Ontario.

I found my own mother dead on her bedroom floor. She, herself, lost her husband Tom very suddenly. My good old Algebra teacher at St. Patrick's College, Leo Byrne, born and bred in Huntley, lost his father and sister in a train crash in Arnprior. Carmelita had been accepted as a Sister of St. Joseph in Pembroke and her father was taking her there on that fatal day. A missionary retreat master once told me of a newly ordained priest, who after giving his final blessing at his first Mass, dropped dead.

I knew a seminarian of the Scarboro Foreign Missions. We used to play ball together at St. Augustine's Seminary in Toronto. After eight years of training, he was ordained and assigned to Japan. On his way there, his plane crashed and his life here was over! All of us have experienced the meaning of the Spanish maxim: "Death is as certain as life is uncertain!"

Fate is never more fickle than in matters of romance! How many first romances fizzle? How many engagement rings are returned? How many doors of love are seemingly closed only to have windows open on truer romance.

How strange it was that my mother from "little old Corkery" married a man from Glasgow, Scotland! Her first engagement to an Ottawa man had ended disastrously; he continued to harass her after the breakup, even resorting to lies to get even. She ran to Toronto to her sister Mary to escape his intentions. He followed her. She wrote letters to him threatening police intervention.

Finally he relented and my father entered her life. Although he died after only twenty-four years of marriage, she did find love. The other beau raised a large family. But his wife had a price to pay; her husband was an alcoholic.

My mother's sister, Mary O'Keefe Prudhomme, was also separated from her first serious love — only in a different way. His name was Gregory Mantil, the youngest son of John Mantil and Mary Ann Foley of Panmure. He worked for the Ottawa Dairy and boarded in Ottawa. She was nineteen and he was twenty-seven. According to my mother who told the story to my older daughter, Catherine, Greg and Mary were to be married.

But on August 6, 1920, he had a terrible accident. He was lighting a stove with wood alcohol. It exploded. His clothes caught fire. On August 13, after suffering the most damnable pain imaginable, he mercifully died. His funeral at St. Michael's, Corkery, on August 16, was unparalled in attendance and grief. For Greg was from a large family and like all the Mantils before and since, very popular in the community.

Like Robbie Burns, Mary Prudhomme's betrothed worked in a dairy. Like Burns, she too was separated tragically from her first love. And like Burns, she eventually married a person of French lineage: Burns married Jean Lamour and Mary, Alex Prudhomme from Paris, France. But unlike Burns, Mary found happiness in her marriage. Alex did too! He had come to Canada to escape an unhappy home life. And here he found peace with his Mary.

Perhaps, true happiness in love only follows an unfortunate experience which makes us better appreciate our new found romance. Must we first lose at love if we are to win?

Burns never did find a love to fill the emptiness left by Mary. But, without Mary, he never could have written such lines as:

"As fair art thou, my bonnie lass,
So deep in love am I;
And I will love thee still, my dear
Till a'the seas run dry"

The "Little People" Are Shy

Part of a summer holiday in Ireland for my very Irish cousin Earl Hogan and wife Dorothy included an afternoon jaunt down the main drag of Kilkenny Town. A display in an Irish craft shop had caught their attention when suddenly one of them noticed a reflection in its window of a little old lady scurrying along the far side of the street.

They both turned for a closer look. The lady was about four-foot-two and wore an old-fashioned coloured skirt and bonnet. Over one arm hung a small shopping basket. Her course was dead ahead.

Earl decided to get a picture without getting too close and embarrassing her. He hurried down his side of the street as the basket-lady clipped along on hers. Finally Earl crossed over until he was about twenty-five feet away in the middle of the street and snapped a profile shot. She was alone in the picture.

Sometime the following week, the developed roll came back. Every picture turned out including the one of the street in Kilkenny. Except for one small detail — the basket-lady was not in the picture; nothing but thin air and shop windows where she had been seen.

(Earl Hogan couldn't be more Irish: a descendant of Brian Boru, the greatest All King of Ireland, Earl can also lay claim to being related to "Galloping Mick Hogan", leader of the vigilantes (called the Rapparees by the English). His headquarters were in Clare, but he fought also in Tipperary and Limerick. One night Mick's riders blew up King William's five hundred wagons loaded with gunpowder and supplies destined for the fight in Limerick between James II and William.)

Spirits Leave No Traces

Back in the Twenties an old-timer from the Twelfth Line decided it was time he went to see Doctor Dunn about a persistently sore throat, the irritation of which he himself had long attributed to years of drinking.

When the good doctor said he could find nothing visibly wrong with the throat, the dumbfounded farmer, known for his caustic wit, chided the doctor, "Look again, Doc! There's the price of two farms down there somewhere and there has to be something to show for them!"

200

A Funny Thing Happened After Rekindling the Fire

Buster came to Lanark County as a young man to find work. He felt at home! His roots were nearby. His father had been born on a farm in West Huntley and moved away with his parents after the Great Fire of 1870.

Not long after Buster's arrival, he fell in love with Milly. Unfortunately, Milly had an older brother who couldn't stomach Buster. He tried to break up the romance. He succeeded. Buster simmered and stewed.

One summer, Buster was working at Maurie Williams's farm on the Dwyer Hill Road. They were digging a drainage tunnel in the cellar. The going got tough and they decided to blast. It was around this time that Buster got the idea of making a rocket out of Milly's brother, Archie.

Upon the completion of the work at Williams's, Buster pocketed the remaining bit of blasting powder. Later, at Archie's house in Lanark County, he took down two pieces of firewood from the backshed woodpile. He bore a hole in each block, poured in the powder, stuffed the holes with catalogue paper and put the blocks back on the pile.

As it happened, Milly and Archie went away for a few days in early winter and asked a neighbour to keep the home-fires burning.

No one knows how many trips the neighbour made to the woodpile before picking up a loaded stick. But, one night he dropped a block in the stove, gave the fire a poke, replaced the lids, and put away the poker. As he headed outside, an explosion drove lids, pipes, grates, and red hot embers over walls and ceiling. The neighbour couldn't sit down for weeks and had to be coaxed to stoke a fire again.

Now, Archie didn't have many enemies. So it wasn't long before the finger of justice singled out Buster. The Perth judge must have decided Buster never really intended to kill anyone for he gave him a fairly light sentence.

After his jail term, Buster became a model citizen! He worked from six to six at the gristmill. But it was all over! The brother got the message, but not the *powder*, and poor Buster got both from Milly. None ever married.

Years later, Archie was killed by a train at the crossing near his little white house. To the best of our knowledge, the engineer wasn't Buster.

Did Archie live in fear of Buster?

Did Archie ever light his stove again? Did the neighbour ever lose his fear of woodpiles?

Did Archie frighten away all Milly's suitors?

These queries will never be answered.

And to think it all began in Maurie Williams's cellar in West Huntley.

Thoughts on a Penny

Just a wee deoch and doruis
Just a wee drap that's a
Just a wee deoch and doruis
Before we gang awa

Ignatius O'Keefe once gave me an 1857 copper bank token. It had been found years and years before between two taverns on the Carroll Side Road. Mahoney's Tavern, as mentioned, was in a vale about a third of a mile east of the Burnt Lands' Road and Egan's Tavern was almost adjacent to the Dwyer Hill Road where Angus Carroll now has his home. It's not surprising to find two watering holes only a third of a mile apart: the need for nourishment could be acute in pioneer days when weather and terrain could easily weaken the healthiest traveller. Many a farmer went to Mahoney's just for the mail and had this *weakness* suddenly come upon him.

The bottom half of the large penny had been run over. But aside from a bad bend, its "fine" markings suggested limited usage before its loss. Much larger and thicker than the later Victorian, Edwardian, and Georgian "large cents", issued from 1858-1920, this token had been minted in England for the Bank of Upper Canada which in itself is politically interesting in that Upper Canada as well as Lower Canada ceased to exist under those titles as far back as 1841. In 1841, the two central geographical divisions of East Canada were combined under the name Province of Canada which also included the wide expanse beyond the Great Lakes known formerly as West Canada.

The monetary system, up until 1858, in the British Colonies and Provinces had been the pound sterling: four farthings equalling a penny, twelve pence (pennies), a shilling; twenty shillings, a pound or sovereign; and a pound plus one shilling making up a guinea. The slang "bob" was for a shilling and a "quid" was a pound.

Those were the days when a pound was a pound, in that money was really worth the value of the mineral used in its mintage. The sovereign, guinea and pound were made of gold, the shilling of silver, and the lower valued cents, etc., made of heavy amounts of bronze and copper. Sterling was also used in crowns (five shillings), half crowns, florins (two shillings) and in sixpence and threepence pieces. The less the value of the coin, the smaller its size and silver content. Those were the days too when, both here and in England, sovereigns were for Kings and the rich, and halfpennies and farthings for peasants and the poor.

Naturally Cornelius Mahoney and Michael Egan seldom heard the ring of British coins on their bars. Not only was their clientele too poor, but the British government had severely limited its minting of pennies, tokens, and halfpennies for the Colonies, and later for Provinces of Canada, Acadia, Newfoundland, and Prince Edward Island. In 1851, the reins were loosened a little, albeit reluctantly for the Province of Canada. Large cents and sterling silver five-, ten-, and twenty-cent pieces were minted, mainly to comply with the Canadian trend to the decimal system. In 1870, after another twelve-year moratorium in production, the British again began filling orders, placed this time by the Home Government of the New Dominion of Canada with the understanding, of course, that production costs were borne as usual by the Canadian people.

As a result of these decades of enforced shortage in currency, many colonies, provinces, banks, and corporations, previous to 1851, had made their own coins and tokens. At one point the colony of New France even issued playing cards as currency, since France had also refused to issue coins.

Another alleviation to the money-flow problem was the acceptance of foreign currencies into Canada. The American silver fifty-cent piece gradually became more in demand as the Canadian economy began to pick up around 1870. Another popular silver piece was the Spanish piece-of-eight known as the Mexican dollar while Portuguese doubloons and French livres were also much in evidence.

All monies of course had to be first valued against the British pound which had been the measuring stick of commerce in Canada for centuries. For example, five American silver dollars were rated at $4.86 per pound as were five Canadian single-dollar banknotes (first printed in 1870). The Mexican dollar was worth four shillings twopence sterling, which exactly equalled one dollar under the American-Canadian decimal system. In 1870, the first Canadian fifty-cent silver coins were minted, but only in limited numbers. Mike and Cornelius had to be on their toes with so much foreign and homemade currency floating around their little taverns.

Every day the history of the world and Canada passed through their fingers. For example, among the French monies there was the one-penny token (with the familiar habitant on the obverse) and also the dix-centimes bronze French-Empire coin with its profile of Emperor Napoleon III. From England came the heavy bronze double-chin profiles of Kings George III and IV who reigned over Britain, Canada, and Ireland from 1760 to 1830, those same Georges who barely knew where Ireland was and after whom no Catholic Irishman in his right mind would ever name a child, let alone his donkey.

Other interesting coins would have been the Bank of Upper Canada's halfpenny with its Knight and faithful steed in battle and the large one cent with the sweetly braided laurel-leaved head of a young Victoria, "dei gratia". There was also the one-penny crownless "noggin" of Edward VII, and the intricate Lower Canada "bouquet sous" with their different reverses of roses, thistles, shamrocks and wheat.

How Irish hearts must have stirred at the sight of the "halfpenny-harp" tokens introduced into Lower Canada by Irish sympathizers from

Dublin to challenge the Anglo-Saxons. And what of the nostalgia felt for the "walrus" penny tokens of the Magdalen Islands and the halfpenny "sailing ships" of Newfoundland and Nova Scotia. And how the French must have got their wind up over the copper "propaganda" penny tokens of Field Marshall Wellington introduced into Lower Canada by the British to commemorate (for the French?) the victory over the Corsican-Italian, Bonaparte; as much as to say, "Let that be a lesson to ya!"

Today the penny, cent or "copper" has little value. But up until 1950, many articles, services, foods, and entertainment were measured in cents, not dollars. In the 1930's a Canadian penny bought a handful of jellybeans, gumdrops, or "blackballs". A thirty-ounce bottle of Kik Cola cost five cents. My mother used to buy her groceries in 1935 from Bambrick and Company at 50 George Street in Ottawa where she paid thirty-five cents for two pounds of sausage, twenty cents for two gallons of potatoes, twenty-five cents for half a pound of tea, and twenty cents for two cans of soup. Bing Crosby sang of "Pennies from Heaven" and in another song, kisses and hugs went for a penny. At the circus you could "roll a bowl a ball a penny a pitch" and Penny Arcades attracted young and old.

Tickets in the 1930's on the Britannia Streetcar Line from Holland Avenue to Britannia Park were three cents each, two for a nickel, and ten for twenty-five cents. In the early 1940's, I enjoyed many a Friday lunch of fish and chips for sixty-five cents at Charlie's Bus Diner at Island Park Drive in the West End. Stamps and suckers were a penny and double - dip cones at White's in Britannia only ten cents.

In the summer of 1945, I remember pumping gas at Mel Lockhart's grocery/gas station just outside Almonte. A gallon sold for only twenty-five cents. In Ottawa, I bought my gloves and socks at Woolworth's Five and Ten on Queen Street.

In Egan's and Mahoney's day, the penny token was worth its weight. With whisky going for twenty-five cents a quart, the token similar to the one found by my ancestors would have paid for two stiff shots, since its decimal value was two cents.

Of course, liquid measurement in those days was gallons, quarts, pints, ounces, drams, and drops. A dram was sixty drops and an ounce was eight drams. So whenever a Scotsman or Irishman in answer to an offer of a drink said, "Ah, sure, a wee drop would hit the spot," they were being particularly gracious in their response — a "wee drop", was but one sixtieth of a dram. I had an uncle once who, if you offered him a piece of your chocolate bar, would reply, "Just a taste, thanks!" and then proceed to eat the whole thing. The English language must have a definition for such statements as "going outside for a breath of air" or "taking a step around the block", but I can't find one.

In reality, a snort of whisky, neat, as enjoyed by an able-bodied Corkery farmer was probably at least two ounces (sixteen drams and count 'em, nine hundred and sixty drops). No doubt the liquid measurement served by Egan and Mahoney was "right on" — right down to the last nine hundred and sixtieth drop as it were: full value for hard-earned money. I remember a bartender in Ireland in 1968 drawing Guinness ale for his regulars and filling each tumbler to the very brim with no froth or glass showing. There, a man's ale was a cherished item just as it would have been in those taverns on Mahoney Road.

Who lost this 1857 penny token I hold before me? Was it Michael Hickey, Tom Clancy, William Connel, John Ryan, Edward Kennedy, Matthew Tobin or Michael Grace? Perhaps it was Michael Lynch, James Vaughan, Cornelius Curtin, John Bresnahan or Tom Brown. Or maybe, James Liston, John McNamara, William White, Edward Keefe, Simon McGrath, a Corcoran, Sullivan, Roach, Morrissey, O'Brien, Buckley, Flynn, Forrest, Curran, Delaney, Hogan, Mantil or a McDonald ... all of whom plodded over those limestone hills of Mahoney's Road when Egan and Mahoney were in business.

True, many felt these taverns were "dens of iniquity" and, true, many an Irishman found fuel there for his *sickness*. But all things considered, these taverns among the rocks of Huntley's glens must also have been centres of hospitality for many pioneers: a place to have letters read from home, a rendezvous for yarning, cards, dominoes, darts, checkers... Oh, to hear again the violin's tender Irish cry from round the comfy fires in Mahoney's Inn and watch the mists of Ireland fall unashamedly from Irish eyes ... and how oft'n from there on a winter's night did the spontaneous songs of the grey, calloused and lonely follow the westerly breezes of West Huntley back to the very shores of Bantry Bay.

Local Guides in Ireland

Ask a crofter in County Cork for the directions to Blarney Castle and his answer might go like this:

"G'day, Mister, it's a gran'day, a gran'day, indeed, a fine day to be goin' to, Blarney Castle, did you say? ... Sure I know it well, like the back of my hand... not too far, so it is ... My mither, the Lord ha' mercy on her, oft'n spoke of its beauty and she herself so fair and tak'n from us so early ... So now then, you hold to this road the way you're faced 'til you cross the crik beyond the hill, where ma brither drowned ... Sure t'was just as well, the crature had no life to speak of a'tall, d'ya see? No life a'tall ... Blarney, is it?

"Whar was I? Ah, yes! ... ya come to a cross, but keep on to the cheese factory, shut down now ... not surprisin', the owner's son, a quare if thar ever was one ... laced the cheese one day with some drug setting half the county off its rocker ... I met him once, quare, quare he was ... All before your time, I'd say, poor, poor d'vil ... Well, there you are now, don't give in, you're almost at it ... Keep to the sun and mind the sign, 'Blarney Castle, ten miles' ... God go with ya, Mister! ... What's that ya say? ... Ah, sure, 'tis thanks for nawthin! ... Be off wid ya, now!"

The Great Fire (See map on page 351)

At 8:25 a.m. August 17, 1870, the Canada Central train from above Arnprior had already left Pakenham and was well into its eight-mile run to Almonte.

The almost-new engine tugged its load along the crest of the Mississippi River sending puffs of smoke and spark into summer blue.

On either side, virgin white pine up to four feet thick cast shadows on birch, spruce, beech and elm, and the silver markings of rock and stream set off hard-won clearings of meadow and farm.

In a few minutes the train would pass on its port side an awesome pinery which began on a hill of flatrock limestone and ran some twenty-five square miles across Ramsey Township into West Huntley.

Before the early afternoon was out, this whole section would be forever known as the Burnt Lands. The vegetation had only a few hours to live.

The country round was rugged. A worthy adversary for the Scottish weavers who took it on. A country not much unlike parts of their own Highlands with the colours of all the tartans rolled into a haunting beauty, a beauty that not only gave up its privacy grudgingly but also punished unmercifully those who ignored its laws.

This was the land of the pioneers. Heroes like Lowrey, Wilkie and Muir of 1819 and Snedden, Leckie, Lindsay and McEwan of 1820. Men who built dreams into realities and gave back gainful labour to uprooted clans. And the heroines among them, the good women who with dutiful devotion did it all and succumbed long before the grey had touched their temples.

Soon this Wednesday train to Carleton Place and Brockville would be pulling into Rosebank in Norway Pine Falls. The station was perched on the East Side of the village, just a clapboard shack the size of a chicken coop with the name Snedden displayed beneath one of its pitched roofs. It can still be seen today in a sideyard of Green's house on the Panmure Road waiting for the next train that will never come.

But on that summer's day years ago, the busy station proudly looked westward on a bustling community built around a setting of natural charm.

The village's early success was a tribute to the Snedden brothers who cut it out of a bank in '22 and called it Snedden's Mills. In the 1850's, the name became Rosebank and in 1874, Blakeney. But somehow Rosebank suits it best.

Over the next fifty years, several industries in grist, beer, lumber and tanning sprang up. But it was the little woollen mill in the vale on an island by the rapids that really put Rosebank on the map and brought buyers from near and away to purchase the annual production of over sixty miles of quality tweed.

Even on that morning in August in 1870 at nine standard time, the mill's twenty-five weavers had already put in three hours more of a sixty-six hour work week.

Today, Rosebank deserves a second look. It is due for rediscovery. From Highway 29 the Rosebank road drops into a hidden dale where the Mississippi River divides in three under two bridges before slipping over rippling ramps of rock to secret places.

Once this road went straight up the far eastern embankment, but now it winds contentedly along the valley wall up to the village centre. There, a few crofts still put on their best front alongside a church, store, and the famous Snedden "Stopping Place". With a little imagination, one can see yesterday's children at play, the wagons and horses hitched outside Fenton's Hotel, the farmers round the smithy, the dusty streets and stray dogs, and not far away, the black engine panting white whiskers at the station.

One day at Rosebank, I met an Elmer Foster, whose family are long-time residents. He remembered his father saying he often stopped for lunch at the Snedden Hotel even as late as the Thirties. The house still looks out on the Blakeney Road at a point where traffic from Pakenham, Panmure and Almonte meets at a four-way cross. Old-timers still talk of this "hotel of hospitality", a tribute to its owners, the Snedden family, whose descendants still live in the area. In fact, even after the village's name was changed, the Railroad faithfully adhered to the name "Snedden".

I asked Elmer why a pretty name like Rosebank was ever changed. But he pointed out only half the village became Blakeney. The area on the west side of the river retained the name Rosebank and keeps it even today. It is regrettable that post office officials and town planners are often more political than patriotic, and attach labels to communities that do nothing for nostalgia or the ear. Imagine the pleasure of a sixteen-mile drive on a Sunday afternoon with calls at enticingly named villages like Snedden's Mills, Sheppard's Falls (Almonte), Apple Tree Falls (Appleton) and Morphy's Falls (Carleton Place). Refreshing names, in any language.

The day I met Elmer, I toured a bit out the Panmure Road to an older cross of the Panmure, Rosebank, Pakenham Roads. Not far from there, still on the Panmure Road, I saw nailed on a tree a small sign saying "John Currie". Beside it was a most inviting laneway, a throwback to the Thirties, never running exactly straight at any time, too pretty to last and too true to disappoint.

Sure enough, as I drove along the lane, the shifting shadows suddenly opened out onto acres and acres of naturally groomed greenery running miles away into West Huntley.

In front, capping a rise on the wood's edge was the Currie's white home. A picture of bliss. I had enjoyed similar scenic surprises along the River Lee in Cork and over the Knockmealdown Mountains in Tipperary where hills tumble willy-nilly in grandeur, but somehow this clearing on John Currie's farm had its own special charm. Perhaps such sweet scenes of serenity are not just to be found faraway in foreign lands, but also at home a few miles from our own doorsteps.

Later, I learned regretfully that John Currie had recently died and left a young family. Beauty and tragedy often keep company. A shadow can only fall in the light.

But to get back to that day of August, 1870. While the little engine rested with its yellow-coloured first-, and second-class passenger cars at the Snedden Station, a major topic of conversation among villagers and passengers was the drought upon the land. Hay yields had been small and crops of wheat, corn, potatoes, and turnips were already stunted and ripening before their time.

The green was almost gone from the valley.

Some of the hundred and eighty residents of Rosebank jokingly remembered the record snowfall of 1869 and wished they had some of it now. Snow began to fall that February 11 when Whelan was hanged in Ottawa for the shooting of Darcy McGee and continued to come down for the biblical time of forty nights until the land was unrecognizable.

Now these same unfortunates were in the sixtieth day of a dryness that would crack a rock. A scorching sun and dry wind were sucking the last moisture from the pine. And this day of the 17th looked no different than the others.

In actual fact, it was to be very different. For in just two or three hours, somewhere along the Almonte side of Rosebank, a work-crew of questionable sanity and, as it turned out, squelched identity, was soon to lose control of a brush fire and thereby set off a ring of destruction that would kill twelve people, torch "four hundred" farms in several townships, put two thousand refugees on the roads and threaten the very Houses of Parliament themselves.

Feeding upon dreams and treasures, the fire would strike with swift finality. Like a tidal wave breaking on uneven shores, it would form a massive broken line of crimson zigzagging across the land at the caprice of wind and terrain. Thick stands of pine would take days to burn; open fields were gone in seconds. Flames would "lick up" telegraph posts, railway ties, and fences with the speed of "galloping horses". A few stone houses and churches would stand the test but those of log and shingle would be quickly consumed. At one point, the burning front would be forty miles wide and up to twelve miles deep often running back on itself as if dissatisfied with its devastation.

Terror would run before it and despair in its wake.

Nature would become red with rage.

Hurricane winds would toss sparks from pine top to pine top and the instantaneous-exploding trees were to spew resinous gases and smoke up to "three hundred and sixty miles" away.

"Great, great sheets of flame" ... "still intact" would ride the air "vomiting from clouds of smoke" or "bursting like monsters out of the woods". "Blazing cinders" ... without discrimination "dropped from the air" onto "wagons of belongings" or the dress of a child.

The fire would leave a wasteland: charred trunks with burnt roots fallen across one another in blackened fields; giant smouldering pines, too green to burn, standing like naked sentinels; "the very earth ... ablaze" and "the whole sky ... aflame". And behind the red line, the silence of desolation.

Back at Snedden's Station, that August 17, the mushrooming grey from fresh wood meant the train was ready for the three-mile climb to Almonte. Its red and black trim flashed in the sun. The conductor slipped his Waltham watch into his vest and with a spirited "Alla Boarrd" waved the engineer into action. Sparks fanned out from the spinning wheels as the iron horse shook itself to attention.

Outside town, at what is now McPhail's Side Road, blasts from the whistle sent animals scurrying. In the distance, passengers could see the bonfires of logs and brush where men were literally playing with death.

By 8:10 that evening, about the time the train returned from Brockville, the great pinery where poor John Currie was to settle a hundred years later, would be nothing but a smoking ruin, and further west the communities of Huntley Centre, old Stittsville, Hazeldean, and Bell's Corners would be in ashes.

Some eight miles east of Rosebank, on that fatal day, thirty-one-year-old Mary Anne Gleeson Egan of West Huntley was standing on a hill near her Ninth-Line home. She was watching "the pillars of smoke" rising in the western sky. In her arms, she held her one-year-old twins, Roderick and Patrick.

The one o'clock sun shone relentlessly. It was "sultry", so "calm" ... "not a leaf" was "stirring". The smell of smoke rode "the visible rays" of heat. A weight of approaching danger had settled over the land. She prayed.

Two miles southwest near the little red schoolhouse on the Old Almonte Road, Hugh Kennedy was praying too as he sat nervously astride the top of his father's stable roof. His assignment was to throw water from a big churn on any stray embers, a responsibility he hoped came from his father's trust and not disinterest.

Below Hugh, across the western side of the buildings, Pat Reilly and a dozen hired men were pick and shovelling a fireguard. Pat had raced out some six miles with team and carriage and men from the village of Almonte. Fire was no stranger to him.

As an entrepreneur in Almonte and proprietor of the British Hotel, he had seen or heard about Loyalist Shipman's uninsured losses of his grist and woollen mills in 1852, and, in the same decade, the burn-outs of Bennie's Corners and the Fuller Foundry and Machine Shops in Carleton Place. And, just two years earlier, after one of the hottest and driest summers in memory, he no doubt had witnessed the Christmas-Eve burning of Father O'Malley's Church of the Holy Name of Mary (built 1842). And now poor O'Malley was stationed at St. Michael's, Corkery, with the fire coming straight at him again.

Pat knew that unless the fire turned, it would be upon them in an hour, two at the most. The west wind was presently pushing the fire slightly across and mostly along the Town and Twelfth Lines. Hugh Kennedy's four hundred acres lay directly in its path on the crest beyond the Long Swamp between the Eleventh and Twelfth Lines.

Sitting up there like the proverbial clay pigeon, Hughie Kennedy gazed at the distant dark clouds of smoke whiffing out the sun. He wondered how his neighbours further along the stone-crest would make out: the Flynns, Forrests, Hickeys, Graces, Whites, O'Briens, Morrisseys, Macdonalds, Buckleys, O'Keefes and Mahoneys. And the families in the valley: the O'Keefes, O'Briens, Sullivans, Egans, Hogans, Roches, Manions, Browns. What of them, thought Hughie?

Meanwhile, in that valley, at O'Keefe's Corners, three miles to the north, on the Eleventh Line, my great-grandparents, Tom and Margaret O'Keefe had even less time to prepare than the Kennedys. Already the smell of smoke moved around the buildings.

As a boy on their farm where the Carroll Side Road crosses the Dwyer Hill Road, I experienced the sensual stimulae brought down by those same west to southwest winds: the lonesome wails of the daytime Pembroke Locals and the nighttime Sleepers for the West, the precursory smell of the rains, their swell of sound beating across the Burnt Lands' bush, and the silent puffs of dust exploding on the Eleventh Line as the first heavy drops drew near.

Imagine the terror and turmoil at O'Keefe's! The decisions to be made. To make a run for it? If so, how far could they get with three adults and nine children in one wagon and one buggy? And which direction to go? Up the Mahoney Road (now the Carroll Side Road) across the fire's path to the safety of Almonte? Or down the same route to the Panmure Road behind James Brown's farm and then back to Panmure? Or was it to be directly back the Eleventh Line hoping to reach beyond the fire's avenue of destruction?

And what belongings to take — bedding? utensils? clothes? furniture? And where to put it all in one wagon? Was there time to bury articles and keepsakes? If so, what? Where? And what to do with the livestock? Herd the eight cattle? Maybe the twelve sheep would follow. The six pigs would be on their own. The fourth horse would easily tag along.

210

Or was the idea of escape already too late? Was staying on and making the best of it the only way? — Lying face down in the fields between rows of turnips and potatoes; putting wet blankets on the roof; filling the well half-full of rocks and putting some of the family down there with wet turf and greens thrown over protective planks.

Yet no matter what the decision, to flee or to stay, some system of looking after one another had to be worked out. Perhaps they decided William (20) would help Catherine (8); Edward (15) would care for Michael (5); John (15) to watch over Mary (13); Thomas (11) with David (10), two-year-old Stephen with his mother (40), and Tom (50) and his brother David (60) looking after everybody.

At the end of the O'Keefe lane on the next farm over, Pat and Mary Hogan and their seven children were in their own state of preparations. And no doubt Dave and Bridget Egan, on the property presently owned by Mary and Angus Carroll, had been down to O'Keefe's to discuss the crisis. And John O'Keefe, brother to Tom, living on the East half of Tom's lot, had probably come up from "down below" with some of his four grown children.

Further along the Carroll Side Road and up the Panmure Road to the church, other families like the Browns, Manions, Roches, Corcorans and Finners were busy making ready. Each family was on its own and left to its own ingenuity.

Then, a strange event occurred. Amid all the confusion, heat, bawling, crying, oinking and neighing, Margaret Finner O'Keefe, the mother of nine, made a personal decision, one told me by her grandchild, my aunt, Mary O'Keefe Prudhomme, a few months before she died.

Margaret took an old chipped plaster-of-Paris cross down from its resting place and walked quickly across the brown field towards the Mahoney Road.

As her little feet flew under her heavy skirt, no doubt her heart pounded and her mind raced.

As the oldest of ten Upper Canada children and the mother of nine pre-Confederation ones, Margaret was a seasoned veteran of pioneer life.

She knew men and women can do only so much and that in spite of good intentions and unstinting sacrifices, crises come which can only be resolved by God Himself. And she knew the likelihood of His intervention depended largely, but not always, on the degree of faith and love held for Him by those asking for His help. What she was about to do, showed that Margaret indeed had a strong working relationship with the Father. She was confident that if she, His daughter, asked Him anything in the name of Jesus whose cross she now carried, even the impossible, like the abatement of an uncontrollable fire, would be granted.

Such unwavering faith in Providence was not uncommon among pioneers. God's presence in their daily life was a matter of course for early Huntley families like the Kennedys, Manions, Mordys, Hodgins,

Cavanaghs, Johnstons, Mooneys, Grahams, Acres, McBrides and Rivingtons.

Long before their chapels and churches were built on hopes, prayers and pennies, handfuls of Presbyterian, Methodist, Anglican and Catholic faithful gathered for services as regularly as possible in conveniently chosen homes, barns, and stables. Circuit-riding missionaries periodically came by to conduct services and administer sacraments: Reverend George Farr for the Methodists, Reverend Glen for the Presbyterians, and Reverend Amos Ainsley who rowed the Ottawa River from Quebec to help guide the Anglicans of both March and Huntley. Margaret herself would remember Father MacDonald from Lanark and Fathers Terence Smith and Peter O'Connell from Richmond whose parish boundaries extended to wherever their services were needed.

One favourite stopping place for the Catholic saddle-bagging priests was the Panmure home of "Long" Tom O'Keefe and Mary Foley. Margaret's childhood home was on the Fourth Line of Fitzroy about a mile away. And I'm sure she'd remember the priest staying at the O'-Keefe residence for three or four days in the summer of 1846 performing marriages, hearing confessions, celebrating the Eucharist, and baptizing waiting babies, one of whom was John Currie, the son of her neighbour, Pat.

For God-fearing men in the area like Pat Currie, Tom O'Keefe, Benjamin Finner (Margaret's father), Denis Gallaghan, James Mantil and Edward Lunney, religion was a privilege and a freedom and even a luxury. And while many were tough, rough, and hard-drinking, they still walked through the virgin forests with one hand on the axe and the other in God's. Margaret had their spirit!

From their home on the Mahoney Side Road, Dennis Egan and his wife Bridget Manion would have watched Margaret coming up the tree-lined road. They would have gone out in their yard to greet her. At the top of the first hill they would have seen her stop and turn slightly to her right in the fire's direction. And then they would have knelt and blessed themselves as Margaret held the twelve-inch grey cross high above her head with its image of Christ facing the horizon.

They knew Margaret was praying and they joined her, as did all her family back in her front yard some two hundred yards away.

I saw a picture once of Margaret taken in 1908 at her nephew's ordination celebration back at the Finner homestead. She stood alone for the photographer. Even in her eighties she had that regal bearing and reserved resoluteness so common to many of the Mantil women. I could well imagine her crying out that day into the west wind, "In the name of Jesus, save us!"

Sometime, shortly after Margaret's prayer, the wind did change. Five miles away on the Fourth Line of Fitzroy, just across the road from where Margaret was raised, sixty-one-year-old Pat Currie and his family knew

Four of the finest Irish after lunch at Skerries, a seaside resort north of Dublin, 1970: Marilyn O'Grady Ogilvie, Monsignor Farrell from Drogheda, Ireland, a missionary all his priestly life to the Kingston diocese including Perth, Ontario, Eva O'Keefe Ogilvie, and Sister Margaret Power, a Sister of Martha from North Sydney, Nova Scotia.

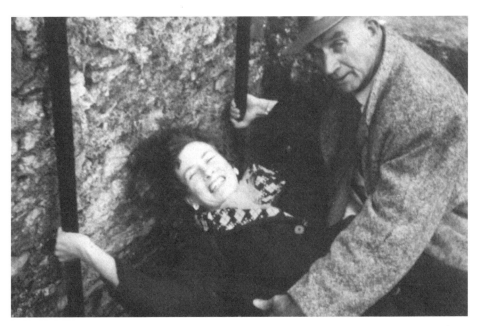

The author's wife kissing the Blarney Stone (underneath the wall) at Blarney castle, home of the MacCarthys, County Cork. The gentleman assisting her has probably held more women than any other man in all Ireland, 1970.

John and Kathleen O'Keefe of Conna, Cork, 1987.

Mr. Dineen opens another Irish grave in Gougane Barra, 1987.

Altar at St. Mary's, Clogheen, Tipperary, where the Murphys, McGraths, and Roches once worshipped, 1987.

More than one hundred coffins were carried on the shoulders of Irish citizens from the town of Cobh to this cemetery some three miles away. The day was May 10, 1915. The Lusitania had been torpedoed three days earlier seven miles south of Kinsale, Cork. Here is one of three mass graves. The house of the O'Donovans lies outside the cemetery wall. Their little daughter Oona was a delight, 1987.

A little lad sits on the Stone of Destiny at Tara in County Meath, the most famous historical site in Ireland. All the ancient monarchs from the Bronze Age to 563 A.D. were crowned here. It was the seat of the All King of Ireland. Conventions with delegates from each province were held here every three years, 1987.

Children climbing a knoll at Tara, County Meath, 1989.

Town of Conna, Cork County, ancestral home of 11th Line O'Keefes and Leaheys, 1981.

St. Catherine's, Conna, 1987.

Julie, Eoin (John), and Bill O'Keefe, children o John and Kathleen, Knockmourne, on the edge Conna, Cork, 1987.

"Dubliner Jacks" on their way home from a St. Patrick's Day parade hold up a large rolled banner, 1968.

Alex, author's caddy at the Royal Dublin Golf Club, 1970. Unfortunately, he knew the layout of the course about as well as the author.

School boys on their way home obligingly pose in front of a creamery stop — Blarney Road, Cork, 1968.

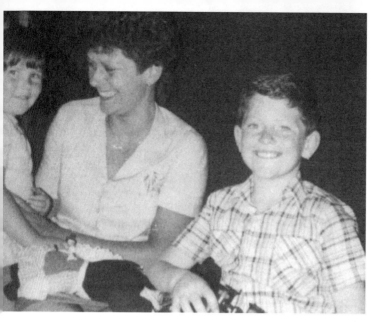

*Anne O'Brien, Joanne an[d]
Dillon, on Galway to Du[blin]
train, 1987.*

*Ninety-three-year-old Father
Gerald Ledey, a Cistercian
monk, in the bookstore at
Mount Melleray,
Cappoquin, Waterford, 1987.*

*Father O'Doherty and
Marilyn, Rathmore Church,
Aug. 15, 1981.*

they were in trouble. The pines on the ridge above their log home were now bending to the north. And the yellowish, black smoke, once billowing towards St. Michael's Church, had turned towards Fitzroy, Torbolton and March Townships.

The Curries prepared for evacuation. They started loading their wagon with precious belongings. Some two miles away, they could see Coady's farm burning on the Western Ridge. Time was at a premium. Finally the last item was atop the load: the family's newly acquired mattress. They were ready to go!

But before they even jumped on, a live ember settled on the mattress and the whole load was lost. Presumably, they ran for their lives up the Fourth Line towards Antrim as the ridge pines puffed into flame, their tops, like fuses of dyna-
mite, lit by flying sparks.

Towards Panmure, Pat and his adult children John, Anne, and Sarah could see the burning of Green's pastures and Checkley's farm. The roads were full of neighbours in various stages of disarray: the Hogans, Cavanaghs, Collins, Finners, Gallaghans, Lowreys, Storys and McGraths who, like the Curries, were to lose everything.

The devastation at Curries was indeed complete — their home, outbuildings, sheep, cattle, horses, Anne's turkeys, bees and geese, and all the

This noble Virgin Pine can be seen in the deep gully of Coady's Creek just west of the north end of the Burnt Lands' Road.

swine except one big sow later found rooting in the smouldering rubble.

The spent pines were like smokestacks. The ridge was so bare the top of St. Michael's Church six miles away could now be clearly seen. The flatrock glistened in the haze, its thin soil burnt to a crisp and carried away forever on the hurricane winds that blew up later on that fatal August 17.

The fire's shape resembled an inverted *V*, its sides growing and slowly spreading like a fan. The left arm continued to eat up the lower part of Fitzroy on its way to Crown Point at the north corner of Torbolton on the Ottawa. North of Currie's, the Diamond Hill School burned. Surrounding wildlife was wiped out. As far north as Fitzroy Harbour, four bears died from smoke inhalation. Dead pigeons and partridge littered the plains. Poisonous odours of pine and cedar rode the oxygen-depleted air. Cattle bellowed the terror felt by all nature!

On the southeast flank, the fire had indeed turned away from the Kennedys, Egans, and O'Keefes, but not before it had most likely burned out Tom White on the Twelfth Line. The two farms directly west of the Egans and O'Keefes on the Mahoney Side Road were also struck, because the census taker for the summer of 1871, in referring to the bushels produced in 1870, wrote in his chart "burned" (under the "wheat, potatoes and turnips" columns) for the West 1/2 of Lot 17, 11th Concession. But surprisingly for the Egans on the East 1/2 of the same lot and the O'Keefes on Lot 17 of the 10th Concession, there was no such negative designation. The fire had come within a half-mile of Margaret's. It had definitely taken a course slightly to the northwest side of her farm.

If a line is drawn from Mahoney's farm to St. Michael's Church, it is obvious that what was once the left side of the fire approaching East, had by reason of the stronger winds from the South become the right side of the fire, just far enough North to spare the Egan and Tom O'Keefe residences. In fact, all of West Huntley Valley was spared.

Up on the Eastern Ridge, however, near the church, the pines were torched. Andrew Manion, across from the church was burnt out, and the horsesheds on the Church's north side were destroyed.

Actual historical data on the fire is sketchy. No cameras captured the damage. No artists roamed the fields to depict the devastation.

Town weeklies like *The Carleton Place Herald*, *The Carp Review*, *The Perth Courier*, and *The Almonte Gazette* lacked the manpower to provide firsthand coverage. Even *The Ottawa Times* relied on reporters from *The Montreal Gazette* for early news on the fire's destruction.

Aside from the report of the Beaver Insurance Investigator, burdened with the disheartening task of settling eighty-two claims, plus a few fragmentary accounts from eyewitnesses, the full extent of the fire's rampage will never be known.

Most small farmers and their tenants swallowed their losses with silent resignation and set about cleaning up and rebuilding. Many pine and cedar logs used for new outbuildings from 1870 on, bear the fire's black and tan scorches. Angus Carroll's barn (recently blown over) on the Carroll Side Road has a few such logs as do the outbuildings of Armer Howie on the Eighth Line and George Bassett and Bill Howie on the Old Almonte Road in the 7th Concession. Even the barn at Maurie Williams's former farm has a few.

Most log buildings in West Huntley then were built in 1870 or later. The fire cleared the land and provided a handy supply of tall, branchless trees. Unfortunately, it also cleared the land of many settlers who had had their fill of West Huntley's hardships. The home owners, particularly on the Eastern Ridge near the church, were fed up. What little soil they had, had been blown away. Enough was enough. Livings aren't made on rocks!

The real story of this catastrophe (which could easily happen again, given the same conditions) is found in the recorded acts of heroism and charity inspired by the fire. Witnesses tell of men, women and children out in the fields on the afternoon of the fire, digging trenches with shovels, spades, and hoes, pulling fences out of the fire's path, covering roofs with wet blankets, digging holes for precious heirlooms and cash, and helping one another race for the safety of creeks, ponds, and rivers. They speak of the Reverend James Godfrey's (Rector of East Huntley's Christ Church) twenty-mile race for home on horseback to save his family by having them lie face down in potato-patch trenches near their doomed rectory. They speak of a mother standing up all night in Green's pond in Goulbourn bathing the heads and arms of her four children.

Tradition applauds the courage of John Hogan (40) and his son James (9) who wouldn't leave his father's side ... how John buried in the safety of a sod-covered well, his baby (2 months), four other children: Mary Ann (10), Mike (8), William (7), Eliza — and his Dublin-born wife Bridget Quinn ... how John and James and the baby died ... how his wife, after spending the night in the well, resolutely walked next morning to a great rock below the Second Line and stood there looking out over the desolate aftermath in March Township ... how she vowed never to quit the land ... how the government, as it did for many others, gave her family food ... and how her two surviving sons, Mike and William, stayed on, and eventually inherited the deed Bridget refused to surrender.

I visited the Hogan farm and its well in the summer of 1989. It's on the East 1/2, Lot 26, Concession 1 of March Township. There I met two of John and Bridget's great-grandchildren: Delores, a teacher in Sault St. Marie, and Michael, a surveyor who lives on the farm with his two daughters. Their father, Michael Leo, married to Norma Muldoon, was the son of William Hogan. Sadly enough, the present Michael himself was touched by tragedy. He lost his beautiful young wife Patricia to cancer. I knew Patricia and her father and mother, Cecil and Margaret Craig, from Black Rapids near Ottawa, and finer people never walked the floor of heaven.

In a sailor's-delight sunset, I stood over the well, positioned some hundred yards from Michael's white frame home. I felt some of the agony of that early morning in August ... I saw Bridget clawing away at the planks and sod trying to reach her badly burnt husband ... I saw her holding her dead baby, cradling her oldest son's disfigured body and comforting her husband (he died that morning) ... I saw

Mike Hogan,
son of Leo and grandson
of William. William was
in a well, protected by his
father during the fire.
Mike now lives on the
original homestead of
John Hogan.

221

her poised upon that rock framed by the silhouettes of her children, filling the unearthly silence with her tears and prayers and her promise never to allow those deaths to be in vain. Surely this was a woman with the raw courage of the true pioneer, who, with nothing but the rags on her back, her health, her God, her friends, and Irish grit, went on to fulfil her husband's dreams and bring honour to his memory.

As I stood talking to the charming Delores, the friendly Michael, and his two children with the dark-bright eyes of their mother, I realized none would be alive but for a brave man and his manly son who stayed by his dad unto death ... and I thought of another Son who did the same and His mother who later held Her Boy's body in Her arms.

Later that summer I got to wondering about that sad day in 1870 and why John Hogan waited so long that his only means of escape was putting his family in a well. The only logical answer I could come up with was that John did not see the fire as an immediate threat. Its slow movement (two miles an hour) and its northeasterly direction towards Stittsville and Hazeldean had lulled him into mild complacency. Surely he must have heard about the ridge fires in Ramsey and Fitzroy. And he must have known his farm was in the fire's path as the wind continued to blow his direction. But all that was nine miles away. He must have thought he had plenty of time to make the six miles to the Ottawa River. After all, the day was sunny, the winds moderate to gusty, and his escape-route, (the Panmure Road to the river or Constance Bay), right beside his next-door neighbour, Ambrose Carroll. In fact, according to William Hogan, a survivor, interviewed in 1941 by an *Ottawa Citizen* reporter, his father did put the family on a wagon and head towards the North. But they had only gone a half a mile when they found themselves surrounded, as the *Citizen* says, "By the pounding roaring forest fire which had overtaken them with speed almost unbelievable!" (By the way, William also said the fire had been started near Rosebank by a farmer burning out a bees' nest).

What John and so many others did not count on, were the gale winds that blew up around 3:45 p.m. The fire's personality was to change dramatically. It was about to become a crazed killer. Its speed of thirteen miles in the previous four and a half hours was to double. The tall pines on the Carp Ridge some three miles northeast of Carp Village and those some seven miles away around Pinch Hill in the southeast corner of Huntley were easy pickings. On the Fourth and Second Lines of Huntley, Mrs. John Harten and Mrs. James Allen would be its first victims. And not long after, the three Hogans, some three miles northeast of the Carp. No one really guessed the savagery of such a fire. William told his son, Michael Leo, that the fire's unpredictability and voracity was further complicated by the fire's own internally generated thermal winds with a power capable of sending great "burning logs flying through the air". In addition, several other witnesses mentioned how the fire "ran back on itself" seemingly going in several directions at once. Poor John Hogan simply misjudged the fire's swiftness, and waited too long.

By late afternoon, the fire had spread into Torbolton, March, and Goulbourn. The Pakenham stage to Ottawa was stopped at South March, its horses already badly singed. The ferry at Berry's Landing in March had just pulled offshore at 4:00 p.m. when gases and smoke eclipsed the sun. Across the land "white ashes and dust" up to "four inches thick" had settled only to be sucked up by the whipping winds and "smashed", "seething" and "hissing" against buildings. A man could barely stand before its wrath.

By 4:30 p.m., a sickening smudge covered the Ottawa River towards Aylmer. A Mr. Lyon, from his position near South March on the Ottawa, noted for posterity that a "shining day" had been "converted" ... "into swift blackening night"! He said, "I seemed to feel the burden of some awful catastrophe approaching!"

The full realization of the fire's severity had indeed taken hold. Along the Richmond Road, "two thousand" refugees on wagons, horseback, bicycles, and foot sought safety beyond the Jock River. Along the Ottawa River, people took to makeshift rafts and boats; others with less time drove their wagons and buggies into the middle of rivers, ponds, creeks, and small lakes.

With "showers of sparks" everywhere, criers-of-doom blew bugles, rang bells and ran through the streets of Old Stittsville (at the end of the present Carp-Stittsville Road), Hazeldean, Britannia, Nepeanville, Bell's Corners, Rochesterville, Merivale, and Ottawa, shouting, "Fire, Fire, the Fire is coming!" By 8:00 p.m., the streets in downtown Ottawa were deserted except for the odd bear wandering around helplessly.

The Ottawa Fire Department held emergency meetings with City Officials. They posted water wagons and men along Preston and Wellington Streets and then ordered two holes smashed into the wooden St. Louis or (Lewis) dam (roughly in the present vicinity of Dow's Lake), thereby releasing five hundred acres of four-foot-deep water over the Preston and Wellington lowlands. The fire was expected in Ottawa about 11:00 p.m.

Although the dam's flooding saved Ottawa itself and the Parliament Buildings, no adequate defence existed elsewhere against the hurricane winds that hit about 8:00 p.m. Fires were reported in Rochesterville and Mount Sherwood (Bronson Avenue). Ironsides near Hull was burning at 9:00 p.m. A man named Gilmore lost 5,000,000 feet of dressed lumber in Chelsea. Aylmer was soon aflame, and not long after, many other sections of the Gatineau Valley.

What had begun as a spark in Rosebank was to become a raging inferno. It killed men, women, and children in Huntley, March, and Goulbourn. In a fifteen square-mile section of Fitzroy and East Huntley only three houses were left. It destroyed Old Stittsville, Hazeldean (except for Kemp's Hotel — now a restaurant), all of Bell's Corners but for the schoolhouse, two churches and Bell House (partly damaged), and then burned its way across present Knoxdale, Greenbank, Merivale, Black Rapids on into Osgoode and North Gower.

Many descendants of old township families can still recall bits and pieces about the fire's damage; how the only house left standing near the Hogan's was Mountain Pat Kennedy's who took in all the homeless of his area that night; how the Richardson families of March lost several members and everything but their Family Bible and heirloom clock; how the Torbolton-March Union School on the Dunrobin-Panmure Road burned. Ask the folk of South March, the Scissons, Acres, Bouchers, Kellys, Sharpes, Gourleys, Robertsons, and Parkers and each will have a story.

Angus Carroll of Corkery told me he once worked with a Monaghan from Dunrobin who said his grandmother shook holy water all around the outside of her Dunrobin house during the fire and her house was the only one in the area not to burn. A Mr. Monk of March told me of his ancestor Arthur Monk's losses: his farm was almost on the shores of the Ottawa. He also mentioned how the nearby Pinheys saved their home by continuously watering the roof. In Fitzroy, a Mr. Green told his grandchildren of the fire racing along the Third-Line fences. In Gloucester, a Mr. Joyce was quoted as saying he saw cows running wildly around bawling and rampaging!

The present day Griersons of Crown Point and Baskins of Baskin's Beach must have stories about the fire's damage to their properties, and how all of Torbolton, (named after Robbie Burn's wife's place of birth in Scotland), took on new life after the fire's clearance of trees and brush. A Mr. Green in Carp Village remembered his stable roof being blown off by the gales. And someone in the Baird family of Torbolton passed along the story of a relative named Smith watching the fire from his sickbed on a raft anchored in the Ottawa. Another Green, this time from Goulbourn, remembered dead fish floating in the Carp River. And, of course, we've heard from the Curries, Hogans, Egans, Kennedys and O'Keefes.

Three other stories deserve mention. They show how persons react to crises in different ways, sometimes quite irrationally.

The first involves a Robert Grant of Goulbourn, a district councillor, church worker, family man, prosperous farmer, and, some say, the wealthiest man for miles around. His farm was in about three hundred yards on the northside of Highway 7, a mile east of the Old Kemp Hotel, and adjacent to the Carp River. The river begins some three miles above the present Stittsville and crosses Highway 7 on the site of the old Grant farm.

According to the press, Bob Grant died while trying to retrieve his cashbox from his burning stone home. Not only did he have a large sum of his own money, but, in his capacity as secretary-treasurer of his church, he kept in safekeeping much of the parishioners' donations. Mr. Grant entered his burning house twice only to be pulled out each time by his faithful hired man. The third time he entered, no one could follow, and Bob Grant never came out. His wife went on to rebuild the family home and raise her family. People of the area still talk of her courage, and Mr. Grant's, too.

In the same vein, years later on February 3, 1916, Florence Bray and Mable Morin lost their lives in the burning of the Ottawa Parliament Buildings. They were guests of the wife of the Speaker of the House. Both were well on their way to safety when they decided to return for their fur coats. As in Bob Grant's death, it was probably the smoke that killed them. Stone won't burn, but white-pine walls and shelving, and oak beams and maple floors do, especially after years and years of oiling, shellacking, and varnishing. Mr. Grant and the two women took the absence of flame as a sign of safe passage. Seven people died in that Parliamentary Fire, and it destroyed everything but the Library at the back. It started at 8:55 p.m. History buffs might be interested in knowing that the clock-bell of the Peace Tower tolled at 9, 10 and 11:00 p.m. It began the midnight knell, almost finished, and then crashed into the depths of the tower. The building was fifty years old. A German agent may have been responsible for the fire, the papers said.

Another story shows the blind courage of an old lady living somewhere on the Richmond Road in the fire's path. The road before her was full of hundreds trekking west to safety. And there she sat ensconced on her roof disregarding all entreaties to come down. Not even the swirling smoke and eerie horizon nor the panic of others could shake her faith in God's providence. *The Ottawa Times*' report has her answering one rescuer with the words, "No! The Lord has always taken care of me. I don't think He will desert me now!" Now that's faith!

Sara Craig in her delightful book, *Hello Nepean*, tells this third story, an amusing one, about Nicholas Tierney of the Rideau River Road and Bob Taylor on the Merivale Road. Their farms abutted each other, the rear acres of which were unfenced and poorly surveyed. During the winter of 1869-70, Tierney cut seventy cords of wood from the back area and piled it in readiness for the Bytown Market. Taylor then "took the notion" that the wood was rightfully his. He built a lean-to at one end and stationed himself on top the woodpile. He and his trusty shotgun would prevent Tierney from moving the wood.

To protect his interests, Tierney in turn built himself a shelter at the other end and took up his position, also armed to the teeth.

All summer long they manned their posts. The women brought out the meals. It looked like a stalemate. And then along came the Great Fire which settled their differences. It burnt the woodpile and all the bush around, including the so-called fences. As the fella said, "Nobody got nothing!"

The Great Fire of August 17 did not die easily. The August 25 edition of *The Almonte Gazette* reported small earthquakes on August 23 and 24 in Almonte Village. Houses shook, dishes toppled, windows cracked. Some blamed the yellow gaseous smoke still covering the Almonte area; others, the natural contraction of the earth's crust.

On August 22, Ottawa was still covered with smoke. Both sides of the Gatineau River were burning. Aylmer continued to smoulder. Perth was surrounded by flame. Westport was in danger.

Granted not all the fires still burning after August 17 were caused by the Great Fire. Many started up on their own. Some historians, however, go as far as to claim that the Great Fire itself was a collection of smaller ones. This is not entirely true! The Great Fire had its beginning around Rosebank and spread its tentacles over some six hundred square miles in a single half-day. True, it burned in several areas at the same time. True, it jumped from ridge to ridge with fickle abandon leaving certain spaces untouched: a large stand of pine behind the Fitzroy Third-Line (Dwyer Hill Road) School escaped, as did Carp Village, and another smaller village, three miles above Bell's Corners, called Little Cross, which at one point was completely surrounded by flame. But, all considered, the Great Fire was one scenario fought on a giant battlefield with hundreds of skirmishes taking place at hundreds of locations. In fact, it remains as the greatest single natural ecological disaster ever recorded in this area.

Imagine the fire's playground. But for a few patches of green, the land is black ... tassels of smoke rise from the trees as from blown-out candles ... no more squirrels, rats and chipmunks to ravage crops ... no reptiles to plague the traveller ... no bears to paw the doors for food at night ... no wolves to kill the fowl and sheep ... no more berry trees, basswood sprouts, potatoes, turnips and corn ... no wheat for bread ... no grain for feed ... no milk for children ... no pork, beef, or fowl for the table.

Fish float in the streams ... carcasses of cattle, horse, pigs and sheep lie huddled in the fields ... the pheasants and partridge are no more ... the songbirds sing on other shores ... the oak, ash, and pine are edged in black ... the land is the land of the dead ... another Waterloo, Ypres, Mount St. Helen, or Nagasaki.

Yet in West Huntley valley, that day, serenity reigned. Close to fifty homes were burnt in Huntley, but not a hair was singed in the valley. West Huntley itself lost four houses. Various sources give various names of their owners: John Allen, the Whites, Andrew Manion, James Scott, William Corbett and B. Ryan have all been mentioned. But in the valley, no losses of buildings were reported. Not only did the Fire change course, but somehow it jumped the valley to the Ninth-Line Ridge.

Next day, the little Rosebank Train was again heard among the green shades of the valley's trees.

Did the wind change and skip over the valley by chance? Or was it the faith of the people like the Kennedys, Mrs. Egan, and Margaret Finner O'Keefe holding her worn plaster cross before the fire?

Perhaps, He heard Margaret's prayer and He said to his Father, "I have not found greater faith than this in all of Huntley!" And the Father said, "Then, give *her* what she asks!" And He did!

The Ribbon

I had been working for several hours one weekend on a section of this book dealing with the reverence held by the old Irelanders for ribbons of cloth. How they used to tie them to the holy thorn trees as offerings to holiness itself. How they used them to mark off sacred places and objects. How they were symbolic of prayer by holy people.

I finished the article on Sunday evening. Next morning my wife and I attended 9 o'clock mass during which I began thinking again about those ribbons of prayer and how our society still attaches a reverential importance to them: armbands for the dead, ribbons for valour and remembrance, and the ones so lovingly wrapped around bouquets and gifts.

Now my wife happens to be of Irish descent and also, to my way of thinking, a holy person. After mass, as the congregation of twenty or so were filing from the pews, the Irish priest, Father Joseph Muldoon, walked over carrying a very large ribbon obviously left over in a seat from a Saturday wedding.

"Who'd like a ribbon?" he asked. No takers! By the time we had moved outside most people had gone and Father Muldoon, still holding the ribbon, looked like a left-over Christmas box. Suddenly he turned to my wife.

"Marilyn, can you use this ribbon?" "Sure, Father! Thanks!" she replied demurely. And then the priest presented her with a gorgeous pink ribbon.

As I drove home, the coincidence of it all struck me: my writing that weekend about ribbons, my thinking of them during mass, and finally the incident of an Irish priest giving an Irish lady something so historically cherished by the Irish.

It was like a small private ceremony in itself where something holy was given to someone holy from God's holy representative.

All chance? I wonder! If it had been anybody else but Marilyn, I wouldn't have given it a second thought!

Marilyn at Tara,
1988

The Luck of the Draw

Not all marriages are made in heaven. Some are made in hell. Take the Anglo-Irish Coopers and the Celtic O'Briens: a cut of the cards joined them; the toe of a woman ripped them asunder. Cromwell started it all!

In 1649, Cromwell had been sent by the British Parliament to put an end once and for all to religious and political freedom among rebelling Presbyterians, Royalist Anglicans, Catholic Anglo-Normans, and Old-Family Irish Catholics. To indicate its support, the English Parliament appointed him Lieutenant-Governor of Ireland. At Drogheda, some fifty miles north of Dublin, he sent twelve thousand men against the two thousand of Duke Butler. Butler refused surrender. Cromwell's cannonade lasted two days; after three assaults he was successful and he slaughtered the garrison. At Wexford, some seventy miles south of Dublin, he massacred some three thousand troops and all the citizens.

From Leinster, he turned to Munster. Cork City surrendered. Then Youghal. At Cashel, he sacrificed some five hundred to his god in Cormac's Chapel on the great Rock. At Clonmel, Hugh O'Neil stood awhile, but finally surrendered after his ammunition ran out. Next came Athlone and finally Limerick, both defeated by Ireton, the son-in-law of Cromwell. Limerick at the time was full of the plague which Ireton himself fatally contracted a few weeks after his victory.

By mid-1652, the war was over. Cromwell made a new son-in-law, Lieutenant-Governor. All Ireland was confiscated by the English Parliament, war trials were held, executions authorized, and all Irish landowners were stripped of their land so it could be given as grants to Cromwell's soldiers. The entire population of Catholics was told to withdraw to the rockpiles of Connaught by the year 1654. Presbyterians in Down and Antrim lost everything — their new homes became the hills and forests of Leinster. As the saying goes, Cromwell "was a beauty"!

A story has it that one day in the midst of the destruction of Limerick, Cromwell was approached by one Moira O'Brien, the last survivor of the ravaged O'Brien clan, once the masters of all Northern Munster. She said:

"General, you have killed my father and my uncles, my husband and my brothers. I am left as the sole heiress of these lands. Do you intend to confiscate them?"

Cromwell was not without a flair for the dramatic. He once spared a town in Cork because a peasant woman toasted his health outside the town entrance. And now before him was a woman of some presence demanding to know his intentions, which were quite obvious to anyone. So he made her an offer *she couldn't refuse*: marry one of his officers, make him her heir, and her lands would remain hers in the interim. She agreed! But which officer? Cromwell said let the cards decide. The cards were dealt; each officer chose one. An Ensign Cooper was the winner.

A few weeks later, Moira was pregnant. Convinced her child was a male heir, she took revenge on poor Cooper. After getting him drunk, she drop-kicked him into eternity with a fatal blow to the pit of his stomach.

But Moira's gratification was short-lived: the baby boy lived and the Cooper family flourished for centuries. But at a price! According to the poet Robert Graves, (1896-1985), whose mother was a Cooper, the Cooper family was forever cursed by ill-luck, such as early and violent deaths, etc.

Is there a moral to this story? The moralist might proclaim, "Never make a deal with a devil!" — the pragmatist, "Don't gamble with a woman!" — while the realist might say, "Never take your eye off a pregnant woman named O'Brien who's serving free drinks and wearing heavy boots!"

Which card did Cromwell designate as the winning one chosen by Cooper that fatal night? Naturally it was the Queen of Spades!

Cooper got a Queen all right, in spades!

A Letter to the Farm

19 Euclid Ave.,
Westboro, Ont.
April 12, 40

Dear Granny;

I am writing you a few lines on my typewriter hoping they will find you well as we are all o.k. here.

Could I come up to the country for my summer holidays again this year as I had such a good time last year I would certainly like to come again, if I may,

I am not able to pay for my board because I have not started to work yet and have no money but as soon as I grow upaand start to work I will pay it all back,

There is a lot of snow here yet and I bet there is lots in the country too, Mother is busy painting the kitchen and it certainly looks very nice, how are the family up there also Allen and Clarence.

This is all for now I will close,

with love,

Gary XXXXXXXXXX

The Orange Mini-Minor

The young couple at first looked like travelling companions. Their hands entwined around the railing of the ship and each other. Her head rested on his shoulder and they occasionally whispered and shyly kissed as they stared blindly into the light indigo swell of Cork Harbour.

A sudden bustle suggested the weighing of anchor. Last-minute supplies were being loaded. The wooden gangplank was drawn away. The play of the seagulls grew more frenzied. The old *Inishfallen* rumbled and gently eased out into the lovely Lee.

It was a half of six. Destination — Fishguard, Wales. A strong March breeze from Bantry Bay kept the Irish flag billowing. The open sea and sunset were yet three hours away. There the ship would turn east past the lighthouse of Fastnet Rock, the most southerly head of Ireland, and a familiar sight to transatlantic passengers, sailors, and yachtsmen.

Except for ourselves, the rear deck was empty; the young couple had gone.

Not more than a few minutes out of Brian Boru Quay in Cork, my wife and I noticed a bright orange Mini-Minor curling along the eastern shore. At a point some hundred yards ahead of the ship, it stopped and the driver came round front and began waving in our direction. At whom we wondered?

We turned and there standing in the shadows beside the lounge entrance was the same girl we'd seen earlier. Slightly turned from us, she waved back and her loneliness filled the evening with sorrow.

For thirteen miles, until the town of Cobh intervened, the little car lingered with us. And every few miles the young lover would jump out to signal his devotion.

At Cobh, he stopped for the last time. Both waved until distance stole their sight. She never saw him leave; he never saw her go below. Their hearts would hold those final waves until they met again.

Vive l'amour!

54

A Touch of Grace

The last time I saw Leonard Grace we were playing softball together on a summer's Sunday some forty-four years ago. A makeshift diamond was set up on old Tim Scott's land by Highway 44, north of the Corkery Church.

Leonard was just another example of those Irish men who took time to join hands with youth, men like Pat Egan, Basil O'Keefe, Matt and Walter Scott. Sort of big brothers, as it were!

I remember the ball games as being very competitive, but always in fun. No one really cared who won. Equipment was nonexistent. No sweatbands, running shoes or caps. Only the catcher had a glove. Grass stains were evident on flannel pants and white shirts.

Baseball and softball have always been popular with West Huntley men. As far back as the early 1900's, Corkery has fielded such teams. Early photos show players like the Scotts, Carrolls, Kennedys, Sullivans, and Egans bedecked in unbuttoned suitcoats, baggy pants, halfcocked fedoras or heavy peaked caps. These teams played friendly matches with Carp, Pakenham, or Carleton Place.

Like those players of long ago, we had no parks, no stands, and no equipment. But we had a good time on some fine Sundays. And, in addition, we young people had the good example of men like Leonard Grace and Basil O'Keefe who helped us grow up just a little better for knowing them.

When I recently met Leonard at the wake of our mutual cousin, the friendly Ray Mantil, Leonard was in his eighties. Even yet he has that nimble gait and gracious manner that set him apart as a man with a touch of grace.

Burling Along

"To burl" means to take out knots in string or wool, etc. But old John Delaney, born and bred in Corkery, used it in another sense. A neighbour had a harrow for sale and knowing Delaney's was as old as the hills he worked, he offered him his harrow for sale. John agreed to a trial run.

A few weeks later the neighbour thought he'd inquire about the harrow. He knew John was set in his ways and never rushed into anything. "Well, Johnny [both men were about the same age], how did ya take to the harrow?"

"Can't say I noted any difference from my own," said Johnny as he caressed his white goatee. "I guess ya won't be takin' it off me hands then?" said the neighbour. John stood ramrod straight, his gold earrings flickering with each turn of his head. "Thanks be to ya, anyway, Jimmy! But I have burled these hills with my old harrow for forty years and I don't see why I can't burl the same for another forty!" And he probably did! He lived 'til he was ninety-five!

How Irish is Irish?

Most Irish names in West Huntley are old Irish. Their pedigrees go back beyond the coming into Ireland of the Norsemen in 795 and the Normans in 1169.

Names like Kennedy, Egan, O'Brien, Carroll, Flynn, Madden, Kelly, Murphy and Sullivan reach into the darkness of Irish antiquity, into the centuries when "The Island of the Woods" was invaded (in order) by the Parthalonians, the Nemedians, the Fomorians, the Firbolg, the De Danaans, and finally by the Gaels from whom all old Irish names are directly derived.

Tradition (the oral treasury of history) has it that during the final period of Gaelic predominance, nearly all old Irish families could trace their genes to one of three Gaelic sons of the Gael, Milid: Heber, Eremon, Ir, or to an uncle of Milid. All are believed to have settled around the Kenmare River in Kerry County. They were called Milesians.

In these early centuries of Bronze and Iron, most Irish individuals took the names of their tribal chiefs. It was these patriarchal heads who held together the families, often being responsible for as many as one hundred and fifty children, in-laws, grandparents, and grandchildren until death did them part. If the head died, the control went to the most worthy son as chosen by the general opinion of all family members.

Under this system, the family unit had considerable strength. The wealth was held in common by each member except the head who was permitted by the sept (clan in Scottish) to own land and cattle, etc., commensurate with the dignity of his position.

In time, what with the heads' properties being passed along to more and more successors due to the increase of family units, a social rift developed between subjects and heads. The heads solved the problem by creating a special class for heads only, a sort of hereditary-nobility called "rigs" or "kings" who eventually came to rule larger and larger sects.

About this time, since the Irish race found itself facing more and more cultural and environmental changes both from within and without, it apparently decided to work out a better system for preserving Gaelic pedigrees.

As tradition was the only means for recording posterity, each large sept was provided with its own herald, musician, and poet whose sole duties were to keep alive the family history. Smaller septs had storytellers who did their utmost to preserve the heritages of their families. In fact, Irish storytellers were eventually so important in Gaelic society that part of the suppression of the Gaels in Norman times included a law which forbade Normans to allow Irish storytellers into their homes.

Around the Tenth Century, the old practice of taking one's name from the chief was carried one step farther: Irish names came to be inherited from fathers and grandfathers. These names were known as patronymics, really nothing more than nicknames. Gradually they were used more and more frequently under the designation of surnames. And because these surnames were taken from the fathers and grandfathers, the prefixes *Mac* meaning "son of" (later changed to *Mc* outside Ireland to distinguish Irish-Gaelic from the Scottish), and *O* meaning "grandson of" or "close relation to", were added in order to better distinguish the ever-increasing divisions of the septs.

Today, all names beginning with *Mc* or *O* and in some cases *Mac* are either old Irish, pre-Viking, Norman, or British.

Many old Irish family names, however, have been spelt over recent centuries without prefixes. During the *foreign* occupations, part of the forced anglicization of Irish surnames included the removal of these prefixes. Upon coming to North America, some families who had earlier complied with the British wishes, never did get round to returning the prefixes. Such decisions were usually deliberate, especially in Canada, which was very British in the Nineteenth Century.

Now that times are different, perhaps some old Gaelic families in West Huntley and elsewhere might consider putting the *O* or the *Mc* back in Murphy, Carroll, and Egan. To do so would be a statement of nationalistic pride in the old sod.

Be that as it may, the old Irish names found in West Huntley for the last one hundred and seventy years are indeed the Anglicized forms of the old Gaelic patronymics with or without the prefixes. A good thing, too, since a knowledge of Gaelic would be required to pronounce the original spellings.

For example, "Hogan" was once "O'h-Ogain", a descendant of "O-gan" meaning "youth" while the surname "O'Keefe" came from "O'-Caoimhe", a descendant of "Caimh" meaning "gentle" or "noble". The O'Keefes, by the way, were one of the few families to keep the *O* during *the troubles* in Ireland. At the end of the last century, there were five "O'-Keefes" to every one "Keefe" in Ireland and today the "Keefe" surname has become very rare both in Ireland and here.

The study of these old Irish names is fascinating. Usually each name contained in its meaning a quality once thought to be inherent to a sept's nature or history. Such qualities may have been physical as in "O'Brien" from "O'Briain", descendant of "Brian" (Boru) meaning "great strength"; or as in "O'Flynn" from "O'Flainn", descendant of "Flann" meaning "red" and "ruddy" in complexion.

Often, too, the quality behind the sept was a dominant personality trait as in "O'Shanly" from "O'Seanlaoich", descendant of "Seanlaoch" from "Séan" meaning "old" and "laoch" meaning "hero"; or as in "O'-Hennesy" from "MacAenghusa", son of "Aengus" from "Aon" meaning "excellent" and "Gus" meaning "strength".

Other qualities were often based on a sept's trade as in "Morgan" from "O'Muiregain", descendant of "Muiregan" from "Muiregan" meaning "mariner"; or as in "Macdermot" from "MacDairmurd", son of "Diarmaid" from the same word meaning "god of arms". The "O'-Learys" from "O'Laoghaire" were "calf-keepers" and the "Maddens" from "O'Madadhain", meaning "small dog" may have been breeders of the same.

Although most surnames had complimentary meanings, some were a bit nasty. "Foley" from "O'Foghladha" meant "plunderer" and "Quigley" from "O'Coiglegh" stood for "untidy hair". "O'Haggarty" from "Oh Eigceartaigh" meant "unjust" while the "Lalor" or "Lawlor" sept from "O'Leathlobhair" had the unfortunate handle of "half leper".

From 1820 to the present, Corkery and area surnames without the prefixes have been: Boyle, Brady, Brennan, Buckley, Burns, Byrne, Carey, Carty, Casey, Cassidy, Cleary, Coffey, Coghlan, Connell, Conway, Corkery, Corrigan, Cronin, Cullen, Currie, Curtin, Daly, Delaney, Devine, Devlin, Doherty, Dolan, Donoghue, Donovan, Dowling, Duggan, Dunn, Dwyer, Farrell, Finn, Finnerty, Finucane, Flaherty, Fahey, Foley, Gaffney, Gallagher, Galligan (not to be confused with Callaghan or Gallaghan which was a distinct sept), Gleason, Gorman, Higgins, Kavanagh, Kearney, Keogh, Killeen, Leary, Lenihan, Lunney, Maher, Mahoney, Malloy, Manion, McGuire, Meehan, Moriarty, Muldoon, Noonan, Quinn, Rooney, Rourke, Ryan, Shaughnessy, Shea, Sheehy, Sheehan, Shine, Sweeney, Tierney, Twomey and Ward.

The derivation of the name Corkery is of some interest. Also spelled "Corkerry", it was said to be a combination of two counties of Munster province from which the sept came: Kerry and Cork. In actual fact, the word is from "O Corcara" from "Corcair", the Gaelic for "purple" or "ruddy".

Most Corkery and area names are as Irish as Paddy's pipe since most families immigrated from Ireland. But, not all are old Gaelic-Irish: "Brown(e)" is Norman-Irish (Twelfth Century) from the French "le brun"; "Burke" is Norman from the French "de burgo" meaning "of the borough"; "Clarke" is Scottish and English except for some Clearys in Ireland who anglicized Cleary to Clarke; "Cody" is Thirteenth Century from England; "Collins" is mostly from England but many are old Irish; "Cunningham" is normally Scottish in the Seventeenth Century, but many old Irish also took the name; "Dickson" is Seventeenth Century from England and Scotland, but some are old Irish as well; "Fagan" is most likely Anglo-Norman from the Fifteenth Century; "Fleming" is from Flanders in Anglo-Norman times and later in the Seventeenth Century from Scotland; "Forrest" is Norman, English, and Scottish, a nickname for a dweller or worker in a forest; "Finner" is Norman-English taken from the French, "le fineur", a refiner of gold and silver; "French" is from Normandy and England; "Grace" is from the Normans of the Twelve Hundreds taken from French for "grace", "le gras".

"Hilary" is from England; "Lindsay" and "Lockhart" are both Seventeenth Century from Scotland; "Mansel" or "Mansele" is from France by way of England, taken from French word "manse" meaning feudal tenant or occupier of a "manse"; "Mantil" is from Anglo-Norman times meaning "cloak" or "mantel" from the French "le mantel", a nickname from the sept's trade, as in other similar surnames like "Hood", "Carpenter", "Turner", and "Capp"; "Morgan" is old Irish but mostly English and Welsh in the later centuries; "Montgomery" is partly from France but mostly from Scotland in the Seventeenth Century; "Murray" is Scottish, but mostly Irish; "McCabe" is from Scotland around the Fourteenth Century; "Morrissey" is Norman and old Irish; "Nagle" is Norman from the French "de Angulo"; "Neville" is from England, but is also Old Irish.

"Newton" is Scottish and possibly French from "neutone"; "Nugent" is Norman-Irish from the French town of "Le Nogent"; "Roche" is from Flanders and in French means "castle"; "Scott" is from Scotland in the Seventeenth Century; "Sherlock" is from England in the Seventeenth Century; "Vaughan" is from Wales in the early centuries, but mostly old Irish; "Walsh" is old Irish but also Welsh; "White" is from England and Scotland from the Nineteenth Century on; and "Williams" is from England and Wales in the later centuries.

In some cases, Norman and English family surnames around the Thirteenth Century were adopted by old Irish septs. This practice accounts for some surnames being both old Irish and Anglo-Norman. A closer study of geographical origins by a professional student would bring out the true distinctions between these Irish septs with similar surnames.

Unfortunately, the vintage of an Irish surname is no assurance of purity in Gaelic genes. Even the older Irish septs must admit to having a mixture of different racial blood. Truly the Irish of West Huntley are blessed with the name, culture, and appearance of Ireland's children, but as far as Gaelic blood is concerned, the amount present differs with the historical background of each family in Canada, Ireland, and elsewhere.

As the Gaels of the B.C. epoch became more and more numerous, they became more biologically involved with those tribes who had preceded them. In Kerry, old-timers believe the Phoenicians and Carthaginians settled on the Dingle Peninsula and round the Ring of Kerry and that it was with these and other people from the Far, Middle, and Near East that the Gaels bedded down. Traces of Hindu-style writing are found in the Gaelic language and on the stone monuments of the pre-Druid worshippers. Some scholars even maintain that Dan, one of the twelve lost tribes of Israel, came to Ireland long before the Gaels. Many Gael and Druid religious feasts and ceremonies were directly copied from the nations of the ancient world.

Centuries of foreign trade and long-distance fishing also has helped shade the colouring of Ireland's Gaelic complexion. Sailors and merchants from Spain, Portugal, Brittany, Normandy, Scandinavia, and the Mediterranean must have been smitten by all the pretty colleens in the port cities of Cork, Kinsale, Cobh, Dublin, Waterford, Wexford, Drogheda, and Larne. Many an Irish child with the facial tones of Roman, African and Turk has scampered playfully on the sandy strands of Salthill in Galway, Rosses Point in Sligo, Lahinch in Clare, and Rosapenna in Donegal.

In addition, although Roman forces never entered Ireland, raiding parties from either side of the Irish Sea brought home one another's slaves and genes.

Then, of course, the Germanic races of Vikings, Normans, and Anglo-Saxons gave Ireland additional flavourings from the older barbaric German tribes like the Jutes, Lombards, Visigoths, Danes, and Franks as well as the bloodlines of the conquered Etruscans and Romans, many of whom were already partly Celtic and Gaelic.

The Normans and Anglo-Saxons in Ireland naturally worried about their own teutonic purity. Stiff penalties were brought down on the Irish for any philandering or marriage with the French and English nobility.

Two wayward kindred nations of these same Anglo-Normans later practised similar tactics: the Americans suppressed the Blacks and the Third Reichers sought the annihilation of the non-Ayrans. Fortunately, these movements were eventually subdued, and Irish, Jew, and Black now live in relative freedom.

The infiltration of new blood into Ireland continued over later centuries. Scottish immigrants with French, Pict, and Celtic backgrounds crossed into Ulster. German Huguenots were given lands in Limerick and Clare just as the Loyalists were later befriended by the British in Upper Canada. And the human trickle from Wales and England itself never really dried up until after the Industrial Revolution.

Further mixings of races on this side of the Big Pond brought even more pandemonium to the pedigree charts. In Corkery, marriages among the Irish of English, Scottish, Norman, and Gaelic lineage have gone on for a hundred and seventy years. And with the coming of multiculturalism, present homeowners with little or no Irish connections have settled in Corkery almost washing the green and gold from the land.

Genetically, for fun, it's possible to carve up the Irish ancestry of West Huntley and other Irish round the world as follows:

- Five per cent from the Fomorians who were tall and dark-haired from Northern Europe;
- Ten per cent from the Firbolg who were wiry, medium height, dark-haired and dark-eyed from Northern Europe;
- Fifteen per cent from the De Danaans (Picts?) who were tawny-haired, tall with blue or green eyes, and fair-skinned, from the Mediterranean area and possibly Scotland;
- Thirty-five per cent from Celts (Gaels) who were brown and red-haired, grey or hazel-eyed, tall and fair-skinned, and inclined to stoutness, from the Near East or Southern Russia;

– Twenty-five per cent from the Germanic tribes, either the Northerners who were tall, blue-eyed, fair-skinned and blond-haired, or the Southerners, who were short, plump, dark-haired, and brown-eyed.

(All these features in various complexities can also be found, as mentioned, among the French-Normans and Anglo-Saxons who came into Ireland and were the direct descendants of those earlier Germanic tribes, once conquerers of Western Europe including Sicily, Spain, and Portugal.)

– and finally ten per cent miscellaneous with genes anywhere from Africa, Turkey, Greece, and beyond.

Quite a mix if any attempt is made to attach any standard description to a certain group. The bottom line is that Gaelic-Irish Canadians are the descendants of many races and cultures.

What makes true Irishmen, regardless of pedigree or antiquity, is the fact that their ancestors came from Ireland ... and it was while there that Ireland changed them as easily as its hills take the breath from an echo ... its spirit touched them ... its soil nourished them ... its winds put the colour of its sand in their hair ... and on their skin its sun left peaches and cream ... the hues of a thousand rainbows filled their eyes ... and in their hearts its magic left hospitality, merriment, optimism, beauty and strength.

Even today an Irishman can be marked off from the Scot, the Brit, the French, and the German. It's a certain something in the manner, maybe a swagger, a turn of phrase, the cut of the jaw, the glint in the eye.

That's what comes of being Irish ... for Ireland leaves its lore with all its children ... an angel-dust sprinkled on the soul ... a mystique that more often than not sets them apart.

You can still feel their presence in West Huntley ... on the forced roads ... on Foxes' Hill ... in the spirit of those that are gone and those that remain ... in the glens and along the ridges ... in the east wind that blows from Galway Bay.

Come, my friends, let's sit on this stone by Coady's Creek and dream awhile!

A Refreshing Drive

Much of Connemara County skirts the Atlantic Ocean. Between the small but colourful centres of Clifden and Roundstone (a fourteen-mile drive), in the shadows of the half-mile-high Twelve Bens, many a seaside vacation is enhanced by bountiful catches of fresh lobster. And if that isn't enough, the air along this twisting stretch is so exhilarating that the road is known as "the brandy and soda way".

56

Jillen Andy's Son

Her name was Jillen Hayes, but townsfolk called her Jillen "Andy" after her husband long since dead.

She had four sons: two were "enlisted" by the Red Coats (John was killed in India before she went and Andy there too shortly after); then there was Charlie, an amputee, last to die; and finally Tead an innocent boy who couldn't live without her.

Tead was a happy lad, a sort of town clown. He sang Irish ballads and recited Irish prophecies. A great whistler, he even defied superstition by practising the art in bed and around graveyards. Younger boys thought him great fun and often were piggy-backed to and from school by their happy-go-lucky friend. Tead loved to stroll and talk and make people laugh: everybody loved him; even the schoolmaster gave him his due.

Then one day poor Jillen died and Charlie told Tead he would have to see to the burial. There was to be no wake nor funeral because people were afraid of catching the fever, especially when Jillen couldn't afford a coffin.

So Tead took charge! And he thought right away of his little friend O'Donavan Rossa and he went and asked Rossa's mother if the lad could be let come to help. And Tead and Rossa dug the grave; one on the spade and the other on the shovel. And Tead who was never seen crying before, did, and Rossa, too, when he saw his pal so hurt.

Then two older Samaritans came by and helped wrap Jillen in her winding sheet and they all placed her on her kitchen door and took her to the cemetery of Skibbereen. There, boy Rossa stood barefoot in the shallow grave and straightened Jillen and set a rock beneath her head.

At this point, an older man named Jack the Tailor from a nearby town who had been watching, became visibly moved and asked Rossa for the stone. And from his pocket the tailor brought out a great red hankerchief with white polka dots and, unmindful of the wetness on his cheeks, wrapped it round the stone and said, "Here child, set her precious head on this now!" And Rossa did.

Then the old tailor told him to untie her nightcap string and loosen her lace and take away her pin as a gift for Tead, for no person he explained should be buried with tied strings or pointed things which might prevent her or him from returning to earth again. And then the tailor told Rossa to place her apron across her face so the earth would not bruise her lips or blind her eyes.

Slowly Tead and Rossa gently sprinkled the gravel and soil over the wasted form of poor Jillen Andy. And the tailor was torn apart seeing the absolute purity of the "simpleton's" love and how much Tead really did understand and care.

For a while after, Tead looked after Charlie during the days, but during the nights he sat by the grave of his mother "guarding her", he said. Each trip he made there, he carried fluffs of turf to beautify the grave of the only one in this world who had known his true worth. Within a month, Tead himself had gone to meet her.

The little boy Rossa went on to become a great defender of Ireland, even across the sea. But he never forgot his great love for Tead and Jillen Andy and the day they said good-bye. Years later he put their story into a poem, the jist of which I have tried to tell here.

(*O'Donavan Rossa became a great leader of the Fenian Movement in Ireland and the United States. He was born in Ross Carberry, Cork, in 1831. He lectured and toured in England, Ireland and America*).

A Close Call

An Irish cousin, Earl Hogan, wheeled his Harley Davidson into the parking lot of a Motel-Restaurant in the deep South. His five-foot slightly corpulent frame had taken on a big hunger and his subsequent supper of Southern fried chicken, yams and black-eyed peas proved to be so succulent, he decided to overnight at the motel just to savour the next day's culinary delights.

True to form, breakfast and lunch were equally satisfying and he felt it only proper that such fare be given his personal commendation. He said to the owner, "Your chef is such a tremendous cook, a fella might consider marrying her!"

Minutes later, he felt a big hand settle on his shoulder and looking up saw it was attached to a well-endowed large black lady whose tiger eyes were staring him down. She purred, "I hear you wants to marry me, honey!"

Terror enveloped poor Earl... perspiration... weakness... tremors. What seemed like a week in Alcatraz passed before she "sprung" him. With a motherly pat, she cooed, "It's okay, Sweetie, youse is too small for me!" And went away chuckling.

Danny's Boys and Girls

Not all Irishmen, especially those around Cork, shared the national devotion to Daniel O'Connell, the great politician and orator from Kerry. They felt his heart was not really with the Irish.

In fact, they held that if Daniel loved the common man as much as he loved all the women he knew, he would have been a greater person. A saying around some parts had it that a stone thrown over any fence in Ireland would probably hit one of Daniel's children.

57

One Foot on Heaven's Floor

At my grandmother's, the milking was done in a small clearing beside long cords of winter wood just below and in front of her whitewashed logged house. The number to be milked seldom went beyond eight — usually seven. My Uncle Edward milked *about two* and my Uncle Nash and I did the rest.

I say *about two*, for Edward, to the chagrin of Nash his older brother and owner of the farm, never quite finished milking any cow. Nash always claimed the cream came down at the last of the milking and Edward felt the milking was over when the expulsion of any excessive energy produced little results. Nash had some justification for being upset. A cow, not properly finished, tends to become a little lazier each time in her production. And, of course, cream for the dairy brought in extra dollars, so scarce in those late Depression years.

I am sure these battles over the milkings had gone on many summers before my arrival. Usually Nash would end up "stripping down" Edward's unfinished assignments and "dressing down" Edward in mildly desperate tones. Edward's reaction to all these purges was like a kite in the wind. He just rode them out and then went on as he did before.

Up until the time I began teaching, I knew nothing about mental disabilities except my own. But as I worked with students from all walks of life, I soon realized the great gamut of man's basic intelligence.

As a boy, I knew my Uncle Edward was a bit different, but I didn't know why or how. He never read the paper nor wrote letters. He could tell the time but couldn't make change. I saw him as a man of twenty-seven who never hurried, never worried, and seldom took anything seriously. Innate drives for success, perfection, or acceptance were foreign to his personality. The little pocket money he received was convenient to buy a hot dog, chocolate bar, and coke in town. He was gentle with animals, especially dogs. He was cordial with people. His sense of humour was keen. When he laughed his whole body shook. He was slow to anger and never showed grief. One emotion I do remember in those early years was frustration ... he missed going to parties and on dates and being close to a ladyfriend and he wanted dearly to go out on his own. But he knew he couldn't and didn't know why. He too had his dreams and hopes and fantasies that were never to be realized. And I think he knew and cried inside.

Such disabilities as Edward's were never discussed by my relatives. The Irish are like that when it comes to very personal or family matters. Ask them about the shenanigans of local characters and they will "wear out your ear". Humorous anecdotes about Eddy's pet bull, Rose's weird turkeys, or Jimmy's new mare, fly freely from sharp memories. But any references to losses, disappointments, and sufferings are usually taboo.

Occasionally a song will bring a tear, and a wee drop pluck a string of sorrow, but for the most part, the Irish hide their sorrows.

We were an interesting lot on that farm. My grandmother was in her early sixties and physically burnt out. My cousin, Rita Kennedy, niece to my grandmother, had been a victim of polio as a child. Nash O'Keefe was handicapped by a crippled foot which gave his walk a decided limp. I knew next to nothing about farming and less about life. And, of course, there was dear Edward. Nash never ran after cattle because he couldn't; Edward never ran because he wouldn't; and I ran around as fast as my little legs could carry me in any assigned direction.

Yet we had great times! We put up with one another and somehow got the work done. I just hope I was considerate enough of those little saints who bore their scars without complaint or bitterness. Since I had not yet suffered much in my own life, I did not fully understand their sorrows from the distance of youth. I beg their forgiveness for the times I should have known better.

Like the time I hit Edward between the eyes with a rubber ball.

It all began so innocently. Clarence Williams and I playing catch behind the huge manure pile outside the stable. Then Edward chancing along and our breezing the ball dangerously close to his lithe frame, all the time baiting him with boyish taunts. Edward was not amused. He gave us fair warning: if we hit him we would rue the day.

The words were scarcely out of his mouth when my missile found its mark right in the middle of his forehead. Before I knew it, the usually gentle Ned was coming at me like a Comanche at Little Rock. Somewhere he had swept up a three-foot stick and everywhere someone was shouting the word "kill" over and over and I knew it wasn't Clarence. The manure pile saved me. I took the open side. We went around the barnyard twice with the spruce board never more than two feet from my streaking posterior. The situation was serious! My life was at stake! No time for sidestepping or faking. Just straight leather to the grass.

Down towards the house we flew. I could hear Edward's threats and the stick swishing. I knew I couldn't get to the kitchen in time unless someone opened the door. I began screaming for help from my cousin, Rita. Stalling for time at full gallop, I turned left and headed for the pump, the trough and the woodpiles. Something kept warning me to stay out in the open. Once more around the yard. Then, a shriek from Rita that the way was clear. I made a beeline up the hill and through the open doorway without my feet touching the steps. Rita slammed the door and I was saved — I learned a good deal that day: Edward had a violent temper when unduly provoked; Edward could run like an ostrich; and, I would never again use Uncle Ned for target practice.

Only on one other occasion did I see his anger. Someone, not I, called him a fool. The Old Testament says no man should call another man a fool: a fool is someone to be confined to hell's fire and Edward knew the

Bible. His reaction was one of rage and he chased the culprit around the house and up the stairs. Some of his school chums also told me Edward once loosened the teeth of a bully outside church one Sunday and no one ever made fun of him again.

All in all, he was and still is a unforgettable character. I remember more of his one-liners than I do of Shakespeare's. For example, I used to throw large forkfuls of hay up on the wagon where Edward stood building the load. Often the hay would go right off the other side. I would be furious and demand to know where he was. Edward would just wipe his brow and say, "I didn't see it coming, Jack!" or "The wind is really up, Jack!" or "Well, I got some of it, Jack!" meaning about four strands. He was never stuck for an answer. Calling me "Jack" infuriated me!

At the table, his mother would say, "Now go easy on that maple syrup, Edward!" To which he would say, "A little bit won't do me any harm!", or "This is good for what ails ya!" One incident, however, left him tongue-tied. Edward was on the wagon sticking the hayfork into the hay; I was driving the horse pulling the rope for the fork, and Nash was in the barn spreading. Everything was proceeding in an orderly fashion until Edward started shouting loudly, "Whoa! Whoa!" I turned to look and Nash peered through the logs. There before our eyes the floor of the wagon was heading belly up for the stars. Edward jumped to freedom, the hayfork tripped, and hay and wood lay in a pile. He had inadvertently tried to put the wagon and horses in the hayloft by sticking the hayfork under the wagon's floorboards.

To give him his due, Edward was really an asset on the farm. True, he did everything his own way, but he still got the job finished. He harnessed all the horses for wagon, cutter, buggy, or machinery. He fetched and took animals to pasture, sometimes twice a day. He forked manure, hay, oats, peas, wheat, and flax. He built coils and stooks. He trampled and spread. He separated milk and pumped water. He carried hay to the cows, grist to the pigs, and milk to the calves. He dug post holes, stretched wire, and drove home the staples. He cut logs in winter and hay in the summer. He ran errands to the neighbours and went down the lane for the mail. He killed hens and geese for dinners and carried eggs from nests to pantry. He washed milk pails and brought up water for bathing and washing. He cleaned out stables, cowbarns and outhouses. He did all those thousands of little jobs that make up a farmer's routine and he did them for the most part without complaint. He never really owned anything except the clothes on his back. He never knew power or success. He never asked for very much! He did what was asked of him and usually with a smile. He just wanted to be your friend, and if you weren't, he didn't mind.

Now that I am older, I know Edward is a saint ... he lived in the eternal presence of God and still does ... he and others like him are in a state of perpetual innocence ... his passport should read: Country of birth — Heaven! He'll be there long before the rest of us!

58

Three Practical Jokes

The Loose Goose

Bill Kennedy's family was one of the first to get a radio. In the early Thirties the batteries were bigger but weaker and often several were required to bring in a programme. But Bill got good reception. In fact, he was in a rapturous state over the quality of his new toy and at one time or another invited neighbours to share his enjoyment. One evening, a few of the boys settled down in Bill's living room to enjoy the "way-down-yonder" music of Don Messer, all the way from Charlottetown, P.E.I. The batteries had been carefully linked together and then joined to the aerial wire which ran through the windowsill to an iron bar stuck in the ground outside the house.

Basil O'Keefe

Everything was ready. The General Electric knob was turned. The tone was all that Bill had said. "The Little Burnt Potato" never sounded better.

But suddenly the radio went dead, and Bill, who could become fairly emotional about things not going his way, became noticeably upset. His mother immediately blamed the breakdown on her goose allowed to run loose ... she must have crashed into and broken the outside aerial.

What Bill and his mother didn't know was that Basil O'Keefe had arranged with the other lads to sabotage Bill's command performance. Basil had hid outside and cut the aerial at a critical moment. Naturally the men inside, in order to further perplex Bill, responded to the prank by complaining bitterly about their wasted evening.

After a suitable lapse, Basil rejoined the wires and Don Messer returned. Bill said it wasn't the aerial after all, but probably faulty machinery back at the radio station. Basil entered the party to be told by everyone how the radio had failed, but was now working. And the goose continued to run loose.

The Bread, Jam and Beef Caper

It's often a thin line between good taste and bad when it comes to practical jokes. Halloween was always a favourite time for pranksters, a time to paint pigs, move outhouses, or howl like wolves behind bushes on main roads in the wee hours of a moonless night.

One practical joke in West Huntley backfired.

Five men, led by the Welridge brothers, one of whom worked at Maurie Williams's in the early Depression years, having been tipped off that neighbour Martin Ryan would be away visiting the nearby Newtons on Halloween, entered Martin's unlocked house, had a game of cards, a smoke, and partook of Martin's jam, bread, and tea. Before leaving, they lovingly spread jam and bread crumbs between Martin's white sheets and for good measure opened all the livestock gates.

Martin naturally didn't much enjoy chasing down his cattle and getting his fanny covered with preserves. Moreover, his sleuthing proved successful in that one very young culprit squealed and the four others spent thirty days in jail. George Welridge, the leader, was a enigmatic, artistic sort, and he wrote a poem about the prank, laying particular emphasis on the turncoat who brought them all down.

Knowing George, he may have put a curse on him. We'll never know! But the young lad, only in his early teens at the time, to the shock of the whole country, did die accidentally but tragically many years later!

Dummy Up to the Bar, Boys!

R.J. Manion tells of a practical joke played on an irritable, short-sighted, frontier bartender named Jerry. Two lads carried a male window dummy up to Jerry's bar in Fort William and ordered drinks for all three. After Jerry served them, the live ones drank the three drinks and left the propped-up dummy to pay.

Jerry kept waiting for the dummy to reorder or pay up. When his customer refused to pay, or even talk to him, Jerry's temper ignited and he smashed a bottle on the poor lad's head. With the mannequin out like a human, the two instigators rushed into the bar, made a suitable fuss over their friend's plight, and shouted at Jerry, "Jerry, you've killed our buddy!"

Jerry blurted, "I don't give a damn; he tried to pull a *gun* on me!"

Freddie

When Freddie M____ of the Carp boarded the Canadian Pacific "Palace Sleeping Car" at Ottawa's Union Station in the winter of 1906, it was obvious the District Masonic Lodge could not have chosen a finer representative to attend their National Convention in Toronto. In his tailored dark blue-worsted suit, tartan tie, vest, gold watch and chain, fur-collared Scottish-Ulster overcoat, black Derby, and black-thorn walking stick, Freddie could have passed for the Irish ambassador.

On alighting next morning at 7:35 in the Toronto Station, his ensemble caught the eye of an obsequious porter who marked Freddie as a possible guest at the prestigious King Edward Hotel. As the young redcap helped Freddie down the steps, he said to Freddie, "King Edward?" The ever glib, sandy-haired Freddie, never known to miss an opening, pulled himself to full attention, adjusted his collar and politely answered, "Lord, no, lad; sure I'm only Freddie M____ from the Carp!"

59

Name Variations

In spite of the widespread use of surnames as nicknames since the Tenth Century, the old Irish practice of using first names and its many variations has never really ceased.

Around Macroom in West Cork, even as late as the Thirties and Forties, a whole family often went by the father's first name. For example, in one family, Batty Cronin was the husband, his wife was Mary Batty, his daughter, Kate Batty, his son, Seamus Batty, and his mother, Grannie Batty.

In West Huntley, they do much the same even today to distinguish several people with identical names: Mary, the wife of Angus Carroll, is Mary Ang; Mary O'Keefe, the wife of the late Basil O'Keefe, is Mary Basil, and Mary, wife of the late Benny Kennedy, is Mary Benny. In West Cork, years ago, the wife of an explorer who had made several successful expeditions to the Arctic, was called "Lissie Pole". A farmer living near a mountain gap was known as "Teique (Ted) the Pass". Others around, went by "Tom the Devil", "Shawn the Post", "Connie Gougane" (his home area), "Patty the Shoe", and "Jimmy the Spring".

A lad in Bantry named Dan, known locally for his pet saying "Bedam" became "Dan Bedam", just as in Corkery, for the same reason, a Pat Kennedy was given the name "Jesups Pat"! In West Cork a door-to-door salesman was "Jerry the Sack" and in Corkery a resident barber named Johnny Mantil, was "Johnny the Barber". A tailor named Buckley near Gougane Barra in Cork was simply, "The Tailor".

Years ago, these name variations which gradually became known also as nicknames, were more common in West Huntley.

I remember as a boy often meeting a self-effacing, pleasant bachelor named Johnny Kennedy. Johnny was the closest thing to a religious hermit West Huntley ever had. I recall seeing his round-shouldered form moving stealthily among his buildings across from the Eleventh-Line School. It was generally believed that, as a form of penance, he or his father had constructed the entrances to the smaller outbuildings in such a way that anyone entering had to bend almost to the knees.

After Johnny died, I went over to his vacant place and found out the entrances to the hen house, pigsty, etc., were indeed cut very low. Anyway, the people were obviously more impressed by his slyness than his holiness, for they nicknamed him, "Johnny Fox".

Another local character of special interest was Pat Kennedy. He lived on a very high point called Bear Hill just off the Seventh Line. Pat was also extremely holy. I remember seeing him telling the group rosary before Sunday Mass. His ruddy face under wisps of white always seemed at peace. He used to kneel straight as a rolling pin on those painful kneelers with his chubby fingers gently caressing his rosary as it swung back and forward in cadence to his high-pitched nasal monotone voice which always carried slightly above the others.

To everyone, he was affectionately known as "Pious Pat". Lawrence Kennedy, who knew him well, told me Pat was just that and more. Come to think of it, the Popes of Pat's era were all Piuses. I thought maybe the locals were referring to "Pius Pat" like Pope Pius IX, X, XI and XII. I asked Lawrence and he said that it was "Pious Pat".

Some people consider nicknames in poor taste. Certainly schoolyard versions like "gums", "shorty", "dumbo", "gimpy", "fatty", and "doberman" can be real ego-thumpers.

The air was blue one day in the principal's office of a small district school where I once taught, after the drama club's skit in the auditorium had referred to a certain dear lady teacher (not overly blessed with beauty) as old "walrus" face. An ancient history teacher of mine at St. Patrick's High School was named after an Egyptian despot, "Khufu". And a vice-principal I once knew was referred to as "Gazot".

Political nicknames with or without a twist of humour can also be truthfully blunt. Much depends on the political leanings of the listeners. American Democrats for example basked in the embarrassment of the "Tricky Dicky" affair, while in England "Randy Andy" was fair game for the tabloids.

Some loyal royalist once named a drink "Bloody Mary", in memory of the Sixteenth-Century Catholic Queen who persecuted English Protestants. Yet, when it came round to nicknaming Queen Elizabeth I, they called her "Good Queen Bess" even though she was equally cruel to Irish Catholics, Scottish Protestants, and loyal friends. As for the success of her reign, if it wasn't for Sir Francis Drake's naval victories, she would have brought England to economic disaster.

I have often ordered a "Bloody Elizabeth" in restaurants as a retaliatory joke. May I suggest the ingredients: two fingers of Paddy's Whiskey and three dashes each of British tabasco and bitters.

Sir Robert Peel, the British Prime Minister, who was never liked by the Irish even though he gave them the vote in 1829 (rather than face a civil war), as previously mentioned, was nicknamed by the Irish, "Sir Orange Peel"!

His friend, the Duke of Wellington, born, bred, and educated in Ireland was unpopular there too. But in England they christened him the "Iron Duke" and later made him Prime Minister. Someone once asked him about how he became a success even though he was Irish. He replied, "Just because I was born in a stable, doesn't make me a horse!" A close examination of this statement suggests the Duke's brilliance on the battlefield was not extendable to his breeding. Considering that a major bulk of his troops, horses, and money for the Napoleonic wars came from Ireland and that most of his own earlier financial support came from a rich Irish uncle, he should have been more kind to Ireland.

Anyway, he forgot his roots and most Irish have seemingly forgotten him.

Nicknames have also been used to give "bally hoo" to secret Irish political organizations. In 1760, Southern Protestants formed one group called "The Hearts of Steel" and another "The Hearts of Oak" (after the oak leaves on their caps). Around 1790, in the North, political scores were settled by "The Wreckers" and "The Peep-o'day Boys", the latter name suggestive of a membership either always up bright and early and on the job or always just getting back at the crack of dawn after a night of sinister activities.

Another such group in 1920 that made the old IRA look like altar boys was called "The Black and Tans", a collection of some ten-thousand-seasoned-commando-type 1914-18 veterans recruited in England and sent to Ireland by Lloyd George and Winston Churchill to beef up the Royal Irish Constabulary being slowly riddled by the IRA. Dressed in their black and khaki, they quickly went to work in Limerick breaking windows and assaulting civilians, thereby earning the title "Black and Tans" after a local pack of hounds.

On Sunday afternoon, November 21, 1920, in retaliation for Collins's Squad's earlier killing of fourteen British Officers in Dublin, the Black and Tans with another group, "The Auxiliaries", surrounded the grounds at Croke Park in Dublin where the All-Ireland Gaelic football final between Tipperary and Dublin was in progress. They fired on the crowd killing twelve and wounding sixty. Two weeks later they burned the centre of Cork City to the ground.

The Catholic side also had its "hit and run" squads. Disbanded Irish soldiers in 1690 formed "The Rapparees", a nickname for an Irish free-booter (pirate) or plunderer. These men had once been under Officer Patrick Sarsfield who had continued to lead the Irish army against William of Orange after James II was defeated near the *sacred* Boyne River on July 1, 1690. The date of this Protestant victory, cheered by the then Pope for political-religious reasons, was later to become July 12, (presently Orangeman's Day), as the result of a world-wide adjustment to the calendar in that century.

Probably one of the greatest Irish military fighters of all time, Sarsfield left Ireland peacefully after the Limerick Treaty signed by William had guaranteed the defeated Irish officers and people the rights to property, etc., in return for promises of loyalty to the Crown. The Treaty was broken by the British Parliament and Sarsfield died in France, still fighting the English. He and the sixteen thousand soldiers like him who fought into the next century as mercenaries on foreign shores were proudly nicknamed, "The Wild Geese".

Around 1760, another "under-bog" army was "The White Boys". Whatever their successes, their camouflage-techniques weren't much. To the delight of British patrols, "The White Boys" wore white shirts over their coats to mark their membership. The British soldiers, however, evened the odds by wearing scarlet tunics to boost their morale, not to mention their casualties.

"The Ribboners" of the 1850's were Irish vigilantes specializing in executions. If they somehow used ribbons, let's hope they were for purposes of identification and not strangulation. Most likely, however, they did wear ribbons. As already noted, an old religious custom attached magical powers to pieces of rags and clothing. Devout Christians were wont to tie them to bushes and small trees to mark the three thousand holy wells in Ireland. The people believed each rag was a symbol of their prayers offered to God imploring Him to empower the holy waters to take on the ailments of those for whom the prayers were offered. Cures particulary of eye, mouth, lungs and barrenness were not unusual. These wells were usually visited on the first Sunday of each quarter of the Celtic Year, in February, May, August and November.

Even certain trees to which these "vigil" clothes were so lovingly tied had religious significance. Thorn trees for example were believed to be planted exclusively by the "little-people" near hallowed ground, holy wells and cairns. No Irelander would uproot a thorn tree, deface a sacred burial ground, or disturb a holy well. Foolin' around with mother nature was not the same as foolin' around with fairies.

Some years ago in Corkery on the old Forrest property on the Twelfth Line across from the Vaughan Side Road, a new owner decided to put an outbuilding on the top of a small hill near his barn. The backhoe was rented and put in readiness. But every time the motor was turned on, it would run for a short time and then cut out. If the operator got down to check something, the key in the tractor would turn off. If he went away at all from the machine, the same result. Since the owner couldn't get his horses to go near the spot and since he himself was getting more nervous, the project was moved to another site. The locals decided it was probably an old Indian burial ground.

Besides the use of ribbons, another devotional Irish practice was the placing of small, usually white stones near wells, thorn trees and other holy sites, all of which were dedicated to favourite saints. Even today, piles of stones line the roadsides near final resting spots or mark the spots where violent deaths like murders, suicides and accidents occurred. Each passer-by, mourner, or pilgrim would throw a stone on the holy spot as a sort of prayer on top of a prayer until the mound of rocks was a prayer itself.

French Canadians have a similar custom at burials when they throw flowers into the grave ... for the Irish it was stones. It was all they had. They even used them to count their Ave Marias by moving pebbles from one hand or pocket to the other. They also used them for beehive huts, for monuments, sepulchres, and even fences. The stone meant shelter, protection, remembrance, even devotion.

Two final examples of Irish-political nicknames follow, one sacrilegious and the other scandalous. In Ulster today, rugby players apparently compete better when they imagine the game-ball is the Pope. The idea of the Pope being hammered through the posts and booted into the stands brings a smile to Ian Paisly's scowl.

Not to be outdone, in Southern Ireland, the ball becomes Margaret or Elizabeth. Imagine Maggie, the former British Prime Minister, being held close to the chest by Kerry's Tom Manion or the Queen being passed around in the scrum under all those hairy legs; it's enough to shrivel up all those "By Appointment to Her Majesty"-labels pinned on the six hundred Lords of Whitehall.

As a general rule, thank goodness, nicknaming is a complimentary vehicle of identification. It brings personal warmth into human relationships. It breaks down cultural, racial and class distinction. It puts colour into the whitewash of humanity. It gives a camaraderie to groups that surnames and given names cannot convey. Nicknaming proves a man doesn't choose his friends; they choose him.

The use of nicknames in sport and entertainment shows just how far whole towns, cities and nations and even eras will go in taking certain popular individuals into their hearts.

Remember the "Sultan of Swat", Babe Ruth, "Iron Man" Lou Gehrig, Joe Dimaggio, "The Yankee Clipper", "Whitey" Ford, "Sparky" Anderson, "Kid" Carter, "Pee Wee" Reese, "Ty" Cobb, "Mookie", "The Shaker", "Rusty", and "Satchel" Paige. On the gridiron, young people idolized "Knute" Rockne, "Slinging Sammy" Bough, "Broadway Joe" Namath, the "Big Train" Lionel Conacher, and the Chicago Bears' "Refrigerator". Out of the black ghettos, rose boxing greats like "Jersey Joe" Walcott, "Sugar Ray" Robinson and Joe Louis, "The Brown Bomber".

Even the boxer "Kid McCoy" out of Detroit stirred Irish America and indirectly gave us the slogan "The Real McCoy". Apparently, years back, a fella walked up to a bar in Detroit and was told by a friend that the fighter "Kid McCoy" was drinking there. Not convinced of McCoy's identity, the lad engaged the stranger in taunting conversation, the result being that the doubting Thomas ended up on the honky-tonk floor. As he came to, he stood up, rubbed his jaw and acclaimed through aching teeth, "That's the *Real* McCoy all right!" Since then, anything genuine is referred to as the "Real McCoy".

Hockey palaces also rocked to nicknames: Boston's "Kraut Line" of Dumart, Schmidt and Bauer; Montreal's "Toe" Blake, "Rocket" Richard, and "Boom Boom" Geoffrion; Chicago's "Golden Jet" Bobby Hull and Toronto's "King" Clancy, "Teeter" Kennedy and "Hattrick" Primeau. At the old Argyle Street Auditorium in Ottawa the rushend could be heard hollering at "Legs" Fraser and "Butch" Stahan.

In the Forties and Fifties on a Saturday afternoon, the M.J. O'Brien Theatre in Almonte was full of little legs riding dusty trails with "Hopalong" Cassidy, "Doc" Holliday and the "Kids": Billy, Durango, and Ciscoe. For the adults, there were "King" Gable, "Duke" Wayne, Clara Bow, the "It" girl, the "Keystone" Cops, "Fatty" Arbuckle, "Gypsy Rose" Lee, and "Bing" Crosby.

Back on the farm, General Electric, Westinghouse, and Rogers-Majestic radios, with the big red batteries stacked near windows, brought in the music and voices of "Minnie" Pearl, "Red" Foley, "Little" Jimmy Dickens, "Kitty" Wells, "Hawkshaw" Hawkins, "Fibber" McGee, "Fats" Waller, "Guy" Lombardo, "The Little Sparrow of Paris" - Edith Piaf, and "Duke" Wellington. Early television had "Woody" Herman, "The Golden Fog", Mel Torme, "Dizzy" Gillespie, "Chubby" Checker, "Red" Skelton, "Cab" Callaway and Elvis "The King".

Even the funnies had nicknames for its imaginary characters: "Bathless" Groggins, "Popeye" the Sailor, "Little Orphan" Annie, "Dagwood" Bumstead, and "Chief" Wahoo.

In religion, St. Theresa Martin of Lisieux (Lee Soo), France, was known to the Catholic world as the "Little Flower", and every Catholic soldier in the trenches of World War I carried her picture.

In the Spey area of Scotland along the North Sea Coast, the fishermen are known to one another exclusively by nickname. They are called *T* names which are single names descriptive of the owner but never, never derogatory. These names apparently fit their owners to a tee.

West Huntley had many other nicknames such as "Big Pat" and "Little Pat" Egan and "Irish Ned" and "Baldy Ned" Kennedy.

A Johnny Mantil known for his business acumen was called "Pearly Johnny" while Bill Kennedy, the frequent cutter of poplar trees, to be sold for a dollar each for fencing, was known as "Poplar Dollar Bill".

To some, Jimmy Forrest of the Twelfth Line was "Jersey Joe" and to others plain "J.V." He once had the job of cleaning the big bell over the schoolhouse near the Vaughan Side Road. As a calling card, he painted his initials on the bell in large aluminum letters, "J.V.F." From then on, the youngsters, more impressed by his daring than his art, referred to him as "J.V." The "V" stood for his middle name, Victor, and he certainly was to them!

Among the Corkery women, "Muzz" Haggarty lived at the eastern end of the Vaughan Side Road. According to a cousin whose judgement I respect, Muzz and her sisters had the best-looking legs in the country. The lovely Amanda Grace of the Twelfth Line was nicknamed "The Babe", and her sister, the inimitable Rose Loretta Grace was known to everyone as "Mama".

Among the men: "Cheeta" Kennedy must have had beautiful eyes or great running ability, and the only way to distinguish between the two Jack Mantils was by "Big Jack" and "Little Jack". The same for the two Jack Finners and two John Scotts, only it was "Old Jack" and "Young Jack", and "Old John" and "Young John".

In those days, "Lollie" Grace was a popular man-about-the-country, and one had to get to bed early to beat "Sleepy Din", no relation of several other West Huntley "Dins". Across from the Catholic Church on what was once Finner's Hill and is now "Corkery Woods", lived "Blackstrap" Finner. And Martin Ryan was called "Pringle" Ryan after a popular look-a-like pedlar. Various brother and cousin combinations were "Red" and "Black", two hair colours still much in evidence among the West Huntley Irish.

The Irish once put a lot of store into the art of nicknaming favourite sons and daughters. It's regrettable that the practice is disappearing. Perhaps society now takes itself too seriously. A sign of the times — fun and laughter more difficult to come by — more sophistication — more fences between the "boxes piled on boxes, all in a row"!

I still tingle at the remembrance of my days in football and hockey and classes at St. Patrick's College. I was called "Oats" Ogilvie then. As little Tommy Davis broke for a pass in hockey he'd shout, "Hit me, Oats!" and he'd take it from there. The images of those school and sport buddies of mine has never left me: Tom "The Hip" Kelly, Peter "Red" Cunningham, "Willy" Dineen, "Toasty" Brown, "Elbows" Jim Touhey, "Nails" Porter, the Aylmer "White Knight" Darcy Boucher, "Teddy" Powers, "Weiner" Thompson, Frankie "The Fish" Fisher, "Willy" Young, "Wee Charlie" Wicker, "Chuck" Lemenchick, Tony "A.D. Smith" Duggan, "The Sly Fox", Charlie Roberts, "Chuck" Lynch — so many spirited lads who shared my youth and made it better in every way.

And I remember with great affection the best teacher I ever had, Father "Mitch" Mitchell, from Yorkshire, standing like a wet noodle over a front desk where he had sentenced me. He'd have one hand on a hip and the other at the end of a halfcocked Latin text, and his beady brown eyes would stare down over dark horn-rimmed glasses, as his elocutionary perfect voice fired quips at some of the worst Latin students since the Roman Coliseum slaves.

One day my whispered offbeat answers to his needling remarks led him to pin on me the name, "Joker". For three years it was "Joker" this, "Joker" that, always the "Joker". Sounding like Sir Winston addressing his maid after she poured gravy on his best bib and tucker, he'd say something like:

"Joker, [pronounced Joe-C-a-r-e and dragged out for two full seconds], Joker, my apology for interrupting your slumber, but would it be too much of an imposition on you to honour this frazzled, beleaguered instructor and this half-baked, half-awake class with your tantilizing translation of Hannibal's romp over the Alps?"

60

Their Mother's Children

If I were to pick a singular personality trait common to all of my grandmother's seven children, it would be refinement. Not a refinement of stuffiness and snobbery, but one that mirrored a genuine humility. A refinement based on poverty of spirit rather than delusion of grandeur. A refinement that considered it bad taste to put down a neighbour, dishonourable to whine about life's injustices, and improper to bring anything but evenness of disposition before the public eye.

Angus O'Keefe was the youngest child, some ten years my senior. He was my boyhood idol. I followed him like a puppy dog. When he lay down, so did I, right beside him. I shadowed him on his chores. I spent hours trying to wave my hair like his. And for all my pestering, he never once showed discontent.

After Sunday Mass we played music together in the parlour. He had taught me how to play Hawaiian guitar, so I was able to accompany him as he played violin. The parlour in those days was really a music room. Rather a secluded spot: Indian rug, orange upholstered horsehair furniture purchased through the Sears' Catalogue, net curtains, and large charcoal photographs of my grandmother and her husband on the wall opposite the west window. A pump organ gave me another way of accompanying Uncle Angus. And a beautiful Victrola by the Rapier Piano Company provided many hours of enjoyment as I played over and over again those thick twenty-, to thirty-year-old records.

Angus O'Keefe and Grace Mantil,
1945

It was Angus who helped me obtain my first paying job. He was working back at Kinburn at Leo Colton's general store. Since he had no means of conveyance, he used to bring home Colton's big red Ford truck. Naturally, I asked him if I might sometime travel around with him. I had done the same sort of thing with the young Freddie McBride on his milk-run in Carp and with Charlie Finner in his bread truck in and around Almonte.

One day Mr. Colton asked me to help Angus dig ice blocks out of the sawdust insulation. I was only ten, but I did my best and was extremely proud of myself to say the least. Mr. Colton never knew it but I ate my wages in bananas.

Angus and I used to escape the summer heat by having our lunches in the basement of Mr. Colton's store. That's where he kept the bananas. The best-tasting bananas I have ever eaten. Mr. Colton survived to be nearly ninety living out his last years in Westboro Village where he was the President of the Senior Citizen Centre. I wonder if he ever missed those bananas.

Later on, Angus worked for the Woollen Mills in Appleton, first as a bus driver and then as a machinist. His approachable nature made him extremely popular among his fellow workers. He was always a good listener — seldom bringing a story or taking one away. Little boys need heroes and he was one of mine. He was a great example for me — never drank, smoked, or used bad language. I can still see him pedalling in the Eleventh Line to call on his future wife, Grace Mantil. Loaning him my bicycle was the least I could do for such a worthy cause.

Mary, the oldest child, played a big part in my life, too. She lived with her husband Alex Prudhomme and their two sons in the neighbourly town of Renfrew. Their first home in the early Thirties was on the "main drag" and only twenty-five feet from the railway's main line to the West. The sturdiness of this house was proven by its ability to withstand the vibrations from freight trains passing into the frontier at sixty miles per hour.

Just up the tracks was the natural stone CPR station where I spent many comfortable evenings, especially in the winter, waiting for the Pembroke Local. (If a person was slower than the Local, he was very slow) ... I remember the warmth from the central potbellied stove ... the clickety-click of the wireless ... the big mahogany clock with its second hand snapping each movement ... the large comfortable varnished benches ... the smelly washrooms ... the mail wagons on the cement platforms ... the stationmaster looking terribly officious ... the swarthy railgang coming in for respite from the cold.

And two hundred yards farther down the track, before entering the station, the huge engines going West used to wait panting for water ... I remember in particular, the passenger train for Vancouver restless under the water tower at ten o'clock every evening ... and the long waterspout finally swinging away ... and the engineer tooting thanks to the men ... and the great pile of steel awakening with feverish jumps ... I remember the engine, after loading at the station, belching great breaths from top and sides as its huge wheels spun and wrenched each car to attention ... and then the powerful beam expanding on the tapered track ... and the car windows quickly becoming a blur and the caboose's lonely red lantern receding into places known only in boyhood dreams.

Aunt Mary's second home in Renfrew was my favourite. It was on Quarry, a street resplendently bordered on both sides by stately elms and maples. Set slightly back from a sidewalk, this white-stucco home had everything a fine home should possess: verandas, gardens, fruit trees, cement walks, storage shed, umpteen bedrooms, sunny kitchen, and indoor stairs at the front and back of the house — a fine residence well-suited to a fine location in Renfrew.

For years, Aunt Mary opened her home to male boarders. She provided nutritious food, comfortable lodging, and a good deal of motherly affection for young men from all over Ontario, many away from home for the first time. I wish I had a dollar for every lunch pail she packed and every shirt she pressed. Every boarder benefited from his stay with Aunt Mary. Even the lad who went to work one morning leaving the upstairs' bathtub's faucet running over a secured plug. His quick removal that evening from the premises must have improved his bathroom etiquette. He was last seen wearing an iron pot planted over his ears.

The Prudhommes were gracious hosts. Local priests like Fathers Murray, Maloney and Hunt often dropped in during the day for coffee-chats. Relatives such as the Lockharts and Ogilvies arrived on a summer Sunday, Aunt Mary's one free day. I remember the afternoons we'd gorge ourselves on a five-gallon bucket of ice cream from the Maple Leaf Dairy. I remember many happy hours spent with my first cousins Frank and Arnold: movies at O'Brien's, the Fall Fair, card games, and visits to Uncle Alex's big roundhouse where he repaired locomotives. The boys and Aunt Mary were exceptionally good to Uncle Alex who struggled for seven years with Parkinson's disease. He died just two months after Aunt Mary's mother and both bodies had to be kept for spring burial. As a result, she had the painful duty of burying her husband and mother from the same vault on the same day.

Aunt Mary came to Ottawa at age sixty-one to work as a housekeeper at St. Martin de Porres' parish. She stayed twelve years. She did everything but dispense the sacraments: she was cook, janitor, sacristan, custodian, secretary, and confidante to over two hundred priests who came and went from St. Martin's. Not bad for a woman who had already completed a lifetime's work.

I remember Aunt Mary as a woman of great sensitivity to the problems of others. She was constantly giving of herself to the countless people who loved to surround her. Her heart knew no bounds. Many came for solace. Others for advice. During the Depression, they came for food and money. She accepted them all. I remember her as a woman of great faith. She loved the Mass and her rosary. She said novenas like no person I have ever met. She had a zest for life, nay, a sparkle, that permeated even her saddest days. I spent many happy hours in her company and she is not forgotten.

One day, on the anniversary of her death, my wife and I were attending a Mass in her honour at St. Martin's in Nepean. Aunt Mary used to sit at the left front of the church near the side door. Just as the Consecration of the Mass approached, I wondered (and apparently my wife did, too) if Aunt Mary was sitting there that night. As the priest raised the Host, to the exact second, the fire alarm went off.

Ignatius Joseph O'Keefe, the oldest son, became the owner of the farm in 1934. At the risk of sounding effusive, he was much like his namesake St. Joseph: reliable, humble, dedicated. He was always there looking after others: his mother, his cousin Rita, and all the visitors that swarmed around his farm, especially roguish youngsters with nothing but time on their hands. So many visitors surely must have tested his endurance and finances. Yet he never complained. He welcomed everyone with patience, and, until his death, he kept his burly arms around the farm and its people. It is not surprising that his reputation was spotless among his friends, neighbours and relatives.

Of all the O'Keefes, Ignatius took the most pride in his heritage. The family name "O'Keefe" meant much to him and he was very happy when his brother Angus had a son and heir, Gary. Since Nash's death, Gary has also had a son, Sean, to carry on this branch of the O'Keefes. Gary lives on the old O'Keefe homestead!

The last time I saw Nash he had but two days to live. He was in the Almonte hospital, unconscious. I put my chubby hand inside his big mitt of a hand and he responded by squeezing it tightly, just once. Beside his bed, I saw the small brass and ebony crucifix I had loaned him some months before when the cancer first struck. It contained relics of the Little Flower of Lisieux, St. Theresa.

This cross had a history. The first owner was Sister Mary Augustine of the Precious Blood Sisters of Toronto. She gave it to her brother Joe Lee who loaned it in turn to my grandfather Tom O'Keefe. After his death in 1934 it was returned to Joe who presented it to me in 1955. It was many years after Nash's own death in 1972 that I chanced to ask Bill Lee, Joe's son, if he knew the date of Sister Augustine's

Five of Genevieve O'Keefe's eleven grandchildren: Wayne Lockhart, son of Cecilia; Frank Prudhomme, son of Mary; Anne, daughter of Angus; the author, son of Evelyn (Eva); and Gary, son of Angus — In 1990, on Frank's farm in Montague Township.

demise. He wrote back: December 12, 1945. Ignatius O'Keefe, who had her cross all during his sickness, also died on December 12.

Annie O'Keefe lived with her husband Maurie Williams on a farm next to her childhood home. She was blessed with a placid disposition in conjunction with a strong sense of duty that made her an excellent mother and wife. Her motto was "Live and Let Live". It is not surprising that her marriage lasted over fifty years. In fact, no one can ever remember her and her husband arguing together about anything. She was that kind of woman.

Aunt Annie had a way of hiding her good deeds. Only God and His Mother know how many rosaries she said in the privacy of her room. Before she died she told me she had prayed for me every day for fifty years and I was fifty-three at the time of her passing. Not only did she pray for me, but she also gave me a Christmas present every year for twenty-five years.

Many others were recipients of her kindness, the total number never to be known. During lean years her brother and brother-in-law found work on her farm. She welcomed her mother-in-law as a member of the family until the latter's death, and when one of her husband's nieces needed a home, she was raised until she was ready to go to work. As I got older, I grew to appreciate the significance of such a wonderful person as Annie Williams. She was a true friend in her own unobtrusive way and I wish to acknowledge publicly my appreciation about that.

Her children, Clarence, Allan and Shirley, had her friendly way about them, too. Shirley had a happy personality while Allan was as steady as his dad with his own brand of ticklish humour. When his parents suffered poor health in their old age, Allan took on the added responsibility of doing many of the house chores. Later he lived on alone after his parents' deaths, but the necessity of making all their funeral arrangements and visiting lawyers and government accountants to settle their estates was very difficult for him.

Far more of a strain than we knew!

One day in August, 1984, I dropped in on Allan. When I asked him where his dog Spot had got to, he told me he had been killed a few weeks earlier. When I got home, I went downtown and bought him a five-month puppy with a teddy-bear face and a stubby tail, a far cry from his lovable Dalmatian's domino-markings. Some four weeks later, I went by to see how new dog and owner were doing, only to learn that little roly-poly had also been killed by a car. I should have been suspicious then about Allan's future, for I believe deaths of pet animals are sometimes associated with imminent human death. In 597 A.D. in Iona, Scotland, legend has it that St. Columba, the great Irish missionary, while he lay dying, was approached by his old white horse who proceeded to show much agitation about his master. When the attendants tried to drive him away, the saint forbade them, saying: "To this brute beast, devoid of reason, the Creator Himself has clearly in some way revealed that his master is about to go away from him." I know many cases where pets have died within one or two weeks of their owners' deaths.

Some three weeks later, about 10:30 p.m., on October 22, I was out walking. My thoughts were suddenly on Allan. What could my wife and I do to provide him with a holiday with us? Who would run the farm in a three-day absence? I was concerned about him. The next morning I learned that he had died of a massive heart attack during his sleep. Everyone was shocked! What an untimely death for such a good person: a lad who had never done anyone harm, had lived out his life for others, and had quietly kept all his suffering and pain locked within. Even today when I drive onto the Williams' farm, I expect to see him and Spot and wee Stub-tail on the front porch. And I remember the night I thought of Allan at the very time of his last agony when it was too late to help. Ailean Donn, (the brown-haired Allan) had joined his parents.

Clarence Williams, the oldest boy, left home for a career in Auto Mechanics. After many years working in Almonte, he joined the Experimental Farm Machinery Division which he affectionately called the Funny Farm Machinery Division. Clarence inherited a good deal of musical talent. He could play guitar, violin and piano. In the early Forties, his parents bought a grand piano half the size of a boxcar and plunked it in the front parlour. Many an hour I spent there accompanying Clarence's violin renditions of Don Messer's favourites or singing duets with him from the latest Western Music sheets.

I was pleased to be best man at Clarence's marriage to Barbara Ballard. And I have watched with interest the development into adulthood of his six children. He still takes a keen interest in cattle just as his father and Allan did. And he has never lost that infectious sense of humour in spite of life's jarring reversals. Not only that, he remains one of the most honest men I have ever met.

Like Allan and Shirley he is indeed a true friend. Together we four swam, skated, sang, and laughed. One day we'd scale the logs inside Jimmy Kennedy's barn for pigeon eggs — on another, we'd go butternut hunting near the Burnt Lands. Diving from huge crossbeam logs into hay was fun as was the rivalry of shooting vegetable cans off fence posts.

After a day of fun or work, the scrumptious meals of Aunt Annie were eagerly awaited. Could she cook! : large white murphies with their jackets falling off — flaky white bread under whipped butter — tender beef with rich gravy — frosty milk and oatmeal cookies — deep lemon pies — green onions that snapped in your mouth — fresh turnips and carrots. She knew the way to a boy's heart.

Annie Williams was a remarkable lady! She helped in the operation of the farm in every way she could. Her duty at home was her prime concern and home was where she mostly stayed. She was a very private person with the O'Keefean trait of seldom thinking out loud. Like her mother she carried much in her heart.

Her last few years were difficult: her husband was unwell and she herself had a bad heart and lungs. She literally gasped for breath for the last five
years of her life. The final time I saw her she was sitting in a wheelchair in
the Almonte hospital. She was thin and boney. Her hands hid her rosary. As
I left the room, her sad eyes, (an apparent "trademark", some say, of all the
Corkery O'Keefes), dropped away. I knew how much she had suffered and
she knew I knew. Nothing was said. We never met again.

A few days later, on a Monday evening, one set of lights in my
kitchen refused to turn on. The fixture itself had three lights. A check of
the three light bulbs showed all to be in working order. The fuse was not
blown since a similar fixture at the other end of the kitchen (with its own
switch) worked perfectly. A removal of the switchplate indicated no
loose wires. The job was obviously one for an electrician.

Later that night, news came that Annie Williams had died that afternoon. The funeral was to be held on Thursday. On Tuesday, Wednesday, and
until Thursday noon, the lights remained out. Thursday at supper I tried
them again and on they came. It occurred to me at this point that the
lights were out from the time Annie Williams died until the day she was
buried. In twenty-three years, this was the only occasion the switch
failed to work. Nor has it ever failed since, nine years later.

Cecilia Lockhart, the youngest girl of the O'Keefe family, had my
grandmother's compassion. When she put a band-aid on a cut, a person
immediately felt better. In fact, if you had any problem, she would listen
and come up with the right words to set things right.

As a young married woman, she worked at Bryson Graham's on
Sparks Street in Ottawa. Later, in the Forties, she and her husband
opened a small store and gasbar on the edge of Almonte and within a few
years they built a bigger complex across the road on Ottawa Street. A
good portion of their success was due to the professional ease with
which Cely Lockhart met the public.

In the hot summer of 1946, I tended the gasbar and confectionery
stand for ten weeks. Wayne and Gwen, their children, had been born
about a year earlier and I had been called in to relieve the demands on
Aunt Cely. The living quarters at the back of their small bungalow made
the home of the seven dwarfs look huge. I slept on the couch and the
twins were nestled in their crib behind the curtained bedroom. I hardly
slept a wink that summer. The twins cried and cried. I stuffed paper in
my ears and buried my head in pillows. At the end of the season, the
doctor announced that the children had had intestinal infection. Thank
God: I was beginning to think that all babies shrieked at night. To this
day, neither Wayne nor Gwen, dares whimper in my presence.

I should have received danger-pay that summer. Mel Lockhart, as it
turned out, was fearless of electrical storms. During the fiercest ones, and
some real zappers followed the Mississippi, Mel refused to turn off the
electricity to the gas pumps. No amount of pleading from Aunt Cely and
me was heeded. Business was business! Often electric bolts would shear

Mary O'Keefe (1857-1922), daughter of Tom O'Keefe and Margaret Finner, married Tom Rowan. ive of her grandchildren appear above: Alfred, Madeline, Eileen, Orpah and Michael James, c. 1940.

Three grandchildren of John O'Keefe, one of four Irish brothers from Cork. They were born in 'erkins' Mills, children of William O'Keefe and Mary Jane McNulty (of Pointe Gatineau, Quebec).

They are: Gertrude (1884-1964), Lucy (1887-1970), and her twin Agatha (1887-1967).

Margaret, another grandchild of Mary O'Keefe Rowan, and one of the ten children of Mike Muldoon and Annie Rowan. All died young with the exception of Margaret still living in Arnprior. Note the Muldoon smiles.

Above: The blind William O'Keefe, known for his great physical strength, piety, and wisdom, with his sister Mary's son Tom Rowan on the far left, and his brother Tom's three boys, Angus, Ignatius and Edward, c. 1930.

Rita Kennedy and her mother Kate McDermot, wife of Pat Kennedy, c. 1932.

Kate McDermot's older sister, Genevieve O'Keefe and her four daughters, Eva, Cecilia, Mary, and Annie, c. 1953.

Richard Brown and
William Delaney, 1924

Mel Lockhart
and his wife
Cecilia O'Keefe, about
1938

John E. Burns and Edward Grace, 1924

James Carter, 1924

Jack Mantil, 1924

Basil O'Keefe with his wife Mary and daughter, Mary Anne.
The boys at the back are Larry, Donny and Danny; in the middle, David and Michael.

Helen Lee, Ed O'Keefe, Tom Rowan, Angus and Ignatius O'Keefe, and Angus's pet pig, c. 1934. Tom wa the son of Mary O'Keefe Rowan. Helen is a great-granddaughter o Tom Clancy and Mary Lormasne of West Huntley Her mother wa the beautiful Laura McDermo

Mary Mantil Carroll and her mother Rose on the right, and Mrs. J. Carroll on the left.

John Bassett and Archie Currie with his sons John and Michael who escaped the deadly fire that took two of their first cousins. John Bassett married the widow Susan Gosson Scott.

Kate O'Keefe, granddaughter of Benjan Finner and Mary Mantil, with her fir cousin, Joe Finner.

the atmosphere only some fifty yards away and thunder claps shake the little house, but Mel continued to move about undaunted by nature's display. Not once did he ever make a sale in a storm; so we had no idea what he was trying to prove. As far as I was concerned, he was bereft of any nervous system.

I used to get even by eating Peterson's vanilla ice cream off and on during the day. Uncle Mel would say, "I hope you are not eating away the profits in vanilla ice cream?" I would mumble a reply behind spaniel-eyes and go about my duties. But I really did support the Peterson Ice Cream business little by little that summer. It was very hot, and my pay was only ten dollars per week, and I wasn't getting my sleep, and then again, boys will be boys. Mel knew I was anyway!

Cely's compassion went out to all. She helped many others weather life's storms. She stuck by her children and her brothers and sisters whenever they needed assistance. She bore the deaths of her parents, brother, three sisters, and a dear grandchild. Her own battle with cancer was fought with admirable resignation. Never once did she complain about her pain — never once did she become angered by the injustice of her condition. The O'Keefe children were all like that. Her rosary seemed to be her solace — only a few ever were allowed to see it. To say adieu I had to whisper in her ear — her parched lips murmured a reply.

Cely was the most mystical of the O'Keefes. After my mother's funeral, Aunt Cely and my wife and I returned to mother's bungalow in Westboro. The house held an awful emptiness that day. Its gentle companion of forty-two years had gone. You could hear the loneliness!

Since the house would be empty until such time as it could be sold, I was naturally worried about the safety of its contents. I was particularly concerned about some money my mother held in safekeeping for a next-door neighbour who feared her relatives might take it. I knew my mother always felt very responsible about the safety of this money and had therefore stored it in a safe place.

I asked Aunt Cely and my wife to help me look for it. The bedroom and kitchen were searched with no results. Aunt Cely moved into the small dining room while Marilyn and I were chatting in the kitchen. Suddenly Cely said, "I wish we could find that money!" At that instant, the bottom shelf of the buffet in the dining room gave way and some fifteen dishes from my mother's dinner set fell against the buffet door out onto the carpeted floor. Immediately I told Cely to reach in where the dishes had been and she would find the money. She did and the money was there. To this day, I don't know why I made that statement. In the spill, only one dish was broken but it was the prize of the lot: a beautiful serving plate decorated with petite roses and gold trim. The little miracle had its price! But Cely Lockhart's request was answered, and the neighbour got her money. And my mother was happy.

Edward, the remaining son in the O'Keefe family, has already been discussed in this writing. He of course walks daily in God's garden, the special son of a special mother. Recently, I was visiting Edward at the Fairview Manor in Almonte. We were sitting in one of the television lounges, just the two of us, when a nurse came round to check the area. To my surprise, she turned to me and said, "I see the buttermilk monster has struck again!" I said that was too bad and she added, "Yes, every day our lounges' refrigerators are hit. Someone takes a half a glass of buttermilk from each fridge; we can't seem to catch the culprit!" Through all this, Edward remained completely unconcerned. Jokingly I said that it might be a staff member. And with a smile, she went about her duties.

On my way home, I realized I had missed the whole point of the nurse's remarks. Edward was the buttermilk monster! The nurse knew it and Edward knew it.

The nurse was politely telling me that Edward was the guilty party. She enjoyed Edward's little game and was merely playing along. I doubt if Edward ever really suspected they knew. He continued to raid each fridge at appointed times of the day, never taking more than half a glass at each station and always leaving a dirty glass in each sink. All the facts fitted Edward: he had an insatiable thirst for buttermilk; he could be uncannily deceptive in his own way; and he wouldn't wash a dish if you paid him. An incorrigible *card*! and there he was at the Fairview Manor still indulging in his own brand of chicanery, putting colour into his drab days: "the old buttermilk caper as masterminded by Edward O'Keefe"!

Rare Birds

Having spent many a holiday on his grandmother's farm in Corkery, my cousin Frank Prudhomme is at ease chatting with country folk. He especially enjoys his new neighbours in Montague Township where he has bought a farm. When Frank tells them his grandmother Genevieve McDermot O'Keefe grew up in that area, they become even friendlier.

One day, while chewing the fat with an old codger, a hummingbird flitted by.

Frank remarked, "Henry, I don't believe I've ever seen that species before!"

"I have," says Henry. "It's a new foreign type. Goes by the name of Humgarian."

"Really," remarked Frank, not sure if Henry was pulling his leg. "Humgarian, did you say?"

"You've got it, son! Right on! It's the very rare Humgarian hummingbird!"

•

Being sorely pressed by too many duties, Sir Boyle Roche once said in Parliament, "Not being a bird, I cannot be in two places at once!"

61

Four Strange Deaths

Stephen

The Grim Reaper has always found bizarre ways of going about his business. One such death came to Stephen O'Keefe, my grandfather's brother and youngest of nine. He lived alone down the Vaughan Side Road on the Ninth Concession. He rented out a threshing machine with his brothers William and Edward and also went about the country sheering sheep. All the O'Keefe boys kept flocks of sheep, especially David on the Mahoney Road.

Stephen, however, had one talent not shared by his brothers. He was one of the finest fiddlers in West Huntley. Angus, his nephew, has never forgotten the "sweetness" of Stephen's technique, his way of showing the other side of a usually staid personality.

One afternoon in 1933, a Johnny H_____ found Stephen face down in the tall grass of his farmyard. He had been dead for two days. On his kitchen table, they found several bottles of crab-apple preserves. One had been opened. Its contents had caused his death. The "mother" on top had developed into a lethal poison caused by too little sugar in the recipe or improper sealing. Stephen never had a chance.

My grandmother often warned us to scoop carefully away the top of any freshly opened bottle of preserves. Now I know why. Stephen's death had been a lesson to the whole country.

Josephine

Josephine Curtin's death also served as a warning. My mother, her first cousin once removed, used to caution me about my excessive use of vinegar on food. It will thin your blood and even kill you, she would say. She never told me how she knew!

But as I learned later, apparently that's how Lawrence Curtin and Ellen Clancy lost their grown-up daughter Margaret Josephine. She had developed a craving for vinegar, often drinking a half a glass at a time. She died of a blood condition! My mother would have been about sixteen. She never forgot Josephine's cause of death and never let me forget it either.

Homer

The Manions have had their share of tragedies. Patsy Manion and Elizabeth Tierney's son Homer died at the end of a team of horses. One spring, he was drawing logs around Chelsea, Quebec. He took the team with his empty wagon down to the shore for water. He remained standing on the wagon. Suddenly, the shoreline caved in and the horses pulled Homer to his death into the deep icy waters of the Gatineau River.

Maggie

Every family has one member who holds it together. A steadying personality in times of sorrow and disharmony. The one the other members look to for direction. The one who listens attentively and puts lives back together.

Such a person was the comely Catherine Hickey. Born the year Abe Lincoln took up his cross, she was the last child of Michael Hickey and Mary Sweeney. Somehow the family made a living on that rugged range of rocks and brush between Con Mahoney's and Buckley's on the Twelfth Line. Its lunar condition not surprisingly inspired next-door neighbour Dan Buckley to enter the counterfeiting business.

Somewhere in her twenties, Catherine went to work in Carleton Place. Around that time her family started to unravel. In 1883, her older brother Dennis drowned (33); in 1885, her sister Bridget died; and in 1888, Mary Sweeney died at age sixty-three. For Mary, forty-three years in that deserted spot had been enough. Catherine no doubt looked after all the arrangements.

In keeping with her sense of responsibility to family, Catherine erected a suitable monument in St. Michael's Cemetery some time after her father's death in January, 1900. She had done her duty by leaving a fitting memorial to her parents and brother and sister.

But Catherine's work was not done. Tragedy often comes in large doses. That same year, Catherine Hickey also raised another stone in a different section of the cemetery, a stone which in its own way also meant a great deal to her. It was dedicated to Maggie Ellen Grace, one of the first children of her older sister Ellen who had married Peter Grace in 1877.

In the old days, aunts and uncles often unofficially adopted nieces or nephews to help alleviate the burden of a brother's or sister's large family. Once when I was visiting the ninety-seven-year-old Julia Scott O'Reilly, a young lady dropped into the Fairview Manor to see her. Julia said, "This is my grandniece, Martina, the daughter of Carmel Killeen, my niece; you know Carmel, my sister Cecilia Carroll's daughter. Martina came to live with me when she was about ten. I needed the company after my husband died, and as you know, Carmel had her hands full with eight other children. She lived with me 'til she married. She's a daughter to me. I don't know what I would have done without her!" Julia never had any children of her own.

My own grandmother welcomed her sister Catherine Kennedy's daughter, Rita, into her home in 1935. She was about ten. She stayed twenty years. Annie O'Keefe took in her husband's niece. Stella Kennedy raised the three young ones of her dead sister, Mary O'Connell.

Catherine Hickey did likewise.

Probably around the time Mary Sweeney died. Maggie would be about seven. Catherine twenty-eight. There must have been a closeness there before Catherine chose her. And then their love had grown over the next twelve years and continued to grow long after Maggie's agonizing death on July 7, 1900, just five months after Catherine buried her father.

Her sickness had begun innocently enough. A bruised or cut leg while climbing an apple tree in the fall or was it that spring? And then the dreaded disease of tuberculosis infecting the wound and beginning to multiply its contagious spores. And Catherine watching her chosen daughter suffer each day, dying a little with her.

They buried Maggie on a Monday after the ten o'clock Mass for the Dead sung by Father Patrick Corkery. Peter and Ellen, their children, relatives, and neighbours like the O'Briens, Whites, Morrisseys, Flynns, O'Keefes, Kennedys, Forrests and Curtins would be there! And also at the grave, the tall, gaunt frame of Catherine who had seen something special in her little Maggie so many years before. Ellen also understood. Maggie had been the daughter of both, don't you see?

Few gravestones have verses in St. Michael's Cemetery ... but Margaret's stone near the Whites in front of the site of the old church has one ... it sounds like Catherine ... doing things with dash ... helping where she could ... trying to leave a fitting tribute to Maggie ... getting the mason to cut her feelings into stone so you and I would know of her love and her loss ... and perhaps more important, leaving for posterity an adulation to the Maggie that was her Maggie ... whose charm had so moved her on that first day Catherine saw her in January, 1882.

The words read:

> *"Sleep on my dear, in calm repose,*
> *Though parted now, a while*
> *In yonder realm we'll join in praise*
> *And greet your happy smile"*

Wouldn't it be something if we all could have seen that smile?

What Did William See?

Cecilia O'Keefe Lockhart told this story about the death of her Uncle William O'Keefe. On January 19, 1936, on an early Sunday morning, he lay dying surrounded by his sister-in-law, Genevieve O'Keefe, Cecilia and two or three other nephews and nieces. As noted, William had been blind for twenty-six years and lived all that time with Genevieve and his brother Tom. Known for his piety and wisdom, he was loved by all the O'Keefe family. Perhaps his own appreciation for them accounted for this strange occurrence.

Just before he died, he raised his head from the pillow and turned it around slowly to look into the eyes of each one present. Then he expired. It was as if, they said, his eyesight had been restored and that he had seen them all before he went to eternity.

62

The Night Halley's Comet Touched Ireland

On Saturday night, May 21, 1910, in Garrynapeaka in the parish of Iveleary in the Barony of Muskerry, County Cork, an act of devilish intrigue took place. It was a night of smoke and fire and terror on the land, a night to bring an atheist to his knees and a sinner to his senses. It was the night the tail of Halley's Comet swept around the earth, and the night two men brought pandemonium to a wee spot in Ireland.

The code-name was Lollipopus. The players: Buckley the Tailor and his neighbour Cork Echo. Now Cork Echo had heifers nearby on a mountain called Coolclogh just atop the community of Derreenowen. The mountain was rough. So much heather and fern and furze that the heifers often fell into large holes and crevices. Cork Echo wanted to burn the mountain, but since the land was commonly owned, he needed the permission of his neighbours in Derreenowen which approval they refused to give. As time went by, Cork Echo became more agitated, often unburdening his trouble on the shoulders of the crippled tailor.

The tailor you see had a certain genius that attracted people. Not just neighbours, but priests, writers, chemists, and doctors from other valleys, towns and faraway places. All types came to his white cottage on the road to Gougane Barra, not far past Inchigeelagh, but farther from Macroom than from Bantry. Even the great Ripley of *Believe It Or Not* fame never failed to call when he and his wife visited Ireland.

The tailor had some education. He worked as an apprentice-journeyman-tailor in Cork City around 1890-1900, travelled in the British Isles, married a calendar-cover-girl named Anastasia, and moved to his new wife's father's home in Garrynapeaka where he set up business. I passed by the site in 1987 on the way to Gougane Barra over terrain not unlike some side roads in West Huntley. At Gougane Barra cemetery, a grave-digger named Dineen drew my attention to the tailor's impressive seven-foot by five-foot black marble tombstone designed by the tailor's friend, the famous Irish sculptor Seamus Murphy.

A student of life, the tailor became its teacher, able to translate into the language of the people the often stilted Mumbo Jumbo of psychology, theology, history and politics. His peat-smelling kitchen-living-dining room was his classroom. And his regular pupils were men with funny-sounding names like "Jerry the River", "Johnny Faddy", "Mickey the Buck", "Jack of the Roads", and "Jack the Ram". They'd sit around his "office" jawing away the evenings, after which they'd return home with hearts lightened by the tailor's merriment.

That week in May, the talk at the tailor's centred around the Comet. Comets weren't much understood in those days. People saw them as meteorites crashing on earth or portents of wars and plagues. In the Fifteenth Century, an unscientific Church introduced a special prayer imploring God to protect the people from the Devil, the Turk and the

Comet. And in the City of Cork, the *Examiner* of that week had quoted some astronomer as saying that, if the Comet touched the earth, it could burn it up.

As the tailor was reading out all this terrifying news to his illiterate friends on the night of May 20, he could sense the fear in the room. It was then that a plan to save Cork Echo's heifers hit him. Before the evening broke up, he told everyone it might be best to say good-bye to one another in case the Comet burnt them alive in their sleep that night. Then he signalled Cork Echo to remain. He told him of his plan, after which Echo went home.

That night the weather was fine and dry. A respectable breeze cooled Echo's excitement as he sat up at home fully clothed. The hours dragged on like Sunday sermons. Finally he could wait no longer. He would do it!

He scampered over to Coolclogh mountain and he set it ablaze. Then he tore back home and discarded his clothes for a nightshirt and took off for Derreenowen. There he went from door to door like a crazed sleepwalker telling everyone the Comet had struck the mountain. He urged them to pray as they had never prayed before. And the fear of God swept among the people and the *Aves* bombarded heaven.

The next day Cork Echo was a hero. Except for Echo's heifers, which he had carefully removed beforehand and then quickly returned later, the mountain was as bare as Venus. But the people were safe. God had answered their prayers. What courage Echo had shown. What faith! He had made them turn to God. A saint in their midst!

Then the tailor joined the fun. The following Monday when it was time to read the paper to his faithful, he memorized for the occasion a fictitious newspaper story of the Comet's touching the top of the highest mountain in Cork. The eyes of his listeners sparkled like cats' in light as he related how one man spotted the fire and ran almost naked through the damp night warning his friends and leading them all in the Rosary; how the fire suddenly ceased; how the earth was saved; and how the astronomer's prediction had been nothing but poppycock. He topped it all off by saying the Bishop had already sent news of Cork Echo's bravery to the Pope himself.

Next day, Cork Echo came down with a cold. But, from his front door he could see his heifers. And he rested easy!

(Based on a story in Eric Cross's book, *The Tailor and Ansty*)

Battle Cries

Certain septs or clans (families) had battle cries:

The Murphys cried "herroo herroo!" — The Earls of Kildare shouted "crom a boo!" from "cromadh a bu!" meaning "croom [their castle] forever!"

Perhaps, our habit of "booing" is a form of such cries used in reverse.

63

The Northwest Corner of West Huntley (See map on page 347)

The Burnt Lands of West Huntley are in the mid-section of the Twelfth Concession along the valley's western ridge. The Great Fire of 1870 swept easterly across the ridge as far as the Upper Mahoney Side Road before turning away to the northeast.

The land today has a rustic charm! As the thick forests were cleared by the pioneers, they must have been pleased to see how similar the lay of the land was to Tipperary and Cork.

A Sunday drive is best begun by turning north at the corner of the Dwyer Hill Road and Highway 44. At the cross of the Dwyer Hill Road and the Mahoney-Carroll Side Road on the southeast corner, as mentioned earlier, is the original homestead of the O'Keefes. Built in the early or middle 1850's, sixteen O'Keefes were born there over a seventy-year period.

This cross was known for years as O'Keefe's Corners. Three brothers, sons of pioneer Tom O'Keefe, lived on three corners. Today, Tom's great-grandson, Gary O'Keefe, and his wife Connie, live at the end of the old laneway which ran out to the side road. An O'Keefe has lived on this corner since 1847. (See page 361)

Tradition has it (and several unearthings support the belief) that a log schoolhouse once was built on Gary O'Keefe's lot. The teacher in the 1850's and '60's would have been Dennis Egan who lived with his wife Bridget Manion and his father Mike. As noted, Michael ran a tavern-store from his house on the southwest corner. After Michael's death into 1868, Dennis probably kept the business going into the 1870's.

The next stretch along the Dwyer Hill Road gives a good view of the far eastern ridge of West Huntley Valley, dappled with manicured fields, meadows and bushy stands. The western ridge on the left is at first quite dense as the bush has been allowed to expand at will. But soon, the area breathes more freely right back to the Vaughan Side Road.

On this part between the Mahoney-Carroll and the Vaughan Side Roads, the settlers cleared the fields, trunk by trunk and rock by rock: families such as the Kennedys, Gallaghans, Manions, Lynches, Sullivans, Vaughans, Harrolds, Bresnahans, Ryans, Walshs, McGraths, Forrests, Hogans and O'Keefes. Their labour can be seen and felt in the sombre repose of the lands in both concessions.

At the Vaughan and Dwyer Hill intersection, a schoolhouse was open from 1841 to 1964. The last frame school on the northeast corner remains, but has been made over into a home.

In the 1910's, my mother, and her father Tom in the 1870's, trudged the two kilometres from O'Keefe's Corners to this school over roads scarcely wider than a wagon. In the warm seasons, they followed the ribbon of green grass growing in the middle of the gravel road. In the winter, they ran along the snow-packed cutter trails.

If the driver turns left at this school corner, he encounters a fairly long hill at the top of which on the right is the highest point in this area of West Huntley. A rather pronounced crank or Z just beyond the hill is a perfect example of how surveying crews in the 1800's solved the embarrassing problem of two adjacent lots not quite joining together according to calculations.

On this crank, a murder took place and the victim was buried nearby. Local travellers avoided this road at night where their horses were always spooked by some sinister force.

This forced road then sidles down to the Burnt Lands' Road. A right turn and a small but well-kept surface leads the driver along the inner side of the western ridge. The road only lasts three kilometres, but years before, it went further on some hundreds of yards across the old Morrissey farm before quitting at the great gorge of Coady's Creek. Beyond the creek lived the Whalens, Coltons and Mantils. Considering the size of the creek's basin both there and behind old Paddy J. Manion's lot on the Carroll Side Road, this creek was once a river in the days of the great forests and swamps. So wide was it in places, that neighbours couldn't agree how to pay for bridges. As the map on page 350 shows, the farmers were content to build their roads alongside and up to the Creek's branches and leave the bridge-building to other generations.

Just beyond Morrissey's and the Coady Gorge, another old road, (now the Mantil Side Road), ran from west to east to meet the Eastern Ridge Road which used to run across the valley and up along the ridge to St. Michael's Church. At the corner of the Mantil and Dwyer Hill Side Roads, the traveller had several options: turn North to Panmure, go South along the Eleventh Line (Dwyer Hill Road) or head Southeast on the Ridge Road to the Church. On its western side, the Mantil Road stopped very quickly at the Coady gulley.

A worshipper returning from St. Michael's could follow the Ridge Road back to the Vaughan Side Road and eventually meet up with the Western Ridge Road, and then if he wished, proceed along the Burnt Lands' Road to the Mahoney-Carroll Side Road. In my day, the Mahoney Road also ran west across the rocky Burnt Lands to the town of Almonte. These old roads were really the turnpikes for the hayburners. They went as the crow flies.

The Eastern Ridge Road emanating from the Dwyer Hill Road-Mantil Side Road cross no longer exists, but its other section from the Church south to Manion's Corners and beyond, is not only open but almost entirely paved, providing the traveller with a clear view of that portion of the valley. The number of mansion-estates along these three miles attests to the valley's lure.

Back on the Western Ridge, the breadth of this three-kilometre section of the Burnt Lands' Road has accommodated many farms. On the driver's right, settlers like the Keefes, Magnirs, Whites and Forrests built their homes up against the shoulder of the ridge to avoid the northern blasts. Farther along, the hills and dales undulate down towards Coady's Creek hiding the old farms of the O'Briens, Bonsfields, Delaneys, Oakleys, Kennedys, Fultons and Wilsons from all but the most discerning eye.

On the return drive, again on the right side, the pioneer lands of the Hogans and Graces back against a line of pines lying this way and that over the westerly arm of Coady's Creek, their tall branches reaching up hauntingly from the shadows. The Creek basin widens dramatically here due to the once-heavy runoff from the Mahoney area some five kilometres away. Beyond Morrissey's, it joins up with the eight-kilometre-long main branch of the Creek which drains the Great Swamp and Eastern Ridge. Together these branches rendezvous with the Mississippi River near Pakenham to flow into the Ottawa. The pines are historically interesting in that only a few escaped the Great Fire of 1870.

Soon the horizon expands into the rugged landscape of Lanark County and, below, the pastoral clearings are engaging, especially in the evening. These divergent tumblings of land are the back-acres of the early Flynns, Curtins, Whites and Forrests whose homes can still be seen hugging the edge of the ridge.

No mansions à la Corkery Road here! Just some new bungalows mixed with log buildings and some fine 1870-1890 henna-red double-brick homes.

Near the end of the return run is one of the prettiest old farms in West Huntley. Its white siding-over-log house rests under several moody oaks at the end of a long laneway. It's the former home of Tom White and Bridget McNamara who rebuilt here after the Great Fire in 1870. Readers will remember this farm as being the playground of Richard. With patches of grey, sepia bush on its left, the golden vista of open fields on its right, and the silver shadings of logs and outbuildings in the centre, the sight is captivating and one I learned to love as a boy.

Immediately beside this white lane, another one wanders down nearly half a mile over pleasant countryside to the front door of the old Curtin homestead. Both lanes would make coming home always a little more pleasurable. Much like the winding entrances of the Dutch farms around Lancaster, Pennsylvania.

The next kilometre and a half offers a change of pace. The bush closes in. And not long past the Vaughan Side Road, the driver begins to savour the mood of one of the most interesting sections of road in West Huntley as the route drops into Coady's Gorge and up again. Beside him are the old lands of the Flynns, Keefes, Buckleys, Hickeys, Forrests, McDonalds, O'Connells, Mahoneys, and Currans. At the bottom of the gorge, the open fields on the right follow the creek as far as the eye can see. On the left, the effects of the Great Fire are still visible. The little soil left on the limestone has nourished sumach and cedar on a rolling topography.

The driver, keeping well to the right, should drive this two-kilometre section of road, slowly. An interesting blend of landscape! The countryside is in no hurry. Mahoney's Side Road is the next turn on the left. It's not marked, so the driver must be on the lookout.

This Mahoney road is at first intimidating, for its condition is about the same as a hundred and seventy years ago. Large dipping rocks loom up, especially on the first two braes into the Coady Creek gorge. In this first vale on the left was Mahoney's Hotel-Tavern-Store-Post Office. The weeds, brush, and broken fences present a forlorn picture today, but, in my time, the fields were clear and cattle grazed across the meadows.

The road rises from Mahoney's vale on a bed of sand to the top of the Western Ridge. The next half-mile winds down over better surface to O'Keefe's Corners. Just below the last hill on the right was the site of Egan's tavern.

My uncle Angus and I once came over this hill in 1943 on a bicycle. He was steering. I was sitting on the crossbar. By the time we reached the top of this last hill we had built up quite a head of steam since the terrain falls rapidly from the ridge above Mahoney's place. Halfway down this hill, one of Basil O'Keefe's sheep broke across our path. We hit the sheep on its left back hip. The bike stopped on the spot. I landed on my uncle. The crossbar bent with the force. The sheep had to be destroyed. Basil and I "settled out of court". I paid for the bike's repairs. Basil took his loss graciously. One never knows what lies beyond the next hill. Maybe even a crosswalk for sheep!

The Bishop and Bernie

Bishops are important people. What they say usually goes! But not for Father Bernie! Irish Bishop Power had the formidable task of convincing the affable but outspoken Father Bernie to assume the duties of Chaplain at a large Motherhouse of Sisters.

"Now Bernie, you'll love your new placement! The Sisters are eager to have you. You'll have your own suite of rooms, a salary, car, good food cooked to your specifications, and lovely grounds by the ocean for swimming. It's almost a holiday, you'll be having, Bernie! When can you be ready to move in?"

"I'd be thankin' your Reverence for his confidence! But I feel I would be doin' him an unfairness to take such an altogether heavenly appointment. If it's all you say it is, at the Mother-house, your Grace, why don't you take it yourself?"

Tanks for the Thrill

The summer of 1941 saw the Canadian Tank Corps come to West Huntley's hills to test new tanks. Many local lads, this author included, hitched rides in the cramped quarters of those swift, maneuverable, steel-treaded broncos.

The Pineapple Inheritance

The Irish can be just as secretive as anybody. Especially about business. My Uncle Maurice Williams was like that. Tight-lipped about financial matters.

For example, take those green leather packets that arrived in his mailbox every three months for thirty-four years. He had the whole country wondering about their contents. And no one ever became the wiser. Maurie never asked any man his business and he never told his.

The first packet came around 1930, from Connecticut, U.S.A. It was addressed to Mrs. Catherine Williams, Maurie's mother, who had come to visit her newly wedded son and liked the place so much she stayed on until her death in 1937. The packets never failed to arrive.

As everyone suspected, but could not verify, the packets contained money orders. And for considerable amounts, too.

The first packet was worth four hundred dollars, a fortune in the Depression when cows sold for fifteen and many farmers couldn't even meet their mortgage payments. Further shipments levelled off at three hundred dollars and gradually dwindled down to seven by 1964.

The geographical source of the packets was Hawaii by way of Connecticut. They came from Catherine's older brother, James Armstrong, who had found fortune, if not fame, in the pineapple business. Since he had never married, he left his brothers and six sisters his shares in a pineapple plantation.

After Catherine's death, her share of the money fell to Maurie and his brother Howard who had come to live with Maurie shortly after their mother had arrived. By the time the last Armstrong sister (all from March Township) died in 1964 at age one hundred and six, the pot was empty.

Trite as it might sound, Maurie's farm for years was partly run on pineapple juice. And the strawberry-raspberry farm Howard Williams established in the early Forties no doubt also had pineapple-money invested in it. Certainly the use of a pineapple inheritance for the development of a raspberry-strawberry farm was more than appropriate.

Clarence Williams, Maurie's son, told me of the elation at another Armstrong sister's home upon the reception of her first money order. She was married to a James Casey. Both were advanced in years. When James laid eyes on the first four hundred dollars, he sat himself down, took off one boot and then the other, picked them up, fired them in the corner, and hollered, "By God, that's it; I'll never work another day in my life!"

An Irish Greeting

"The top of the mornin' to ya, Murphy!"
"And the rest o' the day to yourself, Kelly!"

A Mother's Parting Gift

This is a story of perseverance, love and courage! About a family on the Eighth Line. There were eleven children: Joseph, Cecilia, Maisie, Beatrice, Louise, Ambrose, Edith, Florence, Delbert, Clayton and Willo. Their father John Leo, now in his nineties, is a "decent, respectable, God-fearing man". He's the son of Tim Scott and Emma Hayes, who lived back the Eighth Line, almost at the Old Almonte Road. Tim and Emma had three children: Mary Liz who married Cecil McIntyre from Douglas, Julia who married Cecil's brother Alex, and John Leo who married Cecil and Alex's sister, Jessie. Old Tim, who lost his wife when she was fifty-two, used to say jokingly years later that if he had married the widowed Mrs. McIntyre from Douglas, he'd have a complete set of "four tyres".

When John Leo married Jessie in 1925 he moved in the Eighth Line closer to Highway 44. Patrick Scott and Annie Curtin had once lived there. They had eleven children but lost them all as babies. The land produced ample crops, but in bad years its gravel base barely supported June grass. People tend to forget the early Thirties was also a time of drought which added to the depressed economy around the world. For example in '33, John Leo sold some four yearlings for six dollars each, and as they left the yard exclaimed, "Them's the lowest-priced cattle ever to leave this farm!" Even good yearlings were going for only nine dollars and cows for fifteen. Times were poor and none was poorer than John Leo and Jessie. No oilcloth on the table for them.

By 1941, Jessie and Leo were beginning to see daylight. They had made it through the dirty Thirties. They had lost little Willo in 1937 but the other ten children aged thirteen to two stayed healthy. John Leo and Jessie were never really poor with such a family around them. Every night after supper they'd say the rosary together, for both Jessie and John Leo had great faith, particularly Jessie who had great devotion to the Mother of God. Old Tim Scott was also there living out his

Jessie
holding her first born, Joseph, 1926

*John Leo
Scott,
1924*

final years, having given up his land for a government pension.

The sustaining force behind the family was bonny Jessie. A taller than average brunette, she was two years younger than her handsome black-haired Jimmy Stewart-type husband born in 1898. She was a teacher, took her training in North Bay, and taught in Moose and Wilno before coming to old #6 at Manion's Corners. She taught about four years in West Huntley. She first boarded at Paddy Carter's red-brick home on the Tenth Line and later with Tom Carroll and Mary Rowan on the Old Almonte Road. She had a testing walk each day particularly from Carter's, but she was no slouch. Teachers, by the way, were considered good marital catches by local lads (they still are) and John Leo certainly caught a good one in Jessie.

In 1940, a government official dropped in on John Leo to request permission to test the quality of some gravel hills. Shortly after, John Leo

Two of Jessie's Boys:
Delbert and Clayton, 1946

276

sold some gravel to help with the construction of the Carp Airport. Things were looking up for the Scott Family. And about time, too.

And then one December day in 1941, everything went topsy-turvy. John Leo suffered his own Pearl Harbour. His spirited, happy Jessie suddenly died.

She had gone to Almonte in horse and cutter to see the dentist and afterwards to buy a few Christmas presents for the children. She never got the presents. The horse and cutter were driven back by a friend into the empty yard of John Leo's life. Jessie had choked to death in the dentist's chair on a stray piece of gauze!

What does a man do with ten children and the heart of his family gone?

Only one with great faith in God could have done what John Leo did. He took stock of the situation. The two youngest, just babies, went to an Aunt in Douglas. Cecilia, only thirteen, was asked to quit school. For the first year she and John Leo kept the family together. In 1943, one baby returned from Douglas and the total family number was then nine.

For seven years, until she married Alonzo Kelly in 1948, Cecilia took her mother's place. People in West Huntley still talk in quiet admiration about the "little mother" from the Eighth Line. She answered this actual "call to arms" with the same pluck as her mother.

She was another Jessie! And she had Jessie's faith. The rosary was said every evening, and Cecilia grew up overnight, working as if everything depended on herself and praying as if everything depended on the Virgin.

Along the way, Beatrice helped and then Louise, Maisie, Edith and Florence. And the boys Joseph and Ambrose pitched in. And slowly the family got smaller and smaller as the little birds flew the nest until John Leo one day looked back on it all and knew Jessie was proud of him and Cecilia and the whole lot.

Jessie never did stop loving her family and watching over them. As often happens after a dear-one's death, particularly one of deep religious faith, a little miracle occurred in the lives of those left behind.

Shortly after her going, the financial burden so heavy for sixteen years, began to ease even faster. More men came to buy gravel from John Leo after 1941, and the trucks leaving the property began to increase and did so all through the Forties and Fifties until John Leo sold the whole pit in 1963 to the Dibblee Construction Company for a tidy sum.

While on earth, Jessie had given them all her love and energy and, above all, her example of deep religious fervour. And now in heaven, she had pleaded for this special favour for her family.

The men coming to buy John Leo's gravel were sent, don't you see, as a parting gift by a loving mother, Jessie McIntyre of Douglas.

66

A Bobby Byrnes

Constable Byrnes was about ready. His weasel eyes ran one last time over his sartorial splendour: uniform, spotless ... creases, like razors ... buttons, sparkling ... boots, spit and polished ... moustache, like down ... face, smooth, scented and powdered. He felt how he looked ... trim and confident. Ballyvourney hamlet in Sullane Valley, Cork County, needed the best in law enforcement and, by King George, thought Byrnes, it had it.

A final check for pencil and "fine" book, a rub of boots on the back of royal blue, a vain adjustment to his chin strap, and William Byrnes, one of his majesty's finest, stepped past his yellow door into the brilliance of a summer Sunday afternoon.

Willy didn't much care for Sundays. Most people had the day off. Besides, it was always the day for road-bowling, an illegal sport played, as Willy's luck would have it, in only two counties of Ireland: Armagh and Cork. A mindless game, thought Willy, where two "eejuts" throw their own twenty-eight-ounce iron ball called the "bullet" over five or more miles of road, the winner being the first to propel the ball across the finish line.

And all the wagering! Quite illegal! Bets up to a hundred and fifty pounds on the match with smaller ones on single shots. Many a cupboard bare because of it, thought Willy, and a poor example for the kids. Not to mention the bother to Sunday travellers with hordes of yelping, leaping supporters lining the route, sweeping around the "hind" thrower and then the "fore", each fan fortified by a belt at Dooley's bar where the "score" began, and not a few with the bulge of a Paddy's mickey on their hips for a bit of strength along the way. Little good were the traffic guards posted by organizers ... it was still a mess of confusion with decent citizens, mostly strangers, greatly inconvenienced.

What really stuck in Willy's craw was that in spite of the whole thundering-tarnation event being against the law, the press still advertised the games.

And this Sunday's match was a big one: only two in the "score", not four; a giant of a man named Flynn from Kilgoran capable of lofting the bullet some seventy yards and running it another quarter of a mile; and his opponent, a pork-barrel figure, named Hammer Hayes from Macroom, known for his accuracy and magical deftness at "englishing" the bullet into every conceivable twist of terrain ... finesse against strength it was ... the short against the tall! And the game had already started some seven miles up the Kenmare Road and would be finishing in a glen beyond the big hill coming into Ballyvourney. And then the final gathering at Noonan's bar for the tallying and more suds.

Usually, Willy would bicycle out to some of these games and issue tickets to bettors and players and then confiscate the bullets. But today, due to the popularity of the event, Willy decided to wait until after the final shots to move in with wetted pencil. It wasn't that he enjoyed spoiling people's fun, but the law was the law and Willy went by the book.

The constable he had replaced had had a soft attitude, but Willy was tougher and meaner and no pushover.

Sure his popularity suffered. Dogs were trained to bark at him; the chatter deadened at Williams' General Store when Willy entered for smokes; even the children were unfriendly.

It hurt to see crayon-graffiti such as "Byrnes a Worm!" or worse still, "Wee on Willy!" It was a lonely, dirty job. But Willy felt he had the disposition for it. And apparently everyone agreed.

The match itself was a fierce one, head to head and muscle to muscle, over curves, bridges and yo-yo terrain. Being the hind shot, Hayes went first ... his final chance for the finish line. It was a cannon! The iron sphere sent sparks flying from the stones as it bit the dust, and his supporters, mostly short people, shouted, "He has lit up the road!" But being off-line, the shot unfortunately drew up a few yards short.

It was Flynn's turn. With his red hair flashing above his pocket of fans some thirty yards from the throwing point, he began his run, each stride longer than the last, every muscle stretched beyond endurance, his hairy arm taking the bullet full circle before letting it fly underhanded into the blue. One spectator gasped, "Sure he's thrown it to heaven's door!"

The Hammer had been nailed down by Flynn!

The cheers told Willy the contest was over; so he started up the hill to do his duty.

It was at this point, the local blacksmith on the far side of the hill went into action. In his hands he had a shovel and in the shovel an iron bullet that he himself had just reddened in the forge. At a signal, he threw the ball gently over the crest and down the hill towards the coming Byrnes. Young lads foolin' with the game-ball thought Willy. He easily stopped the bullet with his shiny boot and reaching down, officiously picked it up with his gloved hand and placed hand and glove and bullet in his trousers' pocket.

No one was sure which came first: the smoke, the smell of leather, wool and skin, or the pain and muffled scream of poor Willy. No road-bowling tickets were given out that day or any other day thereafter. It took two weeks to get a new uniform and months for the burns to heal.

By that time, Willy was a changed man. Even the dogs licked his face and the children held his hand and the boys at Williams' Store would swing out an empty barrel for his pleasure.

And every once in a moon, the lads round Noonan's bar would talk of policeman Willy who became affectionately known in Sullane Valley as their own "Bobby Burns"!

He was the only policeman they knew who had!

67

The Little Troopers

One spring afternoon in 1942, with the freshness of smog-free azure and wild flowers on the land, a motley crew spilled out the front door of Number 8 Eleventh Line School.

At the helm, surrounded by a brood of little ones all reaching at once for the pleasure of holding her hands, was the schoolmistress, Rita Tunney. Not too big herself, she wasn't much older than some of her senior students.

As the children skipped weightlessly along the narrow road strewn with stones and holes from the April rains and heaving frost, Miss Tunney silently took note of their exceptionally good behaviour. No doubt her sharp lecture on the solemnity of their mission had left its mark. She had told them they were on an errand of mercy to pay respect to the dead and bring comfort to the bereaved. She knew quite well that many had never before been to a wake, let alone ever seen a dead person. But she had done her best to prepare them! And now as her barefoot charges apprehensively trooped back the Panmure Road, she found herself singularly moved. They were indeed a fine group. And hearty, too, well-accustomed to the rigours of country living. This day would only take them a step farther in strengthening them for the hard knocks of life.

About fifteen minutes later, they arrived at their destination: the old stone house built by Tim Forrest and Catherine Hendricks. Tom Murphy and Annie Delaney lived there then. Inside the front door, on the left, Annie's father, John Delaney, was being waked in the parlour.

John had seen much of West Huntley's development during his ninety-four years. He had served under ten pastors and watched the number of Catholic families rise to a hundred and thirty in 1870 and fall to a record low of sixty in 1930. He had been baptized in the first log chapel built in the present cemetery (1835-1864). He had been with his mother Elizabeth Hendricks that day in 1860 when Father Vaughan, the first resident priest, said the funeral mass for his father William. His sisters Mary and Catherine were there too and his brother James. In time, he would bury them all.

Years ago, into the same old original Delaney homestead near the Eleventh Line across from the Forrest home, he had brought his bride Mary Jane McDonald. They raised a large family there and a good one. And then came the fatal day in the midst of the Depression when John and Mary and the children stood and watched the homestead burn to the ground. Yes, old John "had paid his dues"!

The little mourners edged into the room and formed a semicircle round the coffin. The Carrolls were there: Theresa, Angus and Gerald, and the Williamses, Clarence, Allan and Shirley; Des and Harry Grace from the Twelfth Line were present, as well as Acquin and Terry Kennedy from the Eleventh. From down the Vaughan Side Road had come

Des Vaughan and Joe Hunt along with his first cousins Muzz and Mary Haggerty.

Miss Tunney led them in the rosary and afterwards they offered their condolences to their classmates, Rita, Helen, Grant and Tony Murphy, the grandchildren of John. In the big kitchen with its big table, laden with goodies, they met more Murphys and Delaneys and other relatives and neighbours who had come by foot, buggy, and car. Then, fortified by sweets and milk, at a signal from Miss Tunney, they quietly dispersed and hit the road back to the schoolhouse. Next day, Saturday, May 1, John Delaney would be

John Delaney
1924

buried, and the children's visit be forever recorded in their hearts as a memorable one!

This practice of school children attending wakes of nearby parishioners when the weather permitted was not uncommon in those "pre-downtown-funeral-parlour days". With the elementary schools of West Huntley already opened since 1843, it can be assumed that this manner of sharing another family's grief had been popular for over a hundred years.

The idea is supernaturally sound! Little children have always been thought to have the ear of the Father. His Son urged us to become as they if we expect heaven, for heaven He said was made up of such. In their innocence they pray with simple faith and total trust. They are very special in God's eyes. That's why He said any scandalization of His little ones would bring down His wrath on the guilty.

Two other class visitations deserve mentioning. In 1937, Carmel Murphy, then an O'Keefe from the Twelfth Line, was a teacher at #8. She recalled the day she took her students back the other way on the Eleventh Line to the wake of Mrs. Hannah Harrold. The log house was lonely that day. Hannah's husband John had died in 1934. Only her adopted son George Stone was left to mourn.

It had been a house used to children. John Harrold, Sr. and his wife Jane Perry had lived there. Patrick Sullivan raised a big family there in the 1850's and, after him, William Forrest, one of fourteen brothers and sisters, reared his own large brood, one of whom, Tom, became a priest.

It was good to have children there again. Charlie Newton and Laura Madden's Rita, Rosie, Dorothy and Margaret had come and two children of Mike Kennedy and Margaret Legree, Leo and Leonard. The Carroll family was once again represented by Angus, Bertha, Joe and Emmett. Rose and Maurice Mantil, Joe Hunt, Jackie Brown, and four of Jim and Gertie Vaughan's family, Gerald, Leo, Francis and Mike rounded out the marchers.

That same year, on a cold St. Patrick's Day, the student body of #6 at St. Michael's Church on the Ninth Line marched nearly two miles to the wake of seventeen-year-old Rita Sarah Scott at her home in the middle of the Seventh Concession. No barefeet that day. The girls had their pullovers and the boys their gum boots and everybody wore socks.

The teacher was Margaret Neville from Douglas. Number 6, founded in 1919 by soldier-priest-teacher Father Stanton, drew its students from the middle of the Tenth Concession to the Seventh Concession and from Manion's Corners to approximately the Carroll Side Road and the Eleveth Line. Jack Killeen and Evelyn Kennedy's Margaret, Evelyn and John were part of the contingent. Sarah and Margaret Forrest, daughters of Frankie and Onaugh Kennedy, were there. The Mantils, Bobby, Margaret, Betty, Mary and Raymond also walked on that windy Wednesday,

as did Rita Kennedy, Mary Mantil, daughter of Gerry and Mary Curtin, Modessa Scott, Joe Manion, and Jimmy Scott, son of Frank and Hannah Delaney. Rita Sarah's sisters, Mary, Tessie, Rosie and Kathleen, along with brothers Matt and Manus, were already at home with their widowed mother Susan to greet Miss Neville and their classmates.

The shock of seeing one so young in death must have left an indelible impression on all the young visitors that day. Then again, their presence and prayers must have meant much to the entire Scott family. And little Rita too! And to all the people of Corkery!

Carmel O'Keefe Murphy with her mother, Nellie Moran O'Keefe, and her sister Viola on the left. Her father was Michael from the Twelfth Line.

The Missing Hour

Years ago, daylight saving time was introduced. Spring ahead and fall back, they would say. My mother never got accustomed to losing an hour's sleep in April. All summer, whenever she was tired, she'd say, "It's that change in time; I still miss that extra hour's rest!"

68

Paddy the Post

Some Irish of old had the habit, the habit of repeating themselves, d'ya see? d'ya see? Friendly people they were, so they were, so they were, who tried hard to please, so they did, so they did.

Now when you had occasion to meet such a type, sure you'd think, so you would, so you would, that he had three heads on the go, on the go, but he didn't, he didn't, he didn't, d'ya see?

"Good day, good day, good day to ya," he'd say. "I'm happy, happy to meet ya, so I am, so I am! Do ya remember me? or do ya? do ya?"

"Ah, but I do, I do, I do remember you! You're Paddy the Post, to be sure, to be sure, I remember!"

"Right! Right! Right on! Indeed, indeed, I'm Paddy the Post himself, himself! You're absolutely right! The one and only, Paddy the Post, they say, they say, so they do!"

"Now Paddy, Paddy, Paddy, my boy," says I, "are you sure? are you sure? are you sure? I sometimes wonder, wonder, so I do, so I do, about the number of you, my Paddy, dear Paddy, I do!"

"Ah sure, sure, I'm the only one, the only one, the one and only its true. And thanks be to God for that, for that, to be sure, to be sure, to be sure! Ah! but I see, but I see it's time to go, I must be on my way. The Post, the Post will not wait, not wait for another day. So I bid you adieu, so I do, so I do, and a fond farewell and a toodle-loo too!"

And off he went as quick as nod, as quick as a nod went he. And I thanked the Lord, so I did, so I did, that I never, never have repeated myself the way poor Paddy, poor Paddy, did.

The Church From Within

The Church in West Huntley has always provided the unity, identity and stability so badly required by Catholic families spread over fifty square miles. And never was its presence more needed than in the years when Corkery had no temple of worship nor pastor in residence to bring the faithful together. In those years from 1821 to 1851, the people of God were His Church. Circuit-riding priests like McNamara from Montreal and MacDonald from Perth came when they could to say Masses and dispense sacraments in the barns and homes of early settlers like the Manions and Kennedys. But, generally speaking, the people were left alone to keep alive their faith. Families said the evening rosary, taught a catechism passed down from mother to mother, pronounced private blessings over the dead to be buried on their own land, conditionally baptized babies, and even married each other by taking their vows before an omnipresent God. Even without God's ministers, they followed His Spirit and were living proof that God's Kingdom and His Church lives on in the hearts of His children.

Who's the Boss?

Two bachelor Irish brothers lived with their parents in West Huntley. One day a neighbour jokingly put this question to the boys, "Lads, who's the boss at your house?"

One lad answered, "Pa has more say, that's for sure!"

"And what do you think?" asked the neighbour of the brother.

The lad thought for a while and replied, "What my brother says is true, but him and me have more say too!"

Recycling at Mahoney's

It was a cold winter's night. Most people in West Huntley were home in bed as were Conn Mahoney and his wife. That is, until two already inebriated wayfarers returning from town decided Mahoney should reopen his hotel for a few nightcaps.

They pounded on his front door shouting for Conn until finally Conn's wife could take no more. She opened up an upstairs window and shouted down at the two culprits, "If it's a drink ya be after, you can have half mine and half Conn's!"

And with that she poured the contents of "you know what" upon the upturned heads of the intruders. When they got home, even their dogs hid in the barn.

Wise But Cheap

Father Gorman decided one day that extra Masses should be said to ask God to send rain to the parched land of West Huntley. In order to procure the sacrifices of the laity towards this worthy cause, he visited some parishioners to seek monetary donations for the Masses.

One parishioner, not known for his looseness of purse, refused to give. Father Gorman admonished him, "You realize, of course, your neighbour, M_____, who has less of this world's goods than yourself, saw fit to support this worthy cause!"

Refusing to be embarrassed, the parishioner, who lived beside this charitable neighbour, retorted, "There ya have it, Father! If it rains on old M_____'s place, it'll surely rain on mine! I may as well keep my money!"

No Contest

As gossoons, Jimmy Scissons and Jerry Price often chin-wagged with Dinny Nolan of Almonte who lived on Gore Street directly behind Jimmy's father's General Store on Ottawa Street. Dinny was from Ireland and a prized employee in one of the Almonte mills, often travelling out of country for his employer. One day Jimmy asked, "Mr. Nolan, if you weren't Irish, what would you rather be?"

And Dinny replied very seriously, "Laddies, I'd rather be dead!"

69

An Angel in Disguise

My grandmother was one of those silent heroes who made it through tough years. But not without paying the piper. Her health was broken by the time she reached sixty. She was overweight and pre-diabetic. Her hair was white, her complexion chalky, and arthritis gave her considerable pain.

*Genevieve
about age seveteen,
1896*

As a young woman, she was attractive. Her facial features were refined. Her soft brown hair was combed straight back and tied behind daintily formed ears. Her eyes were large and peaceful. A quiet determination was apparent in her face.

She was born in 1879 on a farm near Franktown in Montague Township across from the old Catholic cemetery just in off Highway 16 to Smiths Falls. The old house is a barn now. As a young girl, the family moved into the town of Smiths Falls and bought a house a few doors from St. Francis de Sales' church. In her late teens, she came to Almonte to work in the woollen mills. Even then, she loved to attend parties and dances.

She married in 1900, changing her name from McDermot to O'Keefe. By 1908 she had four children; by 1921, seven. For fifty-five years she was the heart of her home, generating a warmth that attracted many relatives and friends.

I have often tried to count the many visitors that came to Tom and Genevieve O'Keefe's inconspicuous little house at O'Keefe's Corners. Literally hundreds and hundreds. Her sisters and brothers numbered nine; her husband's, eight. Her aunts and uncles and cousins were numerous. Her five married children brought their families. And then came the grandchildren, all eleven. Many people who dropped by, often stayed and stayed. Her brother-in-law, the blind William, stayed twenty-six years until his death in 1936. She gave him his own room and the affection of a family who adored him. Her niece, Rita, lived with her for twenty years. Her mother, Mary Clancy McDermot, visited regularly from Smiths Falls until her death in 1923. Dan Clancy, her uncle, came for all the fall hunting seasons. Minnie McDermot Haley visited from Smiths Falls and another sister, Laura McDermot Lee, travelled from Toronto with her husband Joe and some of their children. Her sister Nellie often arrived from Hamilton as did her sister Agnes from Ottawa.

In addition, her mother-in-law, Margaret Finner O'Keefe, often came to visit her son, Tom, at this farm where she herself had lived for over fifty-one years. In 1900, she had gone to live with another son David (at the present site of Angus Carroll's) until she died in 1909. From 1849 to 1955, these two remarkable women, Margaret and Genevieve, between them, raised sixteen children and provided the bond that held two families intact for a century.

Another family often welcomed was that of Lawrence and Ellen Clancy Curtin. Ellen was my grandmother's aunt and she lived on the lot on the southeast corner of the Dwyer Hill Road and Highway 44. I remember her in the late Thirties as a kindly old lady and I remember her son-in-law, Jerry Mantil, who was a perfect gentleman and played a respectable violin.

I would like to have known Michael O'Keefe, my grandfather Tom's brother. My mother and her sisters always spoke highly of him. He often took them to the lawn socials around Corkery and taught them how to dance. My mother won several ballroom dancing competitions around Ottawa in the late Twenties and her Uncle Mike can take some credit for her ability. Uncle Mike and his wife, the grace-full Nellie Moran, had a large family who also came down to see their Uncle Tom and Aunt Vive. Basil, their oldest son and, best looking, he said, held a deep affection for his aunt, and always talked about her with admiration. Another son, John, was a close friend of Genevieve's son, Angus, while Angus's sister, Cely, was a good friend of Viola, Mike's daughter.

Other good neighbours often came by too: the Williamses from across the field, Mike and Margaret Legree Kennedy from back the road, the Pat Kennedys from in the line, Bob and Rose Mantil from around the corner, and Jim and Cecilia Carroll from down the road. I met them all and vouch for the authenticity of their friendship towards my grandparents.

With each generation, new faces and more visitors: the Prudhommes from Renfrew, the Ogilvies from Ottawa, and the Lockharts and O'-Keefes from Almonte. All ages and sizes: the Curries, the Killeens, the Charlebois. I remember people like Alex Grace, Jimmy Flynn, Edmund Newton, Joe Manion, Howard Williams, George Stone, Tom Murphy, Johnny Kennedy, Jack Cybulski, Bill Egan, and Eddie Grace. The little boy in the bare feet never forgot a face and used his big ears to advantage.

While my grandmother was overjoyed to see everyone, she was particularly elated by the arrival of good euchre players.

One favourite guest sure to put the colour back in her cheeks was Lollie Grace, the entertainer. His freckled face was capped by bushy brows over green eyes. His wiry, beet-red hair shone in the lamplight. He was part leprechaun, part carnival barker and part riverboat gambler. He could have become a millionaire selling Dr. Ballard's Cough Medicine from the back of a Prairie Schooner. He could sell matches to the devil. He played the ponies and stud poker. And he filled the air with blarney wherever he went, especially to euchre games in the home of a fighting Irish woman like my grandmother.

My grandmother took on the air of an actress in each game. She loved to make believe that Lollie was cheating. Not only did this assumption give her an excuse for losing, but it also allowed the infusion of a jovial tension by her carefully placed insinuations. Lollie, of course, did not have to cheat to win, but no one doubted he could and would if so inclined. So to add to the chicanery, Lollie did the next worst thing and let on he was cheating. And my grandmother knew he was pretending and played her part to the limit. Here was Lollie baiting and jesting; there was grandma snipping and fending, always seemingly on the verge of a stroke. It became a game within a game — the old kitchen table would bounce as the knuckles of little fingers hammered home the winning trumps.

This art of delivering a hand-winning card with just the right amount of force and sharpness does not come easily. (Come to think of it, all the children of my grandmother were quite adept at its application). First of all, anticipation was important. The striking hand with the key card in it was slowly raised, the elbow halfcocked, and the wrist tucked in behind the ear. Then with just the proper amount of thrust, and a little temper thrown in for good measure, and at the exact moment after all others had played, the arm was whipped down and across the centre of the table in a swishing manner so that the knuckles made suitable contact just as the arm spent its full power in a graceful turn. During the delivery it was also appropriate to say something to underline the intended effect (half before the blow and the other half after) — something like, "S_____ (crash) a d_____! You won't get them all!"

Such command performances, of course, were not wasted on unimportant hands, but were reserved for crucial moments like making or stopping euchres, sweeps and loans, especially on the very last trick. I also remember my grandmother, after she had already lost two tricks to her opponent's sure-fire loan-hand, neatly pitching all her remaining cards on the table with considerable vigour and saying something like, "You dealt those jokers from the bottom; you may as well have the rest!" — the pitching usually coming just before the "have". All in all, everybody had a good time including the spectators. Tea and cake would be served and guests like Lollie promised soon to return. The embers in the grates grew dark and lamps directed the ways to the bedrooms and silence.

As a mother-in-law, my grandmother was very popular with all her sons-in-law. Her daughter Mary's husband was one of her favourites. Alex Prudhomme was a man of consummate style whose refinement was evident in his dress and manners. His face carried wisdom beyond its years. Dressed in stylish business suit with vest and gold chain, this lanky, debonnaire, black-haired gentleman could easily have passed as the French Ambassador to Canada. During the Depression he boarded at my grandmother's and worked at Maurie Williams's as a farm labourer until the railroad was able to recall him to his regular job of locomotive mechanic. Uncle Alex, being especially proficient at carpentry, was always helping around the farm. Hard physical work was always to his liking. I remember his forking hay in the early Forties when he himself was in his fifties, and to this day, I have never seen anyone handle a pitchfork with such grace. His was a class act in everything he did. Even in death: he succumbed, after seven years, to a fatal crippling disease with complete faith in God and resignation to His will.

Mel Lockhart, another son-in-law, whom we met earlier, was the husband of Cecilia O'Keefe. Mel was very typical of those affable, honest men often found in small towns. He was a painter and plumber but spent the greater portion of his working-days as the owner-manager of a general store and gasbar in Almonte. He and his wife were a great consolation to my grandmother, especially in her last years when her health worsened due to diabetes. In fact, she had to have one of her legs removed above the knee just a few years before her passing. In the winter months, she often stayed at Mel's home for short intervals. There, the luxuries of hot water and central heating were welcomed by one whose health was delicate, to say the least. While Grannie was still at her own home, Mel and Cely often drove out to help her with cleaning, baking and laundry. My grandmother always enjoyed Mel's pleasant and good-humoured company.

Maurie Williams
c. 1926

Maurie Williams, husband of Annie O'Keefe, was another good neighbour-son-in-law for some thirty years. My grandmother and he seemed to understand each other. Perhaps they hit it off because they were around the same age and because neither one was an O'Keefe in a world full of them. They both knew they had to keep their identities in order to survive. Maurie's wry sense of humour and colourful stories always made him a welcome guest. He also helped my grandmother in many direct ways: he butchered her pigs and cattle, performed the more common veterinarian operations, and shared or loaned farm equipment. I remember the days when he would trudge over from his adjoining farm with the latest newspapers: *The Farm Herald, The Almonte Gazette,* and *The Ottawa Journal.* In exchange for the papers, he sometimes had his hair cut by Ignatius O'Keefe, the local barber of the area. I thought Maurie always got the "raw end" of the deal since Nash's clippers should have been licensed as a dangerous weapon: cut two strands, pull five — cut four — jam six. Worse haircuts may have been given around Corkery but none that inflicted such pain. But then, they were free and no tipping required. And besides, Nash never claimed he was from Seville.

My father, Tom, treasured my grandmother. He too had been smitten by her warm and merry disposition. They enjoyed each other's company

At the O'Keefe Homestead, 1936

Left to right: Frank Prudhomme, Eva O'Keefe Ogilvie, Arnold Prudhomme, the author, Allan Williams, and Model A.

immensely. And if you put them together in a group of friends, both became more gregarious and the fun would flow.

My grandmother must have seen the many fine qualities in my Dad, some of which I only came to realize much later. A fiercely honest and just Gael, his sense of fair play and moral certitude was never compromised. A strict upbringing by loving Presbyterians in Scotland and later in Montreal left him with a somewhat austere outlook on life which he tempered by a sharp sense for humour. Although his formal education stopped after Grade 8 in Glasgow, an insatiable hunger for knowledge continued to be fed by self-instruction. Books by Emerson, Shakespeare, Hugo, Aurelius, Wells, Dickens, Keats, etc., made up his small library. He was very partial to true adventures about the uncharted sea and unknown civilizations. He enjoyed intellectual bull sessions on religion, politics, philosophy and psychology, and included among his regular combatants, an atheistic medical doctor and one pseudo-agnostic dentist. Above all, he loved the free-for-all fun of a party where he could sing and play piano. Around the farm, he was never happier. Every Sunday during the summer he and mom would drive up to see how I was doing. I used to be so lonely when they were leaving. I can still see them going in the line in their Model A and their waving till the bush shut them from me. But as long as my grandmother was there, I quickly resigned myself to another week of happiness.

Sometimes my parents would come on Saturday and stay over. My father and Uncle Alex often joined forces with my Great Uncle Tom McDermot who had the same jovial temperament as his sister, my grandmother. They built among other things, a fine separator shack and a chicken house. My Dad, like Uncle Alex, was a good carpenter. He built his bungalow in Westboro from "scratch", as well as an eighteen-foot cabin cruiser called the "Nancy Lee". His lathe produced some commendable lamps and tables.

Perhaps the sweetest visit of all for Dad was the one to grandmother's for Christmas dinner. All the O'Keefe children and their families tried to be home so that as many as twenty-four would be divided into two or three sittings.

A little boy's tummy fairly rumbled at the sight of those Christmas dinners: bronzed crisp turkey, creamy spuds, smacking-good gravy, nose-tingling ginger ale, cucumber relish, green tomato pickles, long-stemmed onions, sweetened carrots and tangy turnips. And that was just part of the fare. There were crusty bread, freshly churned butter, yummy cabbage-raisin salad, plump juicy tomatoes, crisp lettuce , cold milk, and cream barely oozing from its pitcher. The desserts were tempting: snowy carrot cake, apple pie à la mode, oatmeal cookies, and grandma's pudding swimming in rich sauce. And if I remember correctly, someone always brought along a box of Laura Secord chocolates.

The family circle was never stronger than it was at those dinners. But as life would have it, the circle would be broken. And broken it was shortly after the Christmas dinner of 1952.

At the table, on my left hand, sat my father, and on my right, little three-year-old Glennie O'Keefe. I can recall the seating because someone snapped a picture of that end of the table. My Dad's head was tilted back in laughter and dear Glennie was eyeing the camera as he enjoyed his food. It was a happy evening — but within fourteen days it all changed. My father died suddenly just two weeks later and within three months Glennie passed away in his father's arms. We were all heartbroken. Both were young and dear. My grandmother had seen so many open graves in her day, she must have wondered if they would ever stop. The older you get, the more difficult it becomes to cushion the shock of life's tragedies. She had had her fill.

Regretfully, I never got to know my father that well. At the time of his death I was twenty-one, and I hadn't had much success in my life, (whatever success is). He really didn't have much to be proud of in me. And he went so quickly; there was no time to say anything. In the hospital, my mother and I were brought into the room where he was dying. He was unconscious. Then, suddenly, quite out of the ordinary, said the doctor, he came to. He looked at my mother and me. And he smiled at me peacefully as I nervously took his hand. He seemed to forgive all my ineptness and shower much love on me in those few moments. It was a time of special grace! He was a good, honest, just, dignified gentleman, and I miss him.

It is not easy to write about yesterday. Embers of sadness are easily rekindled by retrospection. Subconscious delvings can be painful and you feel your heart groaning as you relive the separations from those whose lives so lovingly entwined yours. And the recall process is slow: hazy memories cloud realities. Intellectual and sensual stimulae have been dulled by the passing of too many moons. So you must be patient in your contemplations and wait for the images of the past to unfold in due course.

It is as if you were standing in a maze of flowers, none of which are recognizable. The aroma and colour tells you that you're in the right place, but all is a blur of beauty. And then, as if by release of some unknown power, certain flowers become distinguishable. And you pick this one and that and they turn out to be the people and places and sayings that were most dear to you.

It is as if you are caught up in a swirl of obscure images that run relentlessly out into a distant galaxy of the mind. Suddenly, through no credit to yourself, images and thoughts long since forgotten, break into the freedom of your consciousness. Such reruns of memories from beyond are unique.

Images of my grandmother come like that. I see her churning butter ... she strikes the churn-stick down with surprising strength, and when the cream cracks, the added resistance is met with even a more measured beat ... I see her kneading the dough, lifting it up and over and down, driving her palms into the weight ... I see her fat arms whipping the laundry up and down on the tin washboard and later turning the wringers to squeeze out the water ... I see her sprinkling the clothes with one hand while the other strokes them with the deep heat from a flatiron ... I see her darning thick grey socks that went into black boots cut off at the ankles ... I see her peeling vegetables, washing milk pails and separator dishes, wiping tables and cleaning floors.

Work never ceased for farm women like her. The pressure was relentless. Twenty-one meals per week ... rain or shine ... hardly time to feel sorry for yourself ... mouths to be fed, pickles to be preserved, lamps to be trimmed and fires to be stoked ... sun up, sun down ... eggs to be collected, chickens to be fed, water and wood to be fetched ... day in and day out ... floors to wash, verandas to sweep and hearts to mend. It was a regime that literally drove auburn-haired, silkened-skinned Irish beauties to their early graves.

During her working day, a few precious moments were enjoyed. In mid-morning, time for novenas and rosary. After lunch, a rest and later the newspaper. Before bed, one or two hours of cards or letter writing or conversation. Apart from these pauses, life went on and it didn't matter if she was sick, pregnant, or burnt out.

Genevieve McDermot O'Keefe in 1900 at age twenty-one.

If you don't think such women are the heart of a home, look what happens when they're gone. The very walls cry out the emptiness. Discipline and orderliness break down. Rooms are shut off one by one. Family members drift away. Friends call less often. Laughter dies. Happiness is no more, and sage soon grows round the door.

My grandmother was a great friend. In all our times together she never once spoke a harsh word to me. Never! No scolding or nagging! Not once did she ever hurt my feelings, and goodness knows, I deserved chastisement.

She and I played cards until the cows literally came home. After each load of hay was thrown between the rafters, I would dash to the house for a quick game. We must have played hundreds of games over the summer and winter holidays, each one bitterly fought and immensely enjoyed.

Mary Clancy McDermot 1896

Around a farm, something always has to be done. And while my work load as a very young lad was infinitesimal, I did receive some small assignments from my grandmother, the purpose of which no doubt was to keep me out of trouble. Getting fresh drinking water several times a day was one. A fairly easy task, one would say. But it "weren't necessarily so"! The pump was taller than I. Its mechanical condition was shaky and the well usually at its lowest water level in the summers. Even fanatical pumping on the broken handle often produced nothing but air. So it was on up to the huge rain barrel for primer. And then the rusting pump would hiss and snort as I poured water down its gullet in synchronization to my wild cranking. My reward would be a smile from grandma after each cold sip from her battered tin dipper.

Another job was the control of fly extermination. With flyswatter in hand, I would patrol the summer kitchen bashing flies into instant oblivion. Sure, each farm had its small saucers of poison on the window sills and gluey flystickers hanging from the ceiling, but sometimes the services of a professional fly swatter were needed. It was down one side of the kitchen and back up to the other (the floor boards ran on a slant), as I left a trail of death. Sometimes I would count my kills and with pride announce the grand total. Grannie would nod her approval and again remind everybody to pull shut the kitchen screen door which to my knowledge hadn't worked properly for fifteen years. Then with the devotion of the Lone Ranger holstering his silver gun, I would hang my red swatter on its special swatter-nail and move on to my next assignment.

Which may have been collecting eggs. Again a task not as simple as it sounds for a little guy. What with snakes and pigs and roosters to challenge me on my rounds. I say rounds because there was no hen house as such and the desperate hens wandered about seeking weird hiding places for their eggs: spots such as haymows, tall grass, old baskets, woodpiles, beam joints, even abandoned buggy seats. Indeed, the natural tendency for the preservation of the species is most prevalent in the clandestine operations of this flightless bird. After a couple of hours of nonchalant exploring, I usually traipsed to the house with a few whites and browns piled in my orange enamel pot. And my heroine would smile.

Yet another pastime for little folk was berry-picking. The area provided two main choices in this regard, wild berries and tame. Hunting for the wild ones was more fun. But it also required much more discipline, something I was a bit short of, even then. I remember those days as usually being very hot: south winds ... tree squirrels calling ... hot stones ... scurrying chipmunks ... and the crackle of dead branches as I crept on hands and knees looking for the illusive wild strawberry or bent low to bottle the nodding raspberry. It seemed to take an eternity to fill even a wee jar; the berries were about the size of the tip of my little finger. Naturally, it was necessary to sample the pickings. However, I usually made home with enough so that later in the week grandma could serve delectable jam on scrumptious toast made between wire holders held over the lidless circle of an open fire.

As I grew older, I picked the tame varieties on the farm of Howard Williams. Howard had the proverbial green thumb. And not just for berries. His crab-apple trees and his Northern Spies sagged to the ground. His luscious vegetable garden was a constant temptation for youngsters like me and my cousins Clarence and Allan Williams. It lay across the lane from Jim Lynch's abandoned house and immediately beside a deep pool of spring-fed water. Many an afternoon we spent jumping from the rickety bridge into cool refreshment. Later after dog-paddling ourselves into exhaustion, we'd raid the vegetable garden for a snack. I can still remember shaking the damp soil from carrots as big as spinning-tops. And as for those long rests under the shady oak: "those were the days, my friend; we thought they'd never end!"

But it was Howard's tame berries that were blue-ribbon: unblemished, firm, delicious. His strawberry patch was just to one side of his clapboard house while the raspberry bushes ran row on row down from the tree line at the back of the farm. Howard "tendered" his berries with the same devotion as a Burgundian winegrower "spoils" his grapes.

Every week, Howard took a load of berries down to Turner's grocery in Westboro. He used to take out the back seat of his Reo and load them in. I knew all the lads at Turner's — Big Red, Jimmy and Mr. Charron. Those were the days when sawdust covered the long work areas behind the meat counter. Whenever you went in to purchase meat, the server usually slid into view, sometimes going right on by.

Howard was a self-educated, self-made man. As a veteran of the Boer war and an experienced world traveller, he loved to reminisce in an easy style about the old days. He was never happier than when conversing in his berry shack with the colleens who came to pick.

And could those colleens pick berries! Maybe thirty boxes per day against my twelve or was it seven? Friends like Bert and Mary Carroll and Rosemary and Mary Mantil would earn ten cents per box and then buy ten boxes of berries with their three-dollar earnings. I was lucky to take one home.

Fortunately, the raspberry was easier to pick than the strawberry. Howard provided wire basket-holders that hung from the neck on binder twine. This invention enabled a picker to use both hands. As each basket was amply filled (especially the ones you were going to buy), it was snugly placed in the shade between rows. Later, each person went around and collected the boxes on a large receiving tray for sorting at the distribution centre. Panic sometimes ensued when one couldn't locate one's hiding places.

Grannie didn't preserve all the berries brought home. One quart was usually served with supper under sugar and cream.

My grandmother died in her bed in January, 1955. Word of her death reached me in Toronto where I was attending school. In those days, seminarians weren't allowed to return home for funerals, except in the case of immediate family. So I had to bear my loss alone. I was truly shattered. After several very sad days, my sorrow eased and life went on, but never quite the same.

A favourite vistor to the O'Keefe Homestead was Joe Lee, husband of Genevieve's sister, Laura. Joe is shown here with Edward O'Keefe, 1958

Her loss for my dear mother must have been traumatic. I certainly wasn't much help to her since I couldn't leave Toronto. However, as it turned out, my grandmother's body had been placed in the vault until spring. On April 27, I left the seminary. The very next day, unknown to me, my grandmother was to be buried and I was able to walk with my mother behind her own.

The last time I saw my grandmother was just after Christmas, about ten days before her death. She was sitting in her wooden wheelchair, an empty space where her right leg used to be. We were alone in the living room. The boys were outside and Rita Kennedy, her niece, had left to get married some two weeks earlier.

My Victoria was like a doll in her black dress with its fancy white collar ...the majesty was still there although she had become gaunt in her later years ... her hair was swept back as in her youth ... her hands were joined in her lap ... she was very solemn — not her usual self ... she must have known this was our last time together.

At the door I turned for a final look ... she looked straight at me ... she forced a faint smile but her eyes gave her away ... I closed the door that day on a woman who next to my mother and my wife was my dearest friend!

My grandmother was grand!

And not a living soul who knew her would disagree!

Signs

Many pious souls of West Huntley believe in signs from the supernatural world. These recognizable happenings come in answer to prayer and provide solutions to difficult decisions or problems. Jack Curtin from the Twelfth Line may well have believed in such signs, but he certainly didn't let on that day he went to visit a sick friend at the Civic Hospital.

Jack apparently arrived on a floor at an hour not permitted for visiting. An agitated nurse stopped him in the corridor and said curtly, "Sir! Visiting hours here are strictly enforced! No doubt you have noticed all the signs! "

Not easily put down, Jack retorted, "Madame, I've learnt over the years never to put too much store in signs!"

The nurse walked away thinking his brain was spinning its wheels. Jack, however, felt somewhat vindicated!

Backfire!

It wasn't so much due to rudeness and indifference that the parishioners of Knockmourne's St. Catherine's Church were inattentive during sermons, as much as they had become accustomed over the years to the same sermons delivered in the same drone by the same good father.

One Sunday morning, after a Saturday night dance, a good many more than usual were in a state of stupor, except for one lad affectionately known as Looney Rooney who always sat in the front row with his ears glued to every word from on high.

When the priest saw Looney that morning listening so closely and him only half there, and the rest of them all playing with full decks and out of it altogether, he suddenly stopped and peering down on his flock, pointed in the direction of Looney and half-shouted, "It's too bad that you all couldn't give me your attention as the good Mister Loon—Rooney is doing, instead of sleeping before my very eyes!!"

Looney heard the remark, and not wanting to be divorced from the support of his friends, stood up and proclaimed, "Ah, sure, father, and if I had more sense, I'd be sleepin' too!"

Another Sign

Inside the front door of her poor street-level flat in Belfast, an Irish mother has hung a small plaque. It reads: "Love is Enough".

70

Old Number 6

A dwindling population around Manion's Corners forced the closure of #6 in 1924. Its number, however, was not retired! After eighty years of service, it was deservedly transferred to a new frame Separate School to be built near the Church.

The leadership for this new location came from Father Austin Stanton and the elected trustees: Tim Scott, William J. (Big Bill) Egan and Frankie Forrest. Trustee elections were anything but tame affairs. Cliques had their favourites and final decisions of the electorate were not always unanimously received. Poor losers and gloaters don't mix. Clearer heads often had to prevail!

The present Highway 44 was once a forced road from Carp to Almonte. The locals nicknamed it "the highway". Third, fourth and fifth generation Irish from both sides of this highway between the Seventh Line (Bearhill Road) and the Eleventh Line (Dwyer Hill Road) went to the new school. It also drew youngsters from the Seventh, Eighth and Ninth Lines and part of the Tenth Line up to the Carroll Side Road.

These students, however, didn't have the long walks to school as did their parents. For example, the early families from the Carp side of St. Michael's Church — the Corbetts, Kennedys, Samples, Scotts, Clarks and Caseys — had as many as five miles to go to the Manion School over some Commando-type training ground. (See map on page 352)

In fair seasons, barefoot was the only way to go. The same for catechism classes on Sunday (3 p.m.). In fact, some priests in the Tens and Twenties looked disfavourably on *any* child wearing foot attire. Perhaps, they felt going barefoot was a penance that no child should be deprived of in order to gain supernatural merit. Naturally, a few well-to-do parents took exception to any severe punishment meted out to their padded bairns in this regard and often came to the rectory to stand eyeball to eyeball with the parish priest.

In the cold months of those early years, the boys wore gum boots and the girls red velvet ankle boots "with white toes". The winter catechism classes were held on Sundays after Mass, but still the children had to walk home after the lessons.

But no school placement can be perfect. In 1937, even I had to go a mile to St. George's on Piccadilly Avenue in the West End of Ottawa (and a Public School forty yards from my front door). But I had shoes all the time and ploughed streets and cleared streetcar tracks to run along and, on really cold days, a two-and-a-half-cent ride on the red trolley with a blue-capped motorman who'd say, "Step to the back, folks; it's going the same way as the front!" Some days I ran both ways at lunch time to escape egg sandwiches and catch the radio broadcasts of "Big Sister", "The Road of Life" and the first minutes of Bert Pearl's, "Happy Gang".

But my little jaunts were a cakewalk compared to those endured by the Corkery youngsters of the Twenties and later. Like bees to the hive, they came from all directions. Swinging lunch pails and schoolbags and sometimes small tins of coal for the fire, they scampered over rock, picked their way through swamps and wild growth. From along the highway toward the Carp, came Lizzie and Margaret Egan, the daughters of Little Bill and Lyla Gallagher, accompanied by their first cousins, Walter, Edna and Jimmy Sample, children of Jimmy and Annie Gallagher. From the Seventh Concession on a side road off the Eighth Line came the Caseys, Francis and Bunny, children of Mike and Bridget Ryan.

The Caseys didn't have much: a couple of horses, three or four cows, and a few hens. The father, Mike Casey, suffered from asthma as did many who lived in and round those swampy lowlands behind the Church. Respiratory disease still plagues many descendants of this area. (Tuberculosis was once the curse of the Irish here as well as in Ireland.) But somehow the family got by. Norbert stayed at Tom Carroll and Mary Ann Rowan's back at Manion's Corners and went to school from there, and John Lawrence Casey did the same from the Ninth-Line home of Frank Gallagher. Bridget Casey's brother, Jim Ryan, shared a quarter of all his butchered stock with the Casey family even after they moved to Ottawa. The oldest girl, Margaret Casey (now ninety) went to work at *The Citizen* and pumped money into the family's upkeep. And after the move to Ottawa, Bridget, then a widow, worked for years at St. Patrick's Home. She remained the catalyst of the family, and the children all soon had good jobs. In return, the children bought her a lovely home for her twilight years.

Bridget Ryan Casey often returned to visit in West Huntley. She was a good friend of Susan Gosson Scott, the widow of John Matthew. Their farms had almost backed on each other. Matthew died of asthma at age thirty-nine and left the twenty-nine-year-old Susan with several children. The Scott boys and girls remember Bridget's kindness and encouragement to Susan in those hand-to-mouth days. They were two of a kind, Bridget and Susan. Spirited and unsinkable! The same spunk! And lots of fun! They say Bridget often danced a jig on the rungs of the pole-ladder to the loft-bedrooms of the Scott home.

Bridget also came home to be buried. It was March, 1939. Cold and windy. With no vault at the cemetery, all graves had to be dug out in the winter. Dominic Ryan and James Brown, Bridget's nephews, were there and Pat Mike Kennedy, another nephew by marriage. Using crowbars, picks, and shovels, it took the better part of a day to break through three feet of frost. For over a hundred years, each grave, regardless of weather conditions, had to be made ready by friends and relatives of the deceased. In the case of contagious diseases, the diggers didn't have much time!

Dominic Ryan remembers an even worse day at the cemetery back in January, 1945. The temperature was -25°F. Ned Vaughan (1859-1945), his neighbour, had died. It was so cold they had to build a tent on the site. Jimmy, Ned's son, was there and Dominic and a neighbour, Louis Delaney. It took all day. And if it hadn't been for young Tommy Carter bringing out coffee from town they all might have frozen to death. Bad enough that Jimmy Vaughan had to suffer the cold and all, but to have to dig his father's grave must have been a great strain. As a matter of interest, I am writing this paragraph forty-six years to the day of that digging!

They tell a story about Ned Vaughan. And this is as good a place as any to tell it. Ned was the bartender at an outdoor summer church social back in the 1910's. The exact location of this annual event was at the top of the hill on the southern side of the Vaughan Side Road, just before the crank, away in on the left. Many pre-Thirties' lawn socials were held on this pretty spread of terrain bordering the back bush of old Mike Flynn's farm. Actually it was on Kennedy land. The fun started about one o'clock on a Sunday afternoon with ball games down at the #8 school. Supper followed with tables and blankets dotting the landscape as the families enjoyed their box lunches and hampers of goodies. At dusk, strains of old-time music eased over the valley and soon the wooden platform bounced to the spring of dancing feet. The large cedar half-beams used under the platform are still there as if waiting for the music and fun to come again.

Anyway, Ned was a reliable sort or he'd never have been put in charge of the bar. In fact he was the kind of a man everyone respected. Even Jim Ryan (1852-1950), his neighbour and seven years his senior, addressed him as Mr. Vaughan. Ned obviously was the right man for the job.

As it turned out, five Orangeman from Fitzroy gathered near the bar. A friend whispered to Ned that they were looking for trouble. Ned went on "alert"! Sure enough, one lad made a remark. Whatever it was, Ned saw red, bounded over the bar and supposedly decked the culprit with a stiffening blow. Ned wasn't a big man. But he could handle "his dukes". Like the Vaughan men I knew, he had a boxer's build. Jimmy his son was like that; lean and muscular. And his grandson, Gerald, has sinews like taut E-strings and is every bit as sound as Gordie Howe in his prime.

Ned's battle brings to mind another Orangeman story from Fitzroy. Father Ernie Bambrick, a friend, was pastor at St. Michael's in Fitzroy Harbour. I knew him from St. George's in Ottawa. A rather straight-laced disciplined man, he led a quiet life, part of which included rocking on his veranda every fine evening. He had the habit of speaking out of one side of his mouth so that people on the opposite side of the Church heard very little of his talks. Some parishioners, not terribly interested in his sermons, deliberately sat on the wrong side which for them was the right, but really was the left. Being on the left, they put themselves in a position of never being put right, certainly a wrong attitude in the matter of their salvation.

The first time Father Ernie told me about his experience with the wild-driving Orangeman, I fell on my knees in laughter. The matter wasn't really a laughing one! A priest's life could have been snuffed out! Yet, I couldn't control myself. The good father's eyes expanded as he recalled the details. And his grip tightened on the rocking chair as he edged forward reliving the leap for freedom he never made.

As it happened, a Model A came sputtering down his street one evening and made a *U*-turn just past the church. Bambrick was rocking away puffing on his pipe (the one which accounted for his speaking at a forty-five degree angle). Nor did he blink an eye when the car's snout turned in his direction and began to increase speed across the lawn. The target was still in his chair when the demolition occurred. Father's description of the car and himself under the boards and rafters and the shouting of the driver and the steam and the confusion just left me in stitches. And every time he retold it, I'd break down with the opening line. But he didn't seem to mind, because he really understood, broken leg and all, the incongruity of the situation. If a priest isn't safe on his own doorstep, who is? A bit like an old lady charging into the Commons, grabbing the mace from the Sergeant at Arms and trying to ram Mulroney as she shouts, "You and your GST". Or like a driver on the Popemobile deliberately turning a corner too sharply and throwing the Pope and his shepherd's staff into a herd of sheep.

But to return to the school children of #6. Little Rita Kennedy, daughter of Pat Mike and Katherine McDermot, also came up from Highway 44. They say she brought to school the biggest and juiciest apples ever grown in West Huntley. From back the Eighth Line came enough Scotts to fill two schools. Kathleen, Rita, Walter, Mary, Manus and Matthew, the children of John Matthew Scott and Susan Gosson, walked about two miles as did Tim Scott and Mary Delaney's Edmund, Wilfred, Stanley, Stella and Modessa. John Leo Scott and Jessie McIntyre sent nine children from the same area during the Thirties and Forties.

From the Ninth Line, Big Bill Egan and his wife Maggie Ellen Kennedy (1880-1934) sent Mary, Michael, Andrew, Pat, and Maurice, as well as boarders Jimmy, Bill and Mary Kennedy. It was Big Bill (1877-1963) who received the contract from Father Stanton to deliver the mail in 1924. He and his son Pat were to carry the Royal Mail for forty-three years through rain, mud and snow. The mail came in from Carp at noon and was first sorted into fifty mailboxes at the Egan home.

In the early days of mail delivery, good strong horses had to be in readiness and, when cars came, they had to be kept finely tuned. The coldness was the worst and the long reach to the boxes and the "odd" neighbour who'd refuse to allow them to use his land as a shortcut on the route. In the Thirties, Bill's Whippet touring car was a familiar sight from the Eighth to the Twelfth lines.

It was Big Bill who had gone to Ottawa with his father, Patrick, to testify for the prosecution regarding the murder of Dick Langford, their neighbour. Big Bill was young then, a mere twelve years. But he had seen a suspicious man named Goodwin walking from the murder scene on the evening of the crime, and the Crown demanded his testimony and he went and he did a good job, just as he was to do with the mail for so many years. Goodwin, by the way, (whom many people thought was innocent), skipped bail and disappeared forever.

Another family from the Ninth Line, that of Frank Forrest and Onaugh Kennedy, also had several children at #6 in the Twenties: Sarah, Margaret, Frankie Junior, Joseph and Lawrence. From the Tenth Line came Jack

Father A. Stanton
1924

Killeen and Evelyn Kennedy's daughters Evelyn and Margaret as well as Anna May Brown, daughter of James Brown and Clara Ryan. From the south end of the Line, Angus Killeen and Carmel Carroll sent their nine children — Patrick, Lyle, Carl, Maurice, Merrill, Glen, Mike, Bernice and Martina — while Bob and Rose Mantil on Highway 44 sent Jackie, Raymond and Grace in the Twenties and Bobbie, Margaret, Mary, Betty and Billy in the Thirties and Forties. The Charlebois, Lawrence and Marion, sent eight: Robert, Leo, John, Billy, Terry, Brian, Lawrence and Naomi. Over the years, until its replacement by a Carleton Board Separate School in 1965, #6 had been of inestimable value to this section of West Huntley. All its graduates, and I know many, speak proudly of its spirit.

The young female teachers from faraway places had much to do with this educational success. Many could not only teach, but sang, danced, and played several musical instruments. Frances Ready from Desoronto, a blond-dancing-doll, full of ginger and spice, played accordion, piano and organ. A very eligible Alex Grace from back the Dwyer Hill Road rushed her for a while, but later turned his attention on another pretty teacher, a redhead from Fallowfield named Hilda Kennedy. Alex had an eye for good-lookers with panache!

I remember Hilda. She was a knockout with her flapper-cut ruby hair. Everyone liked her! A good teacher and dedicated member of St. Michael's Catholic Women's League. And I remember the story circulating Corkery of how she had heard two knocks on her kitchen window shortly before she gave birth to her first born, Michael, and how she took them as a warning of death. And I remember how much the country missed her at her passing, not more than a few days after the birth. And how everybody pined with Alex who didn't have an enemy in all of Corkery. Hilda was thirty-six and the year, 1942.

How suddenly life changes ... happiness goes out like a falling star ... doors close ... dreams shatter ... some force beyond our understanding and control disrupts our equilibrium ... misery ... heartbreak! Is it Fate? Luck? The Cosmos? ... Or is it a Power that thinks and loves and rules all ... and if it is such a Being, why? why? why?

And then often, just as mysteriously, when we are at our lowest ebb and even on the brink of despair, suddenly a rainbow ... and those with faith and even those without it, suddenly look out open windows on new vistas ... cease to be despondent ... become revitalized ... and approach new challenges like the vaudevillians of old hitting a new city on new boards before a new house with a new routine and new players ... and before long laughter returns and old hurts ache less.

And so it was with Alex Grace ... somehow he was directed to search out his old flame, the lovely Frances Ready. Was she married? Would she still care? And what of his child Michael?

Well, he found Frances ... and her love was still there ... and they married and lived in Agincourt ... and Michael became a priest ... and a new daughter Mary Anne came to know the gentle Alex ... and at every St. Michael's Cemetery Decoration Day, on those Sunday afternoons when the wind seems harsher, Alex always came back to honour his parents and friends and remember his first darling Hilda ... until he died in 1963.

Other teachers at #6 in the Twenties were Mary O'Neil, Father Austin Stanton and Bridget Neville. Bridget's sister, Margaret, taught during the Thirties. The Nevilles were from Douglas and boarded at the Rectory with Father Gerald O'Gorman. Kathleen Donovan from up past Renfrew came in the early Forties followed by the popular Margaret Mulville (Mrs. Pat Egan) from Westport. For years Margaret directed the senior girls' choir, played the organ for most church services, and sang solo at many weddings and funerals. Margaret was a close friend of another teacher from Westport, Margaret McMartin, who used to play bridge with me and my wife at Joe and Gwen Ryan's in Perth, Ontario, where

Old #6, Manion's Corners, 1894 - 1924. The first #6 was on the site of the present West Huntley Fire Station from 1841 - 1894.

Angus Carroll, author, Theresa Carroll, Baby Killeen, and Edgar Carroll, c. 1939.

Girls from #6 St. Michael's, c. 1928. First row: Rita Sarah Scott, Grace Mantil, Rita Kennedy, Sarah Forrest, Evelyn Killeen, Margaret Killeen, Margaret Forrest. Back row: Stella Scott, Lizzie Egan, Margaret Egan, Anna Mary Brown, Kathleen Scott, Rita Catherine Scott, May Egan.

Walking the bull, very carefully!

Clarence Williams and author in front of milkhouse, July, 1942.

Probably the last class of Old #6, Manion's Corners: Back row: Laura Bassett, Annie Watson, Lula Bassett, Jessie McIntyre, teacher, Annie Carter, Blanche Carter and Zita Carter. Middle row: Emily Bassett, Mabel Sample, Leona Carter, Lillian Daley, Carmel and Mary Carroll. Front row: George Bassett, Hilbot Watson, Bill Sample, Charlie Sample, Jim Watson, and Bob Sample.

The grave of David Dowling from Charleville, Cork, and his wife Mary Mahoney. They settled in Beckwith on the Town Line with Ramsey. The graveyard of St. Mary's on the 12th line of Ramsey is one of the oldest in the area. David and Mary were the great-great-great-grandparents of the author through his grandmother, Genevieve McDermot O'Keefe. David Dowling was born in 1765.

Margaret and I were both teachers. Margaret was a find — happy, open, humorous, and like her friend, Margaret Egan, a competent teacher. They're both gone now and both suffered much before entering into their rewards. One thing for sure: small towns and rural communities certainly produced fine teachers, and still do. Like those two Margarets.

The very first teacher at #6 was Ethel Golden from *Irish* Quebec. She taught for about four years (1919-22) and then married Ned Scott, son of Mike Scott and Mary Ann Kennedy. Ned and Ethel eventually moved to Trenton, Ontario. Ethel had many talents. She organized the first St. Michael's children's choir, and with herself at the organ, she and her little choir sang at all the funerals and weddings during the weekdays. Weddings in those days were not confined to Saturdays.

A fact not widely known is that all the children of #6 attended the weekday funerals and weddings in the middle-Twenties and early-Thirties. Originally the children went because the teacher had to be away from the school to play the organ for these services, but over the years the practice of the entire school taking part, especially at funerals, continued off and on until 1964, long after the teachers were replaced by official church organists and the choir was only comprised of older members. The presence of the children is also understandable since many would be related to the deceased. Certainly the attendance of the children must have been consoling to the bereaved. The weddings would have been fun, for the girls at least. Most men don't even enjoy their own.

By the time my mother left Corkery in 1928, #6 was part of a tidy centre of religious, social and educational Irish culture. Since the arrival of the Kennedys, Manions and Mordys in 1821, the accomplishments of clergy and parishioners were visibly clear. Father Patrick Corkery (1844-1916), born on the Third Concession of Ramsay to Patrick and Mary Donohue, and perhaps the best-loved priest ever to serve at St. Michael's, built on the sound foundations set by O'Malley and Vaughan. Supported by a healthier national economy which continued to improve into the Twenties, Father Corkery built a choir-loft around 1885 and later added hardwood ceilings and a new main altar. In 1891, parishioners donated statues, one of which was a statue of St. Michael.

Father Walter Cavanagh came in 1905. He was the son of Peter Cavanagh of the Sixth Line, Goulbourn. He built a new henna-brick rectory in 1908 and added new drive sheds beside and behind the Church. Father Austin Stanton born in 1887 on the Seventh Line of Fitzroy, the son of Martin (1835-1915) and Honora Moran (1846-1920), arrived in 1914 and in addition to building the school, added two altars, a new tower, pews, furnace and stations of the cross. He also redesigned the old rectory as a hall for meetings, catechism classes, school plays, dances and socials. The young people of the parish in particular appreciated the new hall.

Those three buildings, Church, Hall, and #6 School, helped keep the Irish of West Huntley together and irrefutably preserved the Celtic culture held so dear by the early pioneers. And it was all done by the members of several generations of the same hundred families. Not bad going, to put it mildly.

But everything comes to a close! A new school now nestles low and sleek along the cedars. There are not many old graduates of #6 left! A Grade One student of 1924, if he or she were alive today, would be close to seventy-five and as those of us who are sixty or more realize, the privilege of old age is granted only to the few. The 1919 flu and other contagious diseases were enough to silence the laughter of many #6's now buried across the road in St. Michael's Cemetery, not more than a handball-throw from where they all played at recess, ate their lunches, and reluctantly answered the teacher's clanging handbell.

Such little wooden schools as #6 with their pumps and woodpiles and swings are living testimony that the heart of good education does not lie in the frills of televisions, computers, clocks, projectors, modern facilities and chauffeured transportation. I went to school for forty-nine years during which time I took courses for twenty-eight and taught for thirty. And I can say with absolute certainty that the secret of good education depends almost entirely on the best possible teacher being put in each classroom, a teacher who tries every day to make the children think and analyze and reason, makes them wonder and dream and create, makes them sweat under discipline, challenges their best in an atmosphere of caring, praise and accomplishment, and, above all, gives them solid example based on good moral values. If the teacher is not a gentleman or a lady, especially in an Elementary School, the other qualities won't be there. It would be better that such a person not be in front of any class! Scholarship isn't everything.

The teachers of old #6 (and #7 and #8 and #9) were the best! They weren't saints and they didn't graduate any. But they were ladies and gentlemen and they certainly turned out plenty of those.

In 1964, #6 was officially retired after one hundred and twenty-five years. And #7 and #8 were hung up as well! What a line they made — those two Wingers from the ridges and their Centre from the valley. Their fans will always remember them!

Ripples

Little children have big ears! What adults do and say leaves vivid impressions on their impressionable minds. In the Twenties, a salesgirl named Annie O'Keefe from O'Keefe's Corners in West Huntley worked at West's Department Store on Front Street in Almonte. Dominic Ryan was just a shaver then, but he remembers Annie O'Keefe as being one of the most polite, obliging people he ever met. He said all the people of West Huntley tried to get Annie to serve them because she took a real interest in them. Our kindnesses and good words live on! Some sixty years later, Dominic still carries around a happy remembrance of Annie.

71

Johnny's Place

Johnny Lynch and his wife Catherine, daughter of old Pat Manion and Elizabeth Lindsay, lived in a log house beside Coady's Creek on the Dwyer Hill Road. They married on February 15, 1887. Johnny's father and mother are listed as Michael Lynch and Julia McGochlin (church spelling). A Michael Lynch and Johannah Houragan (church spelling) lived on the property in 1861. Whether this second(?) Michael is Johnny's father is open to conjecture. Michael could have married Johannah after Julia's death in the mid-Fifties.

Johnny Lynch
1924

Monet would have liked Johnny's spot of tranquillity. The laneway in 1940 wasn't much narrower than the Eleventh Line. It fell casually about a hundred yards to a log bridge over the creek and then down past Johnny's cottage set on the right among maple, apple and lilac trees. The creek was about ten feet wide and with the beaver given carte blanche, the water levels were then very high. This small arm of Coady's stream began at the tip of the Big Hill on Highway 44 (once called Clancy's Hill), crossed over to the east side of the Dwyer Hill Road, and then came back onto the west side under a bridge just past Clarence Williams's stone house, (since sold).

Now there was a bridge with character! As long as I could remember as a boy, it defied anyone to repair it. It had the uncanny ability of always being a little out of sorts ... one day, a spread in the logs ... on another, a swelling in its middle ... and sometimes even partial immersion. In deference to its whims, drivers wary of its moods, approached it with the respect it had earned over the years. Strangers to the road, however, had some rude awakenings!

One summer in the middle Forties, the Region agreed to give the bridge a straightening up. The trick was to keep the bridge high enough to avoid ice and flood waters but low enough to keep automobiles from becoming airborne. The result was that the logs were flat all right but still below the road level. Any car hitting the partly hidden bridge was first sucked down, wash-boarded, and then thrown back up. From a mile away, the familiar "thrrumpp, thrrumpp" of another car striking the bridge always brought a smile as I pictured the shaking arms of the driver trying to hold her on the road. Model A's weren't known for their shocks, but the bridge was.

The cottage is but a hole in the ground now, but the old laneway still haphazardly winds up to the outbuildings on the edge of the bush some three hundred yards from the road. Clarence Williams is lucky to own such a pastoral scene. It's the laneway on the left, going to Arnprior, just before the Blackburn stone house, (since sold).

I first noticed Johnny Lynch in a 1924 picture of the Holy Name Society founded by Father Stanton in 1914 to bring respect to the name of God. The Canadian-born priests were great on Societies. Father Corkery (1884-1904) formed the Catholic Women's League which included among its many accomplishments the organization for many years of the Church Socials. He also set up the Catholic Men's Benevolent Association which helped many a farmer get his financial feet on the ground until one day a member took off with most of the funds and the Association never really recovered. Father Cavanagh (1905-1913) founded the League of the Sacred Heart and the Altar Society of Women. Father Gorman (1928-1941) organized the Sodality of the Children of Mary.

But by far the most successful group, in numbers at least, was the Holy Name Society. The above-mentioned picture in question, taken the year of the parish centenary, shows off over a hundred of Corkery's finest Catholic men and boys. And there in the second row, sitting with his hands joined over a rather pronounced corporation, is one member blessed with a most jovial countenance. Its owner's name, as it turned out, was Johnny Lynch. So I thought I'd find out a few things about him.

As they say, neither Johnny (born 1853) nor Catherine (born 1858) were "spring chickens" when they married. They had three children between 1888 and 1892: Jimmy, Paddy and Anna Mary. Jimmy married Edna Vaughan and they lived across the road in a cheese factory owned by Jimmy. The cheese factory was a popular hangout.

Young lads like Herman O'Keefe and Benny Kennedy would drop in after school for a "swig of white curds". Others, like Clarence Williams and Angus Carroll, were given roll-your-own Zig Zag "tobaccy" by Jimmy who'd say, "You young scamps are getting more smokes than I get!" The young lads all remember Jimmy as a good friend. Always glad to see them coming and not too happy when they left. After the cheese factory closed in the early Forties, Jimmy went to live in Ottawa.

Jimmy and Paddy had an awful craving for cards. Before they were "hitched", they used to frequent their neighbour Jimmy Ryan's for games of 500 with Jim's two younger girls, Mary, now Mrs. Harry Grace (in her nineties and a "live wire" if there ever was one), and Annie, the deceased wife of the late Lawrence Kennedy. After the games and some refreshments, Jim Ryan would start eyeing his gold pocketwatch hanging near the door. At eleven sharp, he'd go over to the watch, start winding it and say, "Way past my bed time!" The Lynch boys knew the signal and they'd say, "I'll guess we'll be on our way!" Jim and wife would go upstairs and the two lads would head out the door.

But outside, they would stop. They weren't going anywhere! As soon as Jim's lamp was well out, they'd steal back in and play on until four in the morning.

Jim Ryan probably knew he was being had! He had an understanding turn of mind. He used to say to his children when they were making too much of a din, "Get home with the lot of ya!" and they'd all shout, "But, Daddy, we are at home!" One time Jim was sitting at a wake on one of a long line of chairs. Next to him was a loquacious lady whose desultory ramblings were completely unnerving. Jim finally turned to a gentleman on his other side, a Herrick, I believe, and a relative of the babbler, and asked, "Have ya got a scissors on ya, lad?" "No, what d'ya want with a scissors?" — "I'm gonna cut the tongue out of this woman while I'm still sane!" Herrick almost fell off his chair laughing.

Jim Ryan
1924

After playing cards into the dawn, naturally Paddy and Jimmy were like those "gentlemen Berties who slept 'til ten-thirty". Old Johnny did his best to get them up. Paddy was the worst! One day Johnny finally found the secret words to get Paddy down to the kitchen, words that give an insight into Johnny's sweet disposition. He'd go to the stairwell and shout, "Come on down, Paddy, and I'll bust open a couple-a eggs for ya!" and lickety-split, down would come Paddy!

Paddy married a woman named Butler in Ottawa. He worked in the Chateau Laurier under the direction of congenial Jack Ballard (1897-1975) who was Head Electrician at the Chateau for many years commuting to his job from his home on Highway 44 near the Dwyer Hill Cross. One day at work Paddy cut off one of his fingers with an electric saw. Jack at the time was in another room talking on the phone completely unawares of the accident. Two workers with Paddy succeeded in bandaging up the wound. One, apparently in a state of shock, gathered up the loose finger in a handkerchief, walked into Jack's office to report the incident and threw the finger down on the table in front of Jack, exclaiming, "And what do ya plan on doin' about that?" For years after, all Jack could say about the incident was summed up in the monotone trance-like sentence, "Is it any wonder I got ulcers!"

Paddy and Jimmy left no children. But Anna Mary made up for the lot. Anna Mary (1892-1952) married a neighbour Peter Joseph Liston on September 27, 1917. They called him Zeff. They moved to Grange Avenue in Ottawa West and raised seven girls and four boys. I went to school at St. George's with some of the younger ones — Shirley and Sheila and Larry. They were always cheery and friendly. Larry married a grand bundle of energy called Carmel Corkery from St. Mary's Parish and they named two of their children after Larry's uncles, Patrick and Jimmy.

Once in love with Corkery, always in love with Corkery. Anna Mary and Zeff and their children, as well as Jimmy and Paddy, often came back to the valley to visit Jimmy and Gertie Curtin Vaughan and in the process wore out many a pack of cards. The Lynchs, Listons, Vaughans, Curtins and Manions went back a long way. And what a mixture: from Tipperary, the Manions and Listons; from Limerick, the Curtins; from Sligo, the Vaughans; and from Cork, the Lynchs. Gerald Vaughan, son of Jimmy, remembers them as "great company altogether". Larry Liston, a great-grandson of Johnny, has often talked to me about his happy visits to Corkery with his parents and uncles.

It's a small world. My mother used to call in for the mail from 1911-1919 at Johnny and Catherine's on her way from school! Although the Lynch children were some twelve to fourteen years older, she would have known them all. Later she and Anna Mary attended the same church of St. George's in Ottawa West, as did so many others from Corkery such as Jimmy Curtin, Annie Mantil and Ignatius O'Brien.

I wish I'd known Anna Mary. Her roots go deep in Corkery. Her great-grandfather on her mother's side was the original settler John Manion, and there's a good chance her father's people were Robinson Settlers in 1823.

But, above all, I wish I'd known Tom O'Keefe my grandfather and his neighbour Johnny "bust them open" Lynch.

Tom Ogilvie got a good woman from Corkery in my mother Eva O'-Keefe and so did Zeff Liston in Anna Mary. Tom O'Keefe and Johnny (both died in the early Thirties) would have been the first to agree. They might have said something like, "Ya bad damn right they did!"

I spent many happy days frolicking on old Johnny's property. Somehow it has never lost its charm: the bouquet of a dear old man lingers on!

Pinning It on the Donkey

Gerry Cokely of West Cork owned a small wagon and donkey. He made his living by transporting wood and turf and feed.

With the arrival of the automobile, the local police introduced a law requiring all vehicles on the road after dark to carry a light.

Now Gerry was an honest man, but not much for silly and expensive innovations. Anyhoo, darkness seldom settled over West Cork in summer until 11:00 p.m. and Gerry was usually home by then. In winter, the tourists were scarcer and the police not so touchy.

However, one July night, Gerry found himself caught on the road in the wee hours and he knew his position was delicate.

Sure enough it wasn't long before the police arrived. Only they found Gerry between the shafts pulling the wagon and the donkey tied at the rear.

"Where's your wagon light, Gerry?" they asked.

"How do I know!" says Gerry. "I just do the pullin'. If ya want to know anything about a light, you'll have to ask the driver out back!"

72

Unrequited Love

One early spring in the late Thirties a bachelor named George, whom we met earlier, offered to help a spinster named Maggie plant her potatoes. Over the summer he wore a path to Maggie's garden to nurture the young plants. Maggie's potatoes flourished as never before.

One evening when the summer sun sinks sooner behind Foxes' Hill, George realized he had taken a shine to Maggie. In fact, he had fallen in love. And since he had recently inherited a small farm and money to boot, he felt he had call to ask for Maggie's hand.

And he did!

And she turned him down!

And she took her own sweet time telling him!

Now George was a good-living man, neighbourly, honest, and hard-working. But he was also extremely sensitive and never took too kindly to correction, teasing, or even the mildest insults.

As a child orphaned in England and sent as a Home Boy to abusive foster parents in Lanark County, he had felt once too often the sting of stick and word. Such early wounds never heal. Remain tender to the smallest hurt. Until death!

Certainly then, Maggie's refusal must have been a serious blow to George. The entire episode is not known. But we do know George was upset, so upset that he felt the need to get the matter off his chest.

That's why he dropped in one evening at my grandmother's not long after Maggie's decision. Grandma's sons Ignatius and Edward were there and her niece Rita Kennedy. George was fond of my grandmother. Looked up to her as a mother. Felt comfortable in her old green-coloured summer kitchen round its dozing fire. Knew she understood him and his feelings.

George talked about his romance that evening. How he proposed to Maggie: "I put it right to her in the tater patch!" ... how she asked him to wait for her answer until fall ... how she finally said she wouldn't marry him ... how she waited until after all the potatoes were dug and bagged by George!

The depth of George's anxiety became evident as he laboured through his story. In fact, he became so excited that my young uncles could barely refrain from laughing. They meant no disrespect!

It was just the way George had of talking. Even in ordinary conversation, he had an uncommonly high-pitched voice. Under emotional stress, it tended to rise more and develop modulations in tone, even crackling and rasping. Just understanding him was a chore! Naturally, the seriousness of George's lament squelched the giggles. Everyone realized George was in a trauma over the rejection of his amorous proposal.

Tradition has no more to offer about that evening. George obviously recovered and went on with his solitary life. Neither he nor Maggie ever married.

But my grandmother certainly must have helped George. My guess is she played down the aspect of Maggie using George. That idea may well have been local gossip anyway.

She no doubt twigged to the conclusion that George really loved Maggie and still did. She probably praised Maggie as a good woman and no doubt she was. She probably pointed out that Maggie didn't really love George but had delayed her reply because she wasn't sure.

George would have to accept the fact that Maggie just didn't love him. Nobody can be blamed for that. Not Maggie and certainly not George! It's for the best, she'd say; not in the plans of God. So try to forget her, George. You did your best! Have a cup of tea and a piece of cake!

As he walked out into the night with his lantern swinging to his great strides, George must have felt some relief. Yet, the ensuing nights must have been lonely ... thinking of Maggie and what might have been and trying to fill the emptiness. Eventually, of course, the great healer, time, would soften the blow and gradually ease the hurt.

But I can't help feeling happy for George ... he had experienced the wonderful sensation of falling in love, and that was good! ... he had felt enchantment for someone of his own choosing ... he'd always have that joy, that beautiful memory of being enraptured by Maggie ... and I'm positive he carried this love for her for the rest of his life, even to the grave ... in his reveries, perhaps he often "wandered" hand in hand "through the fields" with his Maggie.

Maggie, too, was lucky ... she had caught the fancy of another's heart ... to be loved by someone is the greatest gift on this earth ... Maggie had that rare honour! ... I just hope she appreciated it!

The Lighted Church

Lollie Grace told this story of how he and a group of young people were returning home from a Saturday night dance back the Ninth Line. The hour was late; it was already Sunday. As they passed St. Michael's church, they noticed the church was all lit up.

The next morning at Mass, Lollie approached the priest and asked why the church was in use at such an ungodly hour. The priest said he not been in the church last night. He added, "You should have wakened me! It must have been another priest who had died before he had said a requested mass for someone's soul. He came back last night to offer up that mass!"

73

No Pomp, No Circumstance, No Sweat

An Irishman doesn't get too excited about details that matter little in the way of things. An analysis of the nutritional ingredients of a glass of Guinness takes the good out of it. Theological thumpings on the ways of God don't always lead to a better appreciation of faith. Organization is important, but not at the expense of fun.

The Irish television announcer at the Galway Races, in three days of giving out the afternoon racing results, never once mentioned the winning time, purse size, or final odds. He confined his comments to the manner in which the race was run, the horses, drivers, and standings.

The driver of the bus from Cork City to Limerick City in 1968 paid little attention to his scheduled time. He left late and arrived in Mallow Town an hour later for a forty-minute lunch stop. Outside of Mallow, he stopped at a country gate. He blew his horn; a face came to the window of a little house well off the road; a young lady came out, mounted her bicycle, and loaded down with parcels drove down the lane and put the bicycle and parcels and herself on the bus. Apparently, this waiting for people was a common practice.

It was important to get to Limerick, but not at the expense of worrying how long it took.

Getting back to the races. The Irish pay little concern to the condition of the racetrack. It's the race that matters. The track at the seaside town of Tramore, Waterford, is a good example. Once a year the horses come to town for a few days. What the tourist sees is what he gets!

Cars are parked facing any direction in open fields outside the entrance. The only rule seems to be to put on the brakes to prevent the auto from rolling into the sea.

Nothing seems flat because it isn't. It's downhill to the ticket wicket, (the size of a speakeasy's window), and then uphill to the viewing area.

Buildings look like abandoned prospectors' shacks. Bets are placed at apertures as small as the leper's eye at Cashel Chapel and as low as a pygmy's navel. Part of the track can be seen; the rest is taken for granted.

Yet, with the coming of the crowds, the whole mishmash seems to stand straighter ... hot meals of chicken and dumplings with boiled potatoes are served in one building — tea, coffee and pie in another — beer and liquor farther along... bobbing bookies flash signs beside colourful tote-boards as slanted as their odds ... people rush about through the puddles and all, some reading programs or scraps of paper ... a loud-speaker excuses itself ... they're ready to go somewhere in the beyond ... there's a hush and then the cry "They're off"!

Once, twice, a flash of colour among the glens ... some fans have chairs, spyglasses or radios and toss off bits of info to the rest of us ... the din gets stronger ... then, they're in the stretch ... where? ... there! ... a desperate look for number and horse ... they're at the wire ... cheers and sighs, torn-up tickets, downcast looks ... organized mayhem, but also fun ... all done with the offhanded spontaneity of the Irish.

Another example of the Irish mind's precision is the use of the beagle's howl as an instrument of measurement. The owner of a potato field might say to his men, "Men, today we're gonna pick in the pasture as far as a beagle's howl." And every man would know just how far to pick.

An Irishman, too, often shows little reverence for pomp and heraldry. In the Montrose Hotel outside Dublin, our small restaurant table was decked out for dinner. One of our guests was a nun still easily recognizable in 1970 by her dress. Some wine had been ordered. As our waiter with the beverage slid slightly past the table to a halt in the usual slap-dash manner of those in his trade, he said to the Sister as he popped the drink before her, "If Mother Superior could *see you* now!" And he was gone!

Enough's Enough

The ancient Gaelic language has no words to translate the English "yes" or "no". The Gael obviously had no need for such expressions. He preferred to be evasive by being non-specific. Perhaps he considered directness and bluntness a form of bad manners.

An Irish farmer, however, one day lost this Gaelic tendency in the face of a belligerent tourist. The tourist had become disenchanted by a litany of directions from the gaffer, and told him so: "Look it, I'm more confused than ever; all this drivel is getting me nowhere!"

Whereupon the maligned "guide" retorted, "Ah, shure, I may be in the drivel, slick, but at least I know where I am and where I'm going! Ya don't know neither!"

Annie's Advice

Annie Sullivan from Sheenboro, Quebec, wife of Jim Ryan of West Huntley, often used an expression very uncommon to this side of the Ottawa Valley.

Whenever her children were going out to a party or dance, she always encouraged them to "be civil and strange" in their dealings with people, especially strangers. The word "civil" implied politeness with indifference, and the word "strange" suggested indifference with reservation. Not bad advice for any age.

More Advice

Little Alexander Grace heard his mother tell him so many times that nobody likes a "smart-alec" that he deliberately failed his first year of school.

74

Two Marys

Willy and Mary   (A Ballad in Prose)

Some years ago, in the town of Tralee in County Kerry, lived a poor Catholic maid named Mary O'Connor.

One evening a Protestant lad of some means named Willy Mulchinich asked Mary for a walk to the Vale of Tralee. To Willy, Mary was as lovely and as fair as a summer rose.

As the sun dipped neath the blue sea and the cool shades moved up the mountain, Mary walked ever so nearer her Willy and listened all smiling to his every word.

Presently, by a waterfall, in the shredding rays of a pale moon, Willy looked into Mary's eyes and saw the light of all his tomorrows and asked her to be his wife.

And Mary said "yes" to being Mrs. William Pembroke Mulchinich and they left the Vale of Tralee full of great joy.

But it was not to be! For Mary soon died of tuberculosis and poor Willy was a broken man.

And then one day it came to him that he must tell the world of his love for Mary. So he put to paper for posterity one of the most tender ballads ever to seep from a broken heart and called it "The Rose of Tralee".

Today that same moon still shines in that same Valley of Tralee by that same waterfall, just as surely as someone, somewhere in the world is now singing Willy's beautiful song, written for his sweetheart, Mary, his Rose of Tralee.

Sick Call for Mary!

Once upon a promise, a Dresden doll named Mary married a golden-tongued-dandy named Johnny. Her life centred around God, family and Johnny. His revolved around career, himself and Mary.

About four years later, Mary contracted the Spanish flu and her life hung in the balance. Slowly she improved and Johnny left for work one morning with his heart a little lighter.

He lilted down the tenement stairs and scurried into the crowded East Side Chicago street. Suddenly, someone grabbed his arm. He turned sharply!

It was a priest. He asked, "Young man, is this the apartment building where a young lady lies gravely ill?"

"Well, as a matter of fact, my wife was. But she is much better now! By the way," said Johnny heatedly, "who sent for you anyway?"

"What floor is she on?" said the priest.

"Second, Number 9 at the back," said Johnny, "but she doesn't need you; who called you?"

The priest went up. Saw Mary. Heard her confession. Gave her Holy Communion and then Holy Viaticum.

That evening Mary died!

To this day no one ever discovered who sent for the priest — in fact, no one in the neighbourhood had ever heard of or seen him before, or since.

A few Sundays later Johnny returned to the Church. And one day he became a priest.

Hospitality

Many "natural" coincidences exist between the religions of the Hindu in India and that of the ancient Druids in Celtic Europe. Both religions placed great store in hospitality. Even the poorest of the poor was expected to do what he or she could for a guest, even one not well-liked.

An old Hindu proverb given much credence in Ireland was: "The tree does not withdraw its shade even from the woodcutter."

Hungry Grass

Across some fields in Ireland lie strips of land where bush and grass grow wild and free. These patches are called "hungry grass". They mark the spot where a famine victim died. The ground is sacred. If anyone knowingly crosses these areas, they claim he or she can become infected with a hunger that no amount of nourishment can relieve.

As we look around West Huntley, we often can see in its fields similar piles of stone, clumps of bush or solitary trees. Could these mark hallowed ground, like fairy hills, holy wells, burial plots, or even "hungry grass"?

Ashes

Ashes carried a hidden power in old Irish ways. Ashes from the Christmas fire were often spread on the seed potatoes before the planting. And it was believed an approaching storm could be turned back by throwing a handful of ashes before its winds.

An Old Anglo-Saxon Battle Cry

Neither "O" ne "Mac" shall strut ne swagger through the streets of Galway.

Rising to the Occasion

Some years back, two ladies of West Huntley had a rather cold-war relationship. One that sometimes erupted.

Good wives, mothers and Christians, they were about as different as June and January. June was more outgoing, a tease, and loved to banter. Jan was more introspective, reserved, and longsuffering. She also imagined June was talking about her behind her back.

In religious matters, the latter followed the letter of the law while June went by its spirit. Jan believed in setting good example in meaningful ways like saying her vocal church prayers with dedicated gusto; June gave no scandal, but took a more lenient attitude and hoped God was not scoring too closely.

One day after Mass, the parish priest was asked to give a talk to the St. Michael's Catholic Women's League. June and Jan were there — Jan up front. Now this parish priest gave sermons that were not always for the fainthearted. He had a way of stirring up sinner and saint.

His talk that day was on his pet peeve: slander. Soon he was turning his wrath on all those who would try God's patience by talking about a neighbour.

Point after punishing point was driven home and Jan was listening ever more closely. And she started thinking about June's treatment of her and how June probably wasn't even listening.

And before long her imagination was fairly flying. And the longer the priest hammered, the more incensed she became about June's treatment of her until she could contain herself no longer. Bounding to her feet, she turned and pointed to June as she proclaimed for all the world to hear:

"Now, do you hear that, Mrs. _____? He is talking to you, you know!"

And the good priest probably called it day.

A Charming Apple

One day long ago another woman accepted an apple from a man and thereby gave the town of Ballyhooly in Cork its name. In the Seventh Century, a Bishop was entering the territory of a certain tribal chief somewhere between Mallow and Fermoy. In order to meet the chief on the other side of the Blackwater River, the Bishop had to wade through a ford and as he did so plucked from the water a floating apple.

Accompanied by his daughter whose right arm was paralysed, the chief approached the Bishop. Presumably as a gesture of goodwill, the Bishop offered the apple to the young lady. As she reached for it with her left hand, the Bishop told her to take it with her right. And she did. And that's how and where the town of Ballyhooly was founded. The Gaelic name "Baile-athá-ubhla" means "the town of the ford of the apple".

Rich Man, Poor Man

In the last quarter of the Nineteenth Century, certain West Huntley families, particularly the long-established ones who came with Robinson or travelled up from Richmond, Eastern Canada, or the States, found it financially within their means to construct some thirty fine stone and brick houses, many still in evidence, as we have seen, in and around the valley. Much of this initial wealth doubled through marriages. As noticed elsewhere, second generation Irish often strengthened their land holdings and liquid capital by the lucrative bonds of matrimony. Not just water seeks its own level.

Research shows much intermarriage from 1830 to 1870 among well-to-do families from Ramsey, Pakenham, March, Goulbourn, Fitzroy, Beckwith, Drummond, Renfrew and West Huntley Townships. A check of the original builders of West Huntley's grand homes (every bit as fine as the Anglo-Saxon-Norman-Irish ones in Ireland) indicates many betrothals among the children of *strong* families such as the O'Briens, Maddens, Sherlocks, McDonalds, Murphys, Manions, O'Connells, Ryans, McDermots, Meehans, Dowlings, Browns, Carrolls, Carberrys, Flynns, Mahoneys, Kennedys, Herricks, Carters, Tierneys, Mordys, Scissons, Foleys, Kellys, Forrests, Curtins, Lindsays, Corkerys, Legrees, Devines and Hendricks. Some stone-house "beauties" were the exception and did marry the "Irish of the Famine", especially towards the turn of the century. But for the most part, the Nineteenth-Century marriages took place among those of the same social and economic structure. It's only natural.

I am not suggesting here any great snobbery by the *better offs* of West Huntley. God knows stiff-necked, big-feeling people come from any race and walk of life. Coolness to neighbours considered *beneath* one is something we are all guilty of at one time or another.

Besides, wealth and position often have little to do with ego-tripping. It's a state of mind! So much depends on how we view ourselves. A brilliant man may picture himself as stupid and a beautiful woman see herself as a reflection of homeliness. The mentally slow are often loaded with confidence and "plain Janes" can fancy themselves as the last word in grace and style. It's a state of mind.

Social puffiness did exist in West Huntley, but it was only superficially noticeable. The Irish always put more worth in a person's character than his purse strings. "Looking down one's nose" at the dregs of the Irish famines certainly would have been rare among West Huntley folk. The Irish had had their fill of being "lorded over" back home.

I must admit though that as I studied the West Huntley's environs in my research, I was indeed amazed at this very large number of brick and stone houses. Not everybody struggled economically, and not everybody starved during the Depression! A definite economic strata did exist!

As a young lad, six to fourteen, however, I never took much notice of the "haves" and "have-nots" in the valley. If any status was attached to one's man's home over another, I was never aware of it. My grandmother and uncles and aunts never discussed one man's fortune and another's loss. They never complained about their own lot and never spoke ill of those "with" or "without" this world's goods. Neighbours were neighbours! Everyone did his best to make a living. Everyone helped the other regardless of imagined or actual worth.

Back home in Westboro, Nepean, it was the same. My Dad's small homemade bungalow never appeared out of place among the more grandiose homes of our area. My parents seemed unaware of any social hierarchy. Maybe it was the Depression that evened things out.

Our neighbours were good folks: the Johnsons, Lees, Cummings, Proulxs, Peebles, Schryers, Macdonalds, Griersons, Hills. And they all lived in big two-storey brick houses with verandas, on lots large enough to hold unattached garages and vegetable gardens. The street names said it all: Melbourne, Tweedsmuir, Churchill, Roosevelt, Euclid, Edison, Princeton — impressive names for stately homes.

Yet, like West Huntley, airs of superiority seemed foreign there. Everyone was socially accepted. Apparently the children of Westboro's homes heard little discussion at table about keeping up or ahead of the Joneses. From what I can see, that "sweet little Westboro of mine" has never changed. Still a place for rich and poor. Unpretentious: a charm and simplicity about it still.

I was lucky to learn no preconceived biases of religion, race, colour or position from my parents, grandmother or neighbours. Corkery and Westboro were good places to be raised. And they still are!

A Change of Heart

One day in the Twenties a hireling of West Huntley came upon some money apparently mislaid by his employer. He took the money and set out for town with every intention of squandering it at the hotel.

On his way, he dropped in to see Mrs. Thos. O'Keefe, a friend to all who ever met her. She noticed the money and quickly deduced it had been stolen. She then convinced the man to leave the money with her and return to his lodgings. Later she returned the money to her neighbour and urged him to limit his punishment of the hired man to a good reprimand.

This story has come down from the son of that neighbour. He also said, "From that day forward, my parents realized that Genevieve O'Keefe was one of the finest women to walk the fields of West Huntley!"

77

Beating the System

Bishop or No Bishop

Patrick Finner and his wife Mary Bresnahan once lived on Finner's Hill where Corkery Woods' Estates are now. Patrick was a blacksmith and his shop was in an ideal spot: the old Ridge Road passed just in front of his house on its way to Panmure, Pakenham and Rosebank from St. Michael's Church, Carp, and Manion's Corners. In 1870, for example, he shod six hundred horses and grossed four hundred and seventy-five dollars.

He was an English-Irishman. His sister, Margaret Finner O'Keefe, was my grandfather's mother. It was only natural then that Patrick named one of his daughters Margaret, or Maggie, for short.

Sometime around 1918, Maggie became the housekeeper for Father Stanton, parish priest of St. Michael's. Both had demolition temperaments, but somehow they stayed together. Even after Father Stanton was transferred to Eastview in 1928, Maggie went with him. That's where I first met her — a comical wee lady with a will like her father's anvil.

My grandfather Tom O'Keefe and Patrick being first cousins, it wasn't long before Tom's wife, Genevieve McDermot, and Maggie became friends. Since Genevieve was also well-thought-of by Father Stanton, Maggie took to having Genevieve come over to the rectory on special occasions to lend a hand with the preparations.

At one such event, the French Bishop was the guest for dinner and Maggie had called on Genevieve for assistance. Maggie had already made a cake and my grandmother thought she'd better taste it, just in case? The cake was unbelievably bad. So she tried to prevent Maggie from serving it. Maggie turned a deaf ear.

Sure as lightning, Maggie's culinary ineptitude drew the ire of the choleric Father Stanton. Out to the kitchen he flew to tell Maggie what he thought of the cake. Maggie never flinched during his tirade. Standing her ground with hands on hips and sparks in her eyes, she let fly, "Father, as far as I'm concerned, it's good enough for thems that's eatin'it!"

God's Tin Ear

St. Mary's parish in Clonmel, Tipperary, is situated in Irishtown which, during *the troubles*, was not surprisingly placed outside the town gates. It was there in St. Mary's vestibule on a Saturday night that O'Hare was surprised to see his old friend McGinty, a parishioner of the Cathedral Church, St. Peter's, which was built inside the town.

"McGinty, ya devil, why aren't ya at your own church for confession? They know you too well, I suppose!"

'Tis a fair query you do be putting to me, O'Hare. I'm here 'cause the likes of me needs an understanding priest like your Father Williams, a man sent by the Holy One Himself; St. Peter couldn't guide me soul better!"

"McGinty, 'tis special care you need all right. The Lord knows ya haven't sown all your oats! Father Williams, ya say? I do notice he gets a bigger lineup than Jimmy the Tap at the Greyhound Meets. Maybe I should give him a try meself."

"O'Hare, it'd be a wise move! But there's just one bit of information I'd be giving ya — nothing really serious enough to bother your head about."

"And what would that be, McGinty?"

"Well, ya see, Father Williams has a wee affliction which thank God in no way affects his priestly duty."

"And what's that?" says O'Hare.

Says McGinty, "The poor man is almost as deaf as a doorknob!"

George

George Welridge and his brother Walter worked for Maurie Williams during the Depression. At one point, George was being pressed by creditors in Ottawa. The situation was serious. A jail term was a certainty. Never at a loss for imaginative schemes, George decided death was the only way out. So he wrote his own obituary for newspaper publication and sent a clipping to the creditors. Maurie copied out the obituary in his scrapbook.

Now George was a master of innuendo and double entendre, and the difference between his fiction and fact not easily determined. His subterfuge was known by the whole county, and everyone shared in the complicity. No one squealed on George and his creditors never wrote again.

The obituary of George L. Welridge was as follows:

"Attended by many friends from the surrounding district, the funeral of George Lionel Welridge was held on Thursday from his home to St. Francis Catholic Church on the Third Line of Fitzroy with interment in the Catholic Cemetery. Rev. Father O'Brien officiated at the Requiem High Mass.

The deceased was in his 81st year and his death came as a shock to his friends and family as up to the time of his death he had been enjoying good health. Mr. Welridge was a life long resident of Carleton County and for the past 25 years he resided on the Eleventh Line of Huntley. A devout Catholic, Mr. Welridge had gained the respect of all who knew him by his ceaseless activity in church affairs. Surviving are six daughters, Mrs. Anastias McGillicuddy and Mrs. Jeremiah Quigley of Detroit, Mrs. William Hunt and Mrs. Jack Carroll of Huntley, Eliza and Martha at home and a son Walter of Huntley. His wife, formerly Miss Marie Thibeau, predeceased him ten years ago. The pallbearers were six of his closest friends: Mr. Martin Ryan, Mr. Dominic Ryan, Mr. Charlie Newton, Mr. Edmond Newton, Mr. George Stone and Mr. Dennis Mantil all of Huntley. The numerous floral tributes and spiritual offerings testified to the esteem in which the deceased was held.

Dated February, 1933."

Prayer and the Mustard Plaster

External practices of piety were more common in the country years ago. Holy water was sprinkled about the house before a storm. Field workers fell to their knees to say the Angelus in answer to the six a.m., noon and six p.m. bells of St. Michael's. Grown men crossed themselves upon hearing disturbing news. Crucifixes were attached to outside verandas or outbuildings. The rosary was regularly said after supper by the whole family.

Another pious practice, popular before my time, was the saying of prayers by neighbours at the bedside of the sick. Frank Prudhomme, my cousin, says it was done frequently by the Irish and Polish in Renfrew, and another cousin, Clarence Williams, remembers such works of mercy around Corkery.

Clarence recalls the time at home when his grandmother, Catherine Armstrong Williams, had pneumonia. His mother Annie had done what she could. Doctor Dunn held out little hope for Catherine's recovery.

One evening during the crisis, neighbours Billy Roche and wife Bridget Doolan dropped in to say the rosary with Catherine and the family. In the middle of the prayer, Catherine (about age 78) asked her daughter-in-law Annie if she had any mustard plasters. She thought she should try them.

Every twenty minutes, all night, Annie Williams changed the plasters and in the morning Catherine's chest had loosened and the pneumonia was beaten.

The Grave on the Crank

They say that "S"-bends in country roads are nothing more than geographical corrections made by two surveying crews meeting each other off-line. At one of these cranks at the top of the hill on the Vaughan Side Road near the late Basil O'Keefe's home, a man was murdered. The spot on his head where he was hit turned snow-white.

The murderer was never brought to trial and the victim was buried somewhere in the crank. Long after, horses coming into the crank at night became highly agitated and travellers were always leery about passing that darkened grave of the murdered stranger with the patch of white hair.

78

The Sleeping Smithy

Hilary Finner from Almonte, like his father Black Jack, was a skilled smithy. But his hunting ability left a little to be desired.

A young Clarence Williams went hunting for deer one day with more experienced "big-gamers", one of whom was Hilary.

Each hunter took his position ... eyes glued, guns readied, hearts aquiver. Slowly the shadows lengthened.

In mid-afternoon, their luck changed. The prey wandered onto the run. And the dogs were soon there directing them towards Hilary's hiding place. It was just a matter of time now thought the other hunters ... they waited for the rifle reports.

Only they never came; just silence after the swish of the deer high-tailing it and the fading yaps of the dogs. They were disappointed. What had happened to Hilary?

But then, the impossible: the hounds were turning them back and again sending the deer towards the Finner stake-out. Surely Hilary would do something this time? An old-hand like Hilary wouldn't let them down again. But, by Jove, he did, and the deer ran free into tomorrow.

Naturally, by this time, the hunters thought Hilary had suffered a stroke. Certainly something serious had to have happened to cause such a drastic lapse in responsibility. Clarence and a few others made directly to the spot.

Hilary was out of the picture all right. But not from malady or accident. It was the outdoor air that had done him in. They found him oblivious to everything, sleeping like Huck Finn on a soft bed of autumn leaves. The sight was almost enough to make the ever-zealous hunter, Edmund Newton, uncock his rifle forever.

While Hilary may not have been the "bees' knees" as a hunter, he was always a popular lad. Not like another local boy of an earlier generation who never once spotted a deer with other hunters nearby, in case he would have to share the kill with them.

Edmund probably only hunted once with him too.

Lowering the Boom on Clancy

Dan Clancy, my grandmother's uncle, was a teller of wild ghost stories, only some of which were true. He knew West Huntley well having grown up on the Dwyer Hill Road, just across and down a little from my grandmother's house. One night he decided to engage in a bit of "ghosting" around my grandparents' home — howling and knocking on windows, etc.

Not long after he got going, one of the Manion boys from down the side road spotted Dan at play and decided to do a bit of ghosting himself. Without a sound, he got within reach of Dan and ever so firmly wrapped his arms firmly around the ghost. They say Dan never went "ghosting" again.

Not All Bliss

"How's you and the new Mrs. getting on?" asked Timothy.

"Fair to middling!" replied Matthew. "She's a corker! A real nicker! A mind of her own, she has! I don't mind tellin ya, it's takin' all of me wits just to survive. It's peace I'm lookin for!"

Ah," says Tom, "it can't be that bad! Surely her mood softens at times?"

"Well, Tim, my boy, it's like this! She has two bad stretches a day. During them times I tread as softly as a fly wearin' mitts! Before breakfast, she's none too good; she can be real ornery!"

"That's just one time, Mat. When's the other?" says Tim.

Whispers Mat, "All the time after breakfast!"

The Prayer

Cecil and Cecilia's long marriage had become a fiery one. One Sunday after Mass, Cecil waited a donkey's age for her to come out of the church. When she finally climbed into the buggy, he blurted, "And what kept you so long? Goin' to confession, I suppose!"

"Whist, thanks to you, I was praying for a special favour!"

"Sure ya have everything, woman! What else could ya be wantin'?"

"Well, if you must know, and may the Lord forgive me, I was asking Him to take one of us, so's I could go and live with my sister!"

You Never Know!

The neighbourhood could never understand why L____'s husband had gone. After thirty years of marriage, he went from the house one day, never to return.

All agreed she had everything a man could want in a wife, a singularly fine woman in every way.

"Why then did Mic up and leave her? Was he a bit daft?" asked a younger lad of his father.

And his father answered, "My Bucko, it's a wise saying, not easy to understand, but well to remember: 'Tis only the man or woman that wears the shoe who knows where it pinches'!"

79

Michael's Tree

One winter's day in 1878, word came from the bush to Sarah that her four-year-old son Michael had been in an accident. And the young mother ran coatless through the drifts to where he lay, his head smashed from its body by a falling tree.

She and her husband John held each other. Their world had gone mad. They knelt beside Michael. The pain cut deep and their sorrow brought nature to a hush!

Much later, Sarah Carroll Scott stood up. She had to be strong. For John's sake and Julie's, their little girl, and for Michael, their first born, now taken. And they brought out a cutter and laid Michael gently down and covered him with John's coat. And then Sarah gathered up his precious face and placed it in her white apron which she held up before her as she walked behind the cutter. As another Mother had done, she walked from her Calvary to the house which seemed a million steps away. And the next day, February 10, they buried Michael.

Not long after, Sarah planted a white birch in the clearing just beyond the kitchen window. And they called it Michael's tree. And it continued to grow in beauty long after she and John and Julie and John Matthew Junior and the other children had joined Michael. Until 1952.

That summer the trees around Sarah's old home were swept to-and-fro by a violent storm. Inside, Sarah's grandchild, the one she called "my little hen" sat huddled in the kitchen with her own children. And suddenly there came a shocking moment of instantaneous light and sound and Michael's tree was split wide open. And the little hen remembered!

She looked down on her own two sons. Both bore the burns suffered in a tragic fire the previous winter that took the lives of her brother's two precious boys and destroyed her house on Highway 44. She held them closer, the one named Michael and the other son John, the latter so severely burnt that he spent several months in hospital and even today carries the marks of his brush with death. And she thanked God for not taking them!

And then she thought of another John who also carried a mark, John Matthew, her father, son of Sarah, and how she asked him one day about a great white Y cut into the back of his head and he told her he had once been struck an almost fatal blow by a tree.

And then the little hen again thought of Sarah and how she must have relived the terror of Michael's death the day they came to tell her that her only other son, this time John Matthew, had also been felled by a tree. And how she must have trembled until she learned he would recover. And thanked God for not taking him!

Then it came to the young widow that perhaps Sarah had been partly responsible for saving John and Michael that fatal night, and that maybe Sarah was always watching over them all.

Perhaps, the rending of Michael's tree was a sign to move on and leave this homestead where both she and her father had once been little children. It was finished!

So one day shortly after, she gathered her small family about her and left the old house to its memories. As she passed Michael's tree she whispered a final prayer, for Sarah, her father, Michael, and them all.

And to this day, no one has ever lived on that property again!

The New Curate

A certain parishioner of a country parish in Kerry was not so daft as to be without cunning.

In fact, he thought himself the self-appointed inquisitor over the parish priest. He even had the unnerving habit of sitting under the pulpit in the very front pew, nodding and gesturing his agreement or disapproval of the priest's every word.

One Sunday he went further and stood beneath the pulpit looking up at the speaker. This was too much, thought the priest, and later he spoke quite firmly to him and suggested he find another place well back in the fold.

The zany parishioner was not pleased with this remark and told the priest he might come even closer unless the priest let him be.

Sure enough, not long after, the priest entered the crowded church to find the pulpit occupied by his tormentor. The parishioners had tried unsuccessfully to get him down. It was up to the priest.

"Come down from there, this instant!" said the priest.

No reaction!

"D'ya hear me talkin to you, boy? This is your parish priest! Get out of that pulpit!"

And the answer boomed across the church, "Ah, no Father! no! no! no! You come on up here with me! Sure this world is so bad, it needs the likes of both of us up here to save it!"

Not a Shaggy-Dog Story

Angus O'Keefe tells the story of his seeing a white dog entering the cellar entrance at the home of his aunt and uncle, Pat and Catherine Kennedy. They lived on Highway 44 towards Carp just down from the church near Jimmy Sample's. The dog was peculiarly large. It entered through a closed door. No one in that settlement in the late 1920's had ever even heard of such an animal.

80

Down But Never Out   (A Summation)

The Gaelic race should have gone the way of the passenger pigeon. By retreating into Ireland during the Bronze and Iron Ages, it escaped, as we have seen, the segregation inflicted on the other Celtic tribes in Europe and England. During these ages in Ireland, the Gaelic branch eventually assimilated so well with the other hostile descendants of prehistoric man already there that its culture and language soon became dominant. The civil wars continued for the next eight centuries, but Irish-Gaelic unity survived.

In the Ninth Century, the Vikings came to Ireland partly by invitation. They caused havoc in Ireland for two hundred years during which time they founded the seaport cities of Cork, Waterford and Dublin. At Clontarf the High King Boru put them on the run. The main force returned to Scandinavia, but the rest remained and settled comfortably into the Gaelic culture. By the late Twelfth Century, the Celtic "sunburst" (the Irish flag) of gold, white and green, shone steadily over a unified Ireland.

And then the Normans came, also by invitation. As the only combatants still intact after eight centuries of turmoil in central Europe, these Normans boasted the fiercest fighting machine ever seen in Western civilization. Their bloodlines told the story: descendants of those barbaric races that moved like hot lava across Europe — the Jutes, Saxons, Angles, Lombards, Goths, Visigoths, and Franks — all powerful Germanic tribes from Upper, Middle and Lower Germany, from those places where not even the ravenous Roman Eagle dared to fly.

After a round-robin-war-tournament lasting a millennium, only two militarily superior races remained by 1066. At the Battle of Hastings, the victor was proclaimed: the Normans finished off the Anglo-Saxons in an historic battle. Prince Hal was dead. Long live King William.

Gradually, the Norman tentacles reached out. By the time they were invited to Ireland to give military support to an Irish Chief who ultimately sacrificed his country for his greed, they had experienced another two centuries of masterminding Europe and England. When they came to Ireland, their arts of manipulation, diplomacy and exploitation had been even more finely honed. The combination of military prowess and cold-war sophistication proved too much for the Gaels already weakened by their own petty jealousies and family battles.

The Normans changed Ireland. They built towns and villages, and castles, moats and fences. They decimated the remaining families and kings who refused to give in. They drove out the last vestiges of the Gaelic tribal ways. But alas, they also fell prey to Ireland's beautiful maidens and handsome blades. They married into some of the most prestigious old families of Ireland. And soon, like the Vikings, they became more Gaelic than the Gaels. The Irish nation was very French but still mainly Gaelic. It was enjoying its last taste of unity and freedom before the four-hundred-year holocaust to follow.

What eventually happened was that Norman power also weakened in England. The Anglo-Saxon tenacity "to rule, and not be ruled", "to own and not to share", soon gave them military and political control. It wasn't long before the Anglo-Saxon monarchy, parliament, and economy extended their reach into Norman-Irish Ireland.

The Irish had rebounded onto their feet after the Viking and Norman conquests. But the Anglo-Saxon-English were different — sharing their power and wealth with other races was not in their nature. They brought a meanness to subjugation often imitated in recent centuries but never duplicated. They put the Irish on the ropes, brought them to their knees, and put them on the canvas. They set out to annihilate the Normans and Irish. And they almost succeeded.

For four centuries, the English-Germanic bear squeezed the life from the Gaelic wolf. They carved up the land among their own and dispatched its people as refugees. Up in the far left end of Bermuda, away from the tourist's eye, the gravestones of the Irish sugar-prisoners and slaves stare out to sea. In the outback of Australia, their rusted chains still bake in the sun. On the Isle of Death, Grosse Ile, in the St. Lawrence River just down from Quebec, thousands died, the victims of English deceit and graft, diseases in themselves!

What began as expediency for the English soon became a nightmare and finally an embarrassment. The Irish-question would not go away. It came to the point where the English hated the Irish and everything about them. They had made them what they were and then held them up to ridicule. What Hitler did in *shame* to the Jews, he tried to *hide* from the world. What the English did to the Irish with *rancour*, they *showed off* to the world. They stripped the land of its wealth and the people of their dignity. Those they didn't put on docks and rocks, they put in graves.

They made the Irish the beggars of the Western world. But they never finished them off. They put them down but not for the full count. They never conquered them and never put them under any flag but their own. The Irish survived to the credit of Gaelic pride and the ignominious shame of the British. Down but never out!

An Old Eighteenth-Century Irish Parable

Whang was a miller from Cork with an unnatural love for wealth and the company of men who had it. His measure of any man was his financial worth. So he publicly shunned the poor to walk with the rich.

He loved wealth so much, he even dreamed of it. One week he dreamed for three successive nights that a crock of money was buried in the wall of his mill. Since he believed in dreams, he started digging the very next day. But the loosening of the foundation, proved to be his annihilation, for the stones came down with a bang and that was the finish of poor Whang.

A Mass Stone set into a hillside near Inchigeelagh on the Macroom to Bantry Bay road in West Cork. Mass was said secretly here at great risk to all worshippers, 1987.

Bear on the mountain ranges of the Ring of Kerry near Kenmare, 1987.

The Church of the Nativity, Doneraile , built in 1827. The John Roachs came from Doneraile. Doneraile was once owned by Edmund Spenser, the poet. This church would be known to many Irish immigrants.

St. Mary's, Buttevant, Cork, an example of Norman Architecture. The name is from the battle cry of the Barry's against the MacCarthys: "Boutezen avant", ("push forward"). The clock was erected on the occasion of 150th anniversary in 1986. Many immigrants to Corkery after 1836 would also have known this church. The town is four miles from Doneraile.

81

Con

Was Con Mahoney the oldest postmaster ever to hold this appointment in the Dominion of Canada? He may well have been. He cancelled his first stamp (in writing) at age forty and licked his last at ninety-five.

Con was born in Kilkenny and came to Canada with his parents Patrick and Margaret (both born in 1787) and at least three siblings, brothers John, Michael and sister Ann. Although they were not Robinson settlers, Con claimed the family settled in West Huntley in 1824, on the West 1/2 of Lot 18, Concession 11. Patrick Mahoney may have had two sisters also come out around the same time. A Mary Mahoney arrived in Ramsey with her husband David Dowling in 1823, and a Nora Mahoney came in 1825 to join her husband James White. Both David and James were Robinson Settlers. Pat Mahoney may have travelled under an assumed name. Nora Mahoney did; she came out as a Brunswick.

Con was born on April 2, 1811, and died in his one hundred and second year on September 11, 1912. He was thirteen when his parents set up their Canadian homestead. Before settling down at his parents' house, he followed the lumber business. By 1847, he had married his first of four wives, a Mary Kennedy, daughter of John, brother to Tim, both Robinson settlers.

In 1852, the year before he became postmaster of the Powell Post Office, he and his three-year-old son, Cornelius Francis, lost Mary. She was just twenty-seven. The only Mahoney tombstone in St. Michael's Cemetery at Corkery is the one erected by Con for Mary. Mary may well have been his first and only true love. Their son later moved into Ottawa.

Con's second wife was Margaret Grace, born in 1827. They married the same year Mary died. They had three children: John, Margaret who married John McGrath of Arnprior, and Mary who became the wife of John Grace of Almonte.

In the early Sixties, Con married Emily Malone (1831-1884). They had three children: two sons, George and William, and a daughter who married William Forrest. From 1853 to 1884, it was Emily and Margaret who helped out in the post office-store-tavern operated by Con.

Immediately after Emily's death, undeterred by his seventy-three years, Con remarried; this time he chose Bridget Kennedy, the forty-four-year-old daughter of Tim Kennedy and Mary O'Keefe, daughter of John O'Keefe and Mary Duffy from the Twelfth Line. Bridget and Con ran the business (including the post office) for twenty-eight more years until Con retired in 1907. Then they moved into Almonte after selling the farm.

Con's popularity in the area prompted the *Almonte Gazette* to carry a fine editorial tribute shortly after his death. The paper said, "It was as keeper of the stopping place with which he was so long connected that he became most widely known as a genial, warm-hearted and hospitable son of Erin." The article's accompanying photograph depicts a thin man in his sixties with piercing, deep-set, closely-knit eyes, crescent nose and dark bushy eyebrows. A lack of hair on top is softened by sideburns of fluffy white extending frizzily upwards to large slightly turned-out ears. A heavy growth of hair at the back is as dark as his "flaps down" moustache. He has a look of intensity and determination lightened by traces of understanding and kindness. He appears more intelligent than wise.

Con was a West Huntley institution! In politics, even his strong belief in the Liberal party, smack-dab in the middle of a Tory township, never seemed to be held against him by local politicians. As a tavern keeper, he ran a tight ship. As a father and husband, he appeared indefatigable. His long appointment as a postmaster suggests an unblemished record. Imagine, at ninety-five, still active and still needed.

Although his death occurred in Almonte, he chose to be buried at St. Michael's where he had been an active member all his life. Father Cavanagh conducted the service on Friday, September 13. His grave's location is unknown unless he chose to be interred with his first wife Mary.

If indeed Con was the oldest postmaster ever to hold such an appointment in Canada, it's unfortunate no tangible recognition was ever accorded.

He at least deserved a monument of sorts for having had four wives and three families.

Corkery Trivia

Dennis Hickey drowned in the Mississippi River in Almonte on November 29, 1883. He was only thirty! Rumour had it, however, for many years after, that he was murdered.

•

The old Hickey farm on the Twelfth Line is unique in Corkery. Among its ruins are several stone walls used as fences for livestock. Similar fences are still used in Connemara and Donegal.

•

The members of the Catholic Women's League took turns inviting newly married couples of the parish to Sunday dinner.

•

According to an old-timer, many West Huntley women died during their "change of life" cycles. Their systems seemed to lose all immunity to disease during these critical years.

•

Heavenly-scented lilac trees grew profusely in Corkery. As well as providing windbreaks, they were also conveniently planted near the outdoor washroom facilities.

82

The Good Times

It's okay, Rose would say
Don't you worry none —
We'll have good times by and by
Next fall when the work's all done! (A Popular Song)

Corkery Irish didn't wait for the fall to have good times. Card and dance parties were common all year long. Anniversary celebrations and farewell gatherings were popular. Weddings, showers and wakes brought together friends and relatives. Outdoor pastimes included ball games, ice skating, shinny, horseshoes, hunting and fishing. Lawn socials at St. Michael's Church and surrounding parishes were always well supported. Outdoor dances in all the townships always drew a crowd.

Musical sessions at the homes of local artists attracted fellow players, step dancers, singers and storytellers. Even radio parties were in vogue: Doctor Dunn held one at St. Michael's on September 29, 1924, as part of the Centenary celebration. On the following evening he showed a movie and presented a musical programme by teachers and students of the parish on the parish hall stage.

Christmas concerts at the same hall were standard events. Adults and children recited poems or stories. Doctor Dunn's sister-in-law, Claire Moynihan, dressed in long, flowing, silken gown, came to many of these Christmas parties to sing Irish, Christmas, and Negro songs. Her rendition of "Way Down Upon the Swanee River" is still remembered. The finale of the concert was always a Christmas pageant re-enacting the scene at Bethlehem. Handsome fellows like James Brown and Patrick Egan played Joseph and cute colleens like Kathleen Scott and Margaret Killeen, wrapped under folds of dyed-blue cheesecloth, acted the role of the Virgin.

One family noted for its music ability has been the Williamses. Maurie played fiddle as did his brother Howard. Maurie's son, Clarence, who played lead-guitar and sang for the "Country Pals" western group, is also more than adequate on piano and fiddle. Clarence's son, Andy, is a local singer of Western ballads and his daughter, Mona, was an excellent step dancer. I remember in particular two musical parties at Maurie's.

The first involved the step-dancing-wizard Donny Gilchrist from Ottawa, probably in his time the best on the boards around the Ottawa Valley. His regular job was on Parliament Hill where he was friend to senators, security guards and janitors. He danced at Press Gallery Functions, fairs, celebrations, etc., even on the "Don Messer Show". His timing was superb. His whole body gyrated to the tempo of his flying feet.

I can see him now — his big smile, the concentration, the hunched shoulders, the perspiration, that same 110 per cent effort even after several heart attacks. Everybody loved this man and his passing was felt in every hamlet, all the way to the Hill.

The second party involved the visit of Ward Allen. Ward played the fiddle with Joe Brown's "CFRA Happy Wanderers" for over a decade. Maurie and Clarence first met him at the Torbolton home of Leo Carroll and Loretta Muldoon. Leo, son of Ambrose and brother to Mrs. John O'-Keefe of Almonte, was great on musical parties and Ward and other accomplished Western stylists often agreed to join the festivities. Ward had jet-black hair and a shy brooding smile. A quiet man! Deep! Complex! Friendly! The violin spoke for the man. He died in 1965 at the young age of forty-one. But he left us a song he wrote called "Maple Sugar" that is all it says it is and more. Only a man of tender feeling could have created such a song. It shall stand the test of time!

In Maurie Williams's scrapbook I came across an anonymous poem written by one of Ward's mourners. It has such a simplicity and dignity, as the man it commemorates, that I quote it in its entirety:

A Tribute to Ward Allen

I got up the other morning
and looked out into the sky,
Tho the sun had just arisen
There were dark clouds passing by

Tho it was the third of August
The day was bleak, and cold,
And it seemed as if the universe
was frozen in a mould.

I stared at this bleak picture
Then I slipped into my shoes
And went down to get my breakfast
And to listen to the news.

And what the newsman told me
On the radio that day
Seemed the REASON for the weather
For a star had passed away.

On that cold and silent morning
Here is what the newsman said:
"At his home, WARD ALLEN, Fiddler,
Forty-one, discovered dead"

And the next thing I remember
I was standing on the lawn
Looking skyward to the heavens
Where I knew that Ward had gone.

And as if some hand had shaped them
The clouds were moving in
Twisting, Shaping, Interlocking
Like a giant violin,

And the winds became tremendous
Building to a giant roar
They were playing like a fiddle
I had never heard before.

The tune was MAPLE SUGAR
Music swept across the skies
And I'M sure I SAW Ward Allen
Thru the tears that filled my eyes.

Seemed like Ward was up there playing
When the thunder in the dawn
Built up like a loud ovation
Then the vision was all gone.

I walked slowly, sadly, homeward
Realizing I had seen
Something on that August morning
I would never see again.

But the music of Ward Allen
And my vision on that day
Will remain with us forever:
OH HOW THAT MAN COULD PLAY.

—Anonymous

Dan O'Connell and his sons Jimmy and Lorne were then the best step dancers in Corkery. I saw Jimmy dance on several occasions and "he could sure pick 'em up and lay 'em down". They say Jack Carroll, son of Tom and Mary Rowan, did a sleek routine with a broom, and that Jack Vaughan was a good hoofer. Many others around the country knew a step or two but confined their talents to their parlours.

The best step dancer I ever saw in Corkery was Mona Williams. Besides talent, she had the figure, looks and personality. Mona learned her art at the feet of little Buster Brown who established several schools of step dancing throughout the valley. Buster was much in demand on the circuit and danced several times with Don Messer. He had a more polished, disciplined style than Danny Gilchrist who went at his routines with reckless abandon. Buster was half the size of Danny and probably made five times as much money.

Buster came as a student to the Ottawa school where I was Director of Guidance in the middle-Sixties. In those days we had a vice-principal with a short fuse and the instincts of a doberman. Naturally Buster's teaching duties "up the line" soon got in the way of his attendance, and before long he was a frequent guest in said V.P.'s inner sanctum. Only a wall separated his office from mine and many a day my room rattled to the dressing-downs inflicted on victims.

Buster, however, was not your run-of-the-mill student. His clothes were immaculate; he carried himself with aplomb; you might even say he was brash in a gentlemanly way. He was young and successful and had the world by the tail and you could understand why he wasn't about to take any lip from anybody, let alone a vice-principal who didn't even make half as much money.

Their final meeting was a "dandy". Both stood their ground. No quarter given. With a great crescendo of verbiage, the V.P. finally told Buster his days at this school (few as they were) were over. In return, Buster told him what he could do with his school. With that, Buster walked down to the parking lot and drove away in his spiffy yellow and white hardtop. Secretly, I admired Buster! He had class and, as it turned out, passed much of it along to the young people of the valley. He was just meant to be a teacher, not a student.

The Irish of Corkery loved to dance. Nearly every home had a Victrola. And many a house party was built around such oldies as "Yes, We Have no Bananas", "I'm Just Wild About Harry", "The Sheik of Araby", "Red Sails in the Sunset" and "When the Moon Comes Over the Mountain". My favourite among my grandmother's collection was "Alleluia, I'm a Bum". I remember dancing with my Aunt Cely and my mother at the O'Keefe's.

I remember other dances at Jimmy Zappa's, Gerry Mantil's, Bob Mantil's, Ignatius O'Brien's and at the Green's on the Third Line of Fitzroy.

Two favourite spots for platform-dancing in the Twenties and Thirties were just outside Almonte at Fusty Craigs (about where J.R.'s restaurant now stands), and at Frank Herrick's Black Platform at Panmure where Nellie O'Hara and others before her ran a country store for half a century. Johnny Wilson on the Sixth Line of Huntley held many successful barn dances and the Third-Line School at Fitzroy was popular.

The Cedars on Highway 29 was the home of Charlie Finner's "Hayshakers" during the Forties and Fifties. On a Saturday night, nearly all the young people of Corkery showed up at the Cedars. The Agricultural Halls at Carp and Almonte often staged dances. In later years, the Canadian Legion in Almonte has had dancing every Saturday night. Others went as far away as Lake Dorey in Renfrew.

It was the advent of the automobile that made out of town dances accessible. John Bassett and Pat Egan had their Whippets. Mohr O'Brien had a 1930 Ford. Eddie Grace and Dinny O'Brien also had autos. Maurie Williams had a '30 Chev and his brother Howard a 1928 Reo. Jackie Mantil and Jimmy Vaughan had 1928 Model A Fords. Martin Ryan had a Model A *coupé* with a rumble seat. Syl Finner had an Essex. Benny Kennedy, Leonard Kennedy, Alex Grace, John S. Kennedy and Jimmy Carter were others with wheels. And many I never knew!

The popular musical groups over some forty years were Sandy Barr's orchestra, Milton Symington's band from Almonte, Sammy Moran's group from South March, "The Country Pals" from Perth, and of course, "The Hayshakers".

Charlie Finner's father, Jack, an Almonte blacksmith, was raised on the town line between Almonte and Ramsey near the Panmure Road. Charlie's grandfather was William Finner and his grandmother Catherine Braceland. William and my great grandmother, Margaret Finner O'Keefe, were brother and sister.

Charlie's orchestra was made up of George "Doc" James on guitar or piano, Alan Giles on the fiddle, a lad named Purcell from Carleton Place on guitar or fiddle, and Dell Hudson from Arnprior on fiddle or sax. Charlie played fiddle, sax, or drums and called all the squares.

Charlie had a rich, clear voice. He made other square-dance callers from the Southern States and Western Canada sound like rubber ducks. No swanky hat or bandannas for Charlie ... just a tall, thin, tousledhaired open-shirted gentleman who rattled off his calls with crisp precision. I'd love to hear him sing "My Darling Nellie Grey" just one more time. He brought musical joy to the hearts of hundreds with his orchestra's forty years of picking, strumming, sawing and calling.

Fiddling has always been by far the most popular musical pastime in West Huntley. In addition to the Williamses, there were players like Eddie Grace, James Flynn, Andy Meehan, Pat Mike Kennedy, Norman O'Brien, Louis Delaney, Jerry Mantil, old Johnny Delaney, Danny O'-Connell, and Angus and Stephen O'Keefe.

One of the finest fiddlers in the area was Reggie Hill of Arnprior. When he was mortally ill with cancer, they had a retirement party for him at St. John's Hall in Arnprior. When Reggie played his swansong for the public that evening there wasn't a dry eye in the house.

They also had a party for Charlie Finner at the Agricultural Hall in Almonte. His wife Gertie Bolton was there and all his children and hundreds of admirers. Mrs. Hilary Finner said it was "a beautiful tribute to a beautiful man"! Charlie's son, Bernie, according to my Uncle Angus O'Keefe, is an excellent violinist. Bernie often plays of an evening on his back porch in Almonte sending plaintive melodies across the town. Charlie died in 1974. Bernie helps them remember his dad.

The Irish had other talented people in Corkery: Margaret O'Keefe played piano; Katie Curtin, Margaret Egan and Lois Scott played the organ. Tim Scott was a good singer of songs like "Little Boy in Green". And other men who worked the shanty brought back songs, stories and poems and shared them at parties. Nowadays, young Eddie McCabe and Andy Williams can sing and play guitar with the best.

Of course there were many card parties. I played at Lorne Charlebois', Jim Carroll's, Tom O'Keefe's, Maurie Williams', Ronald O'Connell's and Bob Mantil's. Years before that, card games were a nightly occurrence at Casey's, Scott's, Ryan's, Kelly's, Meehan's and O'Brien's. Evenings of six-

Charlie Finner came from a blacksmith's family — the Finners of Almonte: Back row: "Black Jack" Finner, his brother Louie. Front row: Mrs. Farrell Finner, Mary and Lucy (both became nuns), Charlie, Isaiah, Felix and Hilary.

hand euchre have been played for years at the Parish Hall and now in the school gymnasium at St. Michael's.

The Corkery Irish have had good times. Through the tears and years, they have never forgotten how to laugh and sing and dance and play. A bit of the gypsy in the lot.

Hush now! ... isn't that Norman O'Brien's harmonica and Dinny O'-Brien on the fiddle and Howard Williams on the jew's-harp? ... Gerald Carroll spanking the spoons and some little tyke blowing through paper on a comb? ... what's that they're playing? ... "Cock of the North," you say! ... isn't that the battle cry of the Protestant Boys of Derry? ... well so it is! ... just like them ... still trying to get a rise out of the Orangemen! ... they'll never change! ... and who'd want them to!

Losing Track

In the Nineteenth Century, a new railroad was to be built from Shannon Harbour in County Offaly (where the Grand Canal meets the navigable part of the Shannon) to Portumna in County Galway at the top of Lough Derg, a distance of some twenty miles along the Shannon.

All went well for half the distance, and then the money ran out. The completed section lay unused and untouched for some time.

One day an Irish vagrant was charged by the company with stealing a railroad lantern. At the trial, no witnesses came forward to prove the lantern had been owned by the company and the case was thrown out.

Next morning after the trial, company officials were amazed to discover that the entire railroad, track, equipment and stations had completely disappeared.

You see, the people had been willing to accept the bankruptcy of the company, even its reneging on the final salaries due to them after its dissolution.

But what the people wouldn't swallow was the meanness and embarrassment brought to bear on one of their own (a policy which could be copied by some of today's unions).

Even up to the present day, the fencing and buildings along that ten-mile route are of better quality than usually found around Ireland — an example to all who pass by of a people's stand against pettiness and injustice.

But, then, often, isn't it the little things that sometimes move us to rise up? A slight may trigger revenge far quicker than a whiplash.

The Children of Pain

An historical history by the Belden Brothers written in 1879 gives a rather harsh depiction of West Huntley:

"The great majority of the houses and outbuildings are of a description to which the word 'wretched' might fitly be applied; and a very great bulk of the land ... would rival the Rocky Mountains, if not in their picturesque effect and natural grandeur at least in the rocky character and absolute worthlessness for agricultural purposes of its surface: while the general effect caused by the 'great fire' which left nothing of value of what was once a dense forest, is one of desolation and dreary solitude. Altogether, one is inclined to pity those who were so unwise or so unfortunate as to have located in such a place as Western Huntley, when so many splendid chances lay open to them in other directions and to blame them for remaining there while there is still an acre of 'The Great Lone Land' unclaimed. And they are beginning to feel this way themselves. Emigration commenced some years ago on no small scale ... to the Northwest, and within the past year more have gone forward from Huntley to seek a Western home than in any two years previously."

This evaluation by the Belden investigators sounds like a knell. Makes a person wonder why any stayed on at all!

Many, of course, did "dig in" during these economic difficulties. And as years droned on, each generation became stronger. They developed more skills, worked "out and away" for months at a time, and gradually, with the arrival of better educational opportunities, moved into echelons of the work-force seldom cracked before by West Huntley citizens. Mind you, it took seventy-five years after this Belden report, but with each generation preparing the way for the next, the "wills" found the "ways".

Luckily, the economy after 1870 had never completely faltered. The Irish continued to find work in the ever-increasing number of lumber, carding, woolen and flour mills in Appleton, Carleton Place, Pakenham, Rosebank, Arnprior, Perth, and Smiths Falls.

Many followed the railroad's growth in and around the valley: Prescott to Ottawa (1850-54), Brockville to Franktown (1858), Franktown to Carleton Place (1859), Smiths Falls to Perth (1859), Ottawa to Carleton Place (1869), Carleton Place to Almonte to Pakenham to Arnprior (1869-70), Arnprior to Pembroke (1875) and Pembroke to Nipissing (about 1878).

Chasing jobs was not new for the Irish. From 1826-1832, they were the "mud boys" on the Rideau Canal Project. In 1859, they moved stone for the Ottawa Parliament Buildings. They built the booms and slides, dams and canals, and bulkheads and piers along the waterways of the Coulonge, Petawawa, Madawaska, Ottawa and Black Rivers. From 1880 to 1940, they toiled in the shanties every winter from December to March. They built roads and bridges.

While a few West Huntley Irish children from 1870-1940 went on to become lawyers, sisters, nurses, armed-service personnel, priests, teachers, and even politicians, it is sad to say that the majority never had the time, money or opportunity to go beyond the Elementary School Leaving Certificate of Grade 8. To attend the new Continuation (High) Schools in Almonte, Carp, or Carleton Place, a child needed money for room and board as well as expendability from his or her farm responsibilities. Nearly all my uncles and aunts, those grandchildren of the first settlers, had to leave formal education at age fourteen.

The number of citizens staying on in West Huntley to develop skilful trades and open businesses was respectable. Dennis Egan, a teacher, ran a tavern with his father Mike; John Manion had a store-tavern on the Twelfth Line, and, of course, Con Mahoney had his emporium on the Mahoney Side Road. Several did barbering in their spare time.

The blacksmiths were Patrick Finner, Patrick Scott and Patrick Kennedy, all near the Ninth Line. Shoemakers were Dan and James Buckley (Burnt Lands' Road) and James Garvin and James Brown in the settlement next to Goulbourn and Ramsey. John Curtin of the Twelfth Line and Edmund and James Newton of the Eleventh were harness makers. The James Oakleys, Senior and Junior, of the Tenth Concession, were carpenters and builders as was Michael Corcoran on the Eastern Ridge Road. Tom Brown of the Ninth Concession was a carriage and wagon maker. Tom Ragsdale owned a cheese factory on the Eleventh Line, later owned by James Lynch and then Jack Vaughan.

Many had part-time honorarium-positions or seasonal work with the Huntley Township office. Patrick O'Keefe of the Carroll Side Road and Charlie Newton were members of Council from 1900 to 1930 while Council representatives from the previous quarter-century were Tom Carroll, John Manion and P. J. Manion from the Ninth Line, Robert Clarke from the Eighth, and Edward Kennedy from the Eleventh. Pat Carroll, father of Tom, was a selector of jurors and also an assessor. Tom Brown, Bill Egan, John Manion and James Lynch were postmasters.

In the 1940's and '50's employment opportunities again improved for the West Huntley people. Men rode the rails to the harvesting in the West. Others commuted by automobile to work in the surrounding towns. Raymond Mantil joined the Hydro — Herman O'Keefe worked for Canadian Pacific — Mike Vaughan and John Kennedy drove commercial buses — Edmund Newton worked on bridge construction — Basil O'Keefe and Archie Currie became stationary engineers — Allan O'Keefe was with the Road Department of the Township — Jackie Mantil joined the Carleton County Road Crew — John O'Keefe, Bobby Mantil, Angus Carroll and Gerald Carroll were carpenters at the Rifle Range at Shirley's Bay.

Lawrence Grace was a cattle dealer and gasoline station owner — Howard Williams grew strawberries and raspberries — Clarence Williams and Alex Grace became auto mechanics — Angus O'Keefe worked at the Appleton Woollen Mills — Lyle and Carl Killeen were electricians — Cecilia Lockhart owned and operated a store-gas business in Almonte — Edgar Carroll sold cars — Benny Kennedy worked at the Almonte Dairy — Jimmy Newton returned from the war and became a lawyer — Theresa Murphy and Della Carter were nurses — Mary Kennedy, Mary Mantil and Carmel O'Keefe became teachers — Edmund Scott drove for Smith Transport — Maurice Egan became a priest, his brother Andy a teacher, and another brother Wilfred joined the military — many young ladies entered the Sisterhood in Orders across Canada and the United States — Billy Mantil became a successful businessman in California — Michael Grace and Wilfred Scott became priests. And the list goes on, beyond my knowledge and research.

In truth, making a living on a small farm from the 1950's on had become almost next to impossible. Working at two jobs became common practice. Eventually, increased incomes enabled farmers to send more children to advanced education. Gradually the old moulds gave way and a new generation of Irish evolved. It took one hundred and fifty years before all the effort and energy expended by so few, bore fruit.

Today all around the province you can find the new breed of West Huntley Irish. They are working as managers, accountants, teachers, priests, journeymen, engineers, nurses, dietitians, broadcasters, social workers and businessmen. Ask them for their names and they say Brown, O'Connell, Kennedy, Murphy, Killeen, Delaney, O'Keefe, O'Brien, Carroll, Ryan, Forrest, Kelly, Manion, Williams, Mantil, Egan, Scott, Grace, Vaughan, and Flynn.

These young people, wherever they are, have never forgotten their roots. They love to go back home. Whether near or far, they return for visits to the homesteads.

Especially on weekends: farmyards are filled with cars and trucks ... raiding parties hit the pantries ... lawnchairs dot front lawns ... ball games start up ... little people frolic ... animals are spoiled ... favourite beverages are cracked open and bantering fills the day.

Sunday suppers bring back old memories ... everyone happy to be together ... sharing and experiencing special thoughts ... and when the day is over and all have gone to their homes, the grandparents, in spite of their exhaustion, are already looking forward to everyone's return on another Sunday not too far down the road.

Presently, as the rest of the world, West Huntley has become multicultured ... Corkery's 90% Irish purity has gone forever. But wait, all is not lost.

A check of the Almonte phone directory shows the Irish are still on the Rural Routes of Corkery. Gertie and Jim Vaughan's grandchild lives in the homestead. Bob and Rose Mantil have two grandchildren on the Twelfth Line. Two O'Keefe boys are there too and another on the Mahoney-Carroll Side Road. Three Killeens live on the Dwyer Hill Road.

And here and there you find, Browns, Charlebois, Carrolls, Williamses, Kellys, Forrests, O'Connells, Ryans, and Flynns.

Yes, Irish blood still flows in Corkery's arteries. Irish men work the land. Irish mothers rock the cradles.

Their problems are not hunger, isolation, disease and environment as faced by their ancestors. Their difficulties are of a different kind and far more sinister: inflation, chemical abuse, immorality and religious indifference, social and family upheaval, even the fear of annihilation.

But those left will also overcome ... they will meet these challenges ... they will not fail ... they must not fail ... they cannot fail ... for they were born in pain and nurtured in pain ... *they are the children of pain!* ...

And to think, they all lived *once upon a country lane* where I had the privilege of meeting and knowing and loving so many of them ... and for that, I am *eternally* thankful!

Epilogue

Somewhere, beyond the veil, the pipes and flutes will call together all the clans. Families, relatives, and friends will be together.

That's what will make heaven, *heaven*: being forever with the Creator, his Angels, and Saints, and our loved ones.

Appendices

Maps and Drawings

(i) Carleton County

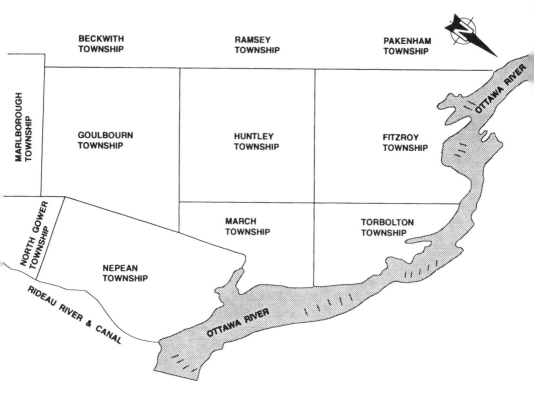

IN 1837-38, THE TOWNSHIPS OF GOULBOURN, HUNTLEY, FITZROY, MARCH, TORBOLTON AND NEPEAN WHICH WERE PART OF CARLETON COUNTY WERE TRANSFERRED TO THE DISTRICT OF DALHOUSIE FROM THE DISTRICT OF BATHURST. IN 1822, CARLETON COUNTY HAD BEEN PLACED IN THE DISTRICT OF BATHURST. ORIGINALLY IT HAD BEEN PART OF THE DISTRICT OF JOHNSTOWN (1791).

IN 1974, HUNTLEY, FITZROY, AND TORBOLTON BECAME ONE TOWNSHIP.

(ii)   *Ireland — Provinces and Counties*

(iii) *Southwest Ireland*

Between Mitchelstown, Fermoy, Mallow, and Buttevant are found the towns of Doneraile, Castletownroche and Kilworth. Newmarket is five miles northwest of Kanturk and Liscarrol some six miles northwest of Mallow. The Ballygiblin Hotel is halfway between Kanturk and Mallow.

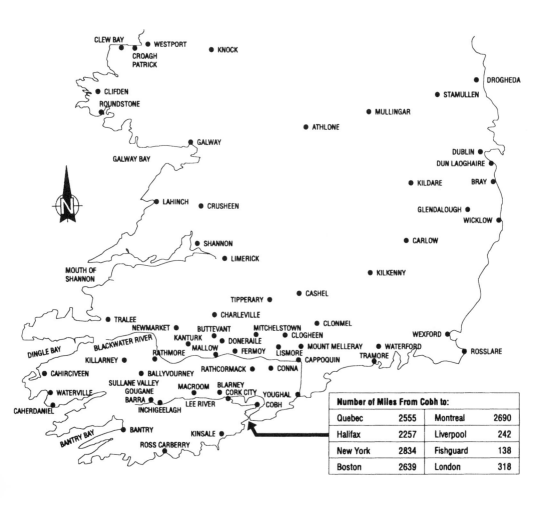

Number of Miles From Cobh to:			
Quebec	2555	Montreal	2690
Halifax	2257	Liverpool	242
New York	2834	Fishguard	138
Boston	2639	London	318

(iv) The Northwest of West Huntley

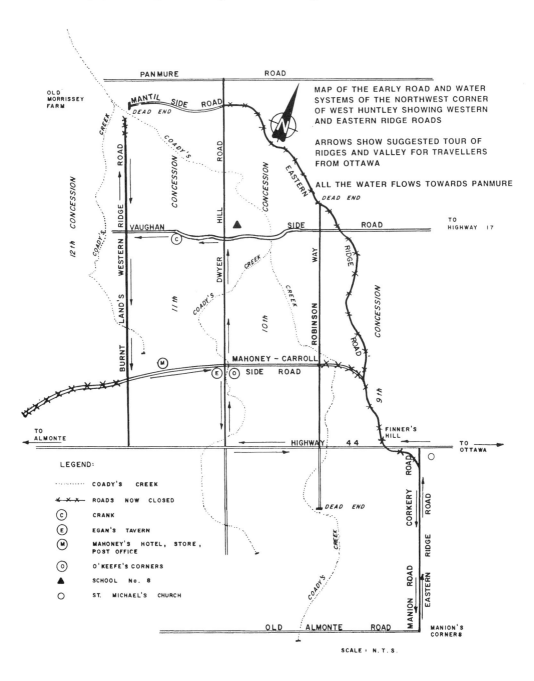

MAP OF THE EARLY ROAD AND WATER SYSTEMS OF THE NORTHWEST CORNER OF WEST HUNTLEY SHOWING WESTERN AND EASTERN RIDGE ROADS

ARROWS SHOW SUGGESTED TOUR OF RIDGES AND VALLEY FOR TRAVELLERS FROM OTTAWA

ALL THE WATER FLOWS TOWARDS PANMURE

LEGEND:

· · · · · · · · COADY'S CREEK

×—×—× ROADS NOW CLOSED

(C) CRANK

(E) EGAN'S TAVERN

(M) MAHONEY'S HOTEL, STORE, POST OFFICE

(O) O'KEEFE'S CORNERS

▲ SCHOOL No. 8

O ST. MICHAEL'S CHURCH

SCALE : N.T.S.

Appendix A

(v) The Southeast of West Huntley (with some 1875 landowners)

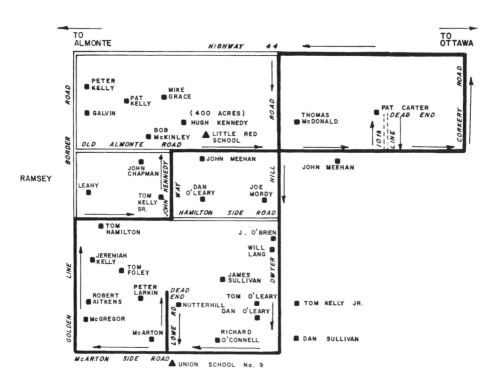

LEGEND :

DWYER HILL ROAD:	11th LINE
LOWE ROAD :	12th LINE
JOHN KENNEDY :	12th LINE
GOLDEN LINE :	TOWN LINE
———▶	ROUTE
■	HOUSE
▲	SCHOOL
≡ ≡ ≡ ≡ ≡ ≡ ≡ ≡	ROUGH ROAD

SUGGESTED TOUR: (FOLLOW ARROWS)

FROM OTTAWA TURN LEFT AT DWYER HILL ROAD AND PROCEED TO THE McARTON SIDE ROAD – TURN RIGHT UP TO THE LOWE ROAD – PROCEED IN AND OUT THE LOWE ROAD TURNING RIGHT BACK ON TO THE McARTON SIDE ROAD – TURN RIGHT AT THE GOLDEN LINE AND PROCEED TO THE HAMILTON SIDE ROAD – TURN RIGHT AND PROCEED TO THE JOHN KENNEDY WAY – TURN LEFT AND PROCEED TO THE OLD ALMONTE ROAD – TURN RIGHT AND FOLLOW ROAD TO THE CORKERY ROAD – TURN LEFT AND PROCEED TO HIGHWAY 44 – TURN RIGHT FOR OTTAWA

SCALE : N.T.S.

(vi) The Old Stittsville-Almonte Road
(approximately, 23 kilometers)

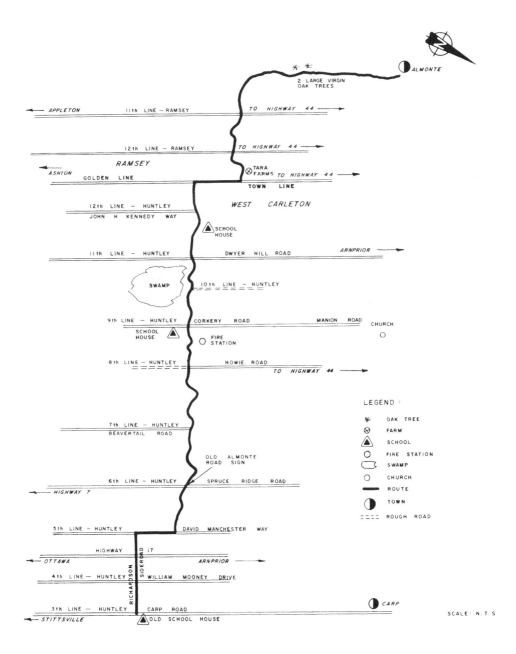

(vii) Old West Huntley Houses (still standing) and Original Owners

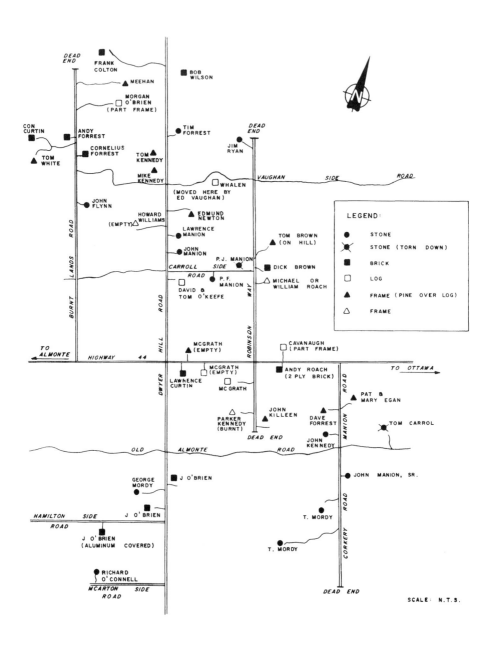

(viii) The Great Fire of 1870

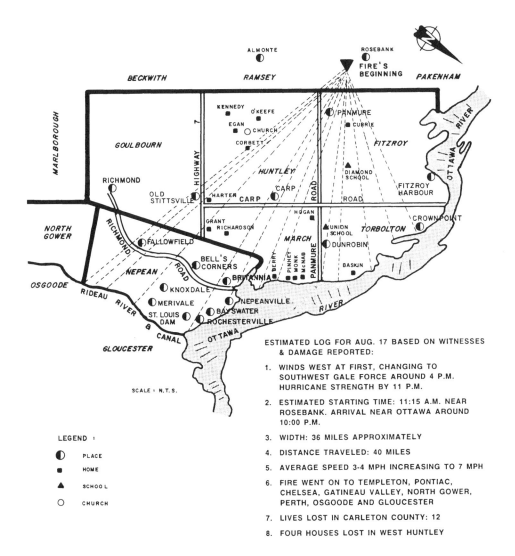

ESTIMATED LOG FOR AUG. 17 BASED ON WITNESSES & DAMAGE REPORTED:

1. WINDS WEST AT FIRST, CHANGING TO SOUTHWEST GALE FORCE AROUND 4 P.M. HURRICANE STRENGTH BY 11 P.M.

2. ESTIMATED STARTING TIME: 11:15 A.M. NEAR ROSEBANK. ARRIVAL NEAR OTTAWA AROUND 10:00 P.M.

3. WIDTH: 36 MILES APPROXIMATELY

4. DISTANCE TRAVELED: 40 MILES

5. AVERAGE SPEED 3-4 MPH INCREASING TO 7 MPH

6. FIRE WENT ON TO TEMPLETON, PONTIAC, CHELSEA, GATINEAU VALLEY, NORTH GOWER, PERTH, OSGOODE AND GLOUCESTER

7. LIVES LOST IN CARLETON COUNTY: 12

8. FOUR HOUSES LOST IN WEST HUNTLEY

LEGEND :

◑ PLACE

■ HOME

▲ SCHOOL

○ CHURCH

351

(ix) West Huntley's School Boundaries (1840 — 1924)

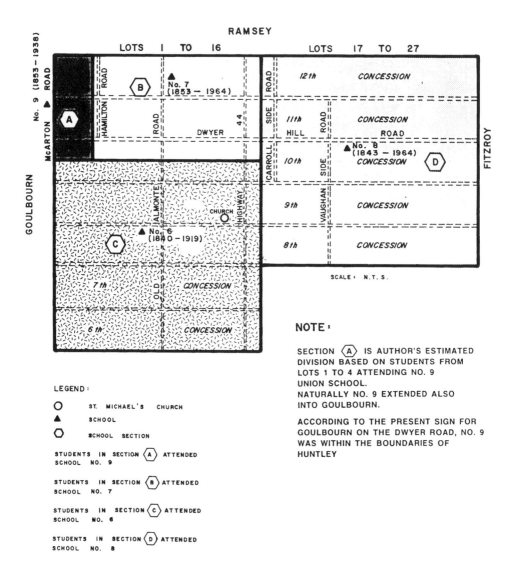

LEGEND:

○ ST. MICHAEL'S CHURCH

▲ SCHOOL

⬡ SCHOOL SECTION

STUDENTS IN SECTION Ⓐ ATTENDED
SCHOOL NO. 9

STUDENTS IN SECTION Ⓑ ATTENDED
SCHOOL NO. 7

STUDENTS IN SECTION Ⓒ ATTENDED
SCHOOL NO. 6

STUDENTS IN SECTION Ⓓ ATTENDED
SCHOOL NO. 8

NOTE:

SECTION Ⓐ IS AUTHOR'S ESTIMATED
DIVISION BASED ON STUDENTS FROM
LOTS 1 TO 4 ATTENDING NO. 9
UNION SCHOOL.
NATURALLY NO. 9 EXTENDED ALSO
INTO GOULBOURN.

ACCORDING TO THE PRESENT SIGN FOR
GOULBOURN ON THE DWYER ROAD, NO. 9
WAS WITHIN THE BOUNDARIES OF
HUNTLEY

(x) Tom O'Keefe's Log House

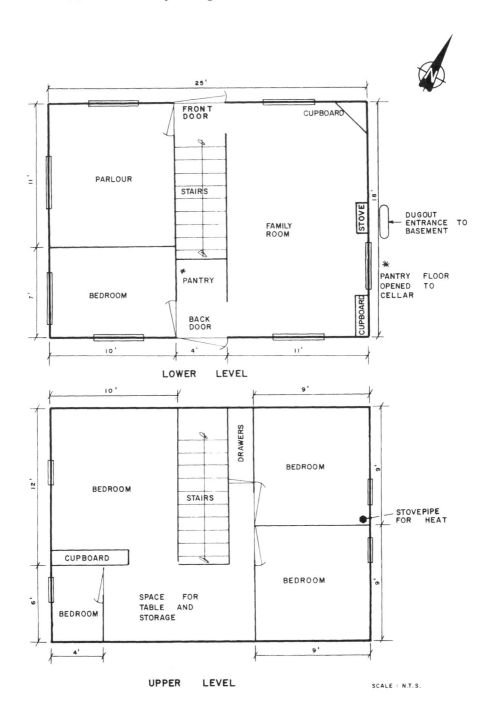

Bibliography

Ahenson, Donald Harman, __The Irish in Ontario - A Study in Rural History__, McGill-Queen's University Press, 1984.

Archives, Ottawa Public, __Census of Carleton County for 1841__.

Archives, Ottawa Public, __Census of Carleton County for 1851, 1861 & 1871__.

Belden, H. & Co., __Historical Atlas of Carleton County, Toronto, Ontario__, Canada, 1879 (new edition).

Bennett, Carol, D.W. McCraig, __Valley Irish__, Renfrew, Ontario, Juniper Books Ltd., 1983.

Bennett, Carol, __Peter Robinson's Settlers, 1823-25__, Renfrew, Ontario, Juniper Books Ltd., 1987.

Bond, Courtney, National Capital Commission, __The Ottawa Country__, Ottawa, Queen's Printer, 1968.

Brown, Howard Morton, __Lanark Legacy__, Ottawa, Ontario, Canada, K.G. Campbell Corporation, 1984.

Bryan, Walter, __The Improbable Irish__, New York, New York, Ace Books Inc., 1969.

Caulfield, Max, __The Irish Mystique__, Englewoods Cliffs, New Jersey, Prentice - Hall Inc., 1982.

Chadwick, Nora, __The Celts__, Middlesex, England, Penguin Books Ltd., 1970.

Childs, Sister Maryanna, __The Sounds of Ireland__, Ohio Dominican College, Our Sunday Visitor, 1969.

Craig, Sara B., __Hello Nepean__, Nepean, Ontario, Canada, Merivale Pioneer Historians, 1974.

Cross, Eric, __The Tailor and Ansty__, Cork & Dublin: Mercier Press, 1942.

Culligan-Hogan, M.J., __The Quest for the Galloping Hogan__, New York, Crown Publishers Inc., 1979.

Currie, T., __St. Michael's Corkery, One Hundred & Fiftieth Anniversary, 1824-1974__, 1974.

Cusack, Mary Frances, __The Illustrated History of Ireland__, Bracken Books, 1987.

Dale, Harrison, __Ireland__, Toronto, Ontario, Canada, MacMillan Company of Canada Ltd., 1919.

De Breffney, Brian, __Irish Family Names__, New York, New York, W.W. Norton & Company Inc., 1982.

Finnigan, Joan, __I Come From the Valley__, Toronto, New Canada Publications, 1976.

Finnigan, Joan, __Legacies, Legends & Lies__, Toronto, Deneau Publishing & Co. Ltd., 1985.

Finnigan, Joan, __Some of the Stories I Told You Were True__, Toronto, Deneau Publishing & Co. Ltd., 1981.

George, Henry, __Progress & Poverty__, United States, Random House, 1879.

Gibbings, Robert, __Lovely is the Lee__, New York, H. Wolff, 1945.

Gibbings, Robert, __Sweet Cork of Thee__, London, J.M. Dent, 1952.

Giffard, Ann, __Towards Quebec__, London, Her Majesty's Stationery Office, 1981.

Godley, A.D. & Humphrey Milford, __Poetical Works of Thomas Moore__, London, Oxford University Press, 1915.

Graves, Robert, __Good-bye To All That__, Cornwall, N.Y., Cornwall Press, 1930.

Grehan, Ida, __Irish Family Names__, Belfast, The Appletree Press Ltd., 1985.

Hall & Dodds, __A Picture History of Ontario__, Edmonton, Alberta, Canada, Hurtig Publishers, 1978.

Haxby, J.A., and Willey, R.C., __Coins of Canada__, Racine, Wisconsin, Western Publishing Company, 1982.

Haydon, Andrew, __Pioneer Sketches in the District of Bathurst__, Toronto, Ryerson Press.

Herstein, H.H., Hughes, L.J., Kirbyson, R.G., __Challenge and Survival__, Scarborough, Ontario, Prentice Hall of Canada, Ltd.

Huntley Young People, __Beginnings - A Brief History of Huntley Township__, 1819-1930, Carleton Place, A.B. Graphics, 1974.

Irish Tourist Association, __Tourist Guide of Ireland__, Dublin, circa 1920.

Johnston, Edith, __Ireland in the Eighteenth Century__, Dublin 1, Gill & MacMillan Ltd., 1974.

Johnston & Spencer, **Ireland's Story**, Cambridge, Riverside Press, Houghton & Mifflin Company, 1923.

Kirkland, Hal, **Joe Baye, A Genuine Canadian & Other Stories**, Almonte, *Almonte Gazette*, 1971.

Lamond, Robert, **A Narrative of the Rise & Progress of Emigration**, Ottawa, Canadian Heritage Publications.

MacGregor, Jimmy, **The Moray Coast, Speyside & Cairnsgorms**, London, B.B.C. Books, 1987.

MacLiammoir, **Ireland**, London, Thames & Hudson, 1966.

Malet, Hugh, **In the Wake of the Gods-On the Waterways of Ireland**, London, Chatto & Windus, 1970.

Manion, Dr. R.J., **Life is An Adventure**, Toronto, The Ryerson Press, 1936. (available in Ottawa Public Library)

McDowell, R.B., **The Social Life in Ireland**, 4 Bridge Street, Cork, Ireland, Mercier Press.

McGiffin, Verna Ross, **Pakenham, 1823-1860**, Pakenham, Ontario, Mississippi Publishers, 1963.

McGiffin, Verna Ross, **Pakenham, 1860-1900**, Pakenham, Ontario, Mississippi Publishers, 1967.

McGill, Jean S., **A Pioneer History of the County of Lanark**, Bewdley, Ontario, Clay Publishing Company Ltd., 1968.

McWade, Robert M., **The Uncrowned King**, Edgewood Publishing Company, 1891.

Muir, Richard, **Traveller's History of Britain and Ireland**, London, England, Michael Joseph Limited, 1983.

Muirhead, Russell, **Muirhead's Ireland**, Chicago, Rand, McNally & Company, 1952.

O'Brien, Rev. C.M., **Finn Barr of Gougane**, Killarney, Ireland, Killarney Printing Works Ltd., 1902.

O'Brien, Edna, **Mother Ireland**, New York, London, Harcourt, Bruce, Jovanowich, 1976.

O'Donovan, Rossa, **Rossa's Collections**, New York, Mariner's Harbour, 1898.

O'Faolain, Sean (John O'Flynn), **The Irish**, Great Britain, Hazell, Watson & Viney Ltd., 1947.

Old St. Mary's, The Biography of the Church of the Holy Name of Mary, Almonte, Ontario, Reproduction Carrière, 1969.

Ontario, **The Pioneer Years**, Toronto, Cannon Books, 1983.

Opportunities for Youth, **March Past**, Kanata, Ontario, 1972.

Plunkett, James, **The Gems She Wore**, A Book of Irish Places, London, Hutchinson, 1972.

Ranelagh, John, **Ireland, An Illustrated History**, New York, Oxford University Press, 1981.

Roche, Aloysius, **A Bedside Book of Irish Saints**, London, England, Burns, Oates & Washbourne Ltd., 1941.

Scherman, Katherine, **The Flowering of Ireland**, Boston, Toronto, Little, Brown & Company, 1981.

Spalding, Henry D., **The Lilt of the Irish**, Middle Village, New York, Jonathan David Publishers, 1978.

Stittsville Women's Institute, **Country Tales**, Tweedsmuir History Committee, 1973.

Upper Canada in the 1830's, Toronto, Ontario, Canada, The Ontario Institute for Studies.

Uris, Jill & Leon, **Ireland-A Terrible Beauty**, Toronto, New York, London, Bantam Books, 1975.

Walt, John, **The Church in Medieval Ireland**, Dublin, Gill & MacMillan Ltd., 1972.

Watt, John W., **The Church and Two Nations in Medieval Ireland**, London, Syndics of Cambridge University Press, 1970.

Woodham-Smith, Cecil, **The Great Hunger**, Hamish Hamilton Ltd., 1962.

Yeats, William Butler, **A Treasury of Irish Myth, Legend and Folklore**, New York, Avenel Books, 1986.

West Huntley's Roots (*See map on page 346*)

Due to quota restrictions in certain areas of Ireland, many emigrants of 1823 and 1825 may have moved to localities where the chances of being selected were better. For example, Patrick O'Keefe and son Tom listed their home as Lismore Parish, Waterford, but in reality were from Convamore, Cork, according to the application forms of the rest of the family who followed in 1825.

In Bathhurst District, here in Canada, some settlers dissatisfied with their assigned claims, moved around as other land parcels became available. Some even changed townships and districts. Others moved away to the United States.

The following summary of West Huntley's Irish-family roots is based on Peter Robinson's records, tombstone information, and the writings of Doctor Dunn, a local doctor.

Corkery was made up of immigrants from many counties of Ireland. The largest number came from Tipperary and Cork, but other counties represented are Limerick, Kerry, Cavan, Clare, Carlow, Kilkenny, Sligo, Mayo, Waterford and Tyrone.

The majority of Robinson settlers of 1823 and 1825 came from Mallow Townland in Cork County in an area north of the Blackwater River. The river begins its wanderings in Kerry, moves across Cork, down into Waterford and then into the Celtic Sea. In Ireland, most settlers lived within a few miles of one another and naturally would have tried to travel together. Most came from within a thirty-mile radius of the town of Mallow.

Name	Date of Arrival in West Huntley	Irish Village/ Town/City/ Parish	County In Ireland
Bresnahan, Dan	1823	Liscarroll	Cork
Brown, Tom	before 1847	Lismore	Waterford
Brown, James	1823	Lismore	Waterford
Buckley, Dan	1823	Churchtown	Cork
Burns, Patrick	before 1847	—	Carlow
Carroll, Patrick	before 1847	—	Wexford
Carter, James	before 1847	—	Tyrone
Casey, John	before 1847	—	Tipperary
Clancy, Tom	probably 1846	—	Cork
Cleary, John	before 1847	—	Tipperary
Colton, Owen	before 1847	—	Tyrone
Cronin, Michael	1823	Mitchelstown	Cork
Curran, James	1823	—	Tipperary
Curran, John	1823	Lismore	Waterford
Curtin, Cornelius	before 1847	—	Limerick
Curtin, Lawrence	before 1847	—	Limerick

Delaney, William	before 1847	——	Wexford
Egan, Dennis	before 1847	——	Tipperary
Egan, Michael	before 1847	——	Tipperary
Egan, Patrick	before 1847	——	Tipperary
Fitzgerald, Bill	1823	Kilworth	Cork
Flynn, John	before 1841	——	Limerick
Flynn, William	1823	Mallow	Cork
Foley, Pat	after 1823	Charleville	Cork
Forrest, Cornelius	1823	Newmarket	Cork
Forrest, James	1823	Newmarket	Cork
Forrest, Richard	1823	Newmarket	Cork
Forrest, Tim	1823	Newmarket	Cork
Gallaghan, William	1823	Kanturk	Cork
Grace, James	before 1847	——	Tipperary
Grace, Patrick	before 1847	——	Tipperary
Hickey, Bill	1823	Mitchelstown	Cork
Hogan, John	before 1847	——	Tipperary
Hogan, Michael	before 1847	——	Tipperary
Keefe, Pat	1823	Convamore	Cork
Keefe, Tom	1823	Convamore	Cork
Kelly, Michael	before 1847	——	Carlow
Kelly, Patrick	before 1847	——	Carlow
Kennedy, John	1821	——	Tipperary
Kennedy, John	1823	Charleville	Cork
Kennedy, Tim	1823	Charleville	Cork
Leahey, John	1823	Conna	Cork
Leahey, Pat	1823	Conna	Cork
Liston, James	1842	——	Tipperary
Lynch, Michael	1823	Castletownroche	Cork
Magnir, James	1823	Mallow	Cork
Maher, Dan	after 1823	——	Tipperary
Mahoney, Patrick	in 1820's	——	Tipperary
Manion, Andrew	1823 (?)	——	Tipperary
Manion, James	1823 (?)	——	Tipperary
Manion, John	1821	——	Tipperary
Manion, Martin	1823 (?)	——	Tipperary
Mansele, Lawrence	1823	Mitchelstown	Cork
Mansele, Martin (really Mantil)	1823	Mitchelstown	Cork
Mantle (il), James	1823	Castletownroche	Cork
Mantle, John	1823	Castletownroche	Cork
McGrath, Michael	1823	——	Tipperary
McGrath, Simon	1823	——	Tipperary
Meehan, John	1823	Clogheen	Tipperary
Meehan, Michael	1823	Clogheen	Tipperary
Mordy, Tom	1821	——	Tipperary
Nagle, Garrett	after 1823	Fermoy	Cork
O'Brien, Jeremiah	before 1847	——	Tipperary

357

O'Brien, Tim	before 1847	—	Tipperary
O'Keefe, David	1846 or before	Conna	Cork
O'Keefe, Ed	1846 or before	Conna	Cork
O'Keefe, John	c.1857	Conna	Cork
O'Keefe, Tom	1846 or before	Conna	Cork
O'Leary, Sam	before 1847	—	Tipperary
Roach, Michael	1823	—	Tipperary
Roach, William	1823 (?)	—	Tipperary
Roche, James	1823	Mitchelstown	Cork
Roche, John	1823	Charleville	Cork
Ryan, Benjamin	before 1847	—	Tipperary
Ryan, Martin	1823	Sixmilebridge	Clare
Scott, Mike	in the 1830's	—	Tipperary
Sullivan, Charles	1825	Kilworth	Cork
Sullivan, John	1823	Mallow	Cork
Sullivan, Michael	1823	Mitchelstown	Cork
Vaughan, James	before 1850	—	Sligo
Walsh, William	1823	Mallow	Cork
Whalen, Peter	before 1847	—	Tipperary
White, James	1823	Shannahan	Tipperary
White, William	1823	Shannahan	Tipperary

Two Islands of Death

The above list not surprisingly shows no emigration to West Huntley in 1847. It was the year of the great famine and fever in Ireland, the year when Nature joined the men of greed to snuff out Irish lives, a year not much unlike the Great Plague of the Fourteenth Century that claimed one-third of Europeans. On Grosse Isle, thirty miles downriver from Quebec City, a one hundred and twenty foot Celtic Cross of granite stands atop Telegraph Hill. To this tranquil spot, once called the Isle of Grace, came eighty-four Irish ships in 1847 carrying one hundred thousand refugees. Already infested with typhus, dysentery, scurvy and malnutrition, one in five that year never realized their dreams of freedom.

Their bodies now rest in Quebec City, Montreal, New Brunswick, Kingston, and on Grosse Isle (five to ten thousand) amid its verdant glades of turf, wildflowers and rocky inlets of raw beauty. A great hill, reminiscent of Newgrange and Tara, cradles the Irish who never made it, victims of disease and pestilence, or of what one man named Whyte shouted out in vengeance over his wife's freshly dug grave: the avarice and indifference of the landlords of Ireland. Under the Cross, a plaque commemorates these poor souls. Written in English, French and Irish, it also remembers the countless French, English, Scottish and Irish nurses, nuns, doctors, priests and ordinary citizens who died in the cause of comforting those wretched wayfarers. Canada opened its heart in 1847 as it has done so many years before and since.

Sample Notice of Acceptance for Emigration with Peter Robinson

No. <u>138</u>

NOT TRANSFERABLE

Ireland, 18th April, 1825

<u>Convamore</u> County of <u>Cork.</u>

THESE are to Certify that the undermentioned Persons of the parish of <u>Lismore</u> in the County of <u>Cork</u>, Ireland, have been received by me, as Emigrant Settlers, to be conveyed to UPPER CANADA, and placed upon their Lands at the Expense of His Majesty's Government.

NAME	AGE	
		Head of the Family.
Mary Keiffe		Wife to Pat Keiffe taken out last June. [1823]
Mary	17	
John	15	

{Superintendent of Emigration from
{the South of Ireland to Canada.

Pat Keiffe and son Tom, age 19, came out with Peter Robinson in 1823. Pat's wife Mary and his two children had to reapply for acceptance in 1825, because, for some reason, they were deleted from the passenger list in 1823, probably due to sickness.

Before embarking, the pilgrims usually heard Mass and then bid farewell to any relatives who had accompanied them from home. Most final meetings were held at the nearest cross from the homestead.

The harbour of Cobh from which many emigrant Irish boats sailed is thirteen miles from Cork City. Not surprisingly, it has been called "The Port of Tears". The *Titanic* made its first and last call at Cobh (and any other port) in April of 1912.

Many *Lusitania* victims were brought to Cobh and carried in their coffins up the great hill and across three miles of open country to the City's graveyard. The investigation into the responsibility for the *Lusitania's* supposedly wrong course was handled by the Irish authorities, thereby preventing the British Admiralty from placing the full blame on the *Lusitania's* skipper, a capable man named Turner.

Several historians claim the information uncovered mainly by the Irish, proves that Churchill and his other naval counterparts had deliberately isolated the ship so that a successful German submarine attack on the *Lusitania* would bring the United States into the war.

Mary Keiffe Senior and John and Mary did join Pat and Tom and finally settled in the 30's on the Twelfth Line of Huntley, West 1/2, Lot 23, 11th Concession.

Pat Keiffe was most likely the brother of William O'Keefe of Conna, Cork, whose four sons, Edward, David, John and Tom settled in West Huntley at O'Keefe's Corners later in the century. In 1847, Pat Keiffe was a witness at William's son Edward's wedding to Mary Ann White.

Research shows that two days after Mary Keiffe's acceptance for immigration, a William and Margaret Keiffe of Cork also applied, but apparently never received tickets. They also lived at Convamore, halfway between Fermoy and Mallow on the northern edge of the Blackwater River, but later apparently moved some twenty miles southeast to Conna.

Tradition has it that the four boys of William O'Keefe came from the Mallow area (six miles from Convamore, seat of the Earl of Listowel).

Pat Keiffe was involved in the Ballygiblin feud between the Scottish of Morphy's Falls and the Irish temporarily settled in 1824 in the town of Almonte. He appeared on the stand in the Perth Court, but his testimony was given little credence.

The name "Ballygiblin" probably encompasses the Irish who came from an area in Cork slightly northeast of Mallow. The word "bally" means "town", the word "linn" means "pool", and "gib" is a short form for the French name "Gilbert". Therefore, "Ballygiblin" should mean "the town of Gilbert's pool". The area is still quite French-Norman. Many Fitzgeralds, Fitzpatricks, and Fitzgibbons came from there.

The judge given the task of re-examining the evidence at the Ballygiblin trials was strangely enough an Irishman named Fitzgibbon, (meaning "Fitz" — "son of", "bon" — "good", and "gib" — "Gilbert"). His conclusions indicated the trial was anything but fair, and he more or less exonerated the Irish.

Pat and his son Tom rolled logs on the St. Lawrence. Tom joined the militia and died shortly after, in 1831 at age 27. William and Margaret never did make it to Canada.

O'Keefe's Corners

O'Keefe's Corners was at the crossroads of the present Dwyer Hill Road and the Carroll Side Road. An Edward O'Keefe settled there in 1847. In February of that year, he married Mary Ann White, daughter of James White and Hanora Mahoney. A son Edward was born in 1848, the same year his father died.

Edward probably came in 1846 from Conna, Cork or possibly Convamore, Cork. Convamore is close to Mallow, Cork, and tradition has it that these O'Keefes came from Mallow Townland. Edward was accompanied by two younger brothers, Tom and David. David bought the farm from Mary Ann O'Keefe around 1849 and settled there with his brother Tom who had married Margaret Finner from Fitzroy.

By 1880, O'Keefes lived at three corners. David, Tom's son, lived across from the father, and John, another son, lived kitty-corner to the homestead. Tom O'Keefe, another son, took over the homestead in 1890, married in 1900, and left the farm to his son Ignatius in 1934. Ignatius's nephew, Gary O'Keefe, lives at the Corners on the Carroll Side Road. An O'Keefe has lived at O'Keefe's Corners for one hundred and forty-five years.

The author and his wife owned the O'Keefe homestead from 1972 to 1981. This one hundred acres included fifty acres on the east which once belonged to John O'Keefe, a fourth O'Keefe brother who came to Canada with his young children about 1857. His son Patrick lived there for years. Pat married Catherine Flynn and had ten children, the last of whom stayed on until the late Thirties.

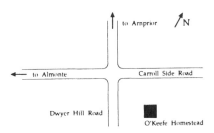

The homestead is still intact. It was probably built around 1855. It is the only log house with a whitewash in all West Huntley.

To find O'Keefe's Corners, coming from Ottawa, turn right on the Dwyer Hill Road off Highway 44. The Corners is the first intersection. The O'Keefe homestead is on the southeast corner.

Father Charlie Finner

Father Finner was a second cousin of this writer. He was born on October 13, 1877, in the parish of The Holy Name of Mary, Almonte. His father was William Finner, born in 1834, son of Ben Finner and Mary Mantil. Mary Mantil lived in Fitzroy, the daughter of John Mantil and Ellen Horrigan. Mary was born in Ireland. She is the great-great-grandmother of the writer.

Father Charlie's mother was Catherine Braceland (Breslin or Braceline). She was married in 1864. Two brothers of Father Charlie were Jack and Sylvester Finner. He entered the Holy Cross Order on June 14, 1900, at Notre Dame, Indiana, U.S.A. (Brother André of Montreal was a Holy Cross religious).

Father made his profession on July 2, 1906, in Washington and was ordained on June 26, 1908, at the Catholic University, Washington. He served in Bengal, India, (same province as Mother Theresa) from February 12, 1918 to June 13, 1932.

He died on April 24, 1936, in Dallas, Texas (he suffered from diabetes). He was buried in the community cemetery in Notre Dame. The report from Bengal at the time of death said:

"A soldier of Christ's foreign legion called home! May his reward for years of service in which he shared India's hardships, poverty, and unrelenting heat be a great one.

A priest of Holy Cross he lies for the long rest, beneath the shadows of Notre Dame, the home which, next to his India Mission, he loved best. In 1932, Father Finner, broken in health came back to the United States, physically doomed. Yet, in the intervening years, he managed to do still a little more work for the community.

Though long expected, death came to him suddenly, and this was kind, for it is well said that when death comes, it is not so much the things we have done as the things still to be done that trouble us. Father Finner, with true missionary spirit, would have felt that there was much more to be done. May his soul rest in peace; in that peace of Christ which as a missionary priest he gave to many tortured souls."

Father Charlie was said to have the power of healing. Genevieve McDermot O'Keefe always claimed she was cured of a heart ailment by Father Charlie after his return from India.

Some Enchanted Places

The enchantment of Ireland can be seen in its colourful names for villages and towns. Here are a few guaranteed to entice the inquisitive traveller:

Avondale	(W)	Killymoon	(Ty)
Ballyhooly	(Co)	Kilmeedy	(Co)
Ballylickey	(Co)	Kinnitty	(O)
Ballyroney	(D)	Knockninny	(F)
Carnalea	(D)	Lisdoonvarna	(Cl)
Clogheen	(T)	Muckish	(Don)
Coomcallee	(K)	Portnoo	(Don)
Crusheen	(Cl)	Rathfarnham	(Du)
Derrylin	(F)	Reenabanny	(Co)
Dingle	(K)	Rineanna	(Cl)
Donnybrook	(Du)	Rosapenna	(Don)
Doolin	(Cl)	Scattery Island	(Cl)
Dooks	(K)	Scrabby	(C)
Dún Ailinne	(Ki)	Shillelagh	(W)
Glendalough	(W)	Slieve Mish	(K)
Hazelwood	(S)	Slieve Anierin	(L)
Hollywell	(R)	Tara	(M)
Inchigeelagh	(Co)	Taghadoe	(Ki)
Inchydoney	(Co)	Ticroghan	(M)
Inishnee	(G)	Tinarana	(C)
Inishannon	(Co)	Toomevara	(T)
Innisfallen	(K)	Tinnahinch	(Ca)
Kilbaha	(Cl)	Tralee	(K)
Killaloe	(Cl)	Vinegar Hill	(Wex)
Kilcoo	(D)	Whiddy Island	(Co)

Codes for Counties

(C)	Cavan	(F)	Fermanagh	(O)	Offaly
(Ca)	Carlow	(G)	Galway	(R)	Roscommon
(Cl)	Clare	(K)	Kerry	(S)	Sligo
(Co)	Cork	(Ki)	Kildare	(T)	Tipperary
(D)	Down	(L)	Leitrim	(Ty)	Tyrone
(Du)	Dublin	(M)	Meath	(W)	Wicklow
(Don)	Donegal	(Ma)	Mayo	(Wex)	Wexford

Irish Proverbs, Folklore, Maxims and Humour

The reason the Irish often fight one another is they can't find any other worthy opponents.

•

Sweet is wine — bitter its payment.

•

A borrowed saw will cut anything.

•

The devil's children have the devil's luck.

•

If you lie down with dogs, you will get up with fleas.

•

A kettle that boils over often cleans the hearth.

•

It's a poor crow that can't lift a stick.

•

A man stole so many parts from his trolley company employer in Belfast, that at the sound of a bell, his whole house started moving down the block.

•

A woman working at the Ford Motor plant in Cork City had so many parts hidden on her person on her way home one night, that when someone gave her a push, she started up and hasn't been seen since.

•

A stalking tree was usually in a field away from the barn. Its branches would be used to hold the ropes, etc., of a hayfork so as to remove hay from wagons and drop it on an adjacent stack. A relative of mine in West Huntley had a stalking tree cut down by a neighbour. No explanation was given, and they never spoke again.

•

Tally sticks have been used by many cultures. In Scotland, identical numbers of notches in two sticks served as a means of auditing a person's payments for produce. When a customer came to pay an instalment, the store owner would cut a nick in the customer's stick and then one in his own.

•

In Ireland, during the suppression of the Gaelic language, the use of Gaelic was forbidden at home and at school. To be sure of a child's compliance at home, parents were told to cut a nick in a stick (supplied by the government) each time Gaelic was used by the child. At the end of a week, a child returned the stick to the teacher who meted out punishment according to the number of infractions; sort of a cut for a cut, so to speak. One wonders why parents, especially Irish ones, would squeal on their children. But apparently some did! Or did they?

•

True faith is like a bird at night always feeling the light of dawn and continuing to sing in the darkness.

•

The grass may grow over a battlefield, but never over a scaffold.

•

When the world becomes decadent, it is the women who suffer the most.

•

Your son's your son 'til he takes a wife; your daughter's your daughter all of your life.

•

It doesn't pay to disturb the natural order. In Ireland, farmers have learned to respect nature. Take magpies, for instance. If a magpie's nest is robbed of its young, the magpies in retribution will kill every one of a farmer's chickens and goslings. Apparently, the magpies only method of capturing man's respect is by retaliation. Perhaps, God uses the same means with man.

•

Mary McCree went on a spree, and came back home as Mother McCree.

•

An Irishman was heard to comment about his first trip on a train, "You come across some fine people on a train, but the first time you meet them, they're kinda like strangers!"

•

A Bessie Foley startled her euchre companions when she announced, "I'd rather be caught dead than allow myself to be cremated!"

•

If the holiest man in the world was to have his sins written on his forehead, he'd always wear his hat down over his ears.

•

It's better to walk without shoes and save your dignity than wear them and lose it.

•

If the crow flies with the wind, there'll be no rain that day.

•

Talk is cheap, but it still takes money to buy whisky.

•

The eyes show what you are; the mouth what you have become.

•

Never trust the hoof of a horse, the horn of a bull, or the smile of a Saxon!

•

Ted Carnochan, a fine Vice-principal at Perth Collegiate, decided to speak to the students about theft, and said, "Since I've come to this school two years ago, I have noticed a marked increase in stealing!"

•

'Tis a bad hen that won't scratch for itself.

•

Death is the poor man's doctor.

•

A weak cat maketh a proud mouse.

•

When I die of old age, you'll be shaking with fear.

•

Never use a hard word when a soft one will do.

•

In the Eighteenth Century, the time taken by a six-horse, ten-seat stagecoach to travel the hundred miles between Belfast and Dublin was three days. If a foreigner wondered why the journey was unusually long, probably no one told him that the Irish mile, in those days, was four hundred and eighty yards longer than the English mile, almost twenty-five per cent farther. John Wesley, the founder of Protestant Methodism, was probably such a victim. After a day's journey on his way to Kilkenny in 1750, he stepped down from his springless barrel on wheels and sighed, "I think this was the longest day's journey I ever rode!" And it probably was! No one had likely told him about the mileage difference. Certainly an Irish Catholic teamster wouldn't!

•

Annie was giving her lad a tonguing after she heard he had bought a motorcycle, "Don't you come runnin' back to me for help, after you've run that thing into a stone wall somewhere!"

•

R.J. Manion heard a new member of the Canadian Parliament tell the members they were "like ostriches with their heads in the sand whistling to keep their courage up!"

•

Never talk ill of a priest. If you do so, don't talk longer than you can hold your finger in fire.

•

Putting new shoes on a bed, shelf, or table, brings poor luck.

•

Never whistle in bed, in a graveyard, or in a plane.

•

When shoes were rare in Ireland, a family had a nightly ritual of washing their feet. (Shades of Biblical times.) A common pot on the kitchen floor was used by each family member, the youngest male going first.

•

Sir Boyle Roche, a pompous but well-meaning Irish member of the British Parliament once said in the House, "The cup of Ireland's misfortunes has been overflowing for centuries and it's not full yet!"

•

It's a long road that doesn't have a turn in it.

•

A black hen can lay a white egg.

•

The eye of a friend is a good mirror.

•

A crow thinks its own young white.

•

Better to be sparing at first, than last.

•

There never came a gatherer, but a scatterer came after him.

•

A sharp tongue invites a split lip.

•

When the hand ceases to scatter, the mouth ceases to praise.

•

The young thorn is the sharpest.

•

A closed hand gets but a shut fist.

•

You're never poor until you go to hell.

•

Tears can be swallowed only so long; one day they must be shed.

•

Melodious is a closed mouth.

•

Celtic vocal organs were unable to say the letter "J". Thus, John became "Sean" or "Shain", and James, "Shamus". "Sean" from "Eoin" was used by the gentry, and "Shawn" by the peasants. If a person named John spelt his name Sean and was not of the gentry, then the locals considered him a social climber and called him a "shoneen" meaning "a little gentry John". A more direct word for him was "upstart".

•

It ain't Irish, but it's a good one. To the suggestion that Venetian gondolas be used on the Ottawa Rideau Canal for the Tourist Trade, an alderman at City Hall advised his peers the enterprise should be started cautiously. He suggested Council first buy only two gondolas, a male and female, and let nature do the rest.

•

Expressions Used Around West Huntley in the 1940's

"Judas Priest!"

"Useless as ___ on a bull!"

"Dear Child of Grace!"

"Sweet, Lifting J____!" (not always a prayer)

"Speak of the devil!"

"Don't trip over the hall light!"

"Get the lead out of your a____!"

"Pay him no mind (or heed)!"

"I'll show him where the bear got in the buckwheat!" (a threat, usually in cards)

"May the Saints preserve us!"

"Keep your shirt on!"

Running around "like a fly in a mitt"!

"A snake in the grass!"

"I have half a mind to!"

"Put your thinking cap on!"

"There's the fly in the ointment!"

"J____, Mary, Joseph!" (not always a prayer)

"Look what the cat dragged in!"

"A little bird told me!"

"Stuck in your craw!"

"Put the whistle in your pocket!"

"You're a sight for sore eyes!"

"More excuses than a cat has kittens!"

"As crooked as a dog's hind leg!"

"You can bet your sweet petootee!"

"God is good!"

"Skill, my backside!" (used in cards)

"Skill, my big toe!" (used in cards)

"Skill, my foot!" (used in cards)

"By hook or by crook!" (two places in Ireland)

"A watched kettle never boils!"

"Don't put all your eggs in one basket!"

"Squealing like a stuck pig!"

"Cute as a fox!" (sly)

"Horse of another colour!"

"Will-o'-the-wisp!"

"He's the devil's!"

"Head like a tack!"

"Horse feathers!"

"Feather your nest!"

"Feather in your cap!"

"Mind you, I've said nothing!"

"So much hogwash!"

"Between them be it!" (don't get involved)

"The poor crature!"

"May the Lord have mercy on him!"

"It wouldn't draw flies!" (poor attraction)

"Where's it all going to end?"

"Going to a shindig!" (festive occasion)

"There's no flies on her!"

"That'll be a frosty Friday!" (no frost in Ireland, usually)

"Nothing to write home about!"

"A holy terror!"

•

"Slow as molasses in January!"

•

"Would you believe?"

•

"Put that in your pipe and smoke it!"

•

"Two steps ahead of a fit!"

•

"Top of the mornin' to ya!"

•

"You're not just whistling Dixie!" (a person means what he says or will stand behind his promise ___ implies a person not only willing to carry his country's flag but also willing to fight for it ___ a patriotic remark based on deep southern convictions during the Civil War ___ a "dix" or "dixie" was a 10-pound note used in Louisiana before the Civil War ___ thus the remark suggests the idea of putting "your money where your mouth is")

•

"Ignorant as Paddy's pig!"

•

"Sit down and take the load off your feet!"

•

"Don't be an old fogey!"

•

"Don't dilly-dally!

•

"Don't dawdle!"

•

"What's the stir?"
(what's the news?)

•

"I don't give a tinker's damn!"

•

"Not worth a tinker's damn!"

•

"Thick as hairs on a dog's back!"

•

"Nosey Parker!"

•

"Feeding your face!"

•

"Bull Roar!" (end of discussion)

•

"Full of himself!"

•

"A big wheel!"

•

"To leave in the lurch!"

•

"Give him a few skites!" (soft blows)

•

"A real ripsnorter!" (a "snort" is a single shot of neat liquor taken in one swallow ___ also used to apply to anything out of the extraordinary ___ the "rip" part seems to be added for emphasis as in "that storm was a ripsnorter")

•

"No spring chicken!"

•

"Saved our bacon!"

•

"All gussied up!" (prettied up)

•

"Thund'ring tarnation!"

•

"Here's to you!"

•

"A devil in the home; an angel in the street!"

•

"A hoot and a holler!"

•

"Think of that now!" (imagine that!)

•

"Wait 'til I tell ya!"

•

"I mind the time!"

•

"Knee-high to a grasshopper!"

•

"Raining cats and dogs!"

•

"Shake a leg!"

•

"Sit up in your boat!"
(pay attention)

•

"Bless my soul!"

•

"Glory be to God!" (not always a prayer)

•

"Hold on to your hat!"

•

"Why you young whippersnapper!"

•

"Go away with you!"
(I don't believe it!)

•

"Keep your nose clean!"

•

"Whistling in the wind!"
(wasting time)

•

"Something fierce!"

•

"Go pedal your papers!" (get lost)

•

"Heaven's to Betsy!" (an exclamation. "Betsy" is short for Elizabeth which means "consecrated to God". Literally, the expression means Heaven belongs to Betsy because she's consecrated to God)

•

"A real tartar!"

•

"A blow in!" (new in town)

He pays "no heed".

"What's your hurry?"

•

"Solid Muldoon!" (used around Pontiac, Quebec, and the Upper Ottawa Valley to describe a hefty person. James Muldoon of the early part of the century weighed four hundred and fifty pounds. He was not just fat; he was tall and big-framed. When he died, the neighbours had to remove him through the window frame instead of the door. Thus, a blockbuster of a child might be lifted up by his uncle to the words: "Begora, you're a solid Muldoon!")

•

"Put him through the hoop!" (make him pay the price)

•

"By the skin of our teeth!"

•

"A lame duck!"

•

"One botheration after another!"

•

"He can lump it!" (take or leave it!)

•

"Hide nor hair!"

•

"Talking a blue streak!"

•

"Gift of the gab!"

•

"Going at it hammer and tongs!"

•

"Talking through one's hat!"

•

"The squeaky wheel gets the grease!"

•

He's a "bad actor"!

•

It doesn't "amount to a hill of beans"!

•

"To beat around the bush!"

•

"Go and sit down somewhere!"

•

"Getting all spruced up!"

•

"Until the cows come home!"

•

"Put a damper on it!"

•

"Bust a gut!"

•

"Pull the wool over your eyes!"

•

"The white-haired boy!" (favourite)

•

"The whole shebang!" (the whole thing)

•

"Holy mackerel!" or "Holy Mackinaw!"

•

"Fit as a fiddle!"

•

"Holy smoke!"

•

"I'll be a monkey's uncle!"

•

"A real humdinger!"

•

"I have a good notion!"

•

"What the Sam Hill are you doing?"

•

"What have you got on it?" (asking price)

•

"No great shakes!"

•

"Not to be put upon!"

•

"Don't be a twit!"

•

"Don't be a twat!" (worse than a twit)

•

Went like a "house on fire!"

•

He was "no ball of fire!"

•

"In a flap!"

•

"To work up a lather!"

•

"Take care!" (meaning "step back")

•

"I came over to tell ya!"

•

"How are you diddling?"

•

"How is all your care?"

•

'Hold her, Newt, she's raring"! or
'Hold her Newt, she's heading for the rhubarb!"

•

'How's your old straw hat?"

•

'God will punish you for that!" (used by Irish mothers)

•

'Stick in the mud!"

•

Nothing but a "nit-picker"!

•

He sure "knows his onions"!

•

They were "very great!" (friendly)

•

'To hoof it!"

•

'Full of beans!"

•

'It let go!" (broke)

•

'Rest yourself!" (step back; let me try!)

•

'Cat got your tongue?"

•

'Putting on the dog!"

•

'Getting a snout full!"

•

'Green around the gills!"

•

'You have a lip that would trip a pig!" (sad face)

•

'What's the use in talkin'!"

•

'Rushing a gal!"

•

'Got his goat!"

•

'Blew his stack!" (spontaneous combustion?)

•

'Between you and me and the gatepost!"

•

'Shoot the breeze!"

•

'Best to all your hands!" (all the people at your house)

•

'She, who's she, the cat's mother?"

•

'Having a leg on!" (in cards)

•

'On the verge of a conniption!"

•

"Don't get yourself into a tizzy!"

•

"That'll ruffle his feathers!"

•

Living pretty "high on the hog"!

•

"Nothing to sneeze at!"

•

"Put a lid on it!"

•

"On pins and needles!"

•

"Don't shilly-shally!"

•

"Cute as a button!"

•

"Hold your horses!"

•

"Fair to middling!"

•

"A face that would stop a clock!"

•

"Do you mind?" (introducing an order or request politely)

•

"As crazy as a bedbug!"

•

"Two shakes of a lamb's tail!"

•

"By Jiggers!" or "Jiggers, eh!" (what do you think of that?)

•

"Took off like a bat out of hell!"

•

"That's only the half of it!"

•

"B__ S__ baffles brains!"

•

"Haul off and lambaste!"

•

"That's a corker!"; "Ain't it a corker!"; or "He's a corker!"

•

"She's the cat's meow!"

•

"Under the weather!"

•

"Small potatoes!"

•

"Round the bend!"

•

"Nervous as a tin of worms!"

•

"Black as the ace of spades!"

•

"Snug as a bug in a rug!"

•

"In a month of Sundays!"

•

Marriages (Mostly Early)

1) "c" - suggests "around" the year listed.
2) Some early marriages took place in Ireland.
3) *Spellings of names are taken from Church records at Almonte, Richmond and Corkery and also the Robinson Papers as well as Census Reports.* The same name may have several spellings depending on the family and the priest.
4) Most marriages listed come from baptismal records.
5) Some partners in marriage lived in nearby townships, but were married by the Corkery priest.
6) When the information is available, a child of a marriage is cited in parentheses.

c.1935	Ballard,	Jack & Elizabeth Lawlis (Barbara)
c.1950	Bassett,	John & Susan Gosson
29/7/1942	Beach,	Byron & Inez O'Keefe (Barry)
c.1838	Beahan,	John & Roseanne O'Connor
c.1847	Brasnahan,	Tom & Ann Carnley
c.1825	Brasnahan,	Tom & Hanora Heffernan
c.1882	Brown,	James & Helena Forrest (Annie)
c.1920	Brown,	John & Clara Ryan
c.1830	Brown,	Tom & Ellen Russell
c.1865	Brown,	Tom & Maryanne Scissons (John)
c.1841	Buckley,	James & Mary O'Brien
c.1838	Burke,	James & Anne Tierney
in 1846	Cadigan,	Cornelius & Honoria O'Brien
c.1864	Cahill,	John & Mary Golding
in 1846	Cardinal,	Edward & Margaret Greer
in 1825	Carnley,	Owen & Mary Fitzpatrick
c.1865	Carroll,	Alex & Catherine O'Bryn
c.1840	Carroll,	Alex & Catherine Doyle
c.1920	Carroll,	Ambrose & Maggie Carroll (Ambrose)
15/08/1953	Carroll,	Angus & Mary Mantil (Jim)
31/10/1959	Carroll,	Gerald & Betty Mantil
c.1857	Carroll,	James & Catherine Belson (Bridgit)
28/11/1917	Carroll,	James & Cecilia Scott (Joe)
c.1952	Carroll,	Joe & Kathleen Madden
in 1885	Carroll,	John & Catherine Lowe
c.1847	Carroll,	Michael & Anne O'Leary (Terrence)
c.1860	Carroll,	Pat & Mary Brennan (Sarah)
c.1858	Carroll,	Pat & Margaret Ann Kennedy
c.1836	Carroll,	Patrick & Jane O'Leary (Tom)
in 1871	Carroll,	Tom & Mary Rone (Jim)
c.1863	Carroll,	William & Mary Moran
c.1850	Carter,	James & Elizabeth Kelly (Paddy)
c.1895	Carter,	James & Rose Brown (Jimmy)
c.1840	Casey,	John & Margaret Scott
c.1889	Casey,	Michael & Bridget Ryan
c.1843	Casey,	Pat & Ann Donohan
c.1875	Cavanaugh,	Edward & Mary Curran (Bridgit)
c.1850	Cavanaugh,	Edward & Elizabeth Carey

c.1845	. . Cavanaugh,	. . Matthew & Mary Cunningham (John)
21/04/1884	. . Cavanaugh,	. . William & Mary Hogan
c.1947	. . Charlebois,	. . Lawrence & Marion Carroll (Lawrence)
c.1840	. . Clancy,	. . . . Tom & Mary Lormasney (Tom)
c.1842	. . Cleary,	. . . . John & Mary Teevin (Tom)
c.1838	. . Cleary,	. . . . Michael & Bridget Hogan (Mary)
c.1875	. . Cleary,	. . . . Tom & Bridgit Galligan (Dennis)
c. 1920	. . Coady,	. . . . Tom & Mary Jane Carroll
in 1841	. . Cody,	. . . . Richard & Margaret Mantle
c.1847	. . Collins,	. . . . Daniel & Johanah Flinn
c.1835	. . Colton,	. . . . Francis & R. Henehan
c.1864	. . Connell,	. . . . Richard & Esther Meehan
c.1864	. . Connors,	. . . Michael & Bridget Kelly
c.1864	. . Corbett,	. . . . Patrick & Margaret Murphy
c.1843	. . Corbett,	. . . . Will & Catherine Phelan
c.1924	. . Corkery,	. . . . Anthony & Mary Meehan
c.1844	. . Corkery,	. . . . Pat & Mary Donohue (Penelope)
c.1844	. . Coughlan,	. . . Tom & Catherine Lantry (May)
c.1875	. . Cox,	. . . . . . Micheal & Margaret O'Keefe (Jim)
c.1835	. . Cronin,	. . . Michael & Mary Dolan (Elizabeth)
c.1876	. . Curran,	. . . John & Anne White
c.1880	. . Curran,	. . . John & Margaret White (Tom)
c.1842	. . Currie,	. . . . Pat & Mary Kavanaugh (Catherine)
c.1840	. . Currin,	. . . . James & Julia O'Brien (Sarah)
c.1835	. . Curtin,	. . . . . Con & Margaret Casey (Con)
c.1838	. . Curtin,	. . . . . Cornelius & Ellen O'Connell
c.1868	. . Curtin,	. . . . . James & Elizabeth Kelly
c.1921	. . Curtin,	. . . . . John & Jane Legree
c.1895	. . Curtin,	. . . . . Lawrence & Bridget Lougan
21/05/1868	. . Curtin,	. . . . . Lawrence & Mary O'Malley
22/08/1882	. . Curtin,	. . . . . Lawrence & Ellen Clancy (Tom)
c.1842	. . Day,	. . . . . . Dennis & Bridget Ryan
c.1870	. . Delaney,	. . . . John & Mary McDonald (Mary)
c.1859	. . Delaney,	. . . Tom & Margaret Nowlan
c.1842	. . Delaney,	. . . William & Elizabeth Hendricks (John)
c.1839	. . Delaney,	. . . William & Elizabeth O'Brien
c.1910	. . Delaney,	. . . William & Nora Sullivan
c.1842	. . Devlin,	. . . . Edward & Mary Lahey (Ed)
c.1847	. . Dolan,	. . . . John & Catherine Furlong
c.1842	. . Dolan,	. . . . Patrick & Anne Kennedy
c.1846	. . Donohue,	. . . Bernard & Ellen Nugent
c.1842	. . Doolin,	. . . . . Tom & Anna McGoldric (Mary)
c.1800	. . Dowling,	. . . David, & Mary Mahoney (Edward)
c.1838	. . Dowling,	. . . Edward & Mary Leahey (David)
c.1846	. . Doyle,	. . . . John & Mary Corkery
12/01/1868	. . Doyle,	. . . . Peter & Catherine O'Brien
c.1866	. . Draper,	. . . . R.J. & Sarah Curren
c.1870	. . Egan,	. . . . . . Daniel & Bridgit McCormac (Margaret)
c.1859	. . Egan,	. . . . . . Denis & Bridgit Manion (Denis)
c.1844	. . Egan,	. . . . . . John & Mary Galleran (Mary)
c.1940	. . Egan,	. . . . . . Mike & Rita Meehan (Judith Ann)
c.1860	. . Egan,	. . . . . . Patrick & Mary Anne Gleason (Elizabeth)
c.1886	. . Egan,	. . . . . . William & Elizabeth Gallagher
c.1905	. . Egan,	. . . . . . William & Margaret Kennedy (Pat)
c.1835	. . Fagin,	. . . . Michael & Mary Anne Collins

373

```
        c.1865  . .  Fenlon,    . . . . John & Jane Mantil
     2/8/1986  . .  Fernandes,  . . Drew & Catherine Ogilvie (Laura)
  06/10/1873  . .  Finlay,    . . . . . John & Jane Mantle
        c.1846  . .  Finn,     . . . . . . Dennis & Margaret McGrath
        c.1890  . .  Finner,    . . . . . Ben & Mary Galligan
        c.1828  . .  Finner,    . . . . . Benjamin & Mary Mantil (Margaret)
        c.1860  . .  Finner,    . . . . . James & Johanna O'Donnell (James)
  14/02/1864  . .  Finner,    . . . . . Patrick & Mary Bresnahan (William)
        c.1860  . .  Finner,    . . . . . Patrick & Mary Braceland (James)
      in 1915  . .  Finner,    . . . . . Peter & Catherine Scott
      in 1841  . .  Finner,    . . . . . William & Margaret Donahue
        c.1865  . .  Finner,    . . . . . William & Catherine Bresnahan (Patrick)
        c.1862  . .  Finner,    . . . . . William & Catherine Bracelinn (James)
        c.1830  . .  Fitzgerald,  . . ? & Johannah Mantil
        c.1838  . .  Fitzpatrick,  . . Henry & Mary McGrath (Esther)
        c.1846  . .  Fitzpatrick,  . . Patrick & Margaret Donahue
        c.1940  . .  Flynn,    . . . . . James & Elizabeth Carter (Bridget)
        c.1895  . .  Flynn,    . . . . . James & Ellen White (Bridget)
        c.1862  . .  Flynn,    . . . . . John & Elizabeth Kelly
        c.1890  . .  Flynn,    . . . . . Michael & Dorothy Ryan (Mike)
        c.1847  . .  Flynn,    . . . . William & Ann Dolan
        c.1842  . .  Foley,    . . . . John & Hannah O'Brien (John)
        c.1850  . .  Foley,    . . . . Michael & Elizabeth Corkery
        c.1915  . .  Foley,    . . . . Tom & Ellen Hennessey (Catherine)
  04/07/1867  . .  Forrest,    . . . . D. & Ellen Folley
        c.1890  . .  Forrest,    . . . . Andy & Margaret Ellen Carberry
        c.1850  . .  Forrest,    . . . . Cornelius & Ellen Curran
        c.1849  . .  Forrest,    . . . . Cornelius & Ellen Kennedy (Ellen)
        c.1910  . .  Forrest,    . . . . Frank & Onagh Kennedy (Frank)
 before 1845  . .  Forrest,    . . . . Henry & Catherine Hewitt (James)
  25/11/1879  . .  Forrest,    . . . . James & Susan Manion (James)
        c.1841  . .  Forrest,    . . . . James & Bridgit Kennedy (David)
        c.1941  . .  Forrest,    . . . . Jim & Anita Donohue
        c.1874  . .  Forrest,    . . . . John & Elizabeth Leahey (Andrew)
        c.1867  . .  Forrest,    . . . . Michael & Bridget Gleeson (Joe)
        c.1835  . .  Forrest,    . . . . Richard & Ellen Sullivan
        c.1838  . .  Forrest,    . . . . Tim & Catherine Hendricks (Eleonar)
        c.1844  . .  Foy,     . . . . . . Andrew & Elizabeth Leary (Catherine)
        c.1856  . .  Gallaghan,  . . Dennis & Peggy Cahil (Mary)
        c.1830  . .  Galligan,   . . Pat & Mary Cullen (Mary)
        c.1847  . .  Galvin,    . . . Denis & Maria Walker
        c.1838  . .  Galvin,    . . . John & Jane Connors (Ellen)
        c.1847  . .  Galvin,    . . . Patrick & Elixa Casady
  27/07/1990  . .  Garvey,    . . . Mark & Mary Ogilvie (Kathleen)
  04/10/1845  . .  Gleason,   . . . James & Mary O'Keefe
        c.1854  . .  Gleason,   . . . Michael & Ellen Quinlan (Mike)
        c.1864  . .  Gleason,   . . . Patrick & Bridget McManus
        c.1864  . .  Gleason,   . . . William & Anne Shehan
        c.1895  . .  Going,    . . . . John & Elizabeth Kelly
        c.1900  . .  Grace,    . . . . Bernard & Elizabeth Newton
        c.1820  . .  Grace,    . . . . Henry & Ellen Coffey
        c.1864  . .  Grace,    . . . . James & Mary Foley (Ellen)
        c.1850  . .  Grace,    . . . . John & Betsy Hogan
        c.1857  . .  Grace,    . . . . John & Clara Whelan
        c.1955  . .  Grace,    . . . . Lawrence & Violet Hall
```

374

c.1865	. . Grace,	. . . . . Martin & Bridget Devine
c.1863	. . Grace,	. . . . . Michael & Ellen Mary Foley
c.1885	. . Grace,	. . . . . Michael & Anne McGarry
c.1875	. . Grace,	. . . . . Michael & Mary Mahoney
c.1875	. . Grace,	. . . . . Pat & Bridgit Colton (Roseanne)
01/05/1877	. . Grace,	. . . . . Peter & Ellen Hickey (Rose)
c.1856	. . Graham,	. . . . Richard & Mary McNamara (Minnie)
c.1842	. . Green,	. . . . . John & Anne McGarra (Pat)
c.1841	. . Green,	. . . . . William & Elizabeth O'Connor (James)
c.1864	. . Griffin,	. . . . . Tom & Mary Meaney
c.1940	. . Hickey,	. . . . Anthony & Noreen Meehan
c.1845	. . Hickey,	. . . . Michael & Mary Sweeney (Catherine)
c.1865	. . Hogan,	. . . . . Denis & Mary Devlin (Pat)
c.1844	. . Hogan,	. . . . . Edmond & Bridget Sheehan (Mary)
c.1853	. . Hogan,	. . . . . John & Bridgit Quinn (William)
c.1894	. . Hogan,	. . . . . John & Adeline Deevy
c.1843	. . Hogan,	. . . . . John & Marcella Moran
c.1973	. . Hogan,	. . . . . Michael & Patricia Anne Craig
c.1928	. . Hogan,	. . . . . Michael Leo & Norma Muldoon (Delores)
c.1860	. . Hogan,	. . . . . Patrick & Mary Lynch
c.1865	. . Hogan,	. . . . . Patrick & Mary Cooney
c.1842	. . Hogan,	. . . . . Tom & Mary Fahey
c.1909	. . Hogan,	. . . . . Tom & Ellen Mary Dubroy
c.1900	. . Hogan,	. . . . . William & Helena Brunette
c.1890	. . Hunt,	. . . . . Peter & Ellen Ryan
c.1847	. . Inright,	. . . . Dennis & Catherine O'Neil
c.1880	. . Kavanagh,	. . William & Mary Curran (John)
c.1860	. . Keefe,	. . . . . Maurice & Mary Ann White
c.1865	. . Kehoe,	. . . . . Peter & Mary Slattery
c.1910	. . Kelly,	. . . . . Joe & Mary Anne Mears (Alonzo)
c.1864	. . Kelly,	. . . . . Martin & Mary Anne McDermott
c.1866	. . Kelly,	. . . . . Michael & Ellen O'Brien
c.1853	. . Kelly,	. . . . . Patrick & Mary Reynolds (Pat)
02/02/1865	. . Kelly,	. . . . . Simon & Ellen Mantil (John)
c.1865	. . Kelly,	. . . . . Tom & June O'Leary
c.1865	. . Kennedy,	. . . Andrew & Sarah O'Leary (Onagh)
c.1945	. . Kennedy,	. . . Benny & Mary Horton
c.1867	. . Kennedy,	. . . Ed & Bridget Devine
c.1920	. . Kennedy,	. . . Edward & Catherine Carroll (Jimmy)
c.1865	. . Kennedy,	. . . Edward & Mary Lynch
c.1900	. . Kennedy,	. . . Henry & Catherine Sullivan (Francis)
c.1890	. . Kennedy,	. . . Hugh & Henrietta Carroll (Tom)
c.1875	. . Kennedy,	. . . Hugh & Mary Lynch
10/02/1885	. . Kennedy,	. . . John & Elizabeth Forrest
c.1945	. . Kennedy,	. . . Leo & Katherine O'Callaghan (Colleen)
c.1830	. . Kennedy,	. . . John & Margaret Manion (Andrew)
c.1918	. . Kennedy,	. . . John & Mary Sullivan
c.1920	. . Kennedy,	. . . Lawrence & Mary Elizabeth Curtin
c.1925	. . Kennedy,	. . . Lawrence & Annie Ryan (Mike)
29/01/1884	. . Kennedy,	. . . Michael & Ann Morrissey
c.1890	. . Kennedy,	. . . Mike & Mary Casey
c.1915	. . Kennedy,	. . . Mike & Margaret Legree (Leo)
c.1900	. . Kennedy,	. . . Mike & Jane McGahey (Lawrence)
c.1903	. . Kennedy,	. . . Parker & Elizabeth O'Keefe
c.1915	. . Kennedy,	. . . Pat & Kathleen McDermott (Rita)

c.1850	. . Kennedy,	. . . Patrick & Mary Casey (Pat)
c.1890	. . Kennedy,	. . . Patrick & Maggie Gleason (Bill)
before 1836	. . Kennedy,	. . . Tim & Mary O'Keefe (Tom)
in 1872	. . Kennedy,	. . . Tom & Betsy O'Keefe (Mike)
c.1830	. . Kennedy,	. . . Tom & Catherine Forrest (David)
c.1838	. . Kennedy,	. . . William & Elizabeth Watt
c.1938	. . Killeen,	. . . . Angus & Carmel Carroll (Lyle)
c.1910	. . Killeen,	. . . . Jack & Evelyn Kennedy
18/08/1885	. . Killeen,	. . . . John & Margaret Grace (Herb)
c.1850	. . Killeen,	. . . . John & Bridgit Gallaghan
c.1846	. . Killeen,	. . . . Pat & Bridgit Gallaghan
c.1875	. . Leahy,	. . . . Francis & Elizabeth Cavanaugh (John)
c.1850	. . Leahy,	. . . . John & Elizabeth Nagle
c.1838	. . Leahy,	. . . . Tom & Mary O'Connor (Pat)
c.1839	. . Leary,	. . . . Daniel & Honora Maxwell (Edward)
c.1838	. . Leary,	. . . . Sam & Mary Conboy (Elizabeth)
c.1910	. . Lee,	. . . . . Joseph & Laura McDermott (Mary)
c.1880	. . Lefebvre,	. . . Art & Bridget McGrath
c.1884	. . Lesage,	. . . . Alexander & Elizabeth McFarlane (John Leo)
c.1864	. . Levey,	. . . . Edward & Mary Stafford
c.1900	. . Liston,	. . . . . Daniel & Mary Grace (Patrick)
c.1900	. . Liston,	. . . . . Edward & Alana Grace
c.1860	. . Liston,	. . . . . James & Bridgit Corcoran
c.1878	. . Liston,	. . . . . John & Ellen Carter
c.1887	. . Liston,	. . . . . John & Margaret O'Brien
c.1870	. . Liston,	. . . . . John & Sarah Wells
29/09/1917	. . Liston,	. . . . . Joseph & Anna Mary Lynch (Larry)
c.1877	. . Liston,	. . . . . Martin & Bridget Oakley
c.1872	. . Liston,	. . . . . Michael & Johanna Flannery
c.1885	. . Liston,	. . . . . Mike & Elizabeth Whelan
c.1870	. . Liston,	. . . . . Pat & Sarah Ward
in 1937	. . Lockhart,	. . . Melville & Cecilia O'Keefe (Wayne)
c.1860	. . Lowe,	. . . . . Michael & Ellen Kennedy
in 1840	. . Lunney,	. . . . Edward & Johanna Mantil (John and Peter)
c.1920	. . Lynch,	. . . . . James & Edna M. Vaughan
c.1885	. . Lynch,	. . . . . John & Catherine Manion
c.1856	. . Lynch,	. . . . . Mike & Johannah Horrigan
c.1840	. . Lynch,	. . . . . Michael & Julia Keorrigan
c.1850	. . Lynch,	. . . . . Michael & Julia McGochlin
c.1857	. . Lynch,	. . . . . Pat & Bridget Hogan
c.1846	. . Lynch,	. . . . . Patrick & Ellen Savage
c.1878	. . Lynch,	. . . . . Patrick & Mary Corbett
c.1840	. . Madden,	. . . John & Julia Ann O'Brien (Tim)
c.1900	. . Maher,	. . . . . Dan & Hellen T. McDonald
c.1865	. . Maher,	. . . . . Michael & Susan Teevans
c.1920	. . Maher,	. . . . . Daniel & Mary O'Connor (Roseanne)
03/09/1884	. . Mahoney,	. . . Con & Bridgit Kennedy (Lawrence)
c.1845	. . Mahoney,	. . . Con & Mary Kennedy
c.1850	. . Mahoney,	. . . Con & Emily Malone
c.1880	. . Mahoney,	. . . Ernest & Julia Meehan
in 1881	. . Mahoney,	. . . John & Mary Jane O'Keefe
c.1830	. . Mahoney,	. . . Patrick & Margaret Tobin
c.1860	. . Malley,	. . . . James & Honora Mantil
in 1834	. . Manion,	. . . . Andrew & Margaret Casey (Pat)
c.1838	. . Manion,	. . . . James & Margaret Tierney (Will)

```
    c.1890  . . Manion,   . . . . Joe & Christine Anne Ryan (Martin)
    c.1890  . . Manion,   . . . . John & Mary McKenna (Tom)
    c.1925  . . Manion,   . . . . John & Kitty Mullins (Jack)
    c.1860  . . Manion,   . . . . John & Bridgit Tierney
   in 1888  . . Manion,   . . . . Lawrence & Hannah Devine (Pat)
    c.1843  . . Manion,   . . . . Martin & Mary Forrest (John)
    c.1920  . . Manion,   . . . . Martin & Esther Sullivan (Joe)
    c.1840  . . Manion,   . . . . Pat & Catherine Lindsay (Pat)
22/09/1874  . . Manion,   . . . . Patrick & Mary Anne O'Bryan (Bob)
    c.1874  . . Manion,   . . . . Pat & Elizabeth Tierney (Homer)
    c.1909  . . Manion,   . . . . Tom & Laura Curtin
    c.1935  . . Mantil,   . . . . . Gerry & Catherine Curtin (Mary)
    c.1927  . . Mantil,   . . . . . Jack & Sarah O'Brien
12/05/1958  . . Mantil,   . . . . . Jackie & Marian Greenfield (Mike)
12/10/1912  . . Mantil,   . . . . . James & Catherine Hunt
    c.1840  . . Mantil,   . . . . . James & Margaret O'Brien (John)
   in 1875  . . Mantil,   . . . . . John & Mary Gallaghan (Bob)
   in 1873  . . Mantil,   . . . . . John & Catherine Whelan (Jane)
    c.1886  . . Mantil,   . . . . . John & Mary Ann Foley (Angus)
    c.1800  . . Mantil,   . . . . . John & Ellen Horrigan (James)
26/10/1932  . . Mantil,   . . . . . John & Bridget Killeen (Angus)
29/09/1919  . . Mantil,   . . . . . Robert & Loretta Rose Grace (Jackie)
    c.1860  . . Mantil,   . . . . . Robert & Ann Fermorin (John)
    c.1835  . . Mantil,   . . . . . Robert & Margaret Ann Finuken (Ellen) (John)
    c.1837  . . Mara,     . . . . . James & Mary Dolan
    c.1966  . . Martell,  . . . . John & Shirley Williams (Sheldon)
    c.1865  . . Mayer,    . . . . . Joachim & Sophie Cardinal
    c.1865  . . McAuliffe, . . . John & Johanna Donavan
    c.1846  . . McCouliff, . . . John & Margaret Fitzgerald
    c.1825  . . McDermot,  . Michael & Judy McCarthy
25/08/1873  . . McDermott, . Ed & Mary Clancy (Genevieve)
    c.1840  . . McDermott, . John & Catherine O'Neil
    c.1845  . . McDermott, . John & Bridget Corkery
    c.1875  . . McDermott, . John & Mary Cullan (Caroline)
   in 1846  . . McDermott, . Michael & Mary Walsh
    c.1842  . . McDermott, . Mike & Mary McGill
    c.1830  . . McDermott, . Patrick & Johanna Dowling (Ed)
    c.1837  . . McDonald,  . John & Christina McDonnell (Martin)
    c.1875  . . McGrath,   . . . John & Margart Mahoney (Julia)
    c.1845  . . McGrath,   . . . Michael & Julia Manion
20/08/1883  . . McGrath,   . . . Michael & Ellen O'Brien (Mary)
07/09/1985  . . McGregor,  . Brian & Anne O'Keefe
    c.1846  . . McIntosh,  . . . Donald & Catherine McDonald
    c.1917  . . McKenna,   . . . James & Mary Ellen Mantil (Dorothy)
    c.1830  . . McNamara,  . . John & Honora Graham (Bridget)
    c.1878  . . Meehan,    . . . . Ed & Johanna O'Brien
    c.1855  . . Meehan,    . . . . John & Catherine O'Connell (Richard)
    c.1845  . . Meehan,    . . . . John & Ann Delaney
    c.1878  . . Meehan,    . . . . Michael & Johanna O'Brien
    c.1850  . . Meehan,    . . . . Mike & Esther Manion (Andrew)
    c.1935  . . Meehan,    . . . . Norbert & Stella Scott
    c.1895  . . Meehan,    . . . . Pat & Bridgit Grace (Pat)
    c.1875  . . Meehan,    . . . . Pat & Jane O'Keefe (Theresa)
    c.1900  . . Meehan,    . . . . Richard & Maude Cleary
    c.1843  . . Moran,     . . . . . Francis & Margaret Behan (Mary)
```

c.1875	. . Moran,	. . . . James & Sarah Dooley (Alex)
c.1837	. . Moran,	. . . . James & Mary Dolan
c.1925	. . Moran,	. . . . Sam & Loretta Forrest
c.1875	. . Moran,	. . . . Tom & Jane Duncan (Ellen)
c.1845	. . Morrisey,	. . . John & Bridget Hogan (Tom)
c.1910	. . Muldoon,	. . . Michael & Annie Rowan (Margaret)
c.1925	. . Murch,	. . . . Fred & Catherine Casey
c.1864	. . Murphy,	. . . . Daniel & Anne Sullivan
c.1953	. . Murphy,	. . . . Grant & Teresa Carroll
19/05/1952	. . Murphy,	. . . Jamie & Marguerite O'Keefe
c.1842	. . Murphy,	. . . . Pat & Elizabeth Kelly (Rosanna)
c.1923	. . Murphy,	. . . . Tom & Annie Delanie (Grant)
in 1845	. . Murphy,	. . . . Tom & Margaret Rahally
in 1942	. . Murphy,	. . . . Vernon & Carmel O'Keefe (Leo)
c.1855	. . Nagle,	. . . . . James & Mary Anne Cavanagh (Ellen)
c.1855	. . Nagle,	. . . . . Richard & Mary Madden
c.1880	. . Neill,	. . . . . Thos & Mary Kelly
Jan. 1915	. . Newton,	. . . . Charlie & Laura Madden (Edmund)
c.1945	. . Newton,	. . . . Edmund & Rita McKenna
c.1873	. . Newton,	. . . . Edward & Ann Twins (Matilda)
c.1900	. . Newton,	. . . . James & Mary Margaret Prentice
c.1865	. . Nolan,	. . . . . Thomas & Honora Morrissy
c.1880	. . O'Brien,	. . . . Patrick & Hanah White (Ignatius)
25/10/1920	. . O'Brien,	. . . . Tom & Anna Ellen Mantil
c.1930	. . O'Brien,	. . . . Ignatius & Lyla Moran
c.1925	. . O'Brien,	. . . . John & Anne Mantil (Rita)
06/02/1883	. . O'Brien,	. . . . Morgan & Jane Colton
c.1840	. . O'Brien,	. . . . Morgan & Sara Lynch (Pat)
c.1860	. . O'Brien,	. . . . Pat & Mary Foy (Pat)
c.1880	. . O'Brien,	. . . . Tim & Mary Fitzgerald
???	. . O'Brien,	. . . . Tim & Julia Madden
c.1860	. . O'Bryan,	. . . Jeremiah & Catherine Foley (Susan)
c.1860	. . O'Bryan,	. . . Patrick & Honora Dowling (Maryanne)
c.1875	. . O'Connell,	. . Andrew & Mary Casey (John)
c.1900	. . O'Connell,	. . Dan & Mary Fumerton
c.1865	. . O'Connell,	. . James & Bridgit Donovan
22/11/1883	. . O'Connell,	. . John & Susan O'Brien
c.1875	. . O'Connell,	. . Richard & Esther Meehan (Catherine)
in 1904	. . O'Connell,	. . Ron & Mary Finner
c.1940	. . O'Connell,	. . Ron & Amanda Grace (Ron)
c.1925	. . O'Connell,	. . Ron & Mary Kennedy (Rita)
c.1835	. . O'Connell,	. . William & Margaret Flynn
c.1845	. . O'Hara,	. . . . Richard & Ellen Brennan (John)
23/07/1865	. . O'Keef,	. . . . David & Sera Cavanaugh (Dan)
c.1835	. . O'Keef,	. . . . Mike & Ester Demara
in 1847	. . (O)'Keefe,	. . . Edmund & Mary Ann White (Edward)
c.1837	. . (O)'Keefe,	. . . John & Mary Duffy (Tom)
29/10/1883	. . O'Keefe,	. . . . Alexander & Elizabeth Margaret Liston (William)
28/07/1945	. . O'Keefe,	. . . . Angus & Grace Mantil (Gary)
28/11/1945	. . O'Keefe,	. . . . Basil & Mary Carroll (Mike)
c.1973	. . O'Keefe,	. . . . David & Wendy Geuer (Mathew)
c.1840	. . O'Keefe,	. . . . Edward & Mary Murphy
11/01/1891	. . O'Keefe,	. . . . Edward & Mary Gallaghan (William)
10/08/1974	. . O'Keefe,	. . . . Gary & Connie Liddle (Sean)
30/03/1931	. . O'Keefe,	. . . . Herbert & Cecilia Coffey (Gerry)

```
      c.1970  . . O'Keefe,   . . . . Herman & Helen Cybulski
      c.1865  . . O'Keefe,   . . . . Jeremiah & Ellen Kennedy (Mike)
      c.1983  . . O'Keefe,   . . . . Joe & Vicky Garriock (Jonathon)
    in 1946  . . O'Keefe,    . . . . John & Margaret Carroll (Joe)
    in 1906  . . O'Keefe,    . . . . John & Mary Sheehan
      c.1910  . . O'Keefe,   . . . . John & Mary Hunt (Josephine)
      c.1840  . . O'Keefe,   . . . . John & Ellen Horan
    in 1844  . . O'Keefe,    . . . . John & Bridget Walsh (William)
      c.1835  . . O'Keefe,   . . . . John & Mary Cory (William)
    in 1844  . . O'Keefe,    . . . . John & Bridget Lunney (Mary Ann)
    in 1928  . . O'Keefe,    . . . . Michael & Areilia St. Martin (Mike)
19/06/1906  . . O'Keefe,    . . . . Michael & Ellen Jane Moran (Basil)
      c.1960  . . O'Keefe,   . . . . Michael & Yolande Jolicoeur (Mike)
      c.1838  . . O'Keefe,   . . . . Mike & Mary Nagle (Bridgit)
01/02/1873  . . O'Keefe,    . . . . Patrick & Catherine Flynn (James)
20/02/1858  . . O'Keefe,    . . . . Patrick & Johanna Power (Pat)
    in 1882  . . O'Keefe,    . . . . Patrick & Susan O'Brien (Joseph)
    in 1849  . . O'Keefe,    . . . . Tom & Margaret Finner (Tom)
      c.1885  . . O'Keefe,   . . . . Tom & Katherine Foley (Herbert)
27/11/1900  . . O'Keefe,    . . . . Tom & Genevieve McDermot (Mary)
    in 1884  . . O'Keefe,    . . . . William & Mary Jane McNulty (Mike)
      c.1845  . . O'Leary,   . . . . Dan & H. Maxwell
      c.1878  . . O'Leary,   . . . . Dan & Catherine O'Brien (Mike)
      c.1870  . . O'Leary,   . . . . Pat & Maggy Carroll
         ???  . . O'Leary,   . . . . Patrick & Margaret Mary Muldoon
      c.1843  . . O'Leary,   . . . . Sam & Mary Corbet (June)
      c.1847  . . O'Mera,    . . . . Thomas & Mary Foley
      c.1856  . . O'Neil,    . . . . . Francis & Judith O'Mera
      c.1844  . . O'Neil,    . . . . . John & Mary Driscoll (James)
    in 1843  . . O'Neil,    . . . . . John & Mary Dunne
      c.1844  . . O'Neil,    . . . . . Tom & Mary Murphy (Mary)
      c.1945  . . O'Reilly,  . . . . John & Julia Scott
      c.1840  . . Oakley,    . . . . James & Mary Manion (Mary)
09/08/1958  . . Ogilvie,    . . . . Garfield Thomas & Marilyn O'Grady (Catherine)
27/06/1987  . . Ogilvie,    . . . . Thomas Albert & Tammy Beekmans
11/10/1930  . . Ogilvie,    . . . . Thomas Murray & Evelyn (Eva) O'Keefe (Garfield
      c.1926  . . Prudhomme,   . Alex & Mary O'Keefe (Frank)
      c.1865  . . Plunkett,    . . . James & Bridgit Riley
      c.1844  . . Quigley,    . . . . John & Mary Whelan (Penelope)
      c.1898  . . Roach,     . . . . . William & Bridgit Doolin
      c.1870  . . Roach,     . . . . . William & Mary Manion
      c.1845  . . Roche,     . . . . . Patrick & Ellen O'Connell
    in 1887  . . Rowan,     . . . . Tom & Mary O'Keefe (Annie)
      c.1896  . . Ryan,     . . . . . James & Annie Sullivan (Dominic)
      c.1847  . . Ryan,     . . . . . John & Mary Slattery
      c.1847  . . Ryan,     . . . . . John & Mary Leary (Pat)
      c.1822  . . Ryan,     . . . . . John & Hanora Russell
      c.1846  . . Ryan,     . . . . . John & Ellen Grace
      c.1960  . . Ryan,     . . . . . Leonard & Sandra Kennedy
      c.1840  . . Ryan,     . . . . . Martin & Elizabeth Herrick (James)
      c.1875  . . Ryan,     . . . . . Patrick & Honoria Kennedy
      c.1864  . . Ryan,     . . . . . William & Anne Morrissy
      c.1898  . . Sample,    . . . . James & Annie Gallagher (James)
11/11/1884  . . Scissons,   . . . . Tom & Margaret Ryan
      c.1940  . . Scott,     . . . . . Edmund & Lois Brennan (Tim)
```

c.1917	Scott,	Frank & Hannah Delaney (Frank)
c.1880	Scott,	James & Catherine Carroll (Tim)
c.1914	Scott,	John Matthew & Susan Gosson (Catherine)
08/07/1872	Scott,	John & Serah Carroll (John Matthew)
c.1925	Scott,	John L. & Jessie McIntyre (Cecilia)
c.1890	Scott,	Michael & Mary Jane Kennedy (Cecilia)
c.1845	Scott,	Michael & Julia Banks (Mike)
c.1925	Scott,	Ned & Ethel Golden
c.1870	Scott,	Patrick & Mary Ann Carroll (Pat)
c.1890	Scott,	Patrick (Tattie) & Lizzie Curtin
c.1908	Scott,	Tim & Mary Delaney (Edmund)
c.1890	Scott,	Tim & Emma Hayes (John Leo)
c.1885	Scott,	Tim & Catherine Kennedy
c.1838	Smith,	Dan & Mary Ann Walsh (Mary Ann)
c.1885	Smith,	Mike & Mary O'Brien
c.1841	Sullivan,	Carroll & Anne Manion (Andrew)
c.1864	Sullivan,	Denis & Bridgit Woods (Mary)
c.1855	Sullivan,	James & Anne Egan
c.1875	Sullivan,	James & Mary Nutterville
c.1873	Sullivan,	John & Julia O'Leary
c.1880	Sullivan,	Lawrence & Maria Coughlin (John)
07/01/1861	Sullivan,	Rod & Margaret Tracey
c.1846	Tierney,	Dan & Maria Monahan
c.1842	Tierney,	Mike & Mary Corkery (Johannah)
c.1875	Vaughan,	Ed & Julia Grace (Catherine)
24/10/1953	Vaughan,	Gerald & Bertha Carroll (Lorne)
c.1890	Vaughan,	Jack & Maggie Kelly
c.1855	Vaughan,	James & Mary Walsh
c.1920	Vaughan,	Jimmy & Gertie Curtin (Gerald)
c.1865	Vaughan,	Michael & Mary Egan
c.1865	Walsh,	James & Agnes Mooney
c.1845	Whalen,	Peter & Elizabeth Bonfield
c.1865	Whelan,	John & Mary Mantil
c.1838	Whelan,	Peter & Anna Roach (James)
c.1860	White,	David & Sarah Cavanaugh
c.1845	White,	David & Sarah Loughrea (Bridgit)
c.1867	White,	Francis & Eleonor Rossiter (Joe)
c.1850	White,	James & Alice Lindsay
c.1810	White,	James & Nora Mahoney (Edward)
c.1855	White,	Maurice & Ellen Seymour (Mike)
c.1845	White,	Maurice & Alice Smith (Patrick)
c.1858	White,	Tim & Ann Fagan (Margaret)
c.1900	White,	Tom & Matilda McDonald
c.1863	White,	Tom & Bridget McNamara (Hannah)
c.1840	White,	Pat & Ellen Gorman
c.1835	White,	William & Johanna Forest (Ellen)
c.1865	Whyte,	James & Catherine Sheahan
in 1957	Williams,	Clarence & Barbara Ballard (John)
c.1922	Williams,	James & Mary Cunningham (Joe)
c.1856	Williams,	John & Catherine Armstrong (Howard)
in 1928	Williams,	Maurice & Annie O'Keefe (Clarence)

A Handy Man's Gaelic-Anglo-Irish Glossary

This glossary is based on information from books written by the Irish and printed in Ireland. Every attempt has been made to be exact. The glossary contains Gaelic, Anglicized Gaelic and Irish-English slang. Some words may be helpful in understanding Irish places and names. They may also recall old terms used around Canada in earlier days.

Abu . . . . . . Our hero, our man
Acushla . . . . Little darling
Achadh . . . . A field or open space
Achar . . . . . A flat field or place
Achora . . . . Friend
Aileen . . . . . Eileen
Airy . . . . . . An affected manner suggesting and empty-headed individual
Alanna . . . . A child
Alla . . . . . . A cliff
Ath . . . . . . A ford
Alt . . . . . . A steep side of a glen
Andruim . . . Habitation by the waters
Ard . . . . . . A mound
Aroon . . . . . A pet name, dear
Auneevin, . . Beautiful
Aluinn
Avourneen . . Darling of my heart
machree
Balla . . . . . A wall
Bally, Bal . . . A town or place
Bally-hoō . . . Noisy demonstrations to gain attention — from a small town, Ballyhooly, in Cork
Ban, Bean . . . A woman, a lady
Bána . . . . . A lea (as in meadow)
Banshee . . . . A fairy woman
Barra, Barr . . Top, summit
Baste . . . . . A beast
Beag . . . . . Small
Béal or Beul . A mouth (as a river), an opening
Bedad . . . . . "By gosh!" "By God!" "Bedamned!"
Beldame . . . . An old ugly woman
Berrin . . . . . Burying
Biddy . . . . . Any female servant (from Bridget)
Bile . . . . . . An historic tree
Blackjack . . . A larger container for beverage, usually beer or whisky — sometimes applied to rum
Blarna . . . . A gap (as in a mountain)
Blarney . . . . Flattering talk
Blast . . . . . An infliction said to be caused by fairies or dwarfs

Blasted . . . . Detestable, accursed
Blastie . . . . . A tiny blasted creature
Blathering . . Silly talk
Blatherskite . . A chatterbox
Blithe . . . . . A merry or joyous disposition
Boccagh . . . . A beggar
Bofin . . . . . A white cow
Bog . . . . . . Soft (as in a field)
Bogán . . . . . A soft-shelled egg
Bóinne . . . . The Boyne River
Boireann, . . . A large rock, a stony
Burrin or district
Burren
Bonavs . . . . Piglets
Boreen . . . . . A lane or path (in the country)
Bouchal . . . . A boy
Boyo . . . . . . A lad who hangs around corners
Bráke . . . . . A thicket; brushwood
Brí, Bray, . . . A hill or brae
Bree
Bridgeen . . . A small bridge
Brogan, Bróg . A boot or shoe
Brugh . . . . . A large house
Brusher . . . . A beard
Buaile, ... Place for keeping or
Boola, Boula milking cattle
Buidhe, ... A yellow boy (colour)
buidh
Bull virgin . . To describe a bachelor
Bun . . . . . . The end (of a road), the foot (of a hill), the mouth (of a stream)
Byre . . . . . . Cowbarn
Cairn, Carn . . A heap of stones
Caiseal, ... A stone fort
Cashel
Caisleán . . . . A castle
Caoine . . . . The good people (usually
Maithe good fairies)
Cappeen . . . . A cap
Carraig, ... A rock
Carrick
Cathair, ... A circular stone fort
Cahir, (usually of uncemented
Caher stones)
Caubeen . . . . An Irish, cloth cap

Caunaroon . .	Beautiful haven
Caunmel . . .	A haven of honey
Cauth	Kate
Cead	A hundred
Cead mille . . failte	A hundred thousand welcomes
Cealla, Killy, . Kells	A church
Ceann	The head (of a weir)
Céim, Keem . Keim	A pass
Chaw	Slang for chew
Cill, Kil, Kill .	A church or a cell
Clab	Open mouth — from surprise or laughing
Cladach, . . . Claddagh	A seashore or beach
Claidhe	A fence
Clann	A clan, race, children
Clár, Clar, . . Clare	A plank bridge
Clochán, . . . Cloghan	A stone hut, a beehive hut (pre-historic times)
Cloch, ... Cloagh	A stone
Cloigin	A bluebell
Clonard . . .	A high meadow
Clonmel . . .	A meadow of honey
Cloon	Meadow
Cluain, ... Clon	A meadow, usually isolated
Cnoc, Knock .	A little hill or hillock
Colcannon . .	A mixture of potato, onion and cabbage
Colleen	A young girl, could be Irish
Colleen dhas .	A pretty girl
Columba, . . . Columb	A dove
Cor	A round hill or turn in the road
Corcaig, . . . Cork	A marsh
Corr	A projection or peak
Cothamore . .	Big coat
Cowherd . . .	One who tends cows
Crann	A tree
Crannogs . . .	Stockaded islands found in clusters on lakes — stone houses in the middle of an island or lake
Cró (call for . cattle??)	A cattle pen or hovel
Cromlechs . .	Stone circles near graves, usually isolated; also used to consecrate some spot used for special reverence in religious or judicial functions
Croosheening	Whispering
Cros	A crossroads, a cross
Crosán	A little cross or crossroads
Cuan, Caun .	A harbour or haven
Cúil	A corner
Cúl	A back
Curie-fibbles .	Small artifacts, curios or objects d'art
Currach	An Irish rowboat
Cushla	Darling
D'yarrag, . . . Derg	Red, scarlet
Da Dardeen .	Wednesday
Da Hena . . .	Thursday
Da Mort . . .	Tuesday
Dable	Double
Dacenter . . .	Fine, good, decent
Dair	An oak
Dal	A tribe
Daltheen . . .	A puppy
Dasate	Lies, deceit
Dash	Slosh on, as with paint on a wooden bench
Deoch án . . . dorrus or Duc án Durrus	A wee drink at the door
Dhudeen . . .	A short tobacco pipe
Dia Linn . . .	God be with us
Dia Linn is . . Muire	God and Mary be with us
Dinger	An outstanding person in his career
Dogman . . .	Tax collector on dogs
Dog's Leg . . .	A drink
Dolls	Irish slang for young women
Domhnach, . . donagh, donny	A church (literally means Sunday)
Doon	A fort
Door-cheek . .	The side of the door
Doras	A door
Doreen	A small drop
Droichead, . . Droghed	A bridge
Drop	A whiskey, or any drink
Druim, ... Drum	A long hill, a ridge
Dubh	Black or Dark (as in colour)
Duc	A drink
Dún, Doon . .	A high fort, fortifications, stone huts (usually of uncemented stone)
Dunaroon . .	A beautiful fort
Eadan	Hill-brow
Eas	A waterfall
Eo	A yew
Failte	Welcomes

Fáinne, An	. .	Literally, "the Ring", the members of which promise to speak only Irish among themselves
Faithche, Faha	. . .	A green
Faoilean	. . .	Seagull
Fillet	. . . . .	A narrow band like a ribbon encircling the head
Fiodh	. . . . .	A wood
Fionn, Finn, Fin	.	Fair, clear
Focal	. . . . .	A word
Froster	. . . .	A nail or cleat in a horse's hoof
Gaddying	. . .	Wandering around listlessly
Gaelach	. . . .	Gaelic
Gaeltacht	. . .	The area in West Ireland, mainly made up of Irish-speaking people
Gall	. . . . . .	Stranger (noun)
Galláns	. . . .	Pillar, stones to mark graves or commemorate a happening
Galoot	. . . .	Slang for a sloppy, ill-mannered person
Galore	. . . . .	An abundance of
Galways	. . .	Whiskers running along the edge of the chin
Garrdha, Garry	. . .	A garden
Garryowen	. .	Owen's garden
Gerry-mandering	. . . .	Dividing a district unfairly to gain a political advantage; often used to refer to any form of crookedness by people in power
Girleen	. . . .	Small girl
Gleann, Glen	.	A hollow or glen, a valley
Glenmor	. . .	A big valley
Glynns	. . . .	Woods
Gom	. . . . .	A fool
Gombeen man	. . .	A salesman of meal or a greedy salesman
Gort	. . . . . .	A tilled field
Gossoon	. . . .	A boy (from "garçon" in french)
Grabbers	. . .	Slang for politicians
Grawls	. . . .	Children (peasantry)
Greeshy	. . . .	Embers
Grian, Green	.	The sun
Grianán, Greenan	. . .	A beautiful sunny spot, a bower, a royal palace, a summer house
Groat	. . . . .	An old silver coin worth fourpence
Gully	. . . . .	A large knife
Gutter, gropper	. . . .	Like a gutter-snipe, a bad character
Herroo	. . . .	An exclamation of praise like "hip, hip, hurray", "Murphy, Murphy, herroo, herroo"
Hooey	. . . . .	Slang for nonsense
Hooking it	.	Clearing out, making off
Hubbub	. . . .	Rumpus, uproar, confusion
Hullabaloo	. .	Disturbance
Humbugged	.	Misled or deceived
Hy	. . . . . .	Island
Inch	. . . . .	A low meadow near a river
Inis, Inish	. . .	An island
Inishamel	. . .	An island of honey
Inisharoon	. .	Dear or beautiful island
Inishmar	. . .	Island like
Jaunty	. . . . .	Stylish, showy or sprightly
Jemmy	. . . . .	Jimmy
Keeler	. . . . .	Small tub for cooling butter
Keen	. . . . .	A funeral cry of Irish peasants
Kern, Kerne	. .	A poor peasant, a boor
Killen	. . . . .	A cemetery for suicides and unbaptized babies
Knochard	. . .	A high hill
Ladder	. . . .	Irish for "lather", as before a shave
La luan	. . . .	Monday
Lam (to lam)	.	To beat soundly
Lamhan	. . . .	Hands
Léim	. . . . . .	A leap or pass
Linn	. . . . . .	A pool
Linney	. . . .	A small house at the back of the main house
Loch, lough	. .	A lake
Long	. . . . .	A ship
Longford	. . .	An encampment
Longmel	. . . .	A place of honey
Lug, Lag	. . .	A hollow chimney
Lurga	. . . . .	A long strip of land
"Mac","Mc"	. .	A son of
Ma bouchal	.	My boy
Ma	. . . . . .	My
Macha	. . . . .	High place
Macushla	. . .	My darling
Maol, Mweel, Muil	. . . . .	Bare
Maise	. . . . .	Indeed!
Malarkey	. . .	Obscure speech, baloney
Maneen	. . . .	A boy who acts like a man
Mar	. . . . . .	Like
Mavrone	. . .	My goodness
Mead	. . . . .	Meadow
Merrow	. . . .	The sea
Mick	. . . . .	Irishman, shanty Irishman

Mickey	A white or Irish baked potato — a sweet potato is a sweet mickey
Midden	Garbage dump or manure pile
Mín, Meen . .	Gentle, smooth or level
Mion	Small
Mitching . . .	Skipping school
Moolie	Cow without horns
Moreydoon, Muiredoon	A fort of the Virgin Mary
Moryah	Forsooth
Muc, Much .	A pig
Muileann . .	A mill
Muine, Money	Shrubbery
Muire, Murry, Morey, Wirra	Mary the Virgin
Muirnin . . .	My darling
Mullin	A hillock
Murning . . .	A murmuring
Murrain . . .	The rot
Musha	Exclamation like "really" "in truth"
Nás	A place of assembly
Nature	Slang for kindliness or affection
Nead, Nad, Ned . .	A nest
Neat as in "whiskey-neat" . .	Drinking liquor in its pure form; straight
Nellie	Ellen, Helen
Nightcap . . .	A dark cloud hanging over a mountain, signifying bad weather
Notion	As in "having a notion" (intention)
'O'	Grandson
Obair, Nobber	Work
Ogham	Strange Irish alphabet cut in stone to commemorate dead leaders (1st-5th Centuries)
Oigh	A maid
Oileán	Island
Óir	Golden
Or	Gold
Padraic	Paddy, Pad
Poll	A hole
Pandy	Mashed potatoes
Patheen . . .	A small path
Pathereen . .	An Irish peasant's rosary
Pogue	A kiss
Pooka	A mischievous Irish spirit
Poteen	Irish moonshine

Power	A multitude as in a "power of people"
Praties	Potatoes
Pusheen . . .	Dear, lovable
Quare	Queer
To Rail	To scold harshly; also used to suggest silly babbling in conversation
Randy	Ill-mannered, coarse
Ráth	Clay houses, fortifications of some sort, fort, an earthen fort
Rigmarole . .	Rambling, confused, foolish talk
Rinn	A point of land
Rócán	An old song
Ros, Ross, Rose, Rush . .	A point or a wood, a peninsula
Ruadh	Red
Sacret	Secret
Saul, Sabhal .	A barn
Saw	To move one's arms as if cutting with a saw; e.g., saw off a tune on a violin
Sceilig, Sgeilig, Skellig	A crag, a lofty rock
Scouse	A late flower
Scudda-Hoo, Scudda-Hay .	Calls to a team of horses, mules, oxen, meaning "move along and gee" and "get along and haw"
Sean	Old
Shagh	Irish for tobacco smoked in a two-inch pipe
Shaile	Salt water
Shandon . . .	Old fort, inn
Shanty	From Irish "shan" or "sean" for "old" plus "tigh" for house: an old house
Sharoose . . .	Bitterness, sarcasm
Shebang . . .	Usually associated with "whole" as in "the whole thing"
Shebeen	An illegal tavern or house where liquor is sold
Shenanigan . .	Trickery, mischief
Shillelagh . . .	A black thorn or oak cudgel
Sidhe	Fairies' places or the fairies themselves
Simples	A collection of warm, moist medicinal plants usually applied to the temple
Sinn Fein . . .	Ourselves
Skirt	Irish slang for a young woman
Slainte	Health

Sleiveen . . . . A mean fellow

Sliabh . . . . . A mountain

Slip . . . . . . A young animal or person, as in "just a slip of a lad"

Smidirin, . . . A small fragment
Smithereens

Sna . . . . . . In the fields
poircenna

Soft sawder . . A person trying to butter-up another, like "soft soaping"

Sook, Sookie . A call for animals to drink or eat

Sop . . . . . . Any food dipped in liquid

Souterrains . . Tunnels used for storehouses or hiding places

Spalpeen . . . A boy, lad, rascal, a migrant farm worker

Spavined . . . A large bone growth on the leg of a horse

Spill . . . . . . As a "spill of smoke" — a roll of paper or piece of wood used to start a fire

Splink . . . . . Spark, glimmer

Squicher . . . A contrary mare; sometimes applied to an unruly woman

Squireen . . . A country squire, who is not so big

Sruthán . . . . A stream

Stag . . . . . . Slang for a spy

Station . . . . A home for saying Mass: every year in Ireland (and later in pioneering Canada) certain houses within a parish were named as "stations". The priest might stay for a number of days. He usually ate alone.

Stint . . . . . As in "beyond his stint or limit or capacity"

Stirk . . . . . A young bull or heifer

Stoolins . . . . As in "horse stoolings of dry turf"; perhaps a pile of turf to which a horse is tied

Strames . . . . Streams

Strong . . . . As in "strong" farmer meaning prosperous and well-to-do

Tackling up . . Harnessing an animal

Tantrum . . . A display of ill-temper

Tawney, ... A fresh, green pasture
Tunney

Tay . . . . . . Tea

Teach . . . . . A house

Templemore . . A great church

Thracking . . . As in tracking rabbits

Thrawneen . . A small morsel of food

Tierce . . . . . A cask holding 42 gallons of wine or one-third of a pipe — usually used at big parties in Ireland — bigger than a barrel

Tigh . . . . . . A house
(pronouced
tee)

Tir Eoghain . . Land of Owen, Tyrone

Tir, Tyr . . . . Land, district

Tumuli . . . . Monuments in honour of the dead

Tobar . . . . . A well

Totties . . . . . Irish slang for young women

Touched . . . Slightly unbalanced mentally

Tráigh, Tra . . A strand

Tuam, Tuaim . A mound
Toom

Trom . . . . . Heavy

Tulach . . . . . A hillock
Tully,
Tallow

Turf . . . . . . Peat

Wattle . . . . . A stick or rod that bends easily

Winkers . . . . A horse's blinders

Woodbines . . Creepers that wind around trees

Worse . . . . . More, as in "you think worse of me than her"

Yapper . . . . Freetalker

Yarrow . . . . A herb

Yerra . . . . . Exclamation, probably meaning "get away with ya"; e.g., "Yerra; don't be talking!"

Youse . . . . . Second person plural in Irish

Acknowledgements

My sincere thanks to:

Almonte Library Staff
Andrews, Rod
Bassett, George
Burnett, Rita
Callahan, Charlotte
Carp Library Staff
Carroll, Angus & Mary
Carroll, Gerald
Carter, Joe
Charlebois, Bobby
Charlebois, Lillie
Currie, Terri
Dublin Public Archives
Egan, Pat
Enright, Mary
Finner, Dominic
Finner, Mrs. Hilary
Flynn, Mike
Flynn, Monica
Ganagan, Father Gerald
Grace, Jim
Grace, Mrs. Harry
Hogan, Earl & Dorothy
Hogan, Leo
Hogan, Mike
Kelly, Alonzo & Cecilia
Kennedy, Lawrence

Kennedy, Leo & Kathleen
Kennedy, Stella
Kingston, Father C.
Liston, Larry & Carmel
Lockhart, Cecilia
Lockhart, Wayne & Sue
Lunney, Father Ed
Manion, Joe
Mantil, Bobby
Mantil, Jackie & Marian
Mantil, Mike & Carol
Mantil, Maurice
Maurice, Delores
McManus, Mrs. Margaret
McWattie, Julie
Mormon Seventh-Day
   Adventists' Archives'
   Staff
Naraine, Prem
National Archives of
   Canada Staff
Neff, Jeff
Nepean Museum Staff
O'Brien, Ignatius
O'Connell, Beatrice
O'Keefe, Angus & Grace
O'Keefe, Donny

O'Keefe, John &
   Catherine, (Conna,
   Cork)
O'Keefe, Margaret Carroll
O'Keefe, Viola
O'Neil, Gwen
O'Reilly, Julia
Ogilvie, Marilyn O'Grady
Ontario Public Archives'
   Staff
Orange, Marjorie
   O'Grady
Penny, Father Bill
Perth Museum Staff
Pohlman, Angela
Powers, Canon (Lismore,
   Waterford)
Prudhomme, Frank
Scott, Donna
Scott, Edmund & Lois
Scott, Father Frank
Scott, John Leo
Vaughan, Gerald
Ward, Sharon
Woods, David
Woods, Edna
West Carleton Library
   Staff

Special thanks to Clarence Williams, Herman O'Keefe, Mr. and Mrs. Dominic Ryan, Catherine Scott Guilmette, Gary and Theresa Hewett, Ignatius O'Brien, Basil and Mary O'Keefe, and Mike O'Keefe of North Bay.